Freud's Early Psychology of the Neuroses

FREUD'S EARLY PSYCHOLOGY OF THE NEUROSES

A Historical Perspective

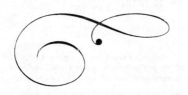

Kenneth Levin

University of Pittsburgh Press

Published by the University of Pittsburgh Press, Pittsburgh, Pa. 15260
Feffer and Simons, Inc., London
Manufactured in the United States of America

Library of Congress Cataloging in Publication Data

Levin, Kenneth, 1944–
  Freud's early psychology of the neuroses.

  Bibliography: p. 285
  Includes index.
  1. Neuroses—History. 2. Psychoanalysis.
3. Freud, Sigmund, 1856–1939. I. Title.
[DNLM: 1. Neuroses. WM170 L665f]
RC530.L47   616.8'52'0710924   77-15734
ISBN 0-8229-3366-7

Grateful acknowledgment is made to Sigmund Freud Copyrights Ltd, The Institute of Psycho-Analysis, and The Hogarth Press Ltd for permission to quote from *The Standard Edition of the Complete Psychological Works of Sigmund Freud,* translated and edited by James Strachey.

Acknowledgment is also made to Basic Books, Inc., for material from the *Collected Papers of Sigmund Freud,* edited by Ernest Jones, M.D.: Volume 1, authorized translation under the supervision of Joan Riviere, Papers I, "Charcot"; II, "On the Psychical Mechanism of Hysterical Phenomena"; III, "Some Points in a Comparative Study of Organic and Hysterical Paralyses"; IV, "The Defence Neuro-Psychoses"; V, "The Justification for Detaching from Neurasthenia a Particular Syndrome: The Anxiety-Neurosis"; VI, "A Reply to Criticisms on the Anxiety-Neuroses"; VII, "Obsessions and Phobias"; VIII, "Heredity and the Aetiology of the Neuroses"; IX, "Further Remarks on the Defence Neuro-Psychoses"; X, "The Aetiology of Hysteria"; XIV, "My Views on the Part Played by Sexuality in the Aetiology of the Neuroses"; and XV, "On the History of the Psycho-Analytic Movement." Volume 3, authorized translation by Alix and James Strachey, Paper I, "Fragment of an Analysis of a Case of Hysteria." Volume V, edited by James Strachey, Papers I, "Hypnotism and Suggestion"; II, "Early Studies on the Psychical Mechanism of Hysterical Phenomena"; and III, "A Case of Successful Treatment by Hypnotism." All published by Basic Books, Inc., Publishers, New York, by arrangement with The Hogarth Press Ltd and The Institute of Psycho-Analysis, London.

Acknowledgment is made to Basic Books, Inc., for material from *Studies on Hysteria,* by Josef Breuer and Sigmund Freud, translated from the German and edited by James Strachey in collaboration with Anna Freud, assisted by Alix Strachey and Alan Tyson, published in the United States by Basic Books, Inc., Publishers, New York by arrangement with The Hogarth Press Ltd., London.

Acknowledgment is made to The Hogarth Press Ltd and to Basic Books, Inc., for material from *The Origins of Psycho-Analysis: Letters to Wilhelm Fliess, Drafts and Notes: 1887–1902,* by Sigmund Freud, edited by Marie Bonaparte, Anna Freud, and Ernst Kris, authorized translation by Eric Mosbacher and James Strachey.

Acknowledgment is made to George Allen & Unwin Ltd and Basic Books, Inc., for material from *The Interpretation of Dreams,* by Sigmund Freud, translated from the German and edited by James Strachey; published in England by George Allen & Unwin Ltd and in the United States by Basic Books, Inc., Publishers, New York, by arrangement with George Allen & Unwin Ltd and The Hogarth Press, Ltd, London.

To the memory of Joseph Levin, my father
and
For Joseph Levin, my son

Contents

Acknowledgments

The study that follows had its source in my work as a doctoral candidate in history at Princeton University. The work at Princeton was supervised by Gerald Geison, to whom I am most grateful for his painstaking consideration of the early drafts of this study and his trenchant criticism and suggestions for revision.

Much of the research, and the writing of the first draft, was done in Zurich, and I am indebted to Professor Huldrych M. Koelbing, Director of the Institute of the History of Medicine at the University of Zurich, for his kind invitation to use the facilities of the Institute and for his continual help during my stay. Dr. Esther Fischer-Homberger of the Institute read the earlier chapters of the first draft and offered a number of very useful comments.

My wife provided invaluable aid and advice at every stage of the work and showed a sporting tolerance in sharing the tribulations which accompanied its writing.

From the fall of 1971 until the summer of 1973, my research was supported by fellowship grants from the Josiah Macy, Jr., Foundation.

Finally, I would like to thank Frederick A. Hetzel, Director of the University of Pittsburgh Press, for his ongoing interest in the manuscript and Eleanor Walker for her editing.

Freud's Early Psychology of the Neuroses

1. Introduction

This study explores Freud's early work on the neuroses and seeks to define, in a manner more comprehensive than previous studies of the subject, the origins of Freud's interest in these diseases, the development of his early theories, and the relationship of his views to relevant concepts current in nineteenth-century neurology, psychiatry, and nonmedical psychology. The period considered begins with Freud's first papers on hysteria and hypnosis (1886), encompasses such major works as *Studies on Hysteria* (1895) and *The Interpretation of Dreams* (1899), and concludes with Freud's *Three Essays on the Theory of Sexuality* (1905). In his publications during these nineteen years, Freud developed an elegant psychology of the neuroses, demonstrated how the same psychology could be used to elucidate normal psychic phenomena, formulated a theory of childhood sexuality as a foundation for his psychology, and elaborated his therapeutic technique for the treatment of neuroses. While Freud undoubtedly revised his theories in major ways in the subsequent thirty-four years of his life, his writings through 1905 can easily be recognized as containing virtually all the fundamental elements of his system.

In tracing the development of Freud's early theories, I will show, in contrast to previous studies, that Freud's interest in the neuroses was shaped by contemporary medical trends towards a greater concern with these diseases, that his early theoretical models were much more closely tied to current medical and psychological literature than has previously been acknowledged, and that, contrary to presently accepted views, Freud, from his first studies of the neuroses, consistently eschewed speculations concerning possible organic explanations for these diseases and concentrated instead on the psychological interpretation of neurotic symptoms.

Much of the literature dealing with Freud's early work on the neuroses, including many of Freud's own later references to his initial studies, tends to perceive these studies as entirely original investigations of previously ignored syndromes. But, in fact, Freud, in his theorizing, consistently drew upon concepts prominent in contemporary psychiatry, neurology, various other medical specialties, and nonmedical psychology. In addition, at the time that Freud first turned his attention to the neuroses, these diseases, particularly hysteria, had for several years been the focus of increasing attention and controversy among academic neurologists and psychiatrists. The controversy primarily concerned a conflict between theories of hysteria (*hysteria* at this time referring either to acute "hysterical attacks," with paroxysms of apparently involuntary gestures, bodily contortions, exclamations; or to chronic symptoms such as hysterical blindness, muteness, paralysis) which traced the syndrome to localized anatomical changes in the brain and alternative models proposed by Jean Martin Charcot. Charcot, who was professor of neuropathology in the Paris Faculty of Medicine and chief physician at the Salpetrière Hospital, agreed that hysteria and related disorders must be caused by some nervous system abnormality. But he insisted that these diseases are not accompanied by anatomical changes and that, therefore, autopsy investigations, no matter how carefully done, would yield no significant findings and throw no light on the nature of the disorders.

This controversy had extensive ramifications with regard to the current state of Continental neurology and psychiatry. There was, in academic medicine generally, an ongoing dispute throughout the nineteenth century as to the relative usefulness of pathological anatomy (following patients to autopsy in order to correlate symptoms with anatomical findings) and physiology (emphasizing experimentation on laboratory animals with the aim of focusing on modes of function rather than on structure) for elucidating the nature of disease processes. The debate was often pursued in rather abstract and philosophical terms, with people disputing, for example, whether a dead human being or a live animal represented a closer approximation to a live human being. But, for the participants, whose views were usually determined by the particular nature of their own educations, the controversy had very practical implications. It touched upon such questions as what relative weight should be given to anatomy and physiology in medical curricula; how much, if any, money should be put into building and staffing physiology laboratories; which type of training should be looked upon more favorably in the context of granting faculty appointments. In Paris, from the time of the French Revolution, greater emphasis was placed on pathological anatomy. Since it was in Paris that psychiatry was first established within the medical faculty as a separate specialty, with its own staff and its own clinical teaching facilities, and since it was consequently from Paris that the major academic texts on psychiatry emanated, the emphasis on anatomical research, which the psychiatrists of the Faculty of Medicine shared with their medical colleagues, came to dominate academic psychiatry on the Continent during the first half of the nineteenth century. From the 1840s onward, the University of Vienna, in contrast to the other major German-language universities, shared the anatomical bias of Paris; in the latter part of the century, as psychiatry became established in Vienna as a university discipline, it too shared the emphasis on anatomy and Vienna soon superseded Paris as the chief center on the Continent of a still dominant anatomically oriented psychiatry.

During these many decades the pathoanatomical method did, in fact, succeed in clarifying the nature of numerous neurologic and psychiatric diseases, and its efficacy accounted in large part for its continuing dominance. But its very success inevitably led to challenges to the approach. For, as anatomical studies effectively removed syndromes from the list of diseases of unknown pathology, they left behind on that list those diseases which were less amenable to the anatomical approach and which now received increasing attention as still-unsolved puzzles. By the early 1880s, numerous neuropsychiatrists, including a number of people originally trained as anatomists, were beginning to challenge the anatomical emphasis and to look for alternative, nonanatomical approaches to these diseases. Hysteria and related neuroses were particularly prominent among the syndromes that had not yielded to anatomical investigations, and they therefore became the subject of widespread study and of much controversy between those who continued to support the anatomical perspective and those who saw a need for new models. Charcot's work on hysteria reflected the effort to develop new explanations for illnesses left unexplained by the anatomical approach. Charcot's own theory of hysteria was that the disease is caused by diffuse physiological abnormalities in the central nervous system and that these abnormalities do not entail any structural changes. Charcot also proposed psychological explanations for a number of hysterical phenomena.

Freud's training in neuropsychiatry was very much in the pathoanatomical tradition and his early career reflected this training. His research prior to 1886 dealt almost exclusively with the microscopic anatomy of the nervous system, and his clinical work centered around establishing the anatomical basis of neuropsychiatric syndromes. When Freud left Vienna in the fall of 1885 for several months of study in Paris, his plan was to continue these anatomical studies. However, while attending Charcot's lectures and teaching rounds at the Salpetrière, he was profoundly impressed by Charcot's theory of hysteria. Freud had done no work on hysteria prior to coming to Paris. His enthusiastic response to Charcot's views was based on the observation that, as Charcot maintained, the symptoms of the hysterical patients hospitalized at the Salpetrière did not fit the picture of symptoms arising from anatomical lesions. Freud's subsequent preoccupation with hysteria was motivated by his sharing Charcot's belief that the disease was of major importance in the general search for new, nonanatomical theories of neuropathology.

But, although he endorsed Charcot's physiological model—the concept that hysteria is due to some diffuse abnormality in nervous system functioning unaccompanied by anatomical lesions—Freud from the start avoided speculation as to the nature of the physiological defect and instead directed his efforts towards developing psychological explanations for those aspects of the disease which seemed amenable to such explanations. He believed that the physiological abnormality was the source of one's vulnerability to neuroses and that this abnormality was also the direct cause of certain specific hysterical symptoms. But he also believed that, in view of the rudimentary state of contemporary neurophysiology, the pursuit of organic models could only result in highly speculative and useless hypotheses. He therefore focused instead on explicating those symptoms which appeared to be the product of psychological factors. He also concentrated on the psychotherapeutic resolution of hysterical symptoms. For many years it has been a generally accepted notion that, to the contrary, Freud initially attempted to develop organic explanations for the pathogenesis of the neuroses and that he only gradually shifted to an emphasis on psychological interpretations. However, I will show that this conception of Freud's early work is erroneous and that, from his first studies of hysteria, Freud consistently placed greatest stress on psychological models and eschewed the development of organic formulas.

The nature of Freud's research and clinical work prior to 1886, in which his emphasis is clearly on questions relating to the structure of the nervous system, is one of the factors that have suggested to observers that Freud must have initially approached the study of hysteria as a search for organic explanations of hysterical phenomena. The various references to the nervous system in Freud's first papers on hysteria have served to reinforce this view. Finally, Freud's "Project for a Scientific Psychology," first published in 1950, has been interpreted as additional evidence that Freud first sought to explain the neuroses in terms of changes in the nervous system. In this manuscript, dating from 1895, Freud attempts to construct detailed neurophysiological explanations for both normal and neurotic mental processes.

Ola Andersson, whose *Studies in the Prehistory of Psychoanalysis* traces the sequence of theoretical modifications in Freud's early work, argues that Freud's move from organic to psychological explanations of neurotic phenomena took place in the early 1890s and was essentially complete by 1894.[1] However, most observers have viewed the "Project" as an indication that in 1895 Freud was still primarily interested in pursuing organic formulas. A more popular opinion has therefore been that the shift from nervous system models to psychological models occurred in 1897 and 1898, and that it coincided with Freud's self-analysis and his discovery of infantile sexuality. This is, for example, the pattern discerned by Ernst Kris.[2]

But the entire notion that Freud first perceived the neuroses essentially in terms of changes in the nervous system, and that he only gradually came to emphasize purely psychological models, distorts the actual direction of Freud's conceptual development. Freud does refer to the nervous system on various occasions in his early papers, and he clearly believed that certain aspects of the neuroses could not be elucidated fully without appealing to physiology. But this position is one which he held throughout his later career as well; and in both the earlier and later papers he refrains from pursuing possible organic models and concentrates instead on those aspects of the neuroses which seemed amenable to psychological explanation. From 1886 until his development of the concept of defense in 1894, Freud consistently emphasized psychological interpretations of his clinical data, and the evolution of his theories of the neuroses during this period was characterized by his repeated appeal to currently popular concepts of psychodynamics and his continued adaptation and modification of these concepts in light of his clinical experience.

The "Project" (1895) is clearly an exception to Freud's pattern of emphasizing psychological interpretations. But this isolated excursion into physiological theorizing can be accounted for in terms of new directions which Freud's studies had taken beginning in 1893. During the early years of his interest in hysteria, Freud had paid little attention to a neurosis labelled "neurasthenia" which was the subject of a large body of literature at this time and was commonly discussed in works dealing with hysteria. Freud's lack of interest was based on the widely held belief that psychological factors played no role in the development of neurasthenia and that the disease was not responsive to psychotherapy. But, with his formulation of the defense theory, beginning in 1893, Freud became convinced that sexuality plays a special role in the etiology of hysteria; and, since neurasthenia was commonly believed to be caused by various pathogenic sexual practices (masturbation, for example, was believed by many to induce changes in the nervous system which led to the disease), Freud began to study neurasthenia with the hope of constructing a general theory of the neuroses based on their origins in sexual life. Over the next two years, Freud devoted considerable attention to neurasthenia, as well as to a related syndrome which he designated "anxiety neurosis," and in 1895 he began to formulate his sexual theory of the neuroses. However, as neurasthenia and anxiety neurosis did not appear to be caused by psychological factors, and therefore did not seem explicable by psychological formulas, Freud concluded that any general model for the neuroses would have to be constructed in physiological terms. Consequently, a physiological interpretation of hysteria seemed indispensable for the development of an integrated theory; this was the major impetus for the "Project."

It soon became clear to Freud that his earlier skepticism was justified and that he could not, in fact, construct a physiological theory which accounted satisfactorily for hysterical phenomena. He then abandoned the "Project." Over the next several years, he once again concentrated on those neuroses which seemed amenable to psychological explication, and he attempted to develop a more exact understanding of the etiology and the psychodynamics of these diseases. During this period Freud constructed a theory attributing the etiology of hysteria and related neuroses to vicissitudes of normal sexual development in early childhood. He also revised his psychodynamic formulas and wrote several works, most importantly *The Interpretation of Dreams*, in which he defended these formulas by demonstrating how they could be used to elucidate normal psychic phenomena such as dreams. But this emphasis on psychological explanations, far from constituting a new direction in his studies as is usually suggested, merely involved a return to the preoccupation with psychological models which had always characterized his work on the neuroses. At the same time, he continued to endorse his original belief that there are aspects of the neuroses that can only be accounted for by physiology.

A somewhat separate problem, which has received extensive attention in recent years and which also pertains to the role of physiology in Freud's work on the neuroses, concerns the source of Freud's psychological models. In *The Interpretation of Dreams* (1899) and in later papers Freud develops psychological theories of mental processes which often resemble contemporary physiological concepts concerning nervous system processes. Various authors have noted this pattern and have concluded that Freud's psychological theories were derived from these physiological concepts. This would suggest that, even if my thesis is correct and Freud did quite consistently emphasize psychological interpretations of neurotic phenomena, physiology nevertheless profoundly influenced his perception of the neuroses. But the arguments propounded by these authors are based on erroneous premises.

Siegfried Bernfeld, one of the first to discuss the significance of physiology for Freud's work on the neuroses, suggested in the 1940s that Freud's medical education introduced him to theories of nervous system functioning which later served as a foundation for his psychological models. Bernfeld emphasized a so-called School of Helmholtz, referring to a group of physiologists (Emil Dubois-Reymond, Hermann Helmholtz, Carl Ludwig, and Ernst Brücke), primarily students of Johannes Müller at the University of Berlin, who had, around 1850, pledged themselves to pursue a physiology based exclusively on chemistry and physics. Brücke was later professor of physiology at Vienna, and Freud did his first research under Brücke's guidance. Bernfeld argued that many of Freud's principles of mental functioning, particularly his concepts of psychic energy, were derived from his training under Brücke and the neurophysiology developed by Brücke and his friends.[3]

The publication of the "Project" (1950) seemed to reinforce Bernfeld's arguments, since a number of concepts which are of major importance in Freud's later psychology are defined in physiological terms in the "Project." In addition, Freud's models in the manuscript closely resemble those presented in a book by Sigmund Exner, who was Brücke's assistant and Freud's university instructor in physiology. These similarities between the arguments of the "Project" (written in 1895) and Exner's *Entwurf zu einer physiologischen Erklärung der psychischen Erscheinungen* (1894) lent still more support to Bernfeld's thesis.

In recent years various authors have elaborated further on this theory that Freud's psychological models were influenced extensively by physiological principles learned from his teachers and invoked in the "Project." Peter Amacher, in *Freud's Neurological Education and Its Influence on Psychoanalytic Theory* (1965), develops this theme at length and maintains that Freud's education in physiology was the most important factor in shaping his psychological concepts.[4] Other writers have supported the same view, including Raymond Fancher and Robert Holt.[5] Holt goes so far as to call for a total restructuring of psychoanalytic theory on the grounds that present theories are based primarily on an outmoded physiology and therefore must themselves be outmoded.[6]

The extreme position taken by Amacher, Fancher, and Holt can be challenged by a number of objections. The essence of Freud's psychology is the notion of a conflict between two psychic systems, and these writers ignore the fact that there was throughout the nineteenth century a well-established psychological tradition—based largely upon the psychology of Johann Friedrich Herbart and quite independent of physiology—which emphasized a conflict between psychic entities. Freud had read widely in this psychology and it undoubtedly exerted an important influence on his models. The concept of splits in consciousness, which played such a prominent role in psychologies of hypnosis during the nineteenth century, was a further source for Freud's theories of multiple psychic systems. Also, there is an ancient and widespread philosophical distinction between "appetites" on the one hand and the psychic forces which control and inhibit these appetites on the other; once Freud had identified sexual ideas and impulses as the key to neuroses, this tradition provided an additional source for his formulations concerning psychic systems in conflict.

Most importantly, Amacher and the others, in their overemphasis of physiology, completely ignore the role of Freud's clinical experience in shaping his theoretical models.[7] Even if one assumes that all of Freud's formulations are based upon earlier theories, whether psychological or physiological, one cannot account for his choices among available theories—why he utilized some concepts and rejected others—without considering his clinical experiences. For example, in attempting to account for Freud's emphasis on sexuality in his theories of the neuroses, one might note that throughout the nineteenth century writers had consistently stressed sexual factors when discussing the etiology of hysteria. But Freud was quite familiar with this literature in 1886, and yet from 1886 to 1894 he rejected sexual theories and insisted that hysteria is primarily hereditary. Consequently, merely citing the earlier literature on hysteria and sexuality does not yield much insight into why Freud ultimately endorsed the sexual emphasis. This can be understood only in the context of Freud's clinical work from 1892 to 1894 and the consistent reappearance of sexual themes in his patients' stories. Similarly, although one can cite numerous theories of intrapsychic conflict which may have influenced Freud, his choice of theory, and the changes in his theory during the course of his early work on the neuroses, cannot be understood without considering his clinical experiences.

However, these observations—that Freud's theories of psychic conflict were shaped primarily by his clinical experiences and by the formulations of contemporary psychology, and that physiology played a very small part in the development of these theories—do not fully resolve the problem of physiological influences on Freud's thought. One must still respond to Bernfeld's argument that neurophysiology provided those principles of mental functioning to which Freud appealed in the "Project" and in *The Interpretation of Dreams* when attempting to imbed his concept of psychic conflict into a general psychology of mental processes. But this argument can also be rebutted. The principles which Freud introduces in physiological terms in the "Project" and which so closely resemble his later psychological models were indeed quite popular in contemporary neurophysiology; they are, in fact, to be found in the works of physiologists throughout Europe and are not particularly related to a special School of Helmholtz, as Bernfeld and Amacher suggest. But these principles were derived mainly from behavioral observations, and the physiologists had in large part merely translated the behavioral material into the language of their science. For example, notions concerning the reflex function of the nervous system and the proportionality between neural stimulus and neural response were inspired to a great extent by well-known behavioral phenomena concerning an organism's tendency to react automatically and in a measured way to disturbances. Further, these concepts appear extensively in the psychological literature of the time and were most often perceived simply as psychological principles. They were expressed in physiological terms in the "Project" because Freud was then concerned with constructing physiological models; but they were in no way intrinsically tied to physiology. Consequently, there is little basis for asserting, simply because these concepts reappear in psychological form in Freud's later work, that neurophysiology has played a major role in shaping Freud's psychology.

The literature which Freud had available to him and upon which he drew in formulating his theories was not limited to works on psychology and psychodynamics, or to the numerous books and articles on the neuroses generated by the widespread interest in those diseases. In this study I review also the literature on dreams, on sexuality, and on other relevant topics, that was similarly available to Freud and that often, as with the works on the neuroses and on psychodynamics, contains concepts and hypotheses that closely resemble Freud's models. However, once having demonstrated the many similarities between Freud's work and that of other writers, one is naturally left with the question of what it is that is unique or special in Freud's formulations and what accounts for the extraordinary and far-reaching impact which his theories have had on modern thought.

Many of the fundamental ideas which figure prominently in Freud's theories and which have come to be associated with his name can indeed be found in the works of numerous other authors. This is true, for example, of the idea of an unconscious and the concept of childhood sexuality. A dissection of Freud's models into a list of basic concepts would, in fact, yield relatively few such concepts which could not be found in some form in the work of earlier writers. It is therefore necessary to go beyond these fundamental concepts in order to gain some understanding of Freud's contribution and some explanation for his tremendous influence. But this observation is hardly surprising. Scientific models in general, no matter how "revolutionary," are built essentially on principles already accepted by the scientific community to whom the models are addressed. This must be particularly true of theories such as Freud's, which receive an enthusiastic reception in relatively short periods of time, since a reception of this sort is inconceivable unless many people are already asking the questions that the theory attempts to answer and are already somewhat prepared for the answers which the theory offers. Freud's models could never have achieved their rapid elevation to such extraordinary prominence in psychiatry had there not already been a widespread interest in the neuroses and had not a number of basic principles, such as the concept of unconscious ideation and the notion of sexual etiologies for neuroses, already emerged as popular themes in neuropsychiatric theorizing.

Of course, Freud's work received a remarkable reception outside of neuropsychiatry as well as within the discipline. Interest in Freud's theories outside of the medical community developed particularly in the wake of his publication of *The Interpretation of Dreams* (1899). But this response would also have been impossible had not a number of Freud's basic concepts converged with currently popular cultural and social themes and with concepts prominent in various nonmedical disciplines such as nonmedical psychology and anthropology. For example, the clash between individual needs and social conventions and restraints, and the related conflict between the nonrational elements of human personality and man as a rational and disciplined being, were prominent themes in the arts and in social criticism during this period, and Freud's work attracted attention in many intellectual circles largely because his concept of a conflict between unconscious sexual impulses and conscious, socially more acceptable thought and behavior seemed to fit well with these themes.

A review of the medical journals reveals that within psychiatry there was considerable interest in Freud's work from the time of his publication with Josef Breuer of *Studies on Hysteria* (1895). This interest increased greatly with the appearance of *The Interpretation of Dreams* (1899) and the *Three Essays on the Theory of Sexuality* (1905). The image presented in Ernest Jones's biography and in many of Freud's own comments, to the effect that these early studies were generally ignored or noticed only to be condemned, is a distortion. These works actually received an impressive and rather exceptional amount of attention in the journals, and the reviews quite commonly contain effusive praise for Freud's formulations.[8] In addition, while various prominent psychiatrists were asserting in such articles that Freud's work represented a significant contribution to the field, a good number of younger practitioners were perceiving Freud's work as considerably more than that, as really pointing to a major new direction for psychiatry. This response accelerated over the next several decades.

If, as I suggest, a widespread interest in such topics as the splitting of consciousness in hysteria and the sexual etiology of neuroses was a necessary prerequisite for this enthusiastic response to Freud's work, the key to that response, and to what is special in Freud's theories, lies in his modification of current formulas concerning these topics and in his integration of the revised formulas into a unified general theory. In contrast to those writers who viewed unconscious ideation in hysteria as the product of some neurological abnormality, or those who interpreted "unconscious ideas" as simply all those ideas temporarily excluded from consciousness because of their irrelevance to one's current line of thought, Freud developed the concept of *defense* and of an unconscious populated by ideas selectively repressed from consciousness due to their particularly painful and disruptive nature. He further insisted that such ideas invariably have some sexual significance and that, even after being repressed, they continue to play a role in psychic life. In *The Interpretation of Dreams* and in several other works, such as *The Psychopathology of Everyday Life* (1901), Freud demonstrated how this model could be used to explain not only neurotic phenomena, but normal psychic processes as well. In addition, he modified and adapted current views on sexuality in childhood and integrated his theory of the sexual etiology of neuroses into a general theory of human sexual development from infancy. In this way, Freud developed a unified, new, and elegant system incorporating theories of the neuroses, of normal psychodynamics, and of sexuality. It is this integration of so many disparate basic elements, this welding of various strands into a consistent and comprehensive system, that was so impressive and so exceptional and that accounts more than any other factor for the tremendous reception Freud's formulations received. It is the major factor in his triumphs both in medical and in nonmedical circles.

Among psychiatrists, the major criticism of Freud's theories was that his formula for the etiology of neuroses was a gross generalization based on insufficient clinical evidence. The critics argued that, whatever might be the situation in some individual cases, it is highly unlikely that all hysteria is due to repressed sexual impulses. But the prospect of a general theory was an attractive one and Freud's formula had considerable appeal, particularly to the many practitioners who already acknowledged the importance of unconscious ideas and whose clinical experience supported the popular association between sexuality and hysteria. This appeal was enhanced by Freud's demonstration of how his concept of repression could be used to explain a variety of normal psychic phenomena. Most important in this regard was *The Interpretation of Dreams,* in which Freud supported his psychodynamic formulas by applying them in an impressive way to the analysis of a large number of dreams. He also demonstrated how his formulas reconciled and integrated the many conflicting theories of dream formation found in the literature, while accounting for all the phenomena which these other models attempted to explain. Freud's theory of sexuality served to further enhance the attractiveness of his neurosis theory. In the *Three Essays on the Theory of Sexuality,* Freud integrated his concept of repressed sexual impulses into a general theory of infantile sexuality and defended this theory by showing how it incorporated current knowledge concerning childhood sexuality, offered a comprehensive analysis of normal sexual development, and provided an explanation for sexual perversions which reconciled the many conflicting views of psychiatrists on this popular subject.

Freud's combined theories of neuroses, of normal psychodynamics, and of sexuality, offering consistent and interlocking explanations for so many complex and fundamental psychic phenomena, were so compelling in their simplicity and their comprehensiveness that they aroused an excited interest among psychiatrists despite the paucity of clinical verification for the neurosis theory and the difficulties and limitations of applying the theory and the analytic technique to the cure of neurotic patients. The total theory elicited, from psychiatrists and from others, a response whose spirit was perhaps best captured in a letter to Freud on his eightieth birthday (1936) from Albert Einstein. Einstein begins:

> You have undoubtedly not made it easy for the sceptical laity to come to an independent judgment [on the correctness of his theories]. Until recently I could only apprehend the speculative power of your train of thought, together with its enormous influence on the *Weltanschauung* of the present era, without being in a position to form a definite opinion about the amount of truth it contains.

Einstein goes on to say, however, that he has recently heard of a number of occurrences which in his view defy any explanation other than that offered by Freud's theories. He concludes: "I was delighted to come across [these instances]; since it is always delightful when a great and beautiful conception proves to be consonant with reality."[9]

2. Pathoanatomical Psychiatry

Historians of psychiatry have often noted that many nineteenth-century psychiatrists perceived pathological anatomy as the key to the explication of mental disorders. Jose Maria Lopez Pinero and Jose Maria Morales Meseguer, in *Neurosis y Psicoterapia,* discuss this trend extensively, particularly as it relates to French psychiatry.[1] Others observe the same trend among some German psychiatrists.[2] This chapter deals with the factors involved in the emergence and development of this pathoanatomical bias, the forces at work in its decline, and Freud's place within the anatomical tradition.

French Psychiatry and the Pathoanatomical Perspective

The emphasis on uncovering anatomical lesions in psychiatric disorders, an emphasis which held a dominant position in Continental psychiatry at the time that Freud began his medical education (1873), can be traced in part to the French psychiatrists of the first half of the nineteenth century. Phillipe Pinel, who, as head of the mental hospitals of the Bicetre and the Salpetrière in the years following the French Revolution, initiated major clinical reforms and established psychiatry as a vital branch of Parisian medicine, did not share the pathoanatomical bias. Nor did his successor, Jean-Etienne Esquirol. But the emphasis on anatomy was endorsed by Esquirol's most prominent students. One such student, Jeanne Pierre Falret, later wrote: "I believed firmly that in all cases, without exception, one could find in the mentally sick appreciable lesions in the brain or its membranes; lesions sufficiently marked and constant as to account satisfactorily for all the various intellectual and affective disturbances in insanity.[3]

Falret and his colleagues were greatly influenced by the current trend towards anatomical studies in general medicine, and particularly by the emphasis which the Paris Faculty of Medicine, virtually from the time of its inception in 1795, placed on pathoanatomical methods. Medical research was understood to mean following one's patient to the dissecting table and discovering lesions which could then be correlated with previously recorded clinical findings. Xavier Bichat, a major figure in the Paris school, wrote in 1801:

> It seems to me that we have entered an epoch where patho-logical anatomy must make a new effort. . . . Medicine was for a long time excluded from the exact sciences. She will have the right to belong to them, at least for diagnostics, when rigorous observation is everywhere combined with ex-amination of [anatomical] changes. . . . What is the value of observation, if one does not know the seat of the disease? You can take notes for twenty years from morning to even-ing at the sick-bed on the diseases of the heart, lung, and stomach and you will reap nothing but confusion. . . . Open a few corpses, and immediately this obscurity, which obser-vation alone would never have removed, will disappear.[4]

Although pathological anatomy was not Bichat's own primary inter-est, his concern with pathological anatomy was the aspect of his work most pursued by his successors. R. T. H. Laennec, another central figure in the Paris school, wrote in 1812 that "pathological anatomy is the torch of nosology and the surest guide for diagnostic medicine."[5] Pathoana-tomical studies dominated the Paris school for the next half century.

Falret, in his *Des Maladies Mentales et des Asiles d'Aliènes,* attests to the influence of current medical trends in attracting young psychiatrists to the pathoanatomical approach:

> As a pupil of Pinel and Esquirol, at the Salpetrière Hospital, I began to study mental alienation under these illustrious masters. At the time when I followed their lessons, a general tendency prevailed in contemporary medicine and naturally had its effect on mental pathology. The young doctors who then studied mental disorders preferred to direct their at-tention to the lesions which were found in the brain and its membranes upon autopsy of the insane. Contrary to the doc-trine of my teachers [who were more eclectic], I yielded like the others to this anatomical direction, which was considered at this time as the true basis of medicine. It is true that I

> fixed my attention on certain special subjects, like suicide, hypochondria, and mania without delirium; but, as a general principle, I soon became convinced that anatomical pathology alone was able to offer an explanation for the phenomena observed in insanity, and that the progress of the science resides in pursuing this study with perseverance.[6]

In addition to being influenced by contemporary medicine, the French psychiatrists were also attracted to the pathoanatomical approach by some early successes of the method in elucidating psychiatric syndromes. For example, many early writers had noted the common occurrence of paralyses among the insane. A. L. Bayle, in 1822, argued that his extensive autopsy studies revealed the presence of specific brain lesions in these patients, and he suggested that the paralyses and the insanity in such patients were really two aspects of a single disease process, both manifestations of the lesions he had uncovered. In 1826, he further characterized the syndrome, which he labelled "dementia paralytica" (disturbances of intellectual function, peculiar grandiose ideation, progressive muscular incoordination and enfeeblement), and he offered additional evidence that both the paralysis and the mental illness were the result of a single disease process and emerged with the development of a specific cerebral lesion.[7] If one considers that dementia paralytica, or "general paralysis of the insane" (ultimately recognized as a late manifestation of syphilis) accounted for perhaps 30 percent of all mental hospital patients,[8] one can appreciate the importance ascribed to Bayle's work and to his success in discovering a pattern of brain lesions in these patients. Bayle's work, and similarly successful anatomical investigations into other neuropsychiatric syndromes, undoubtedly played a role in stimulating further the search for anatomical lesions in mental disorders.

Pathological anatomy continued to prevail in French psychiatry, as it did in French internal medicine, into the latter part of the century. The doctrine of "mental degeneration"—a concept which emphasized the supposed hereditary etiology of mental disorders and which pervaded the etiological thinking of French psychiatrists during this later period—was largely built upon the belief that these inherited disorders typically entail anatomically identifiable brain lesions. Benedict-Augustin Morel, a protégé of Falret and the first major proponent of the degeneration theory, stressed the importance of pathological anatomy for elucidating the nervous system lesions which underlie mental abnormalities.[9] Valentin Magnan, who developed Morel's theories further and played an important role in popularizing them, was particularly interested in associating clinical syndromes with localized pathoanatomical lesions.[10]

Falret, in his 1864 book, speaks of having in later years somewhat modified his views on the role of anatomical studies. This was prompted, he states, by a realization that the anatomical lesions, as important as they are, do not account sufficiently for the great diversity and subtle nuances of the psychic phenomena in insanity. Moreover, he could not, as he had first believed, deduce the prognosis and treatment, as well as the diagnosis, of a mental malady from anatomical considerations alone. But he nevertheless insists: "I still belong to the anatomical school, as I firmly believe in the existence of some structural modification in all mental abnormalities."[11]

Wilhelm Griesinger

The man most responsible for establishing pathoanatomical psychiatry in Germany was Wilhelm Griesinger. Griesinger's impact can be traced in part to his textbook, *Mental Pathology and Therapeutics,* which first appeared in 1845 and was republished in a new edition in 1861. The book, with its anatomical emphasis, received enthusiastic and widespread acclaim. Also of major significance in accounting for Griesinger's impact was his appointment, in 1865, to the first Chair of Psychiatry established in Germany. Griesinger insisted, before accepting the position at Berlin, that the professorship include control of a neurological and psychiatric teaching clinic. He thereby initiated the shift in psychiatric training away from the asylums and into university clinics. With this shift, the leadership in German psychiatry passed from the asylum directors, with their administrative preoccupations and emphasis on patient management, to the university instructors whose orientation was more theoretical and who were more concerned with etiological and pathological models. As a result of this transformation in psychiatric training, Griesinger's theoretical pronouncements and his pathoanatomical orientation were able to exert a much greater influence than would otherwise have been possible. Indeed, there were earlier German psychiatrists whose approach was more strictly anatomical than that of Griesinger; but, so long as psychiatry was not taught in any comprehensive way in the universities and remained, instead, a discipline learned primarily through the practical experience of working in asylums, the impact of any particular theory or approach was necessarily limited.[12]

Griesinger begins his textbook by asserting that "we, . . . in every case of mental disease, recognise a morbid action of [the brain]." He argues that

> testimony in favor of our assertion, that the brain is the
> organ affected in insanity, is furnished by examination of
> the bodies of the insane after death. In many such examina-
> tions, true anatomical changes are found in the brain itself,
> or in its coverings; . . . the circumstance that such changes
> are not always found should not weaken this argument.[13]

While maintaining that the brain is the seat of all mental abnormalities, Griesinger acknowledges in this statement that anatomical examination will not always shed light on the underlying pathology. He
goes on to discuss mental diseases in which changes in the brain "cannot be ocularly demonstrated," but must be postulated "on physiological grounds." Elsewhere, Griesinger concentrates on physiological interpretations of psychiatric disorders, that is, interpretations based on
presumed changes in nervous system functioning without reference to
structural changes. But he nevertheless put particular emphasis on the
pathoanatomical approach to mental disorders and was significantly
influenced by the French anatomical psychiatrists:

> In insanity the observation of post-mortem appearances is a
> department of psychology of the utmost importance. . . . We
> have not only to consider the presence or absence of [ana-
> tomical] alterations generally, not only to establish their inti-
> mate connection with the morbid cause through which [the
> lesion] discovered after death first originated, and to employ
> them for the preservation and treatment of living patients;
> we have also to consider whether a careful examination of
> pathological and anatomical facts will not assist us in forming
> conclusions of a still more comprehensive nature, and
> whether definite fundamental facts cannot be elicited which
> might throw a clearer light on the intimate nature, on the
> mode of progression of these diseases, as well as upon the
> whole physiology and pathology of the brain.[14]

He defends this perspective by referring to recent pathoanatomical
findings: "According to recent investigations, it may be considered a
well-established fact that the majority of post-mortem examinations of
the insane show anatomical changes to exist within the cranium."[15]

In addition, Griesinger elsewhere suggests that those mental dis-

eases which are unaccompanied by anatomical lesions would, if allowed
to progress, eventually display such changes. Indeed, this notion is
central to his whole concept of mental disease. Griesinger received his
basic psychiatric training under the tutelage of A. Zeller at the asylum
at Winnenthal, where he worked for two years (1842 1844). While at
Winnenthal, he adopted Zeller's theory that all mental diseases are
merely various stages of the same psychotic process. In his chapter
"Forms of Mental Diseases," Griesinger suggests two broad classifica-
tions: disorders involving morbidity of emotion and emotional states,
and disorders of intellect and "will." He notes that the former disorders
are often not accompanied by clear-cut anatomical findings. But he also
maintains that, if allowed to progress, these disorders will ultimately
manifest both the symptoms and the consistent anatomical changes of
the latter syndromes:

> In the great majority of cases, those conditions which form
> the first leading group *precede* those of the second group; . . .
> the latter generally appear only as consequences and *termina-*
> *tions* of the first. . . .
>   Pathological anatomy shows us, even at present, that in
> the first group . . . it is rare to find important [anatomical]
> alterations, or such as are not capable of complete removal;
> whilst in the second group, or in the terminal stages, very
> often there exist palpable . . . changes which are incapable of
> cure—particularly atrophy of the brain more or less exten-
> sive, with *œdema* of the membranes, and chronic hydro-
> cephalus. We may say, then, that those cerebral lesions which
> give rise to the first stages of insanity—lesions which are
> certainly not always of an identical nature, and which we, as
> yet, cannot generally characterise anatomically—have this in
> common, that they terminate in very many cases in those
> characteristic consecutive changes in the brain which we
> have spoken of as a stage of permanent anatomical lesion.
>
>   . . . [The] first series includes the forms of melancholy,
> mania, and monomania; the second, the forms of chronic
> mania and dementia.[16]

When later discussing chronic insanity and dementia, Griesinger says
that cases in which no anatomical lesion is found are, in the former,
"rarely observed," and, in the latter, "rare and of no significance." This
thesis, that all mental diseases, if allowed to progress, ultimately de-

velop into chronic insanity or dementia with clearly discernible anatomical lesions, is perhaps based upon observations of patients with
dementia paralytica. Reference has already been made to the large
percentage of asylum patients who were probably suffering from this
disease; and the initial mental aberrations in dementia paralytica would
be those associated with Griesinger's first stage, while the later symptoms of the syndrome would be those of his second stage. Griesinger
(and Zeller) might simply have taken these cases as prototypes of the
natural history of all mental disease. At any rate, Griesinger's notion
that all mental disease represents stages of a single process, with the
latter stages being almost invariably accompanied by clear-cut anatomical lesions, lent added weight to pathoanatomical investigations by
rendering them significant even for those syndromes in which lesions
were not typically found.

In discussing the etiology of mental diseases, Griesinger finds that
"the *psychical causes* are, in our opinion, the most frequent and the most
fertile sources of insanity, as well in regard to preparation as especially
and principally the immediate excitation of the disease."[17] But he then
goes on to develop an organic model for the modes of action of these
psychic factors, explaining how they could result ultimately in anatomical lesions.* Griesinger actually proposes two modes of action: a direct
effect, whereby the psychic disturbances "produce a state of intense
irritation of the brain"; and an indirect effect, involving pathological
changes in respiration, circulation, digestion, and so forth, which in
turn cause lesions in the brain.

Griesinger, in his text, elaborates a complex psychology based on
the psychology of J. F. Herbart and on the reflex concept of nervous
function which then dominated neurophysiological model-building. He
uses this psychology to explain both the psychic causes and the psychic
effects of mental disease:

---

*The pathoanatomical tradition considered in this chapter concerns specifically the
pathology of mental illness, the physical changes in the individual which underlie his
symptoms. It should not be perceived as relating to etiology, that is, to the factors which
induce such changes. Those who shared the anatomical bias generally recognized a
wide range of etiological elements in mental illness, including both psychical factors,
such as emotional shocks, and physical factors, ranging from alcoholism to tumors.
They insisted simply that, whatever the etiology, the symptoms are brought about by
means of pathoanatomical changes. For example, a pathogenic emotional shock, such as
the loss of a loved one, was commonly believed to cause illness by inducing a drop in
blood pressure, which would in turn lead to cerebral ischemia. The ischemia and subsequent cerebral necrosis were, according to this view, the basis of the patient's mental
aberrations.

That there dwells in the psychical life within us an overruling tendency to express itself, to exhibit itself in motions and acts, depends upon this general fundamental fact which meets us everywhere in the nervous system—namely, that peripheral excitations transform themselves in the central organs into motor impulses. . . . The impressions from the whole organism, especially, however, from the viscera, the intestines, the genital organs, etc., under the form of sensuous requirements, give the impulse to action . . . ; in animals they rule uncontrolled, they constitute the principal element of their psychical existence, . . . In man, the immediate transition of these sensations to movement is subject in a higher degree to the influence of the understanding, . . .

. . . If . . . known and definite ideas, by being united to the impulses of movement, exercise an influence upon the muscular movements, this is called *Will.* . . .

In the healthy mind [the Will] urges and impels the individual to express his ideas, to realise them in actions, and thereby to rid himself of them. If this has taken place, the soul feels disburdened and freed; by the act it relieved itself of the ideas, and thus its equilibrium is again established.[18]

But such healthy behavior requires two psychic conditions: "an unobstructed association of ideas" and "a sufficiently strong ego, that can give the decision to its mass of ideas." In insanity of physical origin, the organic disease generates sensations and perceptions which a weakened ego cannot integrate. With insanity of psychic origin, the ego is overwhelmed by sensations and perceptions from outside. In either case, this is the stage of mania and volatile emotions. Ultimately the unintegrated affects and sensations coalesce to form alternate "egos" and the patient sinks into dementia. Griesinger in this way offers an explication of the psychological changes in his two stages of insanity. But, in the course of his psychological discussions, he repeatedly refers to the underlying anatomical lesions. The complete submersion of the primary ego is, for Griesinger, merely the psychological manifestation of the fully developed anatomical abnormality.

Theodor Meynert

Theodor Meynert, Freud's teacher in neuropsychiatry at the University of Vienna and his mentor following graduation, received his own medical training in Vienna during the 1850s and early 1860s. At that time, German psychiatry was being impelled toward a greater emphasis on pathological anatomy by the several factors already noted: the influence of French pathoanatomical psychiatry; the growing response to Wilhelm Griesinger, and particularly to his textbook; and, perhaps most importantly, the impact of new discoveries, especially those concerning neurosyphilis. In Meynert's case, however, there was also the major factor of his training under Carl Rokitansky.

In a period when German medicine was largely dominated by physiologists—most notably Johannes Müller and his students—Rokitansky, a pathologist, founded with Josef Skoda the "new School of Vienna." According to one observer, "they followed largely along the lines laid down by the Paris school. Rokitansky, drawing on an immense body of material, most industriously and systematically continued the study of the pathologico-anatomical changes in the organs which had been undertaken by the French pathological anatomists."[19]

Contemporary accounts confirm the comparison between Paris and Vienna. The common pathoanatomical orientation of the two centers was the subject of a monograph by Carl August Wunderlich, entitled *Wien und Paris* (1841).[20] Rudolph Virchow, in *Cellular Pathology* (1858), speaks of "the Vienna school, for they too, like the French school, [ground] their system of pathology upon pathological anatomy."[21] If there was any significant difference between Rokitansky and the Parisians, it was that, whereas the French generally gave precedence to clinical observation over anatomical studies, Rokitansky "placed anatomical alterations first in the classification of morbid processes and held that the task of clinical medicine was confined to demonstrating these anatomical changes in patients. He thus entirely subordinated clinical medicine to pathological anatomy and made anatomical diagnosis in the literal sense of the word the end and object of his efforts."[22]

Meynert, while still a student, made microscopic slide preparations of autopsy material for Carl Wedl and later did similar work for Rokitansky's assistant, Gustav Scheuthauer. In the course of this work, he became interested in brain anatomy and began doing research in Rokitansky's Pathoanatomical Institute. In 1865, Rokitansky procured for him a lectureship in "the structure and function of the brain and spinal cord with relation to their pathology." In 1870, after Meynert completed his psychiatric training, Rokitansky was instrumental in gaining him a post as director of a psychiatric clinic. In 1875, again with Rokitansky's help, Meynert became director of the newly founded psychiatric teaching clinic at the Vienna General Hospital. This position complemented his appointment as first occupant of the Chair of Psychiatry at the University of Vienna, an appointment based on his accomplishments as a neuroanatomist.[23]

Meynert regarded pathoanatomical research as the key to mental disorders, and he insisted that anatomical studies must take precedence over other approaches to psychiatry.[24] In the introduction to his book, *Psychiatrie* (1884), he defines psychiatry as the medical discipline concerned with diseases of the cerebral cortex, and he speaks of "the necessity of starting from anatomical facts." *Psychiatrie* is actually devoted to a consideration of normal structure and function, which he says is "indispensable to an understanding of the clinical manifestations of mental diseases"; but his theory of normal function is in turn derived from a "close consideration of the pathological anatomy of the organ."

A central concept in Meynert's neuroanatomical orientation is his belief that the various cerebral activities are each carried out within distinct, localized areas of the brain. This thesis is first developed in a monograph written in 1868 entitled "Der Bau der Gross-Hirnrinde und seine ortlichen Verschiedenheiten, nebst einem pathologisch-anatomischen Corollarium." In subsequent years the thesis was reinforced by additional successes on the part of psychiatrists in correlating specific mental symptoms with local anatomical lesions, and by the physiological experiments of G. Fritsch and E. Hitzig, David Ferrier, and others, which succeeded in delineating a specific area of the cortex as the motor center. In *Psychiatrie,* Meynert cites these latter experiments as supporting the evidence offered by pathological anatomy in favor of the cortical localization of functions.[25] With his belief in cortical localization, Meynert saw no limits to the potential for correlating the clinical symptoms of psychiatric disorders with local anatomical lesions.

Griesinger, in considering mental diseases which reveal no anatomical findings, assumed that some anatomical changes are nevertheless present. He did so on the basis of observations that many patients suffering from these diseases eventually progress to more severe syndromes in which anatomical lesions can be readily discerned. Meynert pursues the same line of thought:

> Why can't . . . melancholic and maniacal conditions be based upon fine anatomical changes in the hemisphere? On the contrary, I must insist that anatomical changes are the essence [of these syndromes], because we know that a one-time

melancholia can have an unfortunate termination in permanent imbecility with gross anatomical lesions. A single episode of melancholia is therefore very dangerous for the
brain; and we must conclude, concerning the defect, that the
fore-brain itself has suffered and fine anatomical disturbances are undoubtedly involved.[26]

But unlike Griesinger, who did not specify what these early, as yet
unobservable, anatomical changes might entail, Meynert developed an
explanation of such changes based upon his concept of cortical localization and upon notions concerning cerebral hemodynamics and variations in the blood supply to different areas of the brain. He argued that
psychic aberrations which display no gross anatomical lesions are due
to local cerebrovascular abnormalities and a consequent ischemia, or
impairment in blood perfusion, to the involved areas. Presumably, if
these persist or are allowed to progress, then cerebral necrosis and
gross lesions supervene. These ideas are introduced in Meynert's
monograph of 1868 ("Der Bau der Gross-Hirnrinde"), initially in the
context of normal functional variations. For example, "the surface of
the brain is relatively ischemic in sleep as compared to waking, indeed
in dreamless sleep it is more ischemic than when dreaming." He also
asserts that, during the waking state, those parts of the cortex which
are psychically active at any given moment are comparatively well perfused with blood, or hyperemic, for that moment, whereas other parts
are relatively ischemic. Later in the monograph, after discussing the
various morphological layers of the cortex, Meynert introduces the
pathoanatomical corollary mentioned in the title:

> The large pyramidal cells . . . contain a sharply delineated,
> oval, pustule-like nucleus with a tripartite nucleolus. All pre-
> vious authors described such a nucleus without realizing its
> pathological significance. Instead, the pathological re-
> searcher complained of the lack of morbid changes in the
> carriers of psychic [abnormal] behavior following [the devel-
> opment of symptoms]. . . . and yet, while they complained,
> the most essential, earliest pathological change of the cortical
> substance lay unknown before their eyes.[27]

According to Meynert, changes in these pyramidal nuclei, caused in all
likelihood by some circulatory disturbance, are the pathoanatomical
basis for the first stages of mental illness.

In an 1888 paper, "Über Zwangsvorstellungen," Meynert again
discusses the relationship between mental abnormalities and vascular

disturbances: "With regard to [neuropsychiatric syndromes] which fail to yield either gross or well-established fine microscopic findings, . . . we see the most intense forms emanating from vasomotor disturbances." He goes on to note that "where both anatomically demonstrable disease and vasomotor explanations of the symptoms are lacking, one [has traditionally supposed] some unproveable molecular disturbance of the nerves."[28] This applies particularly, Meynert states, to standard discussions of the early stages of insanity. But he asserts that "it is evident that nowadays this explanation in terms of obscure, purely molecular disturbances is driven too far," and he proceeds to develop a more definitive formula for the psychoses. These supposed "molecular disturbances" are really nutritional disturbances on a cellular level; more specifically, they involve the failure of cortical cells to attract nutritive elements from the blood. The cortical abnormality can be due to some congenital cellular anomaly or to a local vascular abnormality: "The inclination to psychosis . . . is thus based upon the weakness of the nutritive attraction of the nerve cells."[29] Nutritional failure and subsequent degeneration of these cells produce psychic disturbances. Meynert in this way extends the concept of local anatomical changes to all forms of psychosis.

In his 1868 paper, Meynert, after arguing for the localization of psychic functions, proceeds to consider the mechanism of their integration. This integration is brought about by "what I might call the general association system of the cerebral lobes, which by connecting the nearest and most distant areas of the same hemisphere with one another [through 'association tracts'] probably effects an actual total union of cortical areas."[30] It is the association system which accounts for the association of ideas and the construction of trains of thought. The incorporation of associationist psychology into models of brain function had been a fixture in neurophysiology for most of the century, but Meynert was exceptional in his efforts to delineate the association tracts anatomically.

The cortex is thus divided into psychic centers, association tracts, and projection tracts (which connect the cortex to the peripheral nerves and to subcortical centers). In *Psychiatrie*, Meynert then proceeds to a more comprehensive model of brain function. Like Griesinger, he speaks of the essential reflex action of the nervous system, and he regards higher cerebral functions as involving essentially the modification of reflex behavior. Meynert, however, makes the distinction an anatomical one: subcortical centers control reflex acts, while cortical centers work by modifying reflexes.

The influence of the cortex on lower centers is regarded by Meynert as primarily inhibitory, and he goes on to interpret some clinical symptoms in terms of a weakening of inhibitory controls. This concept is not original, but Meynert again proceeds to give it a peculiar anatomical interpretation. In a number of papers he proposes that various syndromes can be explained in terms of ischemia of the cortical centers and relative hyperemia of the subcortical parts of the brain. Meynert argues that the subcortical areas, being closer to the heart, enjoy a higher perfusion pressure than the cortex and consequently the cortex will always be more vulnerable to ischemia and debilitation.[31]

Meynert believed that this model was applicable particularly to a group of neuropsychiatric syndromes—distinct from the psychoses—which were commonly labelled "functional" illnesses. These were diseases for which no clear-cut anatomical lesion had been discovered (including hysteria and related neuroses); and the term *functional* had been introduced earlier in the century to signify changes in nervous system function unaccompanied by changes in structure. But Meynert insisted, of course, that diseases invariably involve structural changes. He suggested that cortical ischemia and subcortical hyperemia are the initial pathological alterations in these syndromes, and that the ischemia and hyperemia are brought about by vascular disturbances. According to Meynert, persistent ischemia leads eventually to cortical necrosis and permanent anatomical lesions, and these lesions are the basis for the fully established "functional" syndromes. Meynert presents this theme in several papers, including "Zum Verstandniss der functionellen Nervenkrankheiten" (1882) and "Über functionellen Nervenkrankheiten" (1883).[32]

Meynert followed Griesinger again by adapting the ego psychology of Herbart, but he once more insisted upon an anatomical interpretation. Herbart wrote of the ego's repression of disturbing ideas. Meynert wrote in 1868:

> The rigid enclosure of the brain permits . . . only limited spatial expansion, so that under the rates of pressure which appear consistent with the unwinding of a conscious process, the spatial expansion of a part of the brain—established through local vascular engorgement—must render more difficult a similar spatial expansion in another part of the brain. The expression of Herbart's: Ideas strive to repress each other from consciousness, can thus be paraphrased by an appreciation of the relative nutrition of the [parts of] the brain.[33]

Meynert in this way reduces the psychological concept of repression to cerebral anatomy and a reciprocal ischemia and hyperemia of different parts of the brain.

The above examples illustrate how Meynert, while adopting the psychological and neurophysiological concepts which were popular in contemporary schemes of brain function, simply integrated them into his anatomical models. These models, built upon the basic notion of the cortical localization of psychic functions, were in turn the foundation of his comprehensive pathoanatomical theories of mental illness. Meynert, in developing this most thorough of pathoanatomical psychiatries, became the acknowledged leader of this type of psychiatry and established Vienna as its chief center.

The Predominance of Pathoanatomical Psychiatry

In the years after the establishment of Griesinger's professorship in Berlin, Chairs of Psychiatry, along with psychiatric teaching clinics, were founded at a number of German-speaking universities; during the last decades of the century these positions were dominated by pathoanatomically oriented psychiatrists. This pattern is particularly striking in the major medical teaching centers. In Vienna, Meynert continued as professor of psychiatry and head of the psychiatric clinic at the Vienna General Hospital from 1875 until 1892. In Berlin, following Griesinger's death (1869), and in Leipzig, Zurich, Munich, and elsewhere, the professorships were held by men who shared Meynert's anatomical approach.

In Berlin, Griesinger was succeeded by Carl Westphal, who continued as professor of psychiatry and head of the psychiatric teaching clinic at the Charité Hospital until 1890. Westphal, in an article on his predecessor written in 1869, criticized Griesinger's occasional psychological and physiological speculations and suggested that psychiatry could be advanced only through the correlation of clinical symptoms with cerebral lesions.[34] He expressed similar views a decade later, in an address entitled "Psychiatrie und psychiatrischer Unterricht" (1880). Westphal states in this address that the task confronting psychiatry is to establish "the connections between the various clinical pictures and . . . anatomical changes, so that the latter can be inferred from the former."[35] He acknowledges that some psychiatric syndromes often do not yield distinguishable anatomical lesions, even with microscopic examination. But he attributes this to the limitations of the microscope and to the brain's ability to make adaptive changes. Westphal later asserts that neuropathological studies are as relevant to the neuroses as they are to illnesses characterized by gross anatomical lesions. He argues that the symptoms of the neuroses parallel those of the latter illnesses, and that one can infer from the gross lesions found in the latter syndromes the probable locus of more subtle anatomical changes in the former.[36]

The professorship of psychiatry at Munich was established in 1872; and the Chair, together with directorship of the university-affiliated asylum, was held by Bernard von Gudden until his death in 1886. Gudden, like Meynert, was primarily a neuroanatomist and owed his academic appointments to his neuroanatomical achievements. These included the delineation of various cerebral tracts and nuclei (the crossed and uncrossed fibers of the optic tracts, the transverse peduncular tract, the interpeduncular nucleus, the tegmental nuclei [dorsal and ventral nuclei of Gudden], and several thalamic nuclei). He is also credited with the important observation that lesions of the cerebral cortex do not cause atrophy of peripheral nerves (Gudden's law).[37] Auguste Forel, who in 1873 was appointed Gudden's assistant at the Munich asylum, writes of their first meeting: "Herr and Frau Professor Gudden welcomed me very amiably, but then Gudden launched without more ado into a discussion of the anatomy of the brain, and was apparently prepared to go on showing me his fine preparations of rabbits' brains until further notice."[38] Through Forel, who had studied under Meynert in Vienna, Gudden became an enthusiastic student of Meynert's recent work in the microscopic anatomy of the brain and of Meynert's theories on the localization of functions. He shared with Meynert the view that psychiatry must proceed by a correlation of clinical symptoms with brain lesions.

The Chair of Psychiatry at the University of Zurich was founded in 1869 and held by Gudden until he moved to Munich. Auguste Forel assumed the post, along with directorship of the Burghölzli mental hospital, in 1879 and continued in these appointments until 1898. Forel, like Meynert and Gudden, received his psychiatric professorship on the basis of his work in neuroanatomy. He studied neuroanatomy under Meynert during the winter of 1871–1872 and, while remaining highly skeptical of Meynert's grand schemes of localization, he became an enthusiastic student of the field. He wrote his doctoral thesis on anatomical studies of the optic thalamus, and in subsequent years was the first to describe the tegmental fields, the zona incerta, and several other brain structures. Much of this work was done while he was Gudden's assistant at Munich, and Forel wrote of his time at the Munich asylum: "Pleasanter than my duties in the ward was my work on the anatomy of the brain, which I eagerly continued. My great series of sections had given me quite a new understanding of the structure of the human brain."[39]

Forel continued to pursue his anatomical studies after his appointment to the professorship at Zurich. His neuroanatomical and pathoanatomical research led, for example, to his independent promulgation of the neurone theory—the theory that the neural cell-body and its appendages comprise a single cellular unit, or "neurone"—published two months after Wilhelm His's famous paper on the same theme (1886).

Paul Flechsig was appointed Professor-extraordinarius in psychiatry at the University of Leipzig in 1877. In 1882 he became director of the newly established university psychiatric clinic and two years later he became the first full professor of psychiatry at Leipzig. He continued in this Chair, as well as in his clinical post, for almost forty years. Flechsig was greatly influenced by Meynert and, according to one biographer, it was Meynert's article on mammalian brain structure in Solomon Stricker's *Handbuch* (1872) that inspired Flechsig to prepare a series of brain sections from human neonates.[40] These sections led to the discovery that, in some nerve tracts in which the nerve fibers have myelin sheaths, the fibers acquire their myelin in a sequential process that actually continues for some time after birth. Neuroanatomists, by subsequently studying brain sections from infants of various ages and observing the sequence of myelination, gained a powerful tool for tracing and distinquishing neural pathways. Flechsig first used the technique to delineate the course of the dorsal spinocerebellar tract (Flechsig's tract) and the pyramidal tract. In later years he turned to investigations of cortical myelination and used his findings to develop his own topography of the cortex.

Flechsig had been made chief of the microscopic anatomy section in Carl Ludwig's Institute of Physiology in 1873, and he is yet another who received his later psychiatric appointments on the basis of his accomplishments as a neuroanatomist. Indeed, his knowledge of clinical psychiatry was so limited that, upon being appointed to the Chair of Psychiatry at Leipzig, he was given several years' leave of absence for travel and study at various psychiatric institutes.[41]

In his monograph *Die Körperlichen Grundlagen der Geistesstörungen* (1882), Flechsig acknowledges that not all forms of mental illness presently yield to anatomical explanations, nor are they likely to in the future. But he argues that "the pursuit of autopsy findings offers gen-

erally the most direct way to advance the recognition of regular relationships between psychic disturbances and brain anomalies . . . because the structural peculiarities of the brain yield far more reference
points for the judgement of psycho-physical mechanisms than all
other . . . experiments relative to the brain."[42]

As new Chairs were established in other universities, they continued to be filled by men whose orientation was towards pathological
anatomy. Prominent examples are Carl Wernicke, who was appointed
professor of psychiatry at Breslau in 1890, and Arnold Pick, who
received the professorship at the German university in Prague in
1886. Wernicke was a student of Meynert's and later Westphal's assistant at the Charité in Berlin. He was perhaps, aside from Meynert,
the most prominent proponent of pathoanatomical psychiatry. In
1874 Wernicke published a paper entitled "Der aphasische Symptomencomplex" in which he argued, on the basis of pathoanatomical
evidence, that the frequently observed phenomenon of sensory aphasia—loss of the power to comprehend spoken words—is caused by
lesions in the posterior part of the first convolution of the brain's
temporal lobe. Wernicke acknowledged in the paper that he was
strongly influenced by Meynert and by Paul Broca, who in 1861 had
presented a paper demonstrating a localized lesion in a patient suffering from loss of the capacity to speak (motor aphasia). Broca's work
had given considerable impetus to arguments concerning the localization of psychic functions and the localization of lesions in mental
disease, and Wernicke's monograph had the same effect. In 1881–
1883 Wernicke published his three-volume *Lehrbuch der Gehirnkrankheiten,* which offers a comprehensive study of the successes thus far
achieved in the correlation of psychic disturbances with local cerebral
lesions. The foreword to the first volume begins: "In the sphere of
brain diseases there is still missing to a great extent the basic material
upon which every clinical discipline is built: good clinical observations
combined with authentic dissection findings."[43] The aim of the book
was to help correct this situation.

In his foreword to the second volume, Wernicke presents extensive
arguments in favor of the localization of cortical functions, maintaining
"that all opposition [to the theory of localization] is specious, was first
shown when, through Meynert's anatomical research, a clear idea was
gained of the structure of the brain and the possible functions of its
cortical layers."[44] Later, Wernicke questions to what extent a focal
symptom warrants the expectation that a localized lesion will be found.
He concludes that, with the exception of some congenital diseases and

some diseases involving diffuse cerebral changes, such lesions can generally be demonstrated.

These citations indicate the extent to which Wernicke adopted Meynert's viewpoint. A neuropsychiatrist who attended lectures by Wernicke adds, in a short biographical sketch: "Meynert's portrait was the only one which hung on the walls of the auditorium in Wernicke's clinic, and his name was one of the few ever mentioned by Wernicke in his lectures."[45]

Arnold Pick, professor of psychiatry at the German university in Prague from 1886, had been an assistant in Meynert's laboratory while still a medical student in Vienna. After graduation, he had worked with Westphal and Wernicke at the Charité in Berlin. Pick did extensive research on the localization of psychic functions based on pathoanatomical studies. His work in pathological anatomy also led to significant clinical contributions, such as the correlation of one form of presenile dementia with a specific pattern of cerebral atrophy (Pick's disease).

Pick, like Flechsig, was not committed to the dogma of pathoanatomical psychiatry—the insistence that all psychic abnormalities are due to anatomical lesions in the brain—in the sense that Meynert, Wernicke, and Westphal were; nor indeed was Forel or Gudden. But Pick, Flechsig, Gudden, and Forel all shared with the others a preference for the anatomical laboratory over the clinic, and a belief that psychiatry's major insights would be won at the dissecting table.

With these men controlling the university Chairs of Psychiatry, the pathoanatomical approach dominated psychiatric education in central Europe through the last decades of the nineteenth century.

Freud and the Pathoanatomical Tradition

Freud's Viennese training, much of it under Meynert, put particular emphasis on anatomical studies, and his early research work was primarily in neuroanatomy. These experiences determined his subsequent medical interests, and throughout his early career Freud envisioned his future contribution to lie in the fields of normal and pathological neuroanatomy.

The extent to which his early research—that done in Ernst Brücke's laboratory as well as that pursued under Meynert—was devoted to neuroanatomy can be seen from a curriculum vitae submitted by Freud in 1897 as part of his application for professorship.[46] Listed are fifteen papers which were written prior to his return from his visit with Charcot in Paris (1886). Of these, nine concern neuroanatomical studies:

1. "On the origin of the posterior nerve-roots in the spinal cord of Ammocoetes (Petromyzon planeri)" (1877)
2. "On the spinal ganglia and spinal cord of Petromyzon" (1878)
3. "Note upon a method for anatomical preparations of the nervous system" (1879)
4. "On the structure of the nerve fibres and nerve cells of the river crayfish" (1881)
5. "The structure of the elements of the nervous system" (1884)
6. "A new method for the study of nerve-tracts in the central nervous system" (1884)
7. "A note upon the inter-olivary tract" (1885)
8. "On the relation of the restiform body to the posterior column and its nucleus with some remarks on two fields of the medulla oblongata"—jointly with L. Darkewitsch (1886)
9. "On the origin of the auditory nerve" (1886)

Three other papers are case histories of patients suffering from well-defined nervous system lesions, together with autopsy findings from the two who succumbed:

1. "A case of cerebral hemorrhage with indirect basal focal symptoms in a patient suffering from scurvy" (1884)
2. "A case of muscular atrophy with extensive disturbances of sensibility (syringomyelia)" (1885)
3. "Acute multiple neuritis of the spinal and cranial nerves" (1885)

(Of the remaining three papers, two are on cocaine and one, his first publication, is a histological study of eel testes.) These anatomical and clinical papers were the basis for Freud's 1885 appointment as lecturer (*Privatdocent*); and the comments of Freud's chief sponsor, Brücke, in favor of the appointment are full of praise for his anatomical work. Brücke was seconded by Meynert and Hermann Nothnagel (professor of medicine), who shared Brücke's enthusiasm for Freud's anatomical research.[47]

Freud's contact with Meynert was, of course, a major factor in his anatomical orientation. Freud was a student of Meynert's in medical school and later served as assistant (*Secundararzt*) in Meynert's psychiatric clinic (May to October, 1883). He also worked for two years (1883–

1885) in Meynert's laboratory. Freud writes in *An Autobiographical Study:* "One day Meynert, who had given me access to the laboratory even during the times when I was not actually working under him, proposed that I should definitely devote myself to the anatomy of the brain, and promised to hand over his lecturing work to me, as he felt he was too old to manage the newer methods.[48]

Freud concurred with Meynert's opinion that he ought to pursue a career as a brain anatomist, and his correspondence is full of references to his current and contemplated work in the field. He was, in fact, warned at one point by Nothnagel, the professor of medicine, that in the interest of a future practice he ought to spend less time in the laboratory and devote more effort to clinical work: "General practitioners, on whom everything depends [for referrals], are prosaic people who'll think to themselves: 'What's the good of Freud's knowledge of brain anatomy? That won't help him to treat a radialis paralysis!' "[49]

Freud's general approach to pathology was, at this time, consistent with his anatomical orientation. *An Autobiographical Study* contains the following anecdote:

> The fame of my diagnoses and of their *post-mortem* confirmation brought me an influx of American physicians, to whom I lectured upon the patients in my department in a sort of pidgin-English. About the neuroses I understood nothing. On one occasion I introduced to my audience a neurotic suffering from a persistent headache as a case of chronic localized meningitis; they all quite rightly rose in revolt and deserted me, and my premature activities as a teacher came to an end. By way of excuse I may add that this happened at a time when greater authorities than myself in Vienna were in the habit of diagnosing hysteria as cerebral tumour.[50]

Freud's concentration on neuroanatomy persisted until the period of his contact with Charcot. In May, 1885, he wrote to his fiancée, Martha Bernays: "I am at the moment tempted by the desire to solve the riddle of the structure of the brain; I think brain anatomy is the only legitimate rival you have or ever will have." In speaking of his planned trip to Paris, he remarked: "What I want, as you know, is to go to Paris . . . [and] have enough leisure to finish my work on the brain.[51]

Freud did, in fact, continue his anatomical studies at the Salpetrière. In his report submitted to the Faculty of Medicine two months after his return to Vienna, he writes:

> I had arrived [in Paris] with the intention of making one
> single question the subject of a thorough investigation; and
> since in Vienna my chosen concern had been with anatomical
> problems, I had selected the study of the secondary atrophies
> and degenerations that follow on affections of the brain in
> children. Some extremely valuable pathological material was
> put at my disposal, but I found that the conditions for making
> use of it were most unfavorable. The laboratory was not at all
> adapted to the reception of an extraneous worker, and such
> space and resources as existed were made inacessible owing to
> lack of any kind of organization. I thus found myself obliged
> to give up anatomical work and rest content with a discovery
> concerned with the relations of the nuclei of the posterior
> column in the medulla oblongata. Later, however, I had an
> opportunity of resuming some similar investigations with Dr.
> von Darkewitsch (of Moscow); and our collaboration led to a
> publication in the *Neurologisches Centralblatt,* bearing the title
> "On the relation of the restiform body to the posterior col-
> umn and its nucleus, with some remarks on two fields of the
> medulla oblongata."[52]

Freud's education, and his subsequent commitment both to basic
anatomical research and to a pathoanatomical approach to neuropsychiatric disorders, clearly place him in the pathoanatomical tradition; and it was undoubtedly quite a jolt for him to hear Charcot
proclaiming in Paris that "the work of anatomy was finished and . . .
the theory of the organic[*] diseases of the nervous system might be
said to be complete."[53]

The Opposition to Pathoanatomical Psychiatry

There was opposition to the pathoanatomical emphasis in psychiatry throughout the period of its ascendancy. In particular, the older
asylum psychiatrists resented the appointment to professorial positions
of men who had been trained essentially in the anatomical laboratory;

Organic was commonly used at this time as synonymous with *anatomical* (signifying
those diseases in which structural changes are readily discerned), and as distinct from
functional (signifying illnesses which were believed by various observers to involve changes
in nervous system function unaccompanied by structural alterations). Whenever, in subsequent quotations, *organic* is used in this sense—rather than in the sense of *physical,* as
opposed to *psychological*—I will note the meaning intended.

and the latter were attacked for their lack of clinical experience and their neglect of the eclectic, humanistic clinical tradition. In Vienna, for example, Meynert was the chief target of such attacks. His conflict with the head of the Lower Austria National Asylum led on one occasion to a demand for his resignation from a clinical appointment.[54]

But the arguments of the asylum psychiatrists had little impact, largely because the professors who controlled university positions were generally research-oriented and felt a greater affinity for neuroanatomists than for men whose interests were primarily clinical and administrative. Consequently, the appointment of brain anatomists to Chairs of Psychiatry continued.

In the early 1880s, however, a more significant opposition began to emerge, one which developed among psychiatrists who were trained in the pathoanatomical tradition and were nevertheless dissatisfied with it. The pathoanatomical approach had remained relatively unchallenged by its students so long as it continued to yield impressive results in the elucidation of various neurological and psychiatric syndromes; but its success merely removed these syndromes from the list of pathological problems and left behind on that list, to receive increasingly more attention, disease entities less amenable to pathoanatomical investigation. Even in those cases where the anatomical approach had succeeded, once psychiatrists had absorbed the information yielded by pathological anatomy, they demanded refinements—detailed explanations of symptoms—which anatomical studies often could not offer. It was these factors which now triggered, among psychiatrists who were students of the anatomical method, the most significant challenges to pathoanatomical psychiatry, and which inspired the formulation of new models and new approaches.

These psychiatrists generally emphasized one of two points. Some did not dispute that anatomical lesions might ultimately be found for all psychiatric syndromes, but they insisted that a greater understanding of the symptoms and the clinical course of mental diseases was needed and that this, at least for the time being, had to be sought through more intensive clinical studies rather than at the dissecting table. Others, focusing on theoretical rather than clinical considerations, noted that, in a number of psychiatric disorders, the anatomists had failed to discover any clear-cut lesions, and they emphasized the need for alternative formulas for the pathology of these particular syndromes.

The most important indictment of pathoanatomical psychiatry from a clinical perspective came from Emil Kraepelin, who had been an assistant to Gudden in Munich and had later worked in Flechsig's neuroanatomical laboratory in Leipzig. In a monograph entitled "Die Richtungen der Psychiatrischen Forschung" (1887), Kraepelin writes:

> At first, to be sure, the fruits of pathoanatomical research in the area of the nervous system were virtually all to the good; and Griesinger energetically proclaimed that this was the approach to diseases of the nervous system from which psychiatry might expect a broadening of its scientific perception. However, one cannot say that up to now the results of pathoanatomical research have in fact essentially advanced the understanding of mental illness.

Kraepelin is in part concerned with the failure of the pathoanatomical approach to cast any light on some forms of insanity; but he also questions the extent of its contribution even with regard to those syndromes for which it has uncovered underlying anatomical lesions:

> To be sure definite changes in the nervous system are known to us as the basis of nervous phenomena, especially paralyses, which accompany particular forms of insanity; indeed, the intensity and breadth of [symptomatic] disturbances appear to display a certain general dependency on the anatomical lesion—unfortunately, however, no definite gains emerge from this for which psychiatry might be indebted to pathological anatomy. Apart from this, the actual relationship between cerebral changes and psychic anomalies remains a complete mystery to us, and the dissection findings, even in a series of the most developed forms of insanity, leave us still totally in the dark.[55]

If Kraepelin seems somewhat acerbic in his denigration of the accomplishments of pathoanatomical psychiatry, he is actually rather sanguine with regard to the potential of the pathoanatomical approach and speaks optimistically of new techniques available to the anatomist. His attack is not directed at pathological neuroanatomy per se, but rather at the tendency of the anatomical psychiatrists to overrate their achievements and to derive fanciful models of symptom formation exclusively from their anatomical findings. His particular target in this vein is Meynert:

> We are today still far from the sought-after goal, further perhaps than is immediately apparent. Here is the point at

which fantasy, unencumbered by the uncomfortable drag of facts, begins to outrace the slow advances of empirical science. . . .

. . . to be sure reference to the current concepts of the rest of medicine gives a certain general direction [to the speculators]; however, the scope which is here offered to speculation is too wide, so the originality of the individual research cannot fully come to expression in these [accepted] concepts. Undoubtedly the most outstanding representative of this type of psychiatry is Theodor Meynert who in a significant manner defines his science as the study of diseases of the forebrain, based on its structure, function and nutrition. Just as in the area of brain anatomy he has conceived and presented with ingenious vision the general structural plan of the central nervous system, despite the most imperfect factual basis, so has he also prophetically attempted to sketch for us a picture of the mechanism of brain pathology.[56]

Kraepelin calls for a greater emphasis on other approaches, particularly careful clinical observation, as an alternative to what he regards as sterile speculation based on inadequate laboratory data. The same argument is made by Richard von Krafft-Ebing, who had received part of his training under Griesinger and in 1889 joined the Vienna faculty.[57] In his inaugural address, Krafft-Ebing attacks Meynert's pretense that mental illness can be "explained" on the basis of recent anatomical discoveries. He states that "the psychiatry of today can only claim the title of a 'descriptive science', not an 'explanatory science' "[58] He insists, with Kraepelin, that more effort must be devoted to careful clinical description.

But Krafft-Ebing, again like Kraepelin, does not see any specific limitations to the potential of pathoanatomical investigation for ultimately discovering structural changes in all forms of mental illness. On the contrary, he states in his textbook, *Lehrbuch der Psychiatrie auf Klinische Grundlage*, that, while there are still many syndromes which have not been correlated with pathoanatomical changes, their number is constantly decreasing and "the hope can be maintained that . . . diligence and destiny, in combination with improved instruments, will with time reduce [the syndromes without identified lesions] to a minimum."[59]

There were others, however, from the ranks of the pathoanatomical psychiatrists who came to regard particular neuropsychiatric syndromes as entirely independent of any anatomical lesion and as therefore unapproachable via pathoanatomical studies.[60] The syndromes most often cited as requiring alternative, nonanatomical explanations were hysteria and related neuroses.

Paul Flechsig, in *Die Körperlichen Grundlagen der Geistesstörungen* (1882), explicitly dissociated himself from those who wanted to "pathoanatomically characterize and classify all forms of mental illness. I am far from believing this presently or generally to be practicable."[61] He referred to the neuroses as a prototype of those mental illnesses which must be regarded as "functional," that is, those which are characterized by a disturbance of nervous activity without any accompanying anatomical lesion. But Flechsig did not undertake any investigations of such syndromes. He remained in the pathoanatomical laboratory and continued to insist that pathological anatomy offers by far the most fruitful approach to psychiatry.

Among the first of the German pathoanatomical psychiatrists to acknowledge the existence of nonanatomical syndromes and to pursue studies in this area was Hermann Oppenheim, Westphal's protégé and favorite assistant in Berlin. In 1884 he published a paper with Robert Thomsen in which he characterized *traumatic neuroses*—nervous system abnormalities which were often found to follow accidents and which clinically resembled hysteria—as constituting a distinct and well-defined syndrome. In his statements of that year, Oppenheim is noncommittal as to whether an anatomical lesion is involved; but in subsequent years he pursued his investigation of traumatic neuroses and consistently rejected pathoanatomical explanations.[62]

Westphal had in 1880 acknowledged that neurotic patients generally yield no anatomical lesions on autopsy, but he expressed a belief that such lesions would ultimately be discovered. A year earlier, at a clinical case presentation, Westphal had considered the pathology of *railway spine,* a syndrome associated with railway accidents in which the patient's physical injuries did not appear severe enough to account for his symptoms (e.g., paralyses, pain, sensory abnormalities). Railway spine was first described by John Erickson in England in 1876 and was the prototype of traumatic neurosis. Westphal suggested that the syndrome is based on a myelitis, an inflamation of the spinal cord. He also intimated that some cases, presumably those which do not fit the clinical picture of a myelitis, may be due to simulation on the part of the patient for the purpose of collecting compensation.[63]

In his book entitled *Die traumatischen Neurosen* (1889), Oppenheim attacks Westphal's position using as his explicit target the neurologist K. T. Rigler. Rigler, like Westphal, had also suggested that traumatic neuroses are due either to a myelitis or to simulation. Oppenheim asserts that

> between the earlier conception, that subsequent to a general physical shock a chronic inflammatory process develops in the spinal cord and in its meninges, and the modern view, there exists so great a difference, that only with emancipation from the older theory could a truly fruitful study of traumatic neuroses begin.

He explains his own views in this way:

> It differs from the older teaching first and foremost in this: that it is hardly a question of spinal shock or spinal disease, but rather the brain, the psyche, is regarded as the only or principal seat of the disease, irrespective of the site of trauma; further, it differs [from the older view] especially in this point—that the basis of the disease is to be sought not in demonstrable pathoanatomical changes, but rather in functional disturbances.[64]

But it was Jean Martin Charcot who was most responsible for promoting the study of the neuroses as disease entities inexplicable in pathoanatomical terms, and his leadership was acknowledged by virtually all contemporary workers in the field, including Oppenheim: "It is an outstanding service of Charcot's to have cast a new light on the essence of these diseases through his campaign, pursued with persevering consistency, in favor of the functional character of all symptoms, and in general to have opened the study of the previously poorly trod field of [these] diseases."[65] Charcot was still in the thick of this controversy over the pathology of the neuroses when Freud embarked for Paris and the Saltpetrière.

3. Charcot, Freud, and the Physiological Model of Hysteria

Charcot on Hysteria

Jean Martin Charcot received his medical education from the Paris Faculty of Medicine, and became professor of anatomy and pathology at Paris in 1872. The pathoanatomical orientation was still firmly entrenched in Paris, and Charcot initially shared this anatomical bias, as shown in the preface to an American edition of his *Lectures on Localization in Diseases of the Brain* (1875):

> In the lectures . . . I have selected, as occasion required, information furnished by normal anatomy, experimental physiology, and clinical observation, illustrated by minute and methodical examination of organic [i.e., anatomical] lesions.
>
> I have always given precedence, however, to the last-mentioned order of testimony, convinced that, although normal anatomy and experimental physiology may serve to indicate the true direction; still, clinical and pathological research is necessary (in the case of the human subject) to a final judgment and the furnishing of proof.[1]

Charcot's reputation as a neurologist was based on his work in elucidating the anatomical lesions associated with a variety of diseases, including tabes dorsalis, multiple sclerosis, and amyotropic lateral sclerosis;[2] and he published several volumes of lectures on the localization of lesions in diseases of the brain and spinal cord.[3]

Charcot's earliest views on the underlying pathology of hysteria were consistent with this background, and he is cited frequently in the neurological literature of the late 1860s and 1870s as having demonstrated anatomical lesions in hysterical patients.[4] In a collection of lec-

tures published in 1877, Charcot argued that hysterical hemianesthesia—the loss of tactile sensation on one side of the body—has the same
etiology as other anesthesias and is due to a "circumscribed lesion of
the cerebral hemispheres"; he presented pathoanatomical evidence
supporting this view.

In a lecture given in 1882, Charcot again asserts his faith in the
primacy of pathological anatomy, noting that "it is often said that the
progress of medicine and of pathological anatomy go side by side. This
is specially true in diseases of the nervous system." But he modifies his
position with respect to hysteria:

> From what has been said it will be understood how much
> importance we ought to accord in our studies to the anatomo-
> pathological method of research. But you are aware, gentle-
> men, that there still exists at the present time a great number
> of morbid states, evidently having their seat in the nervous
> system, which leave in the dead body no material trace that
> can be discovered. [Various illnesses, among them hysteria],
> come to us like so many Sphynx, which deny the most pene-
> trating anatomical investigations. These symptomatic combi-
> nations deprived of anatomical substratum, do not present
> themselves to the mind of the physician with that appearance
> of solidity, of objectivity, which belong to affections connected
> with an appreciable organic [i.e., anatomical] lesion.
>
> There are some even who see in several of these affec-
> tions only an assemblage of odd incoherent phenomena in-
> accessible to analysis, and which had better, perhaps, be ban-
> ished to the category of the unknown. It is hysteria which
> especially comes under this sort of proscription. . . . [But]
> much credit is due to Briquet for having established in his
> excellent book, in a manner beyond dispute, that hysteria [as
> regards the pattern of symptoms found from patient to
> patient] is governed, in the same way as other morbid condi-
> tions, by rules and laws, which attentive and sufficiently nu-
> merous observations always permit us to establish.[5]

Charcot, in the balance of the lecture, pursues this thesis that hysteria,
despite the absence of anatomical lesions, is a clear-cut entity which
follows definite rules. He also offers evidence that hysterical symptoms
cannot be attributed to intentional deception by the patient. (For example, he describes tests done on an hysterical patient who maintained
his arm outstretched, in a "frozen" posture, as one of his hysterical

symptoms. Charcot argues that the patient displayed neither the fine tremors nor the fatigue that a mere simulator would necessarily exhibit.) On the question of simulation he concludes: "A hundred other examples might be invoked which would only show that the simulation, which is talked about so much when hysteria and allied affections are under consideration, is, in the [current] state of our knowledge, only a bugbear, before which the fearful and novice alone are stopped."[6]

While the consistent lack of autopsy findings cast doubt on the presence of anatomical lesions in hysteria, this hardly constituted a comprehensive proof that such lesions do not exist; and Charcot did not base his conviction regarding the absence of lesions in hysteria solely on the autopsy evidence. He also believed that the symptoms of hysteria do not resemble symptoms caused by anatomical lesions. In another lecture from 1882 ("Two Cases of Hysterical Contraction of Traumatic Origin"[7]), as in all his subsequent case presentations of hysterical patients, Charcot is primarily concerned with establishing this point that the patients' symptoms do not resemble those caused by anatomical lesions, but do fit the "rules" of hysteria. He thereby corroborates the absence of lesions on autopsy with clinical evidence that no such lesions are involved; in addition, he reinforces his argument that hysteria is nevertheless a bona-fide pathological entity which presents a consistent clinical picture. His first patient is a female. The demonstration involves: (1) noting hereditary indications of a possible predisposition to mental illness (her father died in a lunatic asylum and her brother is severely retarded); (2) displaying the characteristic, "nonanatomical" nature of the contracture (e.g., hysterical contractures are more intense and more consistent—the intensity does not vary between sleep and waking—than are contractures due to anatomical lesions); (3) pointing out other "typical" hysterical symptoms in the patient (in this case, hemianesthesia, hemianalgesia, and other phenomena). The second case, that of a man, is approached in the same manner.

In rejecting an anatomical basis for hysteria, Charcot shifts to the position that the pathology of the disease involves a neurodynamic abnormality; that is, some purely physiological disturbance of the nervous system. In a lecture given in 1885, Charcot asserts that "the collection of symptoms which have been unfolded, so inexplicable on the hypothesis of an organic [i.e., anatomical] lesion of the brain, spinal cord, or peripheral nerves, admits of a very simple interpretation on the supposition of a dynamic hysterical lesion." And he remarks: "The prognosis naturally follows from the diagnosis, and it is clear that it will be infinitely less grave in cases of this nature [i.e., in diseases caused by neurodynamic changes] than in such [syndromes] as supervene on a destructive [anatomical] lesion."[8]

Charcot then considers the question of what sort of therapeutic intervention might best help to bring this hopeful prognosis to fruition. He suggests that therapy would be most effective if it were "founded on a physiological basis" and were based on a recognition of the mechanism responsible for the patient's difficulties. This leads him into a consideration of hypnosis.

Charcot had been discussing hypnosis in the context of the pathology of hysteria for several years. He believed that hypnosis itself involves physiological changes in the nervous system, or, according to a discussion of Charcot's views by Freud,

> that the mechanism of some at least of the manifestations of hypnotism is based upon physiological changes—that is, upon displacements of excitability in the nervous system, occurring without the participation of those parts of it which operate with consciousness; they [i.e., Charcot's school] speak, therefore, of the physical or physiological phenomena of hypnosis.[9]

Charcot further argued that hypnosis has peculiar manifestations in a person suffering from hysteria, manifestations presumably related to the basic dynamic abnormalities of the nervous system in these people. Charcot labels this type of hypnosis *grand hypnotisme*. To quote again from Freud: "Unlike normal hypnotized subjects, these hysterical patients are said to exhibit three stages of hypnosis, each of which is distinguished by special physical signs of a most remarkable kind (such as enormous neuro-muscular hyper-excitability, somnambulistic contractures, etc.)."[10]

The three stages of *grand hypnotisme* are the lethargic, the cataleptic, and the somnambulic. In a series of lectures given in 1885, Charcot demonstrated how, by means of verbal suggestions to a patient in the somnambulic state, he could artificially produce "a perfect imitation of the monoplegia caused in our two other patients by a process apparently very different, the action of traumatism [i.e., an accidental blow to a limb]."[11] After awakening the patient, so that power was restored to her paralyzed arm, he once again hypnotized her; and, by this time striking her on the shoulder, he again induced a monoplegia exactly duplicating that of his traumatized patients. He concluded:

It may be inquired whether the mental condition occasioned by the emotion, by the Nervous Shock experienced at the moment of the accident [suffered by the other two patients] and for some time after, is not equivalent in a certain measure, in subjects predisposed . . . to the cerebral condition which is determined in "hysterics" by hypnotism. Upon the assumption of this hypothesis, the peculiar sensation felt by our hysterical female in the member submitted to shock, and which we may suppose to have been produced in the same degree and with the same characters in our two male patients by a fall on the shoulder, that sensation, I say, may be considered as having originated, in the former as in the latter, the idea of motor paralysis of the member. But because of the annihilation of the *ego* produced by the hypnotism in the one case, and, as one may suppose, by the nervous shock in the other, that idea once installed in the brain takes sole possession and acquires sufficient domination to realise itself objectively in the form of paralysis. The sensation, in question, therefore, in both the cases plays the part of a veritable *suggestion.* [12]

Charcot thus develops a model for the etiology of hysteria of traumatic origin. In a nervous system conditioned by an hysterical diathesis—that is, an hereditary predisposition to hysteria—nervous shock or fear induces an hypnotic state which renders the victim susceptible to suggestion. The trauma then provides the suggestion of paralysis. Beyond an etiological explanation, Charcot also derives from this model a therapeutic program. He begins regularly to use suggestion, both under hypnosis and without it, as an instrument for relieving hysterical symptoms.

Charcot's work on hysteria was a major step in the revolt against the domination of Continental neuropsychiatry by pathological anatomy. A professor of pathology and anatomy was here explicitly rejecting the anatomical approach and proposing instead a physiological or "dynamic" model. With this work hysteria was established as a key syndrome in the search for new explanations of psychopathology.

Hysteria as a Dynamic Lesion

The concept that hysteria is a functional illness—that it involves a physiological abnormality, but no anatomical lesion—did not originate with Charcot. The physiological emphasis can be traced at least in part to William Cullen who, in the previous century, coined the term *neuroses* and defined them as

> all those preternatural affections of sense and motion, which are without pyrexia as a part of the primary disease; and all those which do not depend upon a topical affection of the organs, but upon a more general affection of the nervous system, and of those powers of the system upon which sense and motion more especially depend.[13]

Cullen's text, *First Lines in the Practice of Physic,* was translated into French by Phillipe Pinel, and both the term *neuroses* and the concept thereby entered French psychiatry, although they received relatively little attention from the anatomically oriented academic psychiatrists. While Cullen's original concept of neuroses covers a large area, including all forms of insanity, the definition was soon narrowed to encompass a small body of diseases among which hysteria held a prominent position.

Through the first half of the nineteenth century, numerous practitioners, in Germany, France, and England, adopted this concept of neuroses and endorsed the view that hysteria and supposedly related syndromes must be understood in terms of diffuse physiological changes in the nervous system, rather than in terms of localized anatomical lesions. In Germany, for example, M. H. Romberg, professor of medicine at the University of Berlin, insisted that many neuropsychiatric syndromes ought to be approached as neuroses; and he bemoaned the fact that "the majority of students [are] attracted by the school which seeks to base the science of medicine exclusively upon pathological anatomy and chemistry."[14]

While emphasizing the neurophysiological aspects of hysteria and other syndromes, these writers, including Romberg, were often either silent or ambiguous on the question of whether any anatomical lesions are, in fact, involved in these ailments. But instances can be cited in which authors speak explicitly of the absence of anatomical lesions on autopsy of hysterical patients.[15]

Examples can also be cited of writers who attributed a role to hypnotism in the therapy of these illnesses. In 1843, James Braid, an English surgeon, wrote in his text *Neurypnology:*

> By the impression which hypnotism induces on the nervous system, we acquire a power of rapidly curing ... many of those distressing affections which, as in most cases they

evince no pathological change of structure, have been presumed to depend on some peculiar condition of the nervous
system, and have therefore, by universal consent, been de-
nominated 'nervous complaints'.[16]

Braid includes hysteria among these diseases, and asserts in a later
work, *Hypnotic Therapeutics,* that "the most striking . . . cases for illus-
trating the value of the hypnotic mode of treatment are cases of hysteric paralysis."[17]

But these predecessors of Charcot had very little impact on the
Continental academic neuropsychiatry of the 1870s and 1880s, the period during which Freud received his medical education. The pathological anatomists' control over university departments of neurology
and psychiatry was then at its height. Among these professors and their
students, the concept of dynamic or functional abnormalities was
largely abandoned, and the relevant diseases were either ignored or
interpreted as reflecting an anatomical lesion. The term *neurosis,* insofar as it was used at all, was reduced to purely nosological significance,
and the early proponents of physiological models of hysteria were generally disregarded and enjoyed little recognition. Their status is illustrated by the case of the Viennese neurologist Moriz Benedikt, who is
often cited as a major precursor of Freud.[18] In a text published in 1868
and entitled *Elektrotherapie,* Benedikt writes:

> Hysteria is thus a modification of physiological being—a di-
> athesis—which is characterized by an excessively labile irrit-
> ability of the nervous system and by an abnormal influence
> of the various parts of the nervous system on one another;
> the latter abnormality, following the former, merely reflects
> an alteration in normal irritability and conductivity. The ab-
> normalities in hysteria manifest themselves primarily in dy-
> namic changes of the nervous system; rarely there appears
> secondarily an anatomical lesion. . . .
>   Many apparently anatomical alterations—for example,
> contractions—can be simulated in the living through hys-
> terical disturbances of innervation.[19]

But Benedikt's views were not shared by his Viennese colleagues, and
one historian writes of him: "Such avant-garde independence was not
received without opposition by the Vienna School of Medicine."[20]
Benedikt was a student and protégé of Johann Oppolzer, who, while
paying lip service to the primacy of pathological anatomy, emphasized

physiology in his own work. Of Oppolzer's position in Vienna, the same historian observes:

> "If Oppolzer clearly places the physiological standpoint above the pathological-anatomical, and does this especially in the establishment of his therapeutic principles, there lies in this a clear deviation from the direction of the Vienna school—indeed, an open criticism of it."[21]

Oppolzer procured a position for Benedikt in the Vienna General Hospital; but when his mentor died in 1871, Benedikt, who remained a maverick throughout his medical career, moved to the "secessionist" General Polyclinic. His status in Vienna is indicated by the fact that although he had been named Professor-extraordinarius in 1869, while still working for Oppolzer, he was not granted the title of full professor until 1899. Finally, Freud's response to Charcot's work, his apparent amazement at the direction that Charcot's research on hysteria was taking, illustrates what little impact Benedikt's work on comparable models had had on his Viennese colleagues.

Similar observations can be made with regard to the work of Paul Briquet, an internist at La Charité in Paris. In 1882 Charcot praised Briquet's book, *Traité clinique et thérapeutique de L'Hysterie* (1859), for having helped to establish hysteria as a distinct and well-defined clinical entity.[22] But Briquet's comments on the pathology of hysteria, his insistence that the disease involves no anatomical lesions, were generally ignored by neuropathologists, including Charcot, in the years following publication of his book.

It was only when the theory of dynamic abnormalities was endorsed by Charcot, whose credentials as a pathological anatomist were so excellent, that the concept began to receive extensive attention in Continental academic neuropsychiatry.[23]

The medical use of hypnosis, like the functional model of hysteria, did not originate with Charcot. Hypnosis had been explored during much of the nineteenth century by various general practitioners, surgeons, experimental physiologists, and other physicians. But, while it was occasionally studied by a neurologist, it had in general received very little attention among neurologists and psychiatrists. This might be due in part to its apparent irrelevance to pathology and therapy when considered from the perspective of a pathoanatomical orientation; but even in England and the United States, where the anatomical bias of the Continent had made little impact, there was virtually no use of hypnotism in neuropsychiatry.

Charcot's own interest in hypnosis derived not from any psychiatric or neurological source, but probably from the work of the physiologist Charles Richet.[24] In 1875 Richet published a paper entitled "Du somnambulisme provoqué" in which he argues that hypnosis involves physiological changes in the nervous system and is, in fact, a form of neurosis. He refutes those who speak of simulation on the part of the subject, and demonstrates the close relationship between hypnotic phenomena and those of other neuroses and of normal sleep. Finally, Richet asserts the usefulness of hypnosis in treating some neurotic patients: "I believe that in certain cases, hypnotism, practised with moderation, can incontestably be effective. Indeed it seemed to me that, in certain hysterical or neurotic subjects, there was a notable remission of symptoms following artificial sleep."[25]

Charcot took up Richet's work on *la neuropathie magnétique*, greatly expanded it, and utilized it in formulating his alternative, physiological model of hysteria. In 1882, he presented to the Academy of Sciences a paper entitled "Sur les divers états nerveux determinés par l'hypnotisation chez les hystériques," in which he describes the three stages of his *grand hypnotisme*.[26] According to Pierre Janet, "it was a tour de force, to bring the Academy of Sciences to recognize hypnotism, which during the past century it had thrice condemned under the name of magnetism."[27] The paper played a considerable role in changing academic attitudes towards hypnosis. But, even before the Academy paper, Charcot's work on hypnotism was spurring a new consideration of the subject in neuropsychiatry. The impact of his hypnosis work paralleled that of his studies on hysteria.

The New Literature on Hysteria and Hypnotism

A look at the literature on hysteria and hypnotism from the last two decades of the century indicates that there was an increasing interest in both subjects and suggests that Charcot's work was largely responsible for this interest.

Index Medicus for 1880 lists thirty-six books and articles published on the Continent on the subject of hysteria. Of these, twenty-six were published in Paris. The thirty-six Continental titles include nine doctoral theses; all nine were written for the Paris Faculty of Medicine. Of the twenty-six Parisian publications, two are by Charcot, another is by Richet, and virtually all of the remainder pursue lines of investigation that were pioneered by Charcot and his coworkers at the Salpetrière. These statistics suggest the degree to which Charcot's interest in hysteria was unique in Continental neuropsychiatry, and they indicate the attention which his work on the subject had received in France. As a result, French studies on hysteria clearly dominated the field.

Subsequent years show a considerable increase in the hysteria literature produced on the Continent, an increase even more remarkable if the number of Continental listings is compared to the number from England and the United States, which remained relatively static. The 1880 *Index Medicus* lists twenty-six English and American titles on hysteria. There are nineteen in 1885, twenty in 1886, and thirty-five in 1895. (The years 1885 and 1886 span the period of Freud's five-month visit with Charcot in Paris; 1895 was the year in which Freud and Joseph Breuer published *Studies on Hysteria.*) Continental titles for the same years number thirty-six in 1880, sixty-seven in 1885, sixty-six in 1886, and eighty-nine in 1895.

The statistics are still more impressive if we exclude the French listings, which were already considerable in 1880, from the Continental titles. The latter now show an increase from six in 1880 to forty-seven in 1895. The French literature increases from thirty titles in 1880 to forty-two in 1895.

The pattern of publications—the initial dominance of the French literature under Charcot's influence, and the subsequent levelling off of French publications while the number of papers from elsewhere on the Continent steadily increased—suggests that the dissemination of Charcot's influence may have been the major spur to the burgeoning literature on hysteria. This view is supported by the testimony of numerous writers on the subject.

In an 1893 obituary article on Charcot, Freud describes the impact of Charcot's work in the early 1880s: "He now pronounced that the theory of organic [i.e., anatomical] nervous illnesses was for the time being fairly complete, and he began to turn his attention almost exclusively to hysteria, which thus all at once became the focus of general interest."[28] Hermann Oppenheim also refers to Charcot's role in inaugurating the new studies on hysteria and related neuroses: "It is an outstanding service of Charcot's to have . . . opened the study of the previously poorly trod field of [neurotic] diseases." Oppenheim acknowledged that there were earlier writers who suggested similar pathological mechanisms for hysteria, but he argued that "it is Charcot's service to have profoundly improved and experimentally supported this theory."[29]

Paul Moebius, a Leipzig neurologist who was one of the major German writers on hysteria and whom Freud refers to as "the best mind among the neurologists," similarly acknowledged the importance of Charcot's work. He speaks of Charcot as the man "to whom more than all others the theory of hysteria is indebted."[30] He also expressed the hope that his own work might be a satisfactory sequel to the insights into hysteria which Charcot first offered.

Freud, Moebius, and Oppenheim were all to some extent followers of Charcot's work on hysteria. But those writers who vehemently opposed functional theories of the neuroses also regarded Charcot as the chief initiator and champion of the new literature, and the rebuttals they offered in response to this literature were most often addressed to Charcot. When, for example, Meynert defends the notion of a local cerebral abnormality in hysteria, in an article entitled "Beitrag zum Verstandniss der traumatischen Neurose" (1888), he does so in the context of a review of Charcot's theories, and his remarks are aimed explicitly at Charcot. Except for a short reference to Oppenheim's work, no other current writer is considered.

The literature on hypnosis from the last two decades of the century reveals a pattern similar to that of the hysteria material. There is a significant increase in publications through the period, and Charcot's work appears to have been the major inspiration for this wide interest in the subject. Again, the importance of Charcot's role is asserted not only by those who accept his views, but also by his opponents. Joseph Delboeuf, professor of medicine at the University of Liege, wrote extensively on hypnotism and supported the theory developed by Hippolyte Bernheim in opposition to Charcot. Bernheim, who was professor of medicine at Nancy, insisted that all the phenomena of hypnosis could be accounted for in purely psychological terms and rejected Charcot's view that hypnosis involves a peculiar neurophysiological condition. This thesis received wide acceptance, and Delboeuf's book, *Le Magnétisme Animal* (1889), is specifically designed as an endorsement of the "Nancy school" and a refutation of Charcot. But Delboeuf nevertheless notes that "M. Charcot is the European scientist who has perhaps best studied nervous diseases, and who has done the most to interest scientists in hypnotism."[31]

The extensive response to Charcot's work on hysteria and hypnotism, and the widespread interest in his studies, can be understood in terms of their significance for neuropsychiatric theories of pathology. The neuroses, as well as other syndromes, had always presented difficulties to pathoanatomically oriented psychiatrists, but some means were generally found to deal with them—either by suggesting possible pathoanatomical mechanisms, or by questioning their status as bona-fide pathological entities, or by putting them aside for the neuroanatomy of the future. But now Charcot, who was perhaps the most respected neurologist in Europe, previously professor of pathology and anatomy in Paris and from 1882 holder of the Chair in Neuropathology especially created for him, was vigorously endorsing a functional model of neuropathology. His work served to establish the theory of hysteria as a major point of confrontation between those who insisted on the comprehensiveness of the pathoanatomical approach and those who wished to pursue alternative, nonanatomical theories of pathology. The theoretical significance thereby accorded to the problem of hysteria can account to a large degree for the attention directed towards the disease during the last decades of the century.

A number of writers who have noted Freud's preoccupation with hysteria during the 1890s, or the general, widespread concern with the disease during this period, have attempted to account for this interest in hysteria by relating it to social and cultural peculiarities of fin-de-siècle Europe. Much has been said, for example, of the European upper middle class during the latter part of the century, with the implication that the life style of this social stratum might somehow have generated cases of hysteria and thereby attracted attention to the syndrome.[32] This has been mentioned particularly in connection with Freud's upper-middle-class Viennese clientele. But this approach runs into immediate difficulties, as cases reported by other physicians were clinically very similar to Freud's and yet were often drawn from very different social groups. The case load at the Salpetrière came primarily from the Paris poor. Hermann Oppenheim in Berlin implied that most of his hysterical patients were also from the lower social strata.

Henri Ellenberger, in *The Discovery of the Unconcious*, suggests that the concern with hysteria and related diseases during the 1880s and 1890s can only be understood in the context of the contemporary social, cultural, and political milieu. In his discussion, Ellenberger offers a detailed profile of the period and considers areas ranging from the rapid change in social structures to the emergence of neo-Romantic and Decadent art. He implies that the peculiar stresses of the social, political, and cultural environment led to a greater incidence of hysterical disorders and a greater interest in the neuroses. But Ellenberger fails to explain how the stresses of this period differed from those of preceding and subsequent decades, or why it was specifically these stresses that generated cases of hysteria and a professional preoccupation with the syndrome.

By recognizing the theoretical importance attributed to studies in hysteria, one can resolve this problem of accounting for the attention accorded the disease. Any phenomenon to which special theoretical significance is attached will attract more attention than it might at other times, or than might seem warranted by external measures of the importance of that phenomenon. Burkitt's lymphoma, for example, receives much more attention in the cancer literature today than can be accounted for in terms of the number of people suffering from the disease. But its frequent appearance in the literature is easily explained in terms of its significance for theories concerning the viral etiology of cancer.

It might be argued that this analogy is unsatisfactory because, in the case of hysteria, there was not only extensive theoretical discussion, but also an unusually large number of reported cases, indicating that the syndrome actually occurred more frequently during this period. But the number of cases appearing in the literature does not necessarily reflect the prevalence of an illness. If interest is generated in a syndrome, more cases will, of course, be sought out and reported in the journals. Moreover, even if we assume that an exceptionally high percentage of people were diagnosed as hysterics, this too can be explained in terms of a heightened theoretical interest. Symptoms that would one day be diagnosed as a bad cold might be labelled influenza a week later if, in the interim, physicians had been made aware of an impending influenza epidemic. Interest in a syndrome can influence numbers of diagnoses as well as numbers of cases recorded in the literature. What might be called hysteria during the period when hysteria was attracting special attention might be labelled simply "nervousness," or "psychosomatic disorder," at some other time.[33]

The widespread interest in hysteria and the extensive reporting of cases of the syndrome may well have been spurred not only by the theoretical significance attached to the syndrome, but by other factors as well. But it seems unwarranted to lay the greater stress on external explanations when considerations within the history of neuropsychiatry can account so fully for this preoccupation with hysteria.

Freud's Response to Charcot

Using a postgraduate travelling grant which he had won the previous June, Freud attended Charcot's neuropathology lectures and teaching rounds at the Salpetrière from October, 1885, to the end of February, 1886. Freud wrote of his motives in going to Paris:

I was bound to reflect that I could not expect to learn anything essentially new in a German University after having
enjoyed direct and indirect instruction in Vienna from Professors T. Meynert and H. Nothnagel. The French school of
neuropathology, on the other hand, seemed to me to prom
ise something unfamiliar and characteristic in its mode of
working, and moreover to have embarked on new fields of
neuropathology, which have not been similarly approached
by scientific workers in Germany and Austria.[34]

But Freud does not seem to have been prepared for the radically
different work being pursued at the Salpetrière (where he expected to
continue his anatomical research);[35] and he wrote to his fiancée from
Paris: "Charcot, who is one of the greatest of physicians . . . is simply
wrecking all my aims and opinions. . . . When I come away from him I
no longer have any desire to work at my own silly things."[36]

Whatever his initial shock, Freud was clearly impressed by Charcot's ideas. Some months later, he devoted the bulk of his report on his
studies abroad to a discussion of Charcot's work on hysteria, writing
that he "left the Salpetrière as Charcot's unqualified admirer."

Freud notes in the "Report":

Charcot used to say that, broadly speaking, the work of anatomy was finished and that the theory of the [anatomical]
diseases of the nervous system might be said to be complete:
what had next to be dealt with was the neuroses. This pro-
nouncement may, no doubt, be regarded as no more than an
expression of the turn which his own activities had taken.
For many years now his work has been centred almost entirely on the neuroses, and above all on hysteria.

Freud then proceeds to relate how up until recently hysteria had not
been well defined. Its symptoms were thought extremely variable, and
exaggerated importance was often attributed to simulation. Charcot
imposed order on this chaos and recognized patterns in the clinical
picture of hysteria. Furthermore,

by making a scientific study of hypnotism—a region of neuropathology which had to be wrung on the one side from
scepticism and on the other from fraud—he himself arrived
at a kind of theory of hysterical symptomatology. These
symptoms he had the courage to recognize as for the most
part real.[37]

Freud was fascinated by these revelations, and he enthusiastically supported Charcot's argument that hysteria is a bona-fide clinical entity. He also accepted the thesis that the disease could not be explained in terms of anatomical abnormalities. He writes that his exchanges with Charcot "led to my preparing a paper which is to appear in the *Archives de Neurologie* and is entitled 'A Comparison Between Hysterical and Organic Symptomatology'." The paper was to deal with the clinical evidence that hysterical symptoms cannot be the result of anatomical lesions.

Freud's enthusiasm was such that he asked Charcot's permission to translate a collection of lectures which Charcot was then preparing for publication. He carried out the task so industriously that the German translation was actually published before the Frer.ch edition.

In October, 1886, Freud presented to the Vienna Medical Society a paper entitled "On Male Hysteria," in which he discussed Charcot's recent work. The text of the paper has not survived, but there are several reviews of it in the medical journals.[38] All concur that Freud stressed three points made by Charcot: that hysteria is a well-defined disease with predictable symptoms, that simulation plays no significant role, and that hysteria in males has the same clinical manifestations as in females. The paper appears to have been mostly concerned with establishing the standard clinical picture of hysteria; but Freud chose to emphasize in the title the last point, that male hysterics present the same picture as female patients. This choice of titles can be attributed to Freud's sharing Charcot's belief that cases of male hysteria, by displaying the same symptomatology as is found in females, provided some of the strongest support for the argument that hysteria is a clinically uniform disease.

The journals also indicate that Freud explicitly associated Charcot's success in his investigations of hysteria with a move away from pathological anatomy. The reviewer for the *Wiener Medizinische Blätter* writes: "He stressed to begin with the great advances made by Charcot in the theory of hysteria, while he emphasized as significant Charcot's altered direction, his shift from pathological anatomist to clinician."[39]

In the discussion which followed Freud's presentation of the paper, comments were made by Meynert, Moriz Rosenthal, Max Leidesdorf, and the meeting's chairman, Heinrich von Bamberger. None of the remarks dealt with the question of the pathology underlying hysteria; but it is indicative of the gap between Charcot's views and those prevailing in Vienna that at least three of those whose comments were reported subscribed to the notion of anatomical changes in hysteria.

Moriz Rosenthal, a neurologist, noted in the discussion that he had written up two cases of male hysteria twenty years before. But Rosenthal's *Klinik der Nervenkrankheiten* (1870), to which he was referring, contains a section headed "The Anatomical Findings in Hysteria," where he states:

> In cases of hysteria, very few people regarded post-mortem examination of the central nervous system as worthwhile; and where it was done (as in the cases of Ollivier, Brodie and Briquet), one was satisfied with a macroscopic examination, and from the negative results concluded somewhat hastily the absence of material changes in the nerve centers. . . . [However,] a gratifying proof that whoever knows how to look will find something here, is provided in a finding discovered by Charcot (*Gazette Hebdom.* Nr. 7, 1865). In a woman, who from the age of fourteen suffered hysterical attacks with later motor disorders, there evolved in the last nine years of her life permanent contractures of all extremities, involving also the muscles of the trunk. Her intelligence remained undisturbed. The patient died of an intercurrent illness, and the autopsy and microscopic investigation revealed sclerosis of the lateral vessels from the bulbus to the lumbar enlargement, together with partial atrophy of the anterior roots.[40]

Rosenthal subsequently acknowledged that localized anatomical lesions are not usually to the found upon autopsy of hysterical patients. But he then suggested that hysteria is caused by cerebral ischemia—that is, a decrease in blood flow to particular areas of the brain—and that, although post-mortem studies may not yield well-marked localized necrosis, one can expect to find in the dissected brain widespread evidence of this ischemia.[41] (Freud later explicitly rejected this thesis, arguing that ischemia "is from its nature an organic [i.e., anatomical] change, the effect of which is determined by anatomical considerations"; and, since the symptoms of hysteria do not conform to those caused by anatomical changes, some quite different mechanism must be involved.[42])

Heinrich von Bamberger, another who spoke in response to Freud's paper, specialized in internal medicine and never wrote on hysteria, and so it is impossible to judge what his views of the underlying pathology were. But a third speaker, Max Leidesdorf, was a psychiatrist who shared Meynert's pathoanatomical orientation. Leidesdorf stated in his *Lehrbuch der Psychischen Krankheiten* that "every psychic disorder is based on an anatomical change in the brain."[43] It seems safe to assume that his notion of the pathology of hysteria differed little in principle from that of Meynert and Rosenthal.

The last of the four physicians cited in reviews of the meeting as having spoken in response to Freud was Meynert. Meynert's views on hysteria remained consistent with his earlier theories of pathology. In 1889, largely in response to the publication of Freud's translation of Charcot's lectures, Meynert submitted a paper to the Vienna Medical Society entitled "Beitrag zum Verstandniss der traumatischen Neurose," in which he develops further his anatomical alternative to Charcot.[44] His principal aim in the paper is to establish the pathology of hysterical paralysis. His thesis is that this pathology involves a localized lesion of the brain, and he argues that

> Charcot . . . completely ignores the relation which the arteries of the Circle of Willis might have to hysterical, or, using the term in a purely descriptive sense, functional paralysis. While he places himself at the height of explanatory knowledge in relation to organic diseases of the brain, the sharp-minded author relinquishes this standpoint in relation to the nevertheless equally clearly localized functional disorders, and allows purely nosological descriptions to suffice with respect to these.

Meynert accounts for Charcot's failure to recognize the anatomical basis of hysterical paralysis by referring to Charcot's scheme of the vasculature of the brain in his lectures of 1875. He notes that Charcot "overlooks, however, [in his] scheme of the basilar arteries, a branch of the internal carotid. . . . This branch, which leaves the carotid below the posterior communicating artery, is the choroid artery."[45]

Meynert then gives an account of the areas of the brain supplied by this choroid artery, and what symptoms might be expected if the artery were occluded; and he argues that these symptoms correspond perfectly to those found in hysterical paralysis:

> I think I have now shown that Charcot's very meritorious and rational attempts to establish, on the basis of arterial distribution in the area, a localization of functions of the brain stem, must remain incomplete because of the omission of the choroid artery from his scheme; as it is this very artery which controls the nutrition of the posterior part of the internal capsule, the area [of the brain] whose function is lost in functional hemiparalysis.[46]

He concludes that cerebral ischemia and necrosis secondary to occlusion of the choroid artery, which in turn is probably due to arteriospasm, are the pathoanatomical basis for this major hysterical symptom. (Freud's reaction to Meynert's thesis appears in his translation of the first volume of Charcot's *Tuesday Lectures* [1892]. Following a section in which Charcot reiterates his autosuggestion formula, Freud states in a footnote: "This is the famous theory of the origin of hysterical paralysis, which Charcot first pronounced in the *New Lectures, 1886.* In opposition to it stands an anatomical theory of Meynert's, which appears to me to be entirely inadequate. [*Wiener klinische Wochenschrift,* 1889]."[47])

Meynert's views on hypnosis, and his response to Charcot and Freud's work on the subject, are in accord with his comments on hysteria. In "Über Zwangsvorstellungen" (1888) he refers briefly to hypnosis as yet another phenomenon that can be explained in terms of localized dysfunction of the cortex due to ischemia.[48] Meynert developed this theme in a separate article entitled "Über hypnotische Erscheinungen" (1888). He argues that patients of the type used in Charcot's hypnotic experiments are already suffering from transient cortical ischemia, and loss of consciousness under hypnotism merely involves a further diminution of cortical blood supply. Meynert addresses particularly the hypnotic tetany (the maintaining of parts of the body in a rigid and "frozen" position while under hypnosis) described by Charcot, and he proposes that this is also due to the cortical defect. He asserts that the cortex is no longer capable of exercising its normal inhibitory control over subcortical centers (which, being closer to the heart, remain relatively well perfused), and that, consequently, prolonged and excessive muscle contraction and rigidity become possible.[49]

Meynert had earlier argued that the physical substrate for the association of ideas and the development of trains of thought involves localized hyperemias in the relevant memory areas of the brain. He now offers a related explanation to account for the effects of hypnotic suggestions. The potency of hypnotic suggestions results from the fact that, due to the general cortical ischemia during hypnosis, no collateral trains of thought are activated to interfere with the suggestions: "The suggested hallucinations appear to be so intense because, as a result of the widespread arteriolar [constriction], no concurrent associations interfere. . . . Should the suggestion involve commands for movements, the motor centers are drawn into the limited field of consciousness . . . and the commands are carried out."[50]

In both "Über Hypnotische Erscheinungen" and "Beitrag zum Verstandniss der traumatischen Neurose," Meynert concludes by condemning the therapeutic use of hypnosis as potentially dangerous and of no lasting value. The latter article, which is, again, primarily a rebuttal of Charcot, contains a note in which Meynert acknowledges his use of Freud's translation of Charcot's lectures. He remarks that Freud is now active in Vienna as a trained practitioner in hypnosis, and he adds dryly that Freud is pursuing suggestion therapy despite his excellent Viennese training.[51]

Freud on the Dynamic Abnormality in Hysteria and Hypnosis

Freud adopted Charcot's physiological model of hysteria and repeatedly endorsed the concept of a functional abnormality as opposed to a localized anatomical lesion. In an article on hysteria written in 1888 for Villaret's *Handwörterbuch der gesamten Medizin,* Freud asserts:

> Hysteria is a neurosis in the strictest sense of the word—that is to say, not only have no perceptible changes in the nervous system been found in this illness, but it is not to be expected that any refinement of anatomical techniques would reveal any such changes. Hysteria is based wholly and entirely on physiological modifications of the nervous system and its essence should be expressed in a formula which took account of the conditions of excitability in the different parts of the nervous system.[52]

Freud insisted that the "ignorance of anatomy" displayed by hysterical symptoms, their failure to reflect the actual anatomical organization of the nervous system (the observation, for example, that in an hysterical anesthesia of a limb the loss of sensation typically involves an area defined by the common-sense demarcation of the limb rather than an area defined by the actual distribution of sensory nerves), effectively rules out the possibility of some localized anatomical lesion and requires an explanation in terms of a diffuse physiological abnormality. This was the theme of that paper comparing hysterical and anatomical symptoms which Freud had first proposed to write after having observed Charcot's work, and which he finally published in 1893; and it is essentially consistent with Charcot's views. Freud does at one point criticize some statements by Charcot about "dynamic lesions," suggesting that they are unfortunate because they might be interpreted as meaning some localized process, such as an ischemia.[53] Ischemia is, of course, exactly the type of process postulated by Meynert, who, in rebuttal to Charcot, insisted that hysterical symptoms can be explained by a transitory decrease in blood perfusion to the affected area of the brain. Freud was concerned that Charcot, by not emphasizing more explicitly the necessarily diffuse nature of the nervous system abnormality in hysteria, was leaving himself open to such counterarguments.[54] But Freud, despite this criticism of ambiguous statements by Charcot, clearly attributed to Charcot the belief that hysteria can only be explained in terms of dynamic changes throughout the nervous system, and he perceived his own work, in the several years after his return from Paris, as essentially amplifying upon the insights attained by Charcot.

Freud defends Charcot's physiological interpretations of hysteria and hypnosis not only against pathoanatomical models, but also against more strictly psychological approaches. This can be seen in his evaluation of Hippolyte Bernheim's theories. Bernheim, in his book *De la suggestion et de ses applications à la thérapeutique,* attempts to dispute Charcot's views on the physiological basis of hypnosis. He argues, first, that all hypnotic phenomena, including those changes which characterize Charcot's stages of *grand hypnotisme,* are merely the result of suggestion:

> As I stated before the Biological Society, suggestion, that is to say the penetration of the idea of the phenomenon into the subject's mind by word, gesture, sight or imitation, has seemed to me to be the key of all the hypnotic phenomena that I have observed. The phenomena said to be physiological or physical, have seemed to me in large part if not entirely, psychical phenomena.[55]

Bernheim insists that virtually all people are subject to suggestion and hypnotizable, and that hypnosis is not a pathological state to which hysterics are specially vulnerable:

> The hypnotic condition is not a neurosis, analogous to hysteria. No doubt manifestations of hysteria may be created in hypnotized subjects. . . . But these manifestations are not due to the hypnosis,—they are due to the operator's suggestion, or sometimes to the auto-suggestion of a particularly impressible subject whose imagination . . . creates these functional disorders which can always be restrained by a quieting suggestion. . . . To prove that the very great majority of subjects are susceptible to suggestion is to eliminate the idea of a neurosis.[56]

Freud translated Bernheim's book in 1888, and in his preface he compares the views of Charcot and Bernheim. He notes that

> if the supporters of the suggestion theory are right, all the
> observations made at the Salpetrière are worthless. . . . The
> hypnosis of hysterical patients would have no characteristics
> of its own. . . . We should not learn from the study of major
> hypnotism what alterations in excitability succeed one anoth-
> er in the nervous system of hysterical patients in response to
> certain kinds of intervention.

Also,

> if suggestion by the physician has falsified the phenomena of
> hysterical hypnosis, it is quite possible that it may also have
> interfered with the observation of the rest of hysterical
> symptomatology: it may have laid down laws governing hys-
> terical attacks, paralyses, contractures, etc., which are only
> connected with the neurosis through suggestion. . . .
>   I am convinced that this view will be most welcome to
> those who feel an inclination . . . to overlook the fact that
> hysterical phenomena are governed by laws.[57]

But, Freud argues, the supporters of the suggestion theory are
wrong. As to hysterical symptoms in general, the conformity of descrip-
tions reported from a multitude of places and at various times in history assures that "in essentials [the symptomatology of hysteria] is of a
real, objective nature and not falsified by suggestion on the part of the
observer." And, as regards hypnosis in hysterical patients,

> already the description of major hypnotism offers symptoms
> which tend most definitely against their being regarded as
> psychical. I refer to the increase in neuro-muscular excitabil-
> ity during the lethargic stage. . . . Anyone who has seen this
> will inevitably assume that the effect must be attributed to
> physiological reasons or to deliberate training and will with-
> out hesitation exclude unintentional suggestion as a possible
> cause.[58]

Freud agrees that suggestion plays a major role in both hypnosis
and hysteria; indeed, suggestion is a key factor in Charcot's model of
hysterical symptom formation. But Bernheim errs, according to Freud,
when he regards suggestion as a purely psychical phenomenon:

> If I say to a hypnotized subject: "Your right arm is para-
> lysed; you cannot move it," I am making a directly psychical
> suggestion. Instead of this, Charcot gives the subject a light

blow on his arm; . . . and his arm drops down paralysed. In [this case] an external stimulus has to begin with produced a feeling of painful exhaustion in the arm; and by this in turn, spontaneously and independently of any intervention on the part of the physician, paralysis has been suggested—if such an expression is still applicable here. In other words, it is a question in these cases not so much of suggestions as of stimulation to *autosuggestions*. And these, as anyone can see, contain an objective factor, independent of the physician's will, and they reveal a connection between various conditions of innervation or excitation in the nervous system. It is auto-suggestions such as these that lead to the production of spontaneous hysterical paralyses and it is an inclination to such autosuggestions, rather than suggestibility towards the physician, that characterizes hysteria.[59]

Freud thus endorses and defends Charcot's concept of physiological abnormalities.

Yet, despite the fact that Freud's interest in hysteria emerged in the context of a conflict between anatomical and physiological models of pathology, and despite his vigorous insistence that hysteria must entail some diffuse physiological abnormality in the nervous system, Freud consistently, from his first works on hysteria, focused his own efforts on developing psychological interpretations of those hysterical phenomena which seemed amenable to such interpretations.

4.

Psychology Versus Physiology in Freud's Hysteria and Hypnosis Papers, 1886–1894

The First Papers, 1886–1891

Freud's early writing on hysteria was devoted largely to establishing the existence of a standard pattern of symptoms. This was a major point in his "Report on My Studies in Paris and Berlin," written shortly after his return to Vienna. It was also, according to the reviews in the medical journals, the main theme of the paper which he presented to the Vienna Medical Society in October, 1886. Freud writes that, at that meeting, "I was challenged by my respected teacher, Hofrat Professor Meynert, to present before the society some cases in which the somatic indications of hysteria—the 'hysterical stigmata' by which Charcot characterizes this neurosis—could be observed in a clearly marked form." Freud took up the challenge a month later with a case presentation of a male hysteric, in which he demonstrates the presence of such standard symptoms as hysterical hemianesthesia, abnormally brisk reflexes, and hypersensitive zones—particularly in the genital area.[1]

In subsequent papers, Freud continued to emphasize the existence of a uniform clinical pattern. In the article on hysteria written for Villaret's *Handwörterbuch* (1888), he endorses Charcot's view that " 'hysteria' is a sharply circumscribed and well-defined clinical picture"; and he asserts that, although the symptomatology of hysteria is "extremely rich," it is "not at all on that account anarchical."[2]

In the preface to his translation of Hippolyte Bernheim's book on hypnosis (*De la Suggestion*, 1888), Freud argues that the uniformity of hysterical symptoms is proof that purely psychological formulas cannot provide a comprehensive understanding of hysteria and that some aspects of the disease require a physiological explanation. But during this period he does not speculate on the exact nature of the physiological abnormality. On the contrary, he states in the Villaret article that, while hysteria must be understood in terms of changes in the conditions of excitability throughout the nervous system, "a physio-pathological formula of this kind has not yet, however, been discovered; we must be content meanwhile to define the neurosis in a purely nosographical fashion."[3]

Freud does go somewhat beyond this cautious approach when he speaks of a "surplus of excitation in the nervous system." But he does not attempt to develop this vague, broad concept further. The notion of a "surplus of excitation" was quite popular at the time, and Freud shared it with numerous other clinicians who thought that they could safely assume some such physiological abnormality on the basis of hysterical symptoms such as contractions, hyperreflexia, convulsive attacks, and hyperirritability, all of which they perceived as manifestations of excessive nervous system activity.

In his discussions of hypnosis, Freud again cites clinical evidence as proof that some of the relevant phenomena can be explained only in terms of dynamic changes in the nervous system, but he once more refrains from speculation on the exact nature of these physiological changes. The need for physiological formulas regarding hypnosis is his major point in the preface to Bernheim's book (1888). This work was followed by several other papers on hypnosis: a two-part review of Auguste Forel's *Hypnotism* (1889), an article "Psychical (or Mental) Treatment" (1890), and a paper entitled "Hypnosis" (1891).[4] In these later papers Freud departs somewhat from Charcot's position on hypnosis. He denies that neurotic patients are more hypnotizable than normal subjects, and he indirectly questions Charcot's concept of *grand hypnotisme*—the notion that there exist particularly profound states of hypnosis which are attainable only by hysterical patients. Freud continues, however, to endorse the concept of the physiological basis of hypnotic phenomena, and he writes in 1891 that, at least in hysterics, "hypnosis comes about in response to purely physiological measures and with all the appearance of a special physical condition."[5] Similar views were expressed by Freud in two lectures on hypnosis delivered in April and May, 1892.[6] But, in all of these works, Freud offers no hypotheses concerning the precise nature of the neurodynamic abnormality.

Freud also avoids neurophysiological speculation in his discussion of therapeutic measures for hysteria and the clinical use of hypnotic suggestion. In a discussion of therapy (1888), Freud divides hysterical phenomena into three categories: (1) the hysterical disposition—that is, the underlying, predisposing hereditary abnormality; (2) standard symptoms—either the standard chronic somatic symptoms, or "stigmata," of hysteria, or the standard acute hysterical attack; and (3) major symptoms of the sort that vary from patient to patient, such as paralysis. In the treatment of the hysterical disposition he prescribes simply constitutional prophylaxis: exercise, hygiene, rest. For the stigmata and the acute attack, which Freud views as direct manifestations of the patient's basic neurodynamic disequilibrium, he prescribes such physical treatments as massage, hydrotherapy, and the Weir-Mitchell rest-cure—a program of regulated diet, rest, and carefully managed exercise. But it is those symptoms which vary from case to case and are therefore distinguishable from the hysterical stigmata that are of most interest to Freud, and it is specifically these which he associates with Charcot's pathogenic model of autosuggestion and which he perceives as amenable to hypnotherapy. Charcot argued that trauma induces a hypnotic state in people who suffer from an hysterical disposition, and that in this hypnotic state the trauma conveys suggestions to the patient—such as that his arm is paralyzed—which subsequently result in symptoms. Freud recommends hypnotic suggestion for the treatment of this last group of symptoms, noting that suggestion is particularly appropriate as it directly addresses the unconcious ideational life which has generated these symptoms.

Freud discusses hypnotic suggestion again in the Bernheim preface and in his three subsequent articles dealing with hypnotism. Except for some general remarks acknowledging that there are indeed physiological aspects to suggestion, his discussions are wholly in psychological terms. Freud, at several points, labels hypnotic suggestion a "causal treatment" with regard to hysterical disorders, because these disorders "are the direct result of a pathogenic idea or the deposit of a shattering experience. If that idea is got rid of or that memory weakened—which is what suggestion brings about—the disorder too is usually overcome."[7]

A number of authors, including Siegfried Bernfeld, Peter Amacher, and Ernst Kris, have maintained that Freud was preoccupied at this stage of his career with physiological models.[8] They suggest various explanations for this emphasis, ranging from Freud's connections with a German neurophysiological tradition to his subscription to supposed contemporary notions that such models were required for scientific legitimacy. These writers would have Freud weaned from this preoccupation with physiology only at some later date. But the general absence of physiological theorizing in Freud's papers on hysteria and hypnosis during these years contradicts such theses.

Freud's position on neurophysiological speculation can be more clearly defined by a comparison with other works on hysteria and hypnotism published at this time. With regard to theories of hysteria, Hermann Oppenheim and Albert Moebius both thought of themselves as Charcot's disciples; yet they differed sharply on whether the task begun by Charcot was one of defining neurodynamic pathways in the disease or of explaining the disease in psychological terms. Oppenheim, in "Thatsachliches und Hypothetisches über das Wesen der Hysterie" (1890), acknowledges that Charcot had established the role of ideas in the formation of hysterical symptoms; but he opposes Moebius's attempt to view hysterical symptoms solely in psychological terms. He argues that, while ideas have a greater impact on the emotional life of hysterics than is the case in normal people, it is the peculiar ease with which this emotional lability is translated into physical symptoms that is the key to hysterical pathology; and he insists that this phenomenon requires a neurophysiological exlanation. He justifies speculation on the physiological abnormality by noting that, while his models are hypothetical, they will nevertheless be of use "if they satisfactorily clarify the primary phenomena, or at least so transcribe them, that they lose the stamp of the wonderful, strange and contradictory."[9]

Oppenheim maintains that hysteria is marked by an "irritable weakness; that is, an abnormal irritability [i.e., excitability] and threshold of exhaustion," which affects all parts of the nervous system. He suggests that this can be explained in terms of some neurological abnormality on the molecular level which renders the nervous system more sensitive to stimulation and less able to modulate neural transmissions. He develops these vague notions somewhat further and then proceeds to account for each of the major symptoms of hysteria by applying his neurodynamic formula.

Moebius, in a rebuttal, argues that most hysterical symptoms are the result of "suggestion" by the pathogenic idea and are therefore amenable to purely psychological analysis. He maintains that, while some symptoms are perhaps not yet fully explicable in psychological terms, physiological speculations are not a satisfactory approach as "our highly scanty knowledge of the neurodynamics of the brain offers no secure foundation" for such hypothesizing.[10]

The emphasis in Freud's writing during these years is much closer to Moebius's position than to Oppenheim's. Freud's comments on the stigmata of hysteria—those symptoms which he regarded as requiring a physiological explanation—are limited to the observation that they establish the physiological foundation of the disease and to the prescrip-

tion of physical modes of therapy for their cure. The bulk of his remarks on hysteria are his psychological discussions of the pathogenesis
of major symptoms such as paralyses and of their amelioration via
hypnotic suggestion. Indeed, these comments, appearing in his hypnosis articles of 1889–1891, are his only published statements on hysteria
for those years. The same emphasis can be seen in his clinical notes on
Frau Emmy von N., written in 1889. Frau Emmy is described by Freud
as a woman of about forty who had been chronically ill for fourteen
years, since the death of her husband. Freud prescribes baths and
massages as a way of ameliorating her constitutional predisposition to
hysteria and treating her hysterical stigmata. But he is primarily concerned with the pursuit of suggestive therapy for those of her symptoms which he perceived to be psychogenic in nature—for example,
her terrifying hallucinations and her ritualistic exclamations (she would
often scream out: "Keep still!—Don't say anything!—Don't touch me!").
Interestingly, a few years later, in a footnote to these clinical notes on
Frau Emmy von N. written shortly before their publication (1895),
Freud refers explicitly to his initial emphasis on psychology. He remarks that, at the time he was treating Frau Emmy, he tended to pay
too little attention to physiological considerations and was too inclined
to give psychological explanations for hysterical symptoms![11]

Contemporary Physiological Models of Hypnosis

The contemporary literature on hypnosis and hypnotic suggestion,
with its frequent development of speculative physiological models, also
presents a sharp contrast to Freud's work.

Meynert's model of hypnosis was an application of his theories
relating neuropsychiatric abnormalities to cerebrovascular changes. He
argued that hypnosis involves a general cortical ischemia, and that this
ischemia is the cause of hypnotic somnolence and posthypnotic amne-
sia. He also maintained that the ischemia is the source of the suggestion
phenomena: it causes a general decrease in cortical activity, and this in
turn prevents the development of the trains of thought which would
normally inhibit the reflex execution of suggestions. Consequently,
hypnotic suggestions trigger unhampered reflex responses. (Meynert
warned that this ischemia, in addition to inducing transient anatomical
changes in the brain, may also lead to necrosis and permanent lesions.)

Rudolph Heidenhain, in *Der sogenannte thierische Magnetismus*
(1880), had considered a model similar to Meynert's, but had rejected it
on clinical grounds. (He noted, for example, that, if hypnotic states are

due to vasoconstriction, they ought to be modified by inhalation of the vasodilator amyl nitrate; but the predicted effect does not occur.) Heidenhain, who was professor of physiology and director of the Physiological Institute at the University of Breslau, proposed an alternative theory. While agreeing with Meynert that the phenomena of hypnotism reflect a diminution of cortical function and of cortical inhibitory control over lower nerve centers, he suggested that the decrease in cortical function is a direct effect of the monotonous sensory stimulation through which the hypnosis is induced: "In the face of all . . . the facts it does not seem to me too rash to suppose that the source of the hypnotic state lies in a functional inhibition of cortical ganglion cells resulting from weak, continuous stimulation of the cutaneous nerves of the face or the auditory or optic nerves."[12]

Wilhelm Wundt, professor of physiology at Leipzig, presented a formula containing elements from both of the above models. Wundt argued, in "Hypnotismus und Suggestion" (1892), that both vasomotor changes and purely neurodynamic factors play a role in generating hypnotic phenomena. He agreed that these phenomena involve primarily a depression of cortical function and a relative increase in the excitability and reflex function of other nervous centers.[13]

The speculations of B. Danilewsky are of interest because the frame of reference for his discussion is a separate tradition of hypnosis research—experiments in the hypnosis of animals. The induction of "hypnosis" generally involved submitting the animals to some sudden change in situation such as turning a frog onto its back and holding it in that position. This usually resulted in a total paralysis lasting for some minutes or even hours. Danilewsky proposed that the cortex is overwhelmed by the quantity of strange sensations triggered by the unfamiliar situation, and that this induces a "reflex inhibition" of cerebral function. He noted that other animal experiments had demonstrated similar reactions resulting from both sensory deprivation and painful stimuli. But he argued that the "reflex inhibition" in these latter situations involve nervous centers other than the cortex. He suggested that there are in fact a hierarchy of "hypnoses," ranging from the subcortical inhibition induced by pain or deprivation, to the cortical inhibition stemming from overwhelming physical stimuli, and, finally, to the case of man where a decrease in cortical functioning can be induced merely by overwhelming psychic stimuli.[14] The experiments and the neurophysiological models of the animal hypnotists influenced the speculations of numerous other writers and is reflected, for example, in Heidenhain's theory.

Even those writers who endorsed Bernheim's thesis—that all the phenomena of hypnotism can be analyzed in purely psychological terms—often felt obliged to offer physiological models. Albert Moll, a Berlin neurologist, insists in his *Der Hypnotismus* (1889) that Bernheim's "suggestion" concept of hypnosis is the correct one and that hypnosis is fully explicable in terms of psychological reflexes. But some hundred pages later he observes that "suggestion," while adequately accounting for the phenomena, does not really explain them; and "we can only expect a real explanation from Physiology."[15] Moll, while offering some physiological speculations, concludes that physiology is not yet capable of giving an adequate account.

Auguste Forel, another supporter of Bernheim, carries physiological speculation a bit further. Forel, who was professor of psychiatry at Zurich, apparently recognized the inconsistency of accepting Bernheim's thesis and yet insisting on physiological models. In the second edition of his book (1891), he attempts to defend his speculations by way of an introductory discussion of *monism*, his term for the thesis which rejects body-soul dualism and maintains that the psyche is merely "that complex of forces . . . whose material substrate is the nervous system, especially the brain." In Forel's view, once the psyche is perceived in this way, there is nothing illogical about arguing that hypnotic phenomena can be fully explained in psychological terms and yet seeking a neurophysiological explanation as more basic.

Forel speculates that the hypnotic state is merely a form of sleep. He argues that, in both sleep and hypnosis, the energy-expending chemical processes which accompany normal cortical activity diminish and a phase of cortical repair supervenes. This chemodynamic shift is accompanied by a depression of those neural connections which are the substrate of normal ideational associations. As a result, the normal associations are weakened and the psyche is subject to domination by suggested associations. Once again, the various hypnotic phenomena are explained in terms of a cessation of cortical inhibitory controls.[16]

Freud, in addition to consistently refraining from speculations such as those noted above, also voiced some criticism of these speculations. In a review of the first edition (1889) of Forel's book, Freud praises the author for avoiding physiological theorizing (the discussions cited above are all in sections added by Forel to the second edition), and he writes that "there can be no doubt that remarks such as those made by Forel . . . have more to do with the problem of hypnosis than have the contrast between 'cortical and subcortical' and speculations on the dilatation and constriction of the cerebral blood vessels."[17] This remark is aimed particularly, of course, at Meynert's thesis. But all the cited physiological models assume that one can largely distinguish between cortical and subcortical functions, and Freud categorically rejects the assignment of higher psychic activities to specific loci in the brain. He writes in the Bernheim preface: "We possess no criterion which enables us to distinguish exactly . . . between an act occurring in the cerebral cortex and one occurring in the subcortical substance."[18] This rejection of the localization of functions leads him to a general refutation of such models:

> The fact that the influence of the cerebrum on somatic functions can be made use of more intensively under hypnosis than in the waking state [contradicts] those theories of hypnotic phenomena which seek to regard them as a "depressing of the cortical activity," a kind of experimental imbecility. But there are a number of other things, apart from hypnotic phenomena, that do not harmonize with this theory, which seeks to understand almost all the phenomena of cerebral activity by means of the contrast between "cortical" and "subcortical."[19]

Freud's skepticism regarding the localization of cerebral functions was undoubtedly a major factor in his general caution with respect to neurophysiological theorizing.

The physiological principles which underlay these various theories of hypnotism were, of course, quite familiar to Freud, and his avoidance of neurodynamic speculations was a deliberate choice, in no way due to an ignorance of the subject. When, some years later, he attempts to develop physiological models of brain function in the "Project," he utilizes the same basic principles as the hypnosis theorists and he displays a comprehensive understanding of the field.

Rudolph Heidenhain, in his hypnosis paper, lists what he regards as the major achievements of experimental neurophysiology: "the discovery of [separate] sensory and motor nerves, the accurate investigation of reflex motions, knowledge of the inhibitory processes within the nervous system, the admittedly still imperfect but nevertheless tolerable establishment of the functions of the individual larger areas of the brain."[20] Of these four factors, the concept of the reflex function of the nervous system (which really embraces the first and second points, since the reflex arc model—whereby a stimulus is conveyed to the central nervous system via a sensory nerve and a motor response is then initiated via a motor nerve—is built upon the differentiation of sensory and motor nerves) and the concept of neural inhibition received particular attention in neurophysiological theorizing. They are the basis of all the physiological theories of hypnosis and hypnotic suggestion cited above and were, in general, very widely disseminated concepts. Freud was well versed in them, and, when he did briefly venture into physiological speculations, he used them as the foundation of his theorizing.

Peter Amacher, noting the use made by Freud's teachers of these and related concepts, traces Freud's understanding of them to his Viennese mentors and, more generally, to the German neurophysiological tradition—the so-called School of Helmholtz—originally discussed by Siegfried Bernfeld.[21] But there are problems with Amacher's thesis. In the first place, neither the reflex model of brain function nor the theories of neural inhibition were the special province of German physiology. Modern reflex theory, the concept of the reflex arc, began with the work of the English physiologist Marshall Hall on reflex functions of the spinal cord (1833). The theoretical extension of the reflex model to cortical functions, while considered by Wilhelm Griesinger in 1843, was independently developed by Thomas Laycock about the same time and subsequently received extensive attention in England.[22] The concept of inhibitory control of lower nervous centers by higher centers was proposed by the earliest proponents of the reflex theory and is discussed at some length in Hall's work.

Of course, the German physiologists could still have made particular application of these principles in subsequent decades, irrespective of where they were first formulated; they could have thereby developed a special tradition in theoretical neurophysiology—a tradition conveyed to Freud by his Viennese instructors. But the neurophysiological literature, including the literature on hypnosis and hypnotic suggestion, indicates otherwise. For example, while all of the authors cited above are German, there are also French and English writers on hypnosis who base their neurophysiological models upon the same principles and yet have no particular connections with German physiology.

Theodule Ribot, professor of psychology at the College de France, was particularly interested in physiological and pathological psychology and was closely associated with the hypnosis researchers working at the Salpetrière under Charcot. He was vice-president of the Société de Psychologie Physiologique (which had been founded by Charcot and Charles Richet in 1885) and editor of the *Revue Philosophique,* the journal which published most of the articles on hypnosis coming from the Salpetrière. Ribot, in *Les Maladies de la Volonté* (1883), speaks of the belief of "all contemporary physiologists, that the reflex is the type and base of all action." The problem, he says, is to explain how actions are inhibited. But he notes the phenomenon of the inhibiting effect of the vagus nerve on the intrinsic rate of contraction of the heart, adding:

> it is a well-known fact that the excitability of spinal reflexes is augmented when [this excitability] is released from the action of the brain. The state of decapitated animals furnishes some striking proofs of it. Without recourse to these extreme cases, one knows that the reflexes are much more intensive during sleep than in the waking state.[23]

There is thus, in Ribot's view, ample grounds for postulating the inhibitory role of higher nerve centers.

In his earlier *Diseases of Memory,* Ribot had made use of these principles when considering the pathology of epileptic attacks. In doing so, he appealed to the work of the English neurologist John Hughlings Jackson, whose neurophysiological theories were based upon the same concepts:

> If amnesia [of the epileptic seizure] arises from weakness in the primitive states of consciousness; how is it that these states, hypothetically weak, inspire determinate acts? According to Hughlings Jackson, there is during the paroxysm an internal discharge sufficient to incapacitate the highest nervous centers. "Mental automatism results . . . from overaction of low nervous centers, because the highest or controlling centers have been put out of use." We have here only a special application of a well-known physiological law: The excito-motor power of reflex centers increases when their connection with the superior centers is destroyed.[24]

Ribot's use of the characterization "well-known physiological law" is indicative of the wide dissemination and acceptance that the principle of cortical inhibitory controls over reflex centers had attained.

Ribot explains hypnotic states, in *Les Maladies de la Volonté,* by means of the same principle. Hypnotic phenomena are accounted for by a decrease in cortical activity. Ribot considers the theory that hypnosis "is produced by a suspension of activity of cortical cells, perhaps by changing the molecular disposition. In this manner the functional movement of the gray substance will be interrupted. . . . As this [hypothesis] is only a statement of facts, we can endorse it."[25] Hypnotic suggestions are merely "the analogue of physiological reflexes" which have been released from the control of the depressed cortex.

The English psychiatrist Hack Tuke, in "Imperative Ideas" (1894), considers those states in which the mind is dominated by a single idea, as in hypnotic suggestion. In assessing the cortical conditions which accompany these states, he refers to "the current doctrine in regard to the control of one portion of the cortex over another," and he concludes:

> Accepting this hypothesis, in addition to Laycock's great fundamental doctrine of the reflex or automatic function of the whole cortex, we seem to find an answer to the question I began with, what are the cerebral conditions accompanying imperative ideas? The most automatic is no longer under the control of the voluntary or least automatic cerebral levels or layers.[26]

Tuke's paper was cited by Freud shortly after its publication.

The principles of the reflex nature of nervous activity and the inhibition of lower reflex centers by higher centers, which Ribot calls well-known and universally accepted, were in fact so widely disseminated that to attempt to trace specific sources for any one writer's use of them is a meaningless task. Moreover, their popular dissemination meant that they were familiar and available to virtually any neurologist, psychologist, and psychiatrist whose interests lay in the direction of neurophysiological theorizing. It might be argued that Freud, when he did choose briefly to venture into neurophysiological theories of the neuroses, did employ a few notions which were particularly associated with the work of his teachers; but this is a matter of details—the broad concepts which lay at the foundation of his speculations were the common coin of neurophysiology.

Freud's Book On Aphasia

In 1891, Freud published a monograph on aphasia which—having appeared a few years after his first papers on hysteria and hypnosis—has received considerable attention concerning its possible significance for his early work on the neuroses. The book is primarily a rebuttal of theories postulating the existence of localized motor and sensory speech centers in the brain. Paul Broca had presented in 1861 a famous paper demonstrating a lesion of the third convolution of the brain's left frontal lobe in a patient suffering from a loss of the capacity to speak. Thirteen years later, Carl Wernicke, on the basis of autopsy evidence, associated another area of the brain with loss of the ability to comprehend spoken words. Wernicke then argued that the speech apparatus consists of a motor center (Broca's area), an auditory or sensory center (Wernicke's area—the posterior part of the first convolution of the temporal lobe), and a system of "association fibers" connecting the two areas.[27] According to Wernicke's model, one's memory of speech sounds is stored in the sensory area and one's memory of the muscular movements necessary to produce speech—the proper movements of jaw, tongue, lips, etc.—is stored in the motor area. There are, in Wernicke's view, three types of aphasia: two "central aphasias," resulting from the destruction of one or the other of the speech centers, and a "conduction aphasia," caused by a lesion of the association tract. In subsequent years, Wernicke and Ludwig Lichtheim developed this model further. In an effort to account for various forms of aphasia which were commonly found in patients but were not explicable in terms of this scheme, they delineated other possible conduction paths to and from the speech centers and argued that lesions of these paths were the cause of the remaining forms of aphasia.

Wernicke was a protégé of Meynert's and fully endorsed both the pathoanatomical approach to neuropsychiatric disorders and Meynert's views on the localization of psychic functions. Wernicke's aphasia paper—which, as Freud notes, "brought him lasting fame"—was regarded as a major success of pathoanatomical psychiatry and a major victory for Meynert's localization theories. Wernicke, in fact, begins the paper by stating that

> the following work is . . . an attempt to put Meynert's brain anatomy to practical use. . . .
> . . . In view of the intimate dependence on brain anatomy which the handling of such a theme requires, it would be impossible to cite Meynert's authorship explicitly at every point. Nevertheless, everything which might be found of value in the following work redounds finally upon Meynert, because the concepts presented here result from the study of his papers and [anatomical] preparations as much as from my own.[28]

Freud's book is a critique of Wernicke's theory. He cites various patterns of aphasic symptomatology which are inexplicable in terms of Wernicke and Lichtheim's models, and he concludes that the division of the speech apparatus into localized centers and conduction paths is untenable. Freud suggests that greater emphasis ought to be placed on "functional" considerations.

Freud uses the word *functional* here in two distinct senses, both of which differ from the meaning we have thus far accorded the term. By *functional* we have signified a type of pathology involving purely neurodynamic changes with no accompanying anatomical lesions.[29] In the aphasia book, Freud uses *functional* to designate, first, the nature of the relationship—as he perceives it—between the brain's structure and its mode of operation. He argues that the speech apparatus is not, as Wernicke maintains, separated into local centers, which store memories, and association paths, which coordinate the retrieval, association, and utilization of those memories. It is not the case, for example, that, on being asked if one is hungry, the memory of such a question, and what it signifies, is aroused in a special sensory speech center, that a transmission to arouse and coordinate an appropriate motor response is then conveyed via the association paths, and that the memory of the appropriate response is then excited in the motor speech center, leading to one's answering yes or no. Rather, Freud suggests, memory storage, on the one hand, and the coordination and utilization of memories, on the other, are in fact inseparable and integrated activities that are performed, not separately by separate parts of the brain, but jointly by all the anatomical units that are involved with the comprehension and utilization of speech. Therefore, a given brain cell cannot be designated a memory cell, or an association fiber; all cells are *functional* (functional$_a$) fibers, taking part in the integrated activity of the speech area.

The second meaning which Freud accords to *functional* in *On Aphasia* has to do specifically with abnormal states and the interpretation of aphasic symptoms. Freud argues that Wernicke and Lichtheim, in attempting to explain aphasic symptoms, have put too much emphasis on the location of the brain lesion. More consideration ought to be given to the severity of the lesion, since a given anatomical unit is capable of operating at various levels below normal, and clinical symptoms are determined as much by the amount of damage to units as by which units are damaged. Freud refers to the various levels of operation of a given anatomical unit as *functional* (functional$_b$) levels.

By stressing these two concepts—the integrated, functional$_a$, organization of the speech apparatus; and the various functional$_b$ levels of damaged cells—Freud believes he can account for those clinical patterns of aphasia which are inexplicable in terms of Wernicke's models.

Various writers have considered the significance of Freud's aphasia book for his studies of the neuroses; they have generally attempted to establish parallels between Freud's rejection of theories of localized pathology in hysteria and his rejection of Wernicke's views on localized speech elements in the normal brain and localized lesions in aphasia. These writers have also stressed the supposed analogy between the alternative, *functional,* concepts developed in the aphasia work and the notion of functional abnormality developed in the hysteria papers.[30]

But Freud's positions on hysteria and on aphasia are hardly analogous to the extent that these writers would suggest. In the hysteria work, Freud's main point is that no anatomical lesion is involved. *Functional* is used to indicate an alternative, neurodynamic type of pathology. Moreover, Freud at this time consistently avoids speculation on what the precise nature of this pathology might be. Similarly, he avoids speculation on how psychic phenomena might relate to brain structure. In his critique of the physiological theories of hypnosis, he explicitly condemns both kinds of theorizing as based on inadequate information and therefore fruitless. In the aphasia work, on the contrary, Freud does not doubt that the overwhelming number of aphasia cases involve localized anatomical lesions. Further, he speculates both on the organization of psychic elements within the speech apparatus (functional$_a$), and on the operative changes within the apparatus under pathological conditions (functional$_b$).

The apparent contradiction between Freud's reluctance to develop physiological models with regard to hysteria and hypnosis and his readiness to formulate such models in the aphasia book is easily resolved. Freud's efforts to construct physiological theories in the aphasia book can be understood in terms of the arguments of the monograph. Freud is insisting that Wernicke's model of speech centers and association paths is erroneous. But, if he merely refutes Wernicke, he leaves himself open to the rebuttal that there is in fact a correspondence between the location of a lesion in the speech area and the symptoms generated, and that this correspondence must be explained. Freud's delineation of an explicit functional$_a$ model of the organization of the speech apparatus, and a complementary model of functional$_b$ changes under pathological conditions, is merely an attempt to complete his argument by demonstrating how Wernicke's observations, as well as observations which Wernicke could not explain, might be accounted for without the assumption of localized sensory and motor centers.

But, while Freud's aphasia work has considerably less in common with his studies on hysteria than many authors would suggest, there are, nevertheless, several points at which Freud's comments on aphasia and on hysteria do converge. This occurs, in the first place, with regard to the question of hysterical aphasia. Freud, from the time of his visit with Charcot, believed that hysterical symptoms demonstrate character-istics by which they can be distinguished from symptoms due to local-ized nervous system lesions; he noted in his 1886 "Report" that he had undertaken to write a paper on the subject.[31] Several years later, in an article on aphasia written for Villaret's encyclopedia (1888), Freud states that hysterical aphasia can similarly be differentiated from apha-sia due to anatomical lesions.[32] What generally distinguishes hysterical symptoms from symptoms caused by anatomical lesions is, according to Freud, the "ignorance of anatomy" displayed by the former; that is, hysterical symptoms take forms which accord to common-sense notions of body organization, but do not accord to actual body structure. An hysterical paralysis of the arm, for example, is usually limited to the arm and entails a complete loss of all movement—a combination of characteristics which, because of the peculiarities of nervous system organization, is not to be found in a paralysis due to neuroanatomical changes. According to Freud's encyclopedia article on aphasia, a similar situation prevails in hysterical loss of the capacity to speak. Hysterical motor aphasia generally involves a total loss of the ability to make sounds; whereas, in the aphasia due to an anatomical lesion, some exclamatory expressions (such as profanities or expressions like "Oh, God!"), or at least some nonverbal sounds, are preserved in the worst cases. Also, whereas an anatomical aphasia invariably also involves an inability to write words (an agraphia), the hysterical form leaves writing ability intact.

Freud does not consider hysterical speechlessness in his book on aphasia, but many of his remarks in the book are relevant to his earlier distinction between anatomical and hysterical aphasias. In particular, Wernicke's concept of a motor speech center, in which the memory of speech movements, or "glosso-kinaesthetic impressions,'" are stored, implies that with destruction of this area of the brain a complete speechlessness ought to ensue. If this were true, then the total speech-lessness of hysterical aphasia would be compatible with an anatomical lesion. But Freud insists that no such center exists. He argues that Wernicke, in postulating speech centers and association paths, is erro-neously projecting a psychological theory, concerning memory units and the association of ideas, onto an anatomical model of brain struc-ture. Elsewhere in the book, Freud discusses the remnants of language usage which are invariably preserved in anatomical motor aphasia, and he cites examples of vestigial speech in patients with aphasia due to anatomical lesions.

Freud's rejection of Wernicke's speech centers is coupled with his insistence that the storage and the coordination of speech impressions are really inseparable elements of an integrated cortical activity involving all the anatomical units of the speech apparatus. He argues that this alternative, functional$_a$ theory can better explain the specific clinical characteristics of aphasia syndromes. But Freud's alternative theory also provides a theoretical basis for his assertion that total speechlessness, as well as a speechlessness in which other language skills remain unaffected, cannot be the result of localized anatomical abnormalities; he thereby strengthens his argument that patients with hysterical aphasia, who typically exhibit a total speechlessness, with other language skills remaining unaffected, are not the victims of local brain lesions.[33] When Freud finally published his article comparing anatomical and hysterical symptoms (1893), he referred back to his aphasia book, and to his functional$_a$ model, as offering a possible explanation for why anatomical aphasia, in sharp contrast to hysterical forms, invariably presents a "mixture of disturbances of various [language] functions."[34]

A second point at which Freud's aphasia and neurosis studies converge has to do with the concept of functional$_b$ variations in the activity of specific cellular units within the brain. Virtually all of the physiological models of hypnosis offered by Freud's contemporaries assumed that the loss of independently initiated behavior in the hypnotic subject, and the subject's exquisite responsiveness to suggestions, indicate the activity of areas of the brain different from those which are involved in normal behavior. The most common formula was that the cortex controlled normal behavior, while hypnosis involved a relative increase of subcortical activity. Freud rejected these physiological models, arguing that the assignment of different behavior patterns to different areas of the brain was an unwarranted assumption. The aphasia work, by emphasizing the concept that individual cerebral areas are capable of operating at various functional$_b$ levels, supported Freud's rejection of models such as the hypnosis theories, and probably contributed to his belief that cerebral physiology was much too complex and too little understood to allow for fruitful speculation on the neurodynamics of hysteria.

The notion of functional$_b$ levels is presented in the aphasia book in opposition to Wernicke's assumption that aphasia necessarily involves a total loss of activity in a circumscribed area. Freud cites an 1887 article by Charleton Bastian:

> Bastian . . . distinguishes three states of reduced excitability of a centre. The smallest reduction manifests itself in a failure of the centre to react to "volitional" stimulation while it

still reacts to stimulation by association with another centre
and to direct sensory stimuli. If function is more severely
disturbed the centre reacts to direct sensory stimulation only,
and finally, at the lowest level of functioning, that reaction
also fails.[35]

This model, according to Freud, is fully supported by clinical evidence.
He notes, for example, that in aphasia "repetition [of something heard,
that is, reaction to direct sensory stimulation] invariably remains intact
longer than spontaneous speech." The analogy between this situation
and that prevailing in hypnosis, where voluntary behavior is supposedly lost while responsiveness to suggestion remains intact, is obvious,
and it is clear how the aphasia work supports Freud's general view that
the notion of separate brain centers for different levels of behavior is
probably erroneous and, at any rate, is certainly not something that can
simply be postulated.

Freud appeals to the work of John Hughlings Jackson primarily as
further corroboration of the concept that the speech apparatus can
assume various levels of functioning under different pathological conditions. Jackson, applying his theory of "disinvolution" (conceived essentially as a reversal of evolution) insisted on the orderliness with
which levels of language skills are lost in aphasia—the most sophisticated being the first to go and the most primitive being preserved
longest. Jackson's evidence in support of this theory served as additional proof that Wernicke's model of memory centers, in which the
loss under pathological conditions is all or nothing, is untenable:

In assessing the functions of the speech apparatus under
pathological conditions we are adopting as a guiding principle Hughlings Jackson's doctrine that all these modes of reaction represent instances of functional [i.e., functional$_b$] retrogression (dis-involution) of a highly organized apparatus,
and therefore correspond to earlier states of its functional
development. This means that under all circumstances an
arrangement of associations which, having been acquired later, belongs to a higher level of functioning, will be lost,
while an earlier and simpler one will be preserved. From this
point of view, a great number of aphasic phenomena can be
explained.[36]

Jackson was, of course, not the first to speak of functional$_b$ retrogression under pathological conditions. The notion underlies, for example, all the physiological models of hypnosis cited above. All of these

theories assume that, with inactivation of a higher brain center, lower, previously inhibited, centers are released and behavior reverts to the level of these lower centers. Theodule Ribot, who cited Jackson extensively and fully acknowledged the importance of his work, nevertheless characterized the notion that pathology involves the liberating of lower levels of activity as a "well-known physiological law." Jackson himself cited numerous physicians who had postulated similar concepts of retrogression, including his former teacher at the York Medical School, Thomas Laycock. Nor was Jackson the first physician to speak of retrogression in ontogenetic and phylogenetic terms. Laycock, for example, writing in the period before Darwin, drew an analogy between functional$_b$ levels in the nervous system and stages in the Chain of Being, with nervous system pathology involving reversion to the level of lower stages.[37] In addition, numerous writers, including Meynert, associated disease processes with retrogression to earlier stages of individual development.

But, in the works of most of these writers, different functional$_b$ levels are more or less explicitly assigned to different areas of the central nervous system. This is particularly true of German authors, and is reflected in the hypnosis theories. Jackson, however, in addition to more fully and consistently developing the entire concept of retrogression, differed from these other writers in insisting that the same cerebral apparatus is capable of functioning at a variety of levels. Disinvolution involves not only reversion to lower centers, but also reversion to lower functional$_b$ modes within the same center: "In all cases of dissolution, there is a reduction to the automatic, more organized, to the earlier acquired of the processes, represented in the centers affected.[38]

It is this aspect of Jackson's theory which renders his work of such importance for Freud's views on aphasia. Jackson's notions of functional$_b$ levels within the same cerebral apparatus probably served also to reinforce further Freud's general skepticism regarding the localization of different psychic functions in separate cerebral areas. As assumptions about the localization of function lay at the foundation of all current physiological theories of hypnosis and hysteria, this increasing skepticism no doubt augmented Freud's resolve to eschew physiological speculations concerning the neuroses.

Josef Breuer on Hysteria

The article on hysteria written for Villaret's *Handwörterbuch* (1888) was Freud's only publication on hysteria for several years. From 1889 through 1891, he limited his writing in the area of the neuroses to a few papers on hypnosis. In 1892, however, he published a paper entitled "A Case of Successful Treatment by Hypnotism," dealing with the resolution of a hysterical patient's symptoms via hypnosis. Then, in January of the following year, he published, in collaboration with Josef Breuer, "On the Psychical Mechanism of Hysterical Phenomena: Preliminary Communication"—the first of his papers to develop a psychological theory of hysteria that goes beyond the autosuggestion theory he had learned in Paris.

Freud's collaborator, Josef Breuer, was a Viennese internist with a distinguished general practice. He was the family physician of Ernst Brücke, Sigmund Exner (Brücke's eventual successor as professor of physiology), Theodor Billroth (the professor of surgery), and many others among the Viennese medical faculty, including Freud.[39] Breuer had begun his career as an assistant in Johann Oppolzer's clinic, where, influenced largely by Oppolzer's physiological orientation, he had done significant work in experimental physiology. In collaboration with Ewald Hering (professor of physiology at the Josephinum, Vienna's military medical school), Breuer in 1868 published a paper on pulmonary "stretch receptors"—neural receptors that respond to expansion of the chest wall and trigger a reflex initiation of expiration—which is recognized as a major contribution to respiratory physiology. The expiratory reflex is still commonly referred to as the Hering-Breuer reflex.[40]

Breuer was appointed Privatdocent in 1868, but his academic career was short-lived. Johann Oppolzer, largely because of his physiological orientation, was regarded as somewhat of an outsider in the Vienna faculty, and his protégés shared his ostracism. When Oppolzer died in 1871, many of his clinical assistants were obliged to withdraw from their appointments in the university hospital. Breuer, upon losing his assistantship, also gave up his post as lecturer and turned fully to private practice. When, some time later, Billroth offered to propose him for an extraordinarius professorship, Breuer asked that the matter be dropped. He continued, however, to pursue physiological research at home, and he published several papers in the 1870s on the physiology of the internal ear. In 1894 he was elected corresponding member of the Vienna Academy of Sciences on the nomination of Sigmund Exner, Ewald Hering, and Ernst Mach.[41]

In 1880, the daughter of a bedridden and terminally ill patient of Breuer's began to develop hysterical symptoms. Breuer undertook her care and followed her illness for nearly two years. Her clinical course is reported, under the name Anna O., as the first of the case histories in Breuer and Freud's *Studies on Hysteria* (1895).[42]

Anna became bedridden in December, 1880, suffering from hysterical paralysis, disturbances of vision, and aphasic symptoms. She also exhibited somnambulic states which came on each afternoon and resolved in the evening. During the latter part of her somnambulism, she would tell stories, on the model of children's stories, to Breuer. She would then sleep and awake refreshed. If Breuer was not present and no story was told, her condition would worsen and the following day two stories would have to be recounted. Anna referred to this pattern as her "talking cure."

Through the early months of 1881, her condition remained stable, except for a worsening aphasia. In March she became completely mute; but, at this point, writes Breuer, "for the first time the psychical mechanism of the disorder became clear." He suggested to her that there was something she did not want to speak about. "When I guessed this and obliged her to talk about it, the inhibition, which had made any other kind of utterance impossible as well, disappeared."[43] The resolution of the aphasia was accompanied by a general improvement with regard to her other symptoms. But the death of her father in April triggered a setback and a significant worsening of her condition.

For the next fourteen months, Anna continued to experience daily somnambulic episodes and continued to recite her stories. But her story-telling soon took on significant new dimensions. Anna began to include, in addition to current fantasies, memories from the earlier months of her chronic illness. Most importantly, she also began to recount events from the six months preceding her full-blown hysteria, that is, from the period June to December, 1880, during which she had devoted much of her time to nursing her severely ill father. It was during these months that she had first developed her symptoms. Breuer soon discovered that, whenever Anna fully related the events and emotions which accompanied the initial appearance of a symptom, that symptom would disappear.

In *Studies on Hysteria,* Breuer describes the first time that, "as a result of an accidental and spontaneous utterance of this kind, during the evening [spontaneous] hypnosis, a disturbance which had persisted for a considerable time vanished,"[44] and he writes of his great surprise at this occurrence. He does not refer to his earlier experience in dealing with Anna's speechlessness, and that experience had apparently not prepared him for the present phenomenon. But, at any rate, he now formulates a therapeutic technique:

These findings—that in the case of this patient the hysterical
phenomena disappeared as soon as the event which had
given rise to them was reproduced in her hypnosis—made it
possible to arrive at a therapeutic technical procedure which
left nothing to be desired in its logical consistency and system-
atic application. Each individual symptom in this compli-
cated case was taken separately in hand; all the occasions on
which it had appeared were described in reverse order, starting before the time when the patient became bed-ridden and
going back to the event which had led to its first appearance.
When this had been described the symptom was permanently removed.[45]

To facilitate this lengthy process, Breuer would hypnotize Anna
each morning and have her summarily run through the occasions on
which the symptom had appeared. He would then return during her
spontaneous somnambulism in the afternoon and use his morning
notes to guide her more detailed reminiscences. In this way virtually all
of her hysterical symptoms were resolved.[46]

Breuer and Freud had met in the late 1870s and had become
professional and personal friends. Breuer began discussing Anna's case
with Freud while he was still treating her, or at least shortly afterwards.
Freud mentions one of these conversations in a published letter to his
fiancée dated July, 1883.[47] But Breuer did not pursue the subject of
hysteria further or attempt to apply his new therapeutic technique
elsewhere. Nor did Freud do very much with Breuer's observations,
judging by his continued preoccupation with pathological anatomy and
diseases associated with anatomical lesions, and by his expressed aston-
ishment in 1885 at Charcot's revelations on hysteria. Freud does report
in *An Autobiographical Study* that he mentioned the case of Anna O. to
Charcot, but it was clearly only in the light of Charcot's lectures that he
developed an interest in pursuing Breuer's experiences.[48]

Breuer and Freud's collaboration developed in the years after
Freud's return from Paris (1886). Breuer did not wish personally to
accept any further cases of this sort for therapy; but he referred hysterical patients to Freud and discussed their cases with him. As Breuer
wrote to Auguste Forel in 1907:

I vowed at the time [of treating Anna O.] that I would not go
through such an ordeal again. When cases came to me,
therefore, which I thought would benefit from analytic treatment, but which I could not treat myself, I referred them to

Dr. Freud, who had returned from Paris and the Salpetrière and with whom I had the most intimate friendly and scientific relations. These cases, their course, their treatment, and whatever contributions to theory arose from them were naturally constantly discussed between us.[49]

The earliest of the cases of hysteria treated by Freud and subsequently reported in the literature is that of Emmy von N., whose therapy began in May, 1889, and whose history is the second of those reported in *Studies on Hysteria*. The chapter devoted to the case in *Studies on Hysteria* contains Freud's original notes, written in 1889, and some addenda together with an extensive discussion, written in 1895. Freud remarks, in a section written in 1895, that he had "decided [in treating Emmy von N.] that I would make use of Breuer's technique of investigation under hypnosis, which I had come to know from the account he had given me of the successful treatment of his first patient. This was my first attempt at handling that therapeutic method." And some pages later, "this was the first case in which I employed the cathartic procedure [Breuer and Freud's term for the method of resolving symptoms by eliciting the events which accompanied their initial appearance] to a large extent."[50] But Freud's notes of 1889 on Frau Emmy von N. show that he was not really basing his therapy on Breuer's catharsis. He did attempt to discover, under hypnosis, the events which surrounded the initial appearance of symptoms; but his therapy involved using hypnotic suggestion to expunge or in some other manner deal with the supposedly pathogenic memories. For example, he worked at tracing Frau Emmy's terrifying hallucinations to their source, to the frightening, essentially childhood experiences which were their original inspiration; but then, as he states in the 1889 notes: "My therapy consists in wiping away these [hallucinations, along with the related memories, via hypnotic suggestion], so that she is no longer able to see them before her. To give support to my suggestion I stroked her several times over the eyes."[51] He clearly did not expect that the mere recollection of the relevant memories would induce a spontaneous cure.

This procedure is consistent with Freud's publications on hypnosis. In the review of Forel's *Hypnotism* (1889), Freud writes that "suggestion . . . satisfies all the requirements of a causal treatment in a number of cases. This is so, for instance, in hysterical disorders, which are the direct result of a pathogenic idea or the deposit of a shattering experience. If that idea is got rid of or that memory weakened—which is what suggestion brings about—the disorder too is usually overcome."[52] Further, in the "Hypnosis" article of 1891, Freud still emphasizes the use of suggestion in dealing with symptoms of psychic origin.

Freud at this time perceived the tracing of hysterical symptoms to initiating events simply as a device for rendering hypnotic suggestion more effective. This approach was, in fact, proposed by various practitioners of suggestive therapeutics. Alfred Binet, one of Charcot's protégés at the Salpetrière, wrote in 1892 that "we shall perhaps find that by taking the patient back by means of a mental artifice to the very moment at which the symptoms first appeared we may make him more susceptible to a therapeutic suggestion." Breuer and Freud, in the "Preliminary Communication," cite this passage from Binet, as well as similar remarks dating from 1889 by the Belgian physician Delboeuf and by Pierre Janet, another of the Salpetrière workers.[53] But the procedure proposed by these authors and utilized for a time by Freud differs profoundly in concept from Breuer's theory of catharsis, whereby, as in the case of Anna O., the very recollection and expression of the pathogenic events is sufficient to induce a cure.

Freud continued to use hypnotic suggestion as a means for resolving hysterical symptoms at least into 1892. In his paper entitled "A Case of Successful Treatment by Hypnotism," which appeared in two parts in December, 1892, and January, 1893, suggestion is the only therapeutic device employed and there is no attempt to trace the origin of the patient's symptoms. In the "Preliminary Communication," which also appeared in January, 1893, Freud and Breuer write that the resolution of pathogenic memories is to be achieved "by introducing [the pathogenic idea] into normal consciousness (under hypnosis) or by removing it through the physician's suggestion."[54] However, by the latter part of 1892, Freud was actually depending more and more exclusively on Breuer's cathartic approach; in the two case histories which date from this period and subsequently appear in *Studies on Hysteria* (Miss Lucy R. and Fraulein Elisabeth von R.), there is no reference at all to suggestive therapy. Symptoms are resolved solely by uncovering the events which accompanied their initial appearance and having the patient fully and vividly describe these events.

The successes of the cathartic method lent considerable support to Charcot's theory of the psychogenic source of hysterical symptoms. But, in addition, they provided the basis upon which Breuer and Freud, in the "Preliminary Communication," constructed a theory of symptom formation in hysteria which differed considerably from the concepts formulated at the Salpetrière.

The Catharsis Theory and the Concept of Abreaction

Charcot viewed the development of paralysis in traumatic neurosis as the prototype of hysterical symptom formation. He constructed a model according to which the pathogenic physical trauma—trauma sustained, for example, in a railway accident—induces a hypnosis-like state in the susceptible patient and at the same time serves as the source of autosuggestions which then generate the patient's paralysis. Hypnosis, in Charcot's view, enables the physician to penetrate to the alternate state of consciousness which was induced by the patient's spontaneous hypnosis at the time of the trauma. New suggestions can then be offered to counter and obliterate the idea of the paralysis.

Freud and Breuer noted that in their patients the events which surrounded the initial appearance of symptoms were uniformly frightful or highly emotional, and they argued that these events constituted a psychical trauma which operated in much the same way as the physical trauma of traumatic neurosis. Charcot had stressed that the key element in physical trauma is the fright, the emotional response, which the trauma produces; the same factor, according to Freud and Breuer, is operative in situations of purely psychic stress:

> *Observations . . . seem . . . to establish an analogy between the pathogenesis of common hysteria and that of traumatic neuroses, and to justify an extension of the concept of traumatic hysteria* [italics in original]. In traumatic neuroses the operative cause of the illness is not the trifling physical injury but the affect of fright—the psychical trauma. In an analogous manner, our investigations reveal, for many, if not for most, hysterical symptoms, precipitating causes which can only be described as psychical traumas. Any experience which calls up distressing affects—such as those of fright, anxiety, shame or physical pain—may operate as a trauma of this kind.[55]

But Breuer and Freud were dissatisfied with Charcot's explanation of symptom formation—the notion that it was simply a matter of hypnotic autosuggestion. Charcot's theory appeared to imply that it was the sequestering of the pathogenic idea in a special state of consciousness, divorced from regular trains of thought, that accounted for the idea's potency, and that bringing the pathogenic idea into association with other thoughts—by, for example, hypnotic countersuggestions—would invariably resolve the symptom. But Breuer and Freud interpreted their own clinical experience as failing to bear this out. Indeed, rendering patients conscious of the source of their symptoms, and thereby bringing pathogenic ideas into association with the ideas of normal consciousness, was one aspect of catharsis; but this alone did not suffice to effect a cure. In Breuer and Freud's experience, a reliving of the original emotional distress that accompanied the pathogenic event was also necessary if a symptom was to be resolved. Breuer noted, for example, that while Anna O. was recounting the earlier appearances of a symptom, that symptom would worsen, and when she told of the symptom's first emergence, the original emotional distress would typically accompany the retelling. Moreover, unless these affective factors—the worsening symptom and the distress—accompanied the procedure, catharsis did not work. Breuer and Freud, on the basis of such observations, remarked in the "Preliminary Communication" (January, 1893) that "recollection without affect almost invariably produces no result."[56]

Breuer and Freud, concentrating on the emotional, affective elements which characterize the initial trauma and must accompany catharsis, developed an alternative pathological model. They argued that emotion-laden experiences normally elicit energetic responses from a person—for example, a frightening experience may elicit a scream or flight—and that, if such responses do not occur, a pathological situation ensues. In hysteria the patient experiences a psychic trauma to which he fails to respond adequately. As a result, the affect-laden memory of the traumatic event persists, although sequestered in an unconscious state. The sequestered memory generates the chronic symptoms, which bear some relation to the initial traumatic event. The memory also produces acute hysterical attacks—sudden paroxysms of apparently involuntary gestures, bodily contortions, exclamations—which, according to Freud and Breuer, essentially involve a partial hallucinatory reliving of the traumatic experience. (For example, Frau Emmy's sudden exclamations of "Don't touch me!" accompanied an hallucinatory reliving of a terrifying childhood experience in which a very ill brother, in a state of delirium, had grabbed hold of her and almost choked her.) The cathartic method works because "it brings to an end the operative force of the idea which was not abreacted [i.e., had not elicited a sufficient response] in the first instance, by allowing its strangulated affect to find a way out through speech."[57]

Implicit in the "Preliminary Communication" is the notion that the more emotion-laden, or affective, the trauma, the greater its potential pathogenicity and the more affective must be the therapeutic catharsis, or the abreaction. Elsewhere the concept of affect is more explicitly quantified. In the fourth section of his paper entitled "Some Points for a Comparative Study of Organic and Hysterical Paralysis," written about the same time as the "Preliminary Communication" and published in July, 1893, Freud speaks of "quotas of affect" and of "the abreaction of accretions of stimulus."[58] In the first of three extant drafts of the "Preliminary Communication," Freud refers to "the theorem concerning the constancy of the sum of excitation." This theorem, as later developed, attributes the need for responding to affective stimuli, and the pathogenicity of failing to do so, to a basic requirement that the level of "excitation" be kept constant.

On several occasions during the latter part of 1892 and 1893, Freud gave cursory neurodynamic interpretations to the quantity of affect and the principle of constancy; but it would be wrong to regard these concepts as derived from neurophysiological considerations. There is no evidence that Freud and Breuer based them on physiological models and such a source cannot be assumed. The quantification of affect seemed justified merely by the fact that there appeared to be a proportionality among the severity—in terms of emotional impact—of the initial trauma, the severity of symptoms, and the degree of emotionality which accompanied catharsis. In addition, it is common usage to speak of emotional psychic states in terms of a force which must be expended. Breuer and Freud cite popular expressions to this effect, such as "to cry oneself out" and to "blow off steam." Anna O. herself spoke of catharsis as a loss of "energy." Another difficulty in insisting on physiological roots for Breuer and Freud's psychodynamics is the fact that comparable models had frequently been developed independently of physiology. Johann Friedrich Herbart, for example, had earlier in the century formulated a psychodynamics that was similar to Breuer and Freud's in a number of respects and was based solely on psychology and mathematics. Herbart was in fact subjected to some criticism for his failure to utilize physiology.[59]

Breuer and Freud's notion, derived from their clinical observations, that the failure to expend accumulated affect yields a pathological situation, immediately suggests the concept of an equilibrium that must be restored. Freud's principle of constancy—his insistence that the organism strives to maintain its sum of excitation at a constant level—merely formalizes the notion of equilibrium, and no physiological considerations need be implicated in his proposal of the principle. (Breuer repeatedly attributes the constancy principle to Freud.)[60]

There is no evidence that physiological considerations played a significant role in shaping Breuer and Freud's model, and the above observations indicate clearly that there is ample basis for developing the catharsis theory, with the quantification of affect and the principle of constancy, independently of physiology. Freud and Breuer were no doubt familiar with physiological concepts, such as notions of cortical reflexes, which bear some resemblance to the abreaction model. But those who therefore assume, as Peter Amacher and others do, that Breuer and Freud's psychological theory must have been derived from physiology, have in fact little grounds for such an assumption.

There are several passages dating from late 1892 and 1893 in which Freud does give a cursory neurodynamic interpretation to the quantity of affect and the principle of constancy. In a lecture given in January, 1893, Freud states:

> If a person experiences a psychical impression, something in his nervous system which we will for the moment call the sum of excitation is increased. Now in every individual there exists a tendency to diminish this sum of excitation once more, in order to preserve his health. The increase of the sum of excitation takes place along sensory paths, and its diminution along motor ones. So we may say that if anything impinges on someone he reacts in a motor fashion. We can now safely assert that it depends on this reaction how much of the initial psychical impression is left. Let us consider this in relation to a particular example. Let us suppose that a man is insulted, is given a blow or something of the kind. This psychical trauma is linked with an increase in the sum of excitation of his nervous system. There then instinctively arises an inclination to diminish this increased excitation immediately. He hits back, and then feels easier; he may perhaps have reacted adequately—that is, he may have got rid of as much as had been introduced into him.[61]

A similar statement appears in the third draft of the "Preliminary Communication," which was probably the joint work of Breuer and Freud. Further, in notes written late in 1892 for his translation of Charcot's *Tuesday Lectures*, Freud defines a trauma as "*an accretion of excitation* in the nervous system, *which the latter has been unable to dispose of adequately by motor reaction* [italics in original]," while "a hysterical attack is *perhaps* to be regarded as an attempt to complete the reaction to the trauma."[62]

But in none of the works from this period does Breuer or Freud attempt to develop these brief neurodynamic references into a more comprehensive physiological theory of hysteria. On the contrary, except for the above remarks, the discussions are totally in psychological terms. In the "Preliminary Communication," there is no reference at all to the nervous system. Nor does Freud's paper comparing anatomical and hysterical paralyses—which is devoted to the theme that hysteria is based on a dynamic or functional abnormality and does not involve anatomical lesions—offer comments on what the neurodynamic abnormality might entail. "Quota of affect" and the notion of constancy are dealt with solely in psychological terms: "Every event, every psychical impression is provided with a certain quota of affect . . . of which the ego divests itself either by means of a motor reaction or by associative psychical activity."[63]

Moreover, in the "Preliminary Communication," Breuer and Freud associate themselves with writers who explicitly reject neurodynamic models of hysteria and insist on emphasizing psychological interpretations. They state in a footnote: "In this preliminary communication it is not possible for us to distinguish what is new in it from what has been said by other authors such as Moebius and Strümpell who have held similar views on hysteria to ours."[64] Moebius argued vehemently that hysteria can be explained wholly in psychological terms. Adolph Strümpell, professor of special pathology and therapy at Erlangen, had been Moebius's chief in the neurological clinic at Leipzig. His position on hysteria differed from Moebius's in that he did not believe the psychological approach would be entirely sufficient. He felt, rather, that the somatic symptoms of hysteria would ultimately require a physiological explanation. However, Strümpell insisted that no such explanation was presently possible. In "Über die traumatischen Neurosen" (1888), Strümpell asserts that neurotic patients suffer from functional or dynamic nervous system abnormalities, but he makes no attempt to develop this theme further and concentrates instead on the psychological causes of the neuroses. In a lecture *Über die Entstehung und Heilung von Krankheiten durch Vorstellungen* (1888), Strümpell does not even mention the nervous system.[65]

Freud and Breuer also state in the "Preliminary Communication" that "we have found the nearest approach to what we have to say on the theoretical and therapeutic sides of the question [of hysteria] in some remarks, published from time to time, by Benedikt."[66] Moriz Benedikt had been writing about hysteria since the 1860s, and had generally emphasized physiological explanations of hysterical phenomena. But, in recent years, he had given increasing attention to psychological factors in hysteria, especially to the pathogenic role of distressing "secrets." He also stressed the therapeutic effects of enabling the patient to unburden himself of such secrets.[67] Freud, although personally acquainted with Benedikt (who had written him a letter of introduction to Charcot in 1885), had not been significantly influenced by Benedikt's early work. He undoubtedly paid greater attention to this work after his return from Paris, since Benedikt concurred with Charcot's view that anatomical lesions play no role in hysteria. But it was Benedikt's psychological formula, his notion of pathogenic secrets, that particularly attracted Breuer and Freud's interest. It was this concept, so closely resembling their own theory of catharsis, which prompted the remark that comments by Benedikt provide "the nearest approach" to their own views. This remark in the "Preliminary Communication" appears in a footnote to the statement "Hysterics suffer mainly from reminiscences"—indicating clearly that Breuer and Freud were thinking specifically of Benedikt's concept of secret memories.

Those few passages in the 1892 and 1893 papers in which Freud and Breuer depart from a strictly psychological approach and introduce neurodynamic interpretations can be accounted for by several factors. First, they served to bring the new psychological formula in line with a currently popular explanation of hysterical phenomena. Standard hysterical symptoms ranging from hyperreflexia to facile emotionalism and what was broadly labeled "nervousness" were perceived by most observers as reflecting a neurodynamic disequilibrium. Freud had merely been echoing a widely held view when he spoke in the 1888 Villaret article of a "surplus of excitation in the nervous system." Interpreting emotion-laden experiences as inducing an increase in nervous system excitation was in part simply an attempt to harmonize the catharsis model with this popular concept of a "surplus of excitation."

More importantly, the references to neurophysiology reflect Freud's continued belief that not all the phenomena of hysteria could be explained solely in psychological terms and that a physiological model would ultimately be required. Freud consistently chose to emphasize psychological explications and insisted that it is impossible, at least presently, to formulate an adequate physiological scheme, but the insufficiency of the psychology seemed to justify brief references to possible physiological factors. Indications that psychology would not suffice came from several directions. First, of course, there was still the issue of the hysterical stigmata. In the "Preliminary Communication," Freud and Breuer speak of aspects of hysteria which, "like the hysterical stigmata," are not accounted for by their psychological model. In addition, nothing has as yet been said as to why the hysterical patient is unable to react adequately to the pathogenic trauma at the time of its occurrence, and Freud was not certain that this could be explained without invoking physiology.

Freud actually became more convinced of the limits of psychological models in the year following publication of the "Preliminary Communication." In particular, his work during that year on obsessions and obsessional neurosis, reported in "The Neuro-Psychoses of Defence" (1894), brought into focus another aspect of hysteria which seemed to require a physiological explanation. In "The Neuro-Psychoses of Defence," Freud argues that the accumulation of affect induced by psychic trauma can lead not only to hysteria but also to obsessional neurosis (which he defines as a separate syndrome, noting that patients suffering from obsessions do not generally exhibit the standard symptoms of hysteria). Whether a pathogenic psychic trauma results in hysteria or in obsessional neurosis depends, in Freud's view, on whether the "sum of excitation," the affect accompanying the trauma, is "converted" into somatic symptoms or merely "transposed" from the memory of the trauma and attached to other ideas, with which the patient consequently becomes obsessively preoccupied. But Freud then must confront the problem of what determines whether a trauma results in "conversion" or "transposition."

The answer, he suggests, lies in the constitution of the patient. Hysteria results when the patient has "the capacity for conversion," which involves "a psycho-physical aptitude for [transforming] very large sums of excitation into the somatic innervation."[68] In this way, the notion that psychic trauma can result in different neuroses, and the distinction between hysteria and obsessions, lead Freud in 1894 toward according neurophysiology a greater role in the explication of hysteria. But Freud makes no attempt to explain what this psychophysical aptitude for conversion involves. Once again he merely indicates a need for a physiological explanation while believing that at present only a psychology of hysteria can be fruitfully pursued. In "The Neuro-Psychoses of Defence," Freud in fact introduces major new concepts regarding a psychology of hysteria and related neuroses, concepts which carry his psychological theories of the neuroses still further beyond those formulas he had learned in Paris.

5. Freud's Theory of Defense

Prior Concepts, 1892–1893

Breuer and Freud maintain in the "Preliminary Communication" (1893) that hysteria is triggered by the patient's failure to respond adequately to a psychic trauma, and they offer two solutions to the problem of why a satisfactory reaction to the precipitating trauma did not occur. In some cases,

> the nature of the trauma excluded a reaction, as in the case of the apparently irreparable loss of a loved person or because social circumstances made a reaction impossible or because it was a question of things which the patient wished to forget, and therefore intentionally repressed from his conscious thought and inhibited and suppressed.[1]

Alternatively, they suggest that the precipitating factor may not be the nature of the trauma, but rather the nature of the patient's psychic state at the time of its occurrence:

> We find . . . among the causes of hysterical symptoms ideas which are not in themselves significant, but whose persistence is due to the fact that they originated during the prevalence of severely paralysing affects, such as fright, or during positively abnormal psychic states, such as the semi-hypnotic twilight state of day-dreaming, auto-hypnoses, and so on. In such cases it is the nature of the states which makes a reaction to the event impossible.[2]

In either situation, the memory of the precipitating event is sequestered from normal consciousness and no adequate reaction occurs.

Nothing is said in the "Preliminary Communication" to suggest that either author preferred one or the other explanation. However, in *Studies on Hysteria* (1895) and elsewhere, the latter formula, the emphasis on special psychic states as the major pathogenic factor, is ascribed particularly to Breuer, while Freud emphasizes a formula stressing the nature of the trauma.

The psychic state hypothesis offered clear advantages in elucidating Breuer's case of Anna O., for Anna's symptoms had been traced to events which were not in themselves especially traumatic, but which had uniformly occurred while she was in her somnambulic condition or some related state. In addition, Anna O. had first developed hysterical symptoms while nursing her dying father, and several of Freud's patients whose histories are given in *Studies on Hysteria* had also become ill while caring for the sick. The psychic state theory could account for this pattern by arguing that the rigors of nursing the sick invariably lead to physical exhaustion, and that this exhaustion predisposes one to abnormal psychic states. This line of argument is actually developed by Breuer in *Studies on Hysteria.*

The psychic state hypothesis is also, of course, similar to Charcot's model for traumatic neurosis. According to that model, some startling experience, such as a railway accident, induces an hypnotic state and, because the patient is in this vulnerable state, a relatively minor event, such as mild trauma to a limb, is capable of producing a symptom such as an hysterical paralysis.

The alternative model, presumably the work of Freud, was motivated by observations which are only briefly referred to in the "Preliminary Communication." Here the authors list cases of "hysterical deliria in saints and nuns, continent women and well-brought-up children," as examples of hysteria in which "the nature of the trauma excluded a reaction." What Freud has in mind can be more clearly seen in two other works written by him during the latter part of 1892: notes to his translation of Charcot's *Tuesday Lectures,* and a paper entitled "A Case of Successful Treatment by Hypnotism." Freud was particularly concerned with hysterical attacks or chronic symptoms which took the form of behavior that was embarrassing to the patient or was regarded as improper. In order to explain such symptoms in a way consistent with the abreaction theory, Freud assumed that the patient had previously inhibited impulses to this type of behavior, and that this inhibition led to an accumulation of unreleased affect which subsequently generated the hysterical symptoms. In this way the nature of the ideas involved—ideas whose inhibition is demanded by the patient's mores, or whose expression would be "unsociable"—determined their pathogenicity.

In his notes to Charcot's *Tuesday Lectures* (1892), Freud comments on Charcot's histories of well-bred boys who had hysterical attacks involving, as one of their characteristics, outbursts of obscene language. Freud writes:

> Can it be a matter of chance that attacks in young people of whose good upbringing and manners Charcot speaks highly take the form of ravings and abusive language? This is no more the case, I think, than the familiar fact that the hysterical deliria of nuns revel in blasphemies and erotic pictures. In this we may suspect a connection which allows us a deep insight into the mechanism of hysterical states. There emerges in hysterical deliria material in the shape of ideas and impulsions to action which the subject in his healthy state has rejected and inhibited—has often inhibited by a great psychical effort.[3]

In his paper "A Case of Successful Treatment by Hypnotism" (1892), Freud discusses similar cases, and he coins the term *counterwill* (*Gegenwillen*) to characterize the generation of hysterical phenomena as a manifestation of inhibited ideas. The major history reported in the paper is that of a postpartum mother who had misgivings about her ability to nurse her child. She strove to repress her doubts and to feed the baby. But she instead developed a number of hysterical symptoms, including hyperesthesia of the nipples, and she was consequently unable to nurse. Freud also cites what he calls his first observation of counterwill. Frau Emmy von N., while caring for a sick child, had made a special effort to keep silent, but during her vigil she suddenly began to make a peculiar clicking sound which eventually developed into a chronic hysterical symptom. Finally, Freud once again mentions the hysterical attacks of nuns and normally well-behaved boys—attacks often entailing obscene language and gestures—as further examples of counterwill.

However, Freud notes that people normally have doubts and misgivings which they try to repress and impulses which they prefer to inhibit and he observes that they generally succeed in controlling these ideas and impulses. What must be explained, therefore, is why the hysteric's efforts at inhibition fail. Freud considers the possible role of physical exhaustion, from which both the new mother and Frau Emmy were suffering at the time their symptoms appeared, but he notes that this type of exhaustion is hardly peculiar to hysterics. He concludes instead that the key factor is a "tendency to a dissociation of consciousness," as a result of which "the distressing antithetic idea, which seems to be inhibited, is removed from association with the intention and continues to exist as a disconnected idea, often unconsciously to the patient himself."[4] Physical exhaustion, which according to Freud may be brought on in part by the very effort of suppressing the antithetical idea, is significant only in that it weakens the primary consciousness and thereby allows the sequestered, suppressed ideas an opportunity to manifest themselves as hysterical symptoms.

The emphasis on a "tendency to a dissociation of consciousness" brings Freud's approach somewhat in line with that of Breuer, for whom the significance of his special psychic states is specifically that ideas and impressions generated during these states are isolated from normal consciousness and lead an autonomous existence (Charcot's thesis of hypnotic autosuggestions conforms to the same model). Both authors can therefore agree that "the splitting of consciousness . . . is present in rudimentary degree in every hysteria, and . . . a tendency to such a dissociation, and with it the emergence of abnormal states of consciousness (which we shall bring together under the term 'hypnoid') is the basic phenomenon of [hysteria]."[5] They differ only in that Breuer emphasizes the spontaneous generation of splits in consciousness and "hypnoid" states, or their emergence in response to fright or exhaustion, while Freud is more concerned with the induction of abnormal states of consciousness, in susceptible people, through an effort at inhibiting particular ideas and impulses.

The theories presented in the "Preliminary Communication" on the nature of the basic abnormality in hysteria can also be found in Freud's lecture "On the Psychical Mechanism of Hysterical Phenomena," published the same month (January, 1893). This work similarly insists that the tendency toward a dissociation of consciousness is the common denominator in hysteria, and that this division can be spontaneous or induced by fright or brought about by an effort at inhibition.

The notion of a split in consciousness had been commonly employed by hypnotists, at least since the beginning of the nineteenth century, to explain hypnotic phenomena. In particular, hypnotists had noted that subjects typically could not recollect the events of their hypnosis when awakened, but displayed a thorough memory of these events during subsequent hypnotic sessions. This was interpreted as indicating the existence of a second consciousness, which was divorced from primary consciousness and in which all the memories of hypnotic episodes were integrated. Such a split in consciousness could also account for why the subject who executed posthypnotic suggestions was unable to give the true reason for his behavior.

Charles Richet, in "Du Somnambulisme Provoqué" (1875), wrote with regard to this theory:

> [Posthypnotic amnesia] is absolutely characteristic, and I have seen no exceptions to this. But, and this is the strange thing, that which happens during [hypnotic] sleep has not completely disappeared, since the reproduction of [hypnosis] recalls the memory. It is this which accounts, I believe, for the division of consciousness of which so many magnetizers speak. The ego consists of the collection of our memories; and when it is limited to a special physical state, it is almost correct to say, theoretically speaking, that the person is different, since she recalls in [hypnotic] sleep an entire series of acts which she ignores completely while awake.[6]

Charcot followed Richet in endorsing the double consciousness concept. In addition, when he applied hypnosis to the elucidation of hysteria, he incorporated the notion of double consciousness into his theory of the disease. Charcot argued that chronic hysterical symptoms are generated by autosuggestion during a spontaneous hypnotic trance and that these suggestions constitute a second consciousness. According to Charcot, the therapeutic value of hypnotic suggestion is based on the fact that the hypnosis penetrates to this second consciousness and the physician's suggestions can then deal directly with the pathological ideas sequestered there.

For both Richet and Charcot, hypnosis is an abnormal neurophysiological state. Hysteria, according to Charcot, occurs only in people who are neurologically vulnerable to such states, and are therefore vulnerable to the formation of a secondary consciousness.

The notion of double consciousness, aside from its prominence in the hypnosis literature, had also achieved considerable notoriety with regard to famous case histories of patients who alternately displayed radically different and to some extent mutually amnesic personalities—histories which are found in the medical literature throughout the century. As the workers at the Salpetrière pursued the double consciousness model of hypnotism and hysteria, they paid increasing attention to these famous cases and sought out similar patients for observation. One such case very often mentioned in the Salpetrière literature is that of Felida X., who was studied for thirty-five years (1858–1893) by Etienne Azam, professor of surgery at Bordeaux Medical School. Azam, who coined the term *dedoublement de la personnalité,* published numerous papers on his patient, as well as a comprehensive study entitled *Hypno-*

tisme, Double Consciousness et Alterations de la Personnalité (1887), which includes an introduction by Charcot.[7] Blanche Witt, a patient at the Salpetrière with a similar history, received so much attention in the literature that Jules Janet refers to her as "an hysteric known to all and justly celebrated."[8]

The most comprehensive expositions of the thesis that hysterics suffer mainly from a splitting of consciousness were those of two of Charcot's protégés, Alfred Binet and Pierre Janet. Binet and Janet both regarded a propensity for the development of secondary personalities as the basic abnormality in hysteria. When Breuer and Freud expressed the same view in the "Preliminary Communication," they noted that "in these views we concur with Binet and the two Janets [Jules and Pierre]."

Binet's two books, *On Double Consciousness* (1890) and *Alterations of Personality* (1891), are devoted primarily to experimental and clinical corroboration of the view that a dissociation of consciousness exists in hysterical patients.[9] This corroboration mainly involves the demonstration of complex behavior of which the patient is unconscious. The complexity of the behavior, according to Binet, demands that we interpret it as the work of a second consciousness. Janet covers essentially the same material in *Psychological Automatism* (1889) and a later book entitled *The Mental State of Hystericals* (published in two parts between 1892 and 1894), which includes a laudatory preface by Charcot.

The second volume of *The Mental State of Hystericals* contains, as a concluding chapter, a paper which had been published separately in 1893 and which was largely inspired by the appearance of the "Preliminary Communication." In this chapter, Janet states that there have been many articles on the subject of the splitting of personality, but "the most important work that has come to confirm our earlier studies is, without contradiction, the article of MM. Breuer and Freud, which recently appeared in the *Neurologisches Centralblatt*."[10]

The thesis that a splitting of consciousness is the key to both hypnotic and hysterical phenomena received considerable attention outside of France, reflecting the wide influence of the Salpetrière studies. The theory underlay much of the work of Frederic Myers and his School for Psychical Research in England, and it appeared frequently in the American literature. In Vienna, Krafft-Ebing endorsed the formula in an 1889 book on hypnotic studies of an hysterical woman.[11]

Some authors attempted to develop physiological explanations for the dissociation of consciousness. Azam, for example, offered a model based on the notion of transient cerebral ischemias. The Salpetrière workers generally agreed that the splitting of consciousness involves some neurophysiological abnormality, but they insisted that attempts to define this abnormality would be purely speculative and fruitless. Binet writes, with regard to hypnosis:

> It is probable, even certain, that these [psychological] altera-
> tions have as a basis material modifications which are pro-
> duced in the nervous centers of the somnambulist and in
> other parts of the organism. But the nature of these purely
> physiological phenomena is quite unknown, and all that has
> been written on this subject seems to me to be fanciful.[12]

Pierre Janet notes that the psychological model does not account for all the symptoms of hysteria. He suggests that perhaps ultimately a neurophysiological model can be obtained which will offer a fuller explanation of hysterical phenomena. But he adds that no such explanation could presently be formulated and that "a psychological definition is, even at this day, the formula best able to sum up, simply from a clinical point of view, the great majority of hysterical symptoms."[13] In the "Preliminary Communication," Breuer and Freud make no mention of a physiological basis for the dissociation of consciousness; they apparently agreed that such remarks would be futile speculation.

Formulation of the Defense Theory

Freud's paper "The Neuro-Psychoses of Defence," which appeared in the spring of 1894, reveals major changes in his approach to the pathology of hysteria. Most important is his introduction of the concept of *defense* and his extension of the hysteria model to embrace other neuroses.

Freud acknowledges in the paper that there are cases of hysteria in which the primary pathogenic factor, leading to a split in consciousness and the absence of normal abreaction to a traumatic event, is Breuer's "spontaneous hypnoid state." But Freud is more concerned with those cases of hysteria where the splitting of consciousness is not spontaneous but is the result of "an act of will on the part of the patient." This second situation he designates "defense hysteria."[14]

The notion of defense hysteria is, of course, closely related to Freud's arguments in the earlier papers that the failure to react normally to a trauma, and the precipitation of a split in consciousness, may be due to an effort at suppression by the patient. But there is an important new emphasis. In the earlier papers, the suppressed ideas generally concerned doubts and misgivings, or repugnant impulses, which did not appear in themselves to be very significant. Freud viewed them as comparable to ideas which are inhibited as a common practice by normal people; therefore, he argued that the pathological aspect was the hysteric's failure at suppression and the return of the inhibited ideas in the form of symptoms. Now, however, Freud emphasizes the importance of the suppressed ideas per se, and he insists that they are uniquely distressful and worrisome to the patient: *"An occurrence of incompatibility took place in their ideational life*—that is to say, . . . their ego was faced with an experience, an idea or a feeling which aroused such a distressing affect that the subject decided to forget about it because he had no confidence in his power to resolve the contradiction between that incompatible idea and his ego by means of thought-activity."[15] Freud no longer regards these incompatible ideas as comparable to the everyday disturbances which normally provoke inhibition. Similarly, he now believes that the suppression of these ideas in hysteria involves a psychological process distinct from normal inhibition. Freud is not prepared to assert that the rejection of a particularly distressing idea can produce hysteria in anyone; he still believes that the sequellae in the hysterical patient reflect a pathological predisposition. But he withdraws from his earlier stress on a "tendency towards a dissociation of consciousness," and notes that, in general, hysterical patients were perfectly healthy prior to their confrontation with the incompatible idea.

The significance now accorded the rejected idea per se is due, in part, to clinical experiences in which patients acknowledged extraordinary efforts at suppression. Freud writes that "the patients can recollect as precisely as could be desired their efforts at defence, their intention of 'pushing the thing away', of not thinking of it, of suppressing it."[16] But probably of greater importance for Freud's development of the defense model was his recognition of the phenomenon of *resistance*. Freud's earliest published comments on resistance appear in *Studies on Hysteria* (1895), but it seems that he first recognized the phenomenon about two years earlier. Freud writes in *Studies on Hysteria* that he had frequently come across patients whom he could not hypnotize, and that he had consequently sought a means by which he could "by-pass hypnosis and yet obtain the pathogenic recollections." He had recalled that, although experiences during hypnosis are ostensibly forgotten in the waking state, Bernheim had succeeded by mere insistence in getting his patients to remember these experiences. Freud states that he had therefore attempted to penetrate the hysteric's second consciousness in an analogous way:

I now became insistent—if I assured them that they *did* know it, that it would occur to their minds,—then, in the first cases something did actually occur to them. . . . After this I became still more insistent; I told the patients to lie down and deliberately close their eyes in order to "concentrate"—all of which had at least some resemblance to hypnosis. I then found that without any hypnosis new recollections emerged which went further back. . . . Experiences like this made me think that it would in fact be possible for the pathogenic groups of ideas, that were after all certainly present, to be brought to light by mere insistence.[17]

This new clinical approach had led to important theoretical considerations:

Since this insistence involved effort on my part and so suggested the idea that I had to overcome a resistance, the situation led me at once to the theory that . . . *I had to overcome a psychical force in the patients which was opposed to the pathogenic ideas becoming conscious (being remembered).* . . . It occurred to me that this must no doubt be the same psychical force that had played a part in the generating of the hysterical symptom and had at that time prevented the pathogenic idea from becoming conscious. What kind of force could one suppose was operative here, and what motive could have put it into operation? I could easily form an opinion on this. For I already had at my disposal a few completed analyses in which I had come to know examples of ideas that were pathogenic, and had been forgotten and put out of consciousness. From these I recognized a universal characteristic of such ideas: they were all of a distressing nature, calculated to arouse the affects of shame, of self-reproach and of psychical pain, and the feeling of being harmed; they were all of a kind one would prefer not to have experienced, that one would rather forget. From all this there arose . . . the thought of *defence.*[18]

Freud does not indicate when he began to use his alternate technique, or when the idea of defense occurred to him. But the new technique is employed in the cases of Miss Lucy R. and Fraulein Elisabeth von R. (the third and fifth cases reported in *Studies on Hysteria*), and these appear to be among the earliest applications of the procedure. Also,

Freud states in a discussion of Elisabeth von R.'s therapy: "In the course of this . . . work I began to attach a deeper significance to the resistance offered by the patient in the reproduction of her memories."[19] Elisabeth von R. is described by Freud as a young lady who exhibited hysterical symptoms of chronic pains in her legs and difficulty walking, and in his report on the case Freud associates her symptoms with her suppression of erotic ideas involving both a brother-in-law and a family friend. Freud comments specifically, in his report, on Elisabeth's resistance to acknowledging her ultimately confessed erotic thoughts and feelings concerning these men.

Both Elisabeth von R. and Lucy R. were first seen by Freud late in 1892, and it seems certain that his observations of resistance in the ensuing months were a major stimulus to his shift to the defense concept and to his preparation of "The Neuro-Psychoses of Defence" (1894).

Freud also records in *Studies on Hysteria* that, after publication of the "Preliminary Communication," he attempted to apply Breuer's catharsis technique (presumably the nonhypnotic version) to other neurotic syndromes and found that the approach proved successful with several types of neuroses. He states that this was true, for example, of obsessional neurosis—a syndrome in which the patient suffered primarily from obsessional ideas. (The absence of standard hysterical symptoms in these patients was proof, in Freud's view, that obsessional neurosis was indeed a distinct syndrome, separate from hysteria.) But the case histories of obsessional neurosis in "The Neuro-Psychoses of Defence" reveal further that Freud encountered the same resistance in these cases as in hysteria. Moreover, his obsessional patients explicitly acknowledged efforts to suppress their pathogenic ideas. These observations led Freud to the conclusion that the pathogenesis of obsessional neurosis specifically paralleled that of defense hysteria—that is, that obsessional neurosis is triggered by the patient's suppression of an extraordinarily distressing idea. The same conclusion is reached with regard to hallucinatory psychoses. These extensions of the defense model generated the notion of an entire family of neuropsychoses of defense and spurred subsequent efforts by Freud to formulate a general theory of the neuroses. Within the next few years, Freud made attempts to integrate various other syndromes—such as anxiety neurosis, melancholia, and paranoia—into the defense theory.[20]

Discussing the mechanisms of symptom formation in different neuroses, Freud argues that the ego, in its effort at defense, attempts to dispose in some way of the quantum of affect which was originally attached to the suppressed intolerable idea. What distinguishes hysteria from, for example, obsessional neurosis is that in the former the affect is converted into somatic symptoms, while in the latter it is merely transposed to another idea, which thereby becomes an obsession. The pathological disposition of the patient determines whether conversion or transposition occurs. As a corollary of this theory, Freud maintains that the characteristic abnormality of hysteria is a "capacity for conversion."

Freud's earlier emphasis on a "tendency towards a dissociation of consciousness" now slips into the background. It had previously been used to explain why the hysteric fails in his effort to inhibit disturbing ideas. But, with the defense theory, the ideas which are suppressed in hysteria are now viewed as of an exceptionally distressing nature and as triggering a pathological process which bears no relation to normal inhibition. Consequently, a "tendency towards a dissociation of consciousness" need no longer be invoked to supply the pathological element. In addition, the realization that other neuroses also involve the formation of a second consciousness indicated that a "dissociation of consciousness" could no longer be perceived as a unique characteristic of hysteria. Finally, Freud cites occasional cases of hysteria where the division of consciousness does not even occur. The "capacity for conversion" thus replaces the "tendency towards a division of consciousness" as the abnormality specifically characteristic of hysteria. Breuer, while not endorsing Freud's defense model, apparently acknowledged that the "tendency towards a division of consciousness" could no longer be regarded as the hallmark of hysteria, and Freud remarks: "In taking this view, Breuer and I . . . are diverging from Janet, who assigns too great an importance to the splitting of consciousness in his characterization of hysteria."[21]

On the Origins of the Defense Theory

Many authors have written about possible sources of Freud's ideas on defense, and they have paid particular attention to comparable notions in the work of the philosopher Johann Friedrich Herbart. A comparison of the ideas of Freud and Herbart was first undertaken by Luise von Karpinska in an article entitled "Über die psychologischen Grundlagen des Freudismus" (1914). The theme was subsequently developed more thoroughly in Maria Dorer's *Historische Grundlagen der Psychoanalyse* (1932).[22] Since the appearance of Dorer's book, a discussion of Herbart's work has been a permanent fixture in papers on the historical sources of Freud's psychology.

Herbart, who from 1809 to 1834 held what had formerly been Kant's Chair in Philosophy at Königsberg, argued that ideas are constantly struggling among themselves to enter consciousness. Those ideas of which one is conscious at a given moment strive to suppress unrelated or antagonistic ideas, while the latter struggle to rise above the "threshold of consciousness" and to replace the former. There are, for Herbart, two thresholds of consciousness: a static one, below which lie ideas that are so successfully repressed that they exert no influence at all on behavior; and a mechanical one, below which lie forceful ideas that are capable of having some influence on behavior even though they are outside of consciousness.

According to Herbart, the equilibrium among concepts is in a constant state of flux due to the impact of new ideas and perceptions. These new perceptions and ideas must be properly absorbed, and a stable equilibrium must be maintained, if sanity is to be preserved. If new concepts are not properly accommodated, mental illness ensues:

> The complex which makes up the self of each person receives incessant additions in the course of life, which are blended together with it in the closest manner. If this blending did not take place, the unity of the personality would be lost, as in many kinds of insanity really happens, inasmuch as a new ego is created out of a certain mass of concepts which act separately, and when the masses, as a result of a change in the organism, enter consciousness one after the other, a changing personality arises.[23]

Much has been written on the subject of Freud's exposure to Herbart's ideas. It has been pointed out, for example, that Franz Exner (Sigmund Exner's father), who was responsible for a comprehensive reform of public school curricula in Austria around midcentury, was a disciple of Herbart, and that Herbart's ideas consequently dominated the philosophical teaching in Austrian schools. An 1898 official history of the University of Vienna states: "The philosophical system, which especially prevailed in Viennese colleges, as well as in the other Austrian colleges, was Herbart's. In this the influence of Franz Exner was especially decisive."[24] More specifically, it has been established that the philosophy text in use at Freud's gymnasium during his last year there was Gustav Lindner's *Lehrbuch der empirischen Psychologie nach genetischer Methode*.[25] Lindner was a student of Franz Exner, and the book is a digest of Herbart's thought. Indeed, Lindner states in his preface that only writers of the Herbartian school are considered in the text.[26] In addition, Robert Zimmermann—who was professor of philosophy at the University of Vienna from 1861 to 1891, and the only full professor in philosophy at Vienna during the fifteen years after Franz Brentano's retirement in 1881—regarded himself as Herbart's disciple and taught Herbart's concepts.[27] (Freud was a student at the university from 1873 to 1881.)

Most significantly perhaps, Herbart's concepts are utilized extensively by Wilhelm Griesinger in his popular textbook of psychiatry and are also mentioned occasionally by Theodor Meynert. It has been noted in numerous works that Freud was exposed to Herbart's ideas, and to their possible application to psychopathology, through these psychiatric sources.

Finally, such observations have led one writer to argue that

> we . . . find that Herbartianism was the dominant psychology in the scientific world in which Freud lived during the formative years of his scientific development. During that time psychologic discussion in Austria was almost exclusively conducted in terms of Herbartian "Vorstellungsmechanik." This held good for not only educators and philosophers, but also for Freud's medical teachers and other scientific contemporaries.[28]

The notion that ideas are constantly being inhibited or repressed was indeed very prominent in psychological thinking during the latter part of the nineteenth century; but, although Herbart's name was often mentioned, there were also other extremely important sources for the same concept. The pervasiveness of the inhibition model can be seen in those physiological theories of hypnosis discussed in the preceding chapter. All these theories, whether propounded by German, French, or English authors, concur in postulating psychic mechanisms which normally inhibit ideas and prevent automaton-like responses to suggestions; also, they all explain the hypnotized subject's responsiveness to suggestions as resulting from the suspension of normal inhibitory controls. It is not very likely that these hypnosis theories were derived exclusively from Herbart's psychology. Indeed, it would be hard to argue that Herbart exerted any influence at all on French and English writers. The hypnosis theorists formulated their psychological mechanisms primarily on the basis of analogies to mechanisms propounded in neurophysiology, according to which the reflex function of lower neural centers is inhibited by higher, cerebral controls. It is true that the physiological model was, in turn, based largely on older psychological concepts concerning behavior and an organism's response to its environment—concepts having to do, for example, with the observation that psychological maturation is accompanied by an increased capacity to inhibit and moderate extreme or stereotyped responses to events in one's environment. But the physiological formula drew upon psychologists other than Herbart. The physiological model was proposed in England quite early in the century and Herbart's psychology played no significant role in its original formulation.

A paper by the Viennese psychiatrist Heinrich Obersteiner, entitled "Experimental Researches in Attention" (1879), emphasizes the importance of the mind's constant inhibition of ideas and perceptions. The paper indicates clearly how the author's ideas were influenced both by Herbart's psychology and by the psychological models derived from neurophysiological inhibitory phenomena. The work is particularly interesting since Obersteiner was a friend of Freud's and directed a sanatorium where Freud was employed for some years beginning in June, 1885. Obersteiner writes that "the current of ideation (Vorstellungsverlauf), or order in which ideas present themselves in consciousness, will be influenced by three factors. Of these the first two act as stimulant (like the accelerator nerves of the heart). . . . The inhibitory influence, that which we have specially to consider, is that of attention." "Attention" for Obersteiner signifies the mind's ability to concentrate on specific psychic phenomena by means of inhibiting extraneous material. He states: "In every mental act whether it be in the domain of sensation, volition, or intellect, there is seen an inhibitory power, essentially the same in all cases. This inhibitory power, on which depends all consecutive mental action, is Attention." Speaking of the inhibition of actions, Obersteiner notes:

> Our actions are conditioned first by sensory perceptions, further through feelings associated with them, and also by revived sensory and motor ideas. We can, however, will that a certain action to which there exists a powerful stimulus should be repressed, and carry out another. By inhibition of the former we concentrate attention on the latter. How difficult it is to repress the motor manifestation of a painful sensation is a matter of everyday observation. Still it is possible, and another action can be substituted for it.[29]

The influence of physiological concepts on Obersteiner's psychological model can be seen in his references to the heart and his discussion of the inhibition of actions. In addition, he quotes several physiologists, including the English researcher Ferrier who had observed: "The centers of inhibition being thus the essential factor of attention, constitute the organic basis of all the higher intellectual faculties." But Obersteiner also cites purely psychological sources. He notes Kant's comments on the inhibition of ideas and accords special importance to Herbart's work: "This subject had already in the year 1822 been carefully investigated by the founder of a psychology based on scientific and mathematical principles, viz. Herbart. . . . Herbart put forward the view that attention consisted in inhibition of ideation."[30]

It is clear, in any case, that due to a variety of influences, most notably Herbart's psychology and the psychology of the physiologists, concepts of psychic inhibition became very popular during this period; it was undoubtedly as a result of these popular views that Freud initially tried to explain the suppression of pathogenic ideas in hysteria in terms of normal psychic inhibition. But there is little basis, other than the general popularity of Herbart's work, for regarding Freud's model as derived specifically from Herbart. Freud's notion of the failure of inhibition did to some degree resemble Herbart's remarks on mental illness. According to Freud's model, the pathogenic ideas in hysteria are not, in fact, inhibited as they ought to be, but are actually separated out into a second consciousness. This concept recalls Herbart's comments on the necessity for properly integrating new perceptions and ideas, and on the pathological results when integration fails and a secondary ego is formed. But more immediate sources for Freud's theories about splits in consciousness and secondary egos were the French writers at the Salpetrière, and it is in fact these sources, rather than Herbart, which are cited by Freud.

Moreover, with his development of the defense theory, Freud no longer viewed the hysteric's suppression of pathogenic ideas as comparable to normal inhibition. Consequently, his new model of hysteria entailed a departure from standard notions of psychic inhibition such as those stemming from Herbart and from the neurophysiologists. The shift in Freud's theory is reflected in a difference in terminology between the papers dating from late 1892 and 1893 on the one hand and "The Neuro-Psychoses of Defence" (1894) on the other. In the earlier papers, *repression* (*Verdrangung*) is used only as a synonym for *inhibition* (*Hemmung*), and *inhibition* is found more frequently. *Inhibition* was the standard term for both psychic and physiological inhibitory processes during this period, and Freud's usage resembles that of Herbart and of the physiologists. *Repression* appears only once in the "Preliminary Communication": "things which the patient wished to forget, and therefore intentionally repressed from his conscious thought and inhibited and suppressed." But in "The Neuro-Psychoses of Defence," a paper about the same length as the "Preliminary Communication," *repression* appears three times and *inhibition* not at all. This change in terminology reflects Freud's insistence, in the defense model, that the effort at suppression in hysteria involves a unique, pathological process distinct from normal inhibition.

In the earlier papers, the term *ego* is used rarely, and it does not appear at all in the "Preliminary Communication." In "The Neuro-Psychoses of Defence," it is found twelve times and is used to emphasize the point that the pathogenic idea in hysteria is particularly distressful and traumatizing to the entire psyche, or ego, and is not comparable to the everyday disturbances or distractions which trigger normal inhibition.

Numerous writers have noted that in the work of Wilhelm Griesinger one finds a concept of ego, and of the ego's suppression of distressing ideas, which resembles Freud's theory. Griesinger, like Obersteiner, explicitly acknowledged both Herbart's influence and the influence of neurophysiology in the formulation of his psychodynamics, but his own models differ significantly from both sources. The impact of Herbart's thought can be seen in this statement by Griesinger on the integration of new material into the ego:

> This assimilation of the new ideas with the pre-existing [ego] does not happen at once—it grows and strengthens very gradually, and that which is not yet assimilated appears as an opposition to the *I* as a *thou*. Gradually it confines itself no longer to a single complexity of ideas and desires which represents the *I*, but there are formed several such masses of ideas united, organised and strengthened; two (and not only two) souls then dwell within the man, and this changes or is divided according to the predominance of the one or of the other mass of ideas, both of which may now represent the [ego]. Out of this, internal contradiction and strife may result; and such actually occurs within every thinking mind. In happy harmonious natures this conflict is spontaneously and rapidly brought to an end, since in all these various complex perceptions, there is developed, in common, several general, . . . fundamental intuitions . . . whereby there is given to all the spheres of the thought and will a harmonising fundamental direction.[31]

But this formulation differs from Herbart's in that for Griesinger the ego is something in addition to the play of idea-forces. The ego consists also of factors—the "fundamental intuitions" mentioned in the quotation—which control the play of ideas. Griesinger states the distinction explicitly when he speaks of "two general conditions necessary to the freedom of human action":

> An unobstructed association of ideas whereby, around the ideas presented, which are transformed into will, other ideas originating may be gathered, and may be opposed to the former . . . [and] a sufficiently strong [ego], that can give the decision by its mass of ideas, strengthening one set of the opposing perceptions, and thereby relatively weakening the other.[32]

Ideas which are inimical to the "fundamental intuitions" of the ego are not integrated into a new harmonious equilibrium as are ordinary ideas and perceptions. Rather, these inimical ideas are suppressed. Whereas for Herbart there is only a single inhibitory process, related to the normal interplay of ideas, Griesinger distinguishes between this process and the ego's rejection of particularly disturbing thoughts.

Freud was almost certainly familiar with Griesinger's text. He writes that during his time in Meynert's clinic he assiduously read the major contemporary works in psychiatry, and Griesinger's book was still a leading text in the field and was also one favored by Meynert. In any case, in his discussion of the derivation of the defense concept in *Studies on Hysteria,* Freud explicitly acknowledges that the notion of the ego's rejection of unacceptable ideas is not an original one. Without naming anyone, he suggests that there were in fact numerous theories of ego censorship comparable to his own. He never refers explicitly to Griesinger, and the only basis for according special importance to Griesinger's theory in shaping Freud's model is the exceptional popularity of Griesinger's text during the period.

But it would be an error to regard either Griesinger's ego psychology or any other contemporary concept of ego censorship as the major inspiration for Freud's defense model. Freud was undoubtedly well acquainted with ego theories, or at least Griesinger's theory, in 1892 and 1893, and yet he chose at that time to explain hysterical phenomena in terms of the normal inhibition of ideas. The defense model developed out of this earlier formula, and was inspired primarily by Freud's recognition of the phenomenon of resistance, and by his realization of the special, particularly inimical nature of the pathogenic

ideas in hysteria. Griesinger's work and other theories of ego censorship might have provided Freud with examples of the type of model he
sought as an alternative to his inhibition model. But the dynamics of
the defense concept were determined by Freud's clinical observations
during 1893 and by the revisions to his earlier theory which those
observations seemed to demand.

Studies on Hysteria: *Breuer Versus Freud*

Freud and Breuer's *Studies on Hysteria,* published in 1895, is divided into four sections: (1) the reprinted "Preliminary Communication"; (2) five case histories—Breuer's "Anna O." and four cases of
Freud's; (3) a theoretical section by Breuer; and (4) a chapter on psychotherapy by Freud.

During the period following publication of the "Preliminary Communication," Breuer had persisted in his view that experiences which
lead to hysteria are rendered pathogenic primarily because of the patient's "hypnoid" state at the time of their occurrence. According to
Breuer, it is usually the presence of a hypnoid state which causes the
memory of an event to be sequestered from normal consciousness and
thereby prevents a normal abreaction to the experience. In his theoretical section in *Studies on Hysteria,* Breuer considers both this hypnoid
state hypothesis and Freud's defense theory, and he insists that the
hypnoid state mechanism is the more important:

> Freud has found in the deliberate amnesia of defence a sec-
> ond source, independent of hypnoid states, for the construc-
> tion of ideational complexes which are excluded from associa-
> tive contact. But, accepting this qualification, I am still of
> opinion that hypnoid states are the cause and necessary con-
> dition of many, indeed of most, major and complex hysterias.

Breuer argues that hypnoid states usually underlie even those cases
which fit Freud's defense model:

> I . . . venture to suggest that the assistance of the hypnoid
> state is necessary if defence is to result . . . in a genuine split-
> ting of the mind. Auto-hypnosis has, so to speak, created the
> space or region of unconscious psychical activity into which
> the ideas which are fended off are driven.[33]

Freud had noted in "The Neuro-Psychoses of Defence" (1894) that
the psychic traumas which lead to hysterical symptoms are almost in-

variably of a sexual nature, and he had argued that this observation is fully explicable in terms of the defense theory. Because of conflicts between sexual desires and social mores, "it is precisely sexual life which brings with it the most copious occasions for the emergence of incompatible ideas."[34] It is therefore sexual life which triggers the greatest efforts at repression and defense. Breuer, in *Studies on Hysteria,* offers several alternative explanations for the prominence of sexual factors in the etiology of hysteria. He argues, for example, that the propensity for developing hypnoid states is derived from an earlier tendency to daydreaming and "absence of mind," and that pathogenic situations occur when affective ideas are introduced into these states of abstraction. Erotic ideas are of such importance partly because they generate dreamlike states and introduce strong affects as well:

> This is the way in which pathogenic auto-hypnosis would seem to come about in some people—by affect being introduced into a habitual reverie. This is perhaps one of the reasons why in the [life history of hysterics] we so often come across the two great pathogenic factors of being in love and sick-nursing. In the former, the subject's longing thoughts about his absent loved one create in him a "rapt" state of mind, cause his real environment to grow dim, and then bring his thinking to a standstill charged with affect.

And some pages later:

> It will be clear here once again how great an influence on the development of hysteria is to be ascribed to sexuality. For, apart from sick-nursing, no psychical factor is so well-calculated to produce reveries charged with affect as are the longings of a person in love.[35]

A second explanation given by Breuer for the special significance of sexuality is a physiological one, which appears in the context of a neurodynamic interpretation of the abreaction theory. This discussion of abreaction represents the first attempt by either Breuer or Freud to give a comprehensive physiological interpretation to their psychology. It was motivated largely by Breuer's desire to support his hypnoid state hypothesis and to offer alternative explanations for those characteristics of hysteria, such as the prominence of sexual experiences among patients' pathogenic traumas, which Freud viewed as best explained by the defense theory.

Breuer begins by insisting that purely psychological interpretations of hysterical phenomena will not suffice. Not all hysterical symptoms are amenable to psychological explanation. In addition, even in the case of those symptoms which can be traced to psychic factors, some physiological explanation is required to account for the ease with which these ideational factors are converted into somatic symptoms. Both of these points had, of course, already been made by Freud. Freud suggested repeatedly that the stigmata of hysteria would have to be explained in neurodynamic terms. He had also argued, in "The Neuro-Psychoses of Defence," that the key to hysteria is a "capacity for conversion" which must be elucidated by physiology. But Breuer now goes further and actually develops a neurophysiological model for the pathogenesis of hysteria.

Breuer argues that "in waking life [cerebral pathways] are in a state of tonic excitation [with the magnitude of this tonic, or baseline, excitation differing for different pathways]. . . . This intracerebral excitation is what determines [each pathway's] conductive capability, and . . . the diminution and disappearance of [this] excitation is what sets up the state of sleep."[36] This tonic excitation, according to Breuer, is necessary for normal cerebral functioning; its diminution in sleep accounts for why dreams display defective and incomplete associations and differ so radically from normal thought processes. During sleep, and in resting states generally, the quiescent brain generates the energy needed to reestablish normal tonic excitation.

Cerebral excitation in the waking state is usually maintained at a constant level:

> The cerebral elements . . . liberate a certain amount of energy even when they are at rest; and if this energy is not employed functionally it increases the normal intracerebral excitation. The result is a feeling of unpleasure. . . . Since these feelings disappear when the surplus quantity of energy which has been liberated is employed functionally, we may conclude that the removal of such surplus excitation is a need of the organism. And here for the first time we meet the fact that there exists in the organism a *tendency to keep intracerebral excitation constant* [italics in original]" (Freud).[37]

This is Breuer's physiological interpretation of Freud's principle of constancy. The notion that nervous energy is maintained at a fixed level appears quite frequently in neurophysiological literature during this period. Breuer himself refers to the concept as an old one and mentions an 1824 passage by Cabanis. In the latter part of the century, the concept is found in the works of French, German, and English writers. John Hughlings Jackson, for example, states that "all actions are in one sense results of restorations of nervous equilibrium by expenditures of energy."[38]

According to Breuer, intracerebral excitation may be increased by physiological needs and instincts and by emotion-laden perceptions and sensations. It is the latter phenomena which are most relevant to hysteria. In situations where the increase in excitation accompanying affective experiences is prevented from being properly discharged, that excitation is converted into somatic hysterical symptoms. This is, of course, merely a translation of the abreaction theory into physiological terms. But Breuer also discusses those increases in excitation which are due to endogenous factors, such as bodily needs and instincts. He refers, for example, to excitation generated by the drives for oxygen and for food and water. Lastly, he discusses sexual drives, arguing that sexuality is the major endogenous source of elevations in cerebral excitation and is therefore particularly well suited for initiating hysterical conversions: "The sexual instinct is undoubtedly the most powerful source of persisting increases of excitation (and consequently of neuroses)."[39] Breuer thus develops another explanation for the prominence of sexual factors in the pathogenesis of hysteria and demonstrates further that this prominence of sexuality need not be interpreted as evidence in favor of Freud's defense hypothesis.

Breuer also uses his physiology of hysteria to support the hypnoid theory more directly. For example, he develops a neurodynamic explication of hypnoid states and demonstrates how easily the hypnoid theory can be integrated into his general physiological model. Breuer argues that hypnoid states, like sleep, involve a decrease in cerebral tonic excitation. But this decrease in tonic excitation results in an impairment of normal associative pathways. As a result, a sudden input of excitation occurring during a hypnoid state cannot be dissipated by normal pathways, and the newly introduced quantum of excitation is therefore available for conversion. Breuer also offers a neurodynamic explanation, in terms of hypnoid states, for the etiological significance of physical exhaustion, which he and Freud had earlier recognized as an important factor in the etiology of hysteria. Breuer now argues that such exhaustion simply serves to lower the level of cerebral energy and thereby facilitates the creation of hypnoid states.

Breuer's physiological interpretations in *Studies on Hysteria* contrast sharply with the absence of such speculations from his earlier joint publication with Freud and from Freud's own papers on hysteria. However, such theorizing is hardly surprising in view of Breuer's earlier work in neurophysiology. Unlike Freud, who had very little contact with physiological research, Breuer had pursued extensive studies in neurophysiology and was highly regarded for his accomplishments in the field. It might be argued that Breuer's interests would naturally lead him towards neurodynamic models, and that perhaps the absence of such models from the "Preliminary Communication" should be attributed to Freud's influence.

But Breuer's attempt to formulate a physiology of hysteria was undoubtedly determined to a large degree by several new factors which had arisen during the two years since the publication of the "Preliminary Communication." First, there was the conflict between his hypnoid theory and Freud's defense concept; it seems certain that support of the hypnoid theory and rebuttal of Freud's defense interpretations were primary motives for Breuer's formulation of his physiological model. A second factor concerned the concept of "capacity for conversion," which had been presented by Freud a year earlier. Freud, in "The Neuro-Psychoses of Defence," argued that a failure of normal abreaction can lead to neuroses other than hysteria, and that hysteria occurs only in patients who possess a capacity for converting affect into somatic symptoms. He suggested that the capacity for conversion is the key to hysteria, stating that "in taking this view Breuer and I are coming closer to Oppenheim's . . . well-known definitions of hysteria."[40] Oppenheim had also insisted that the major characteristic of hysteria is the ease with which psychic disturbances are translated into somatic symptoms. In addition, he had attempted to develop a physiological explanation for this phenomenon. He had spoken of a neurological abnormality on a molecular level which resulted in an "irritable weakness" and an "increased neurodynamic excitability."

Breuer, in his theoretical chapter in *Studies on Hysteria,* endorses Freud's emphasis on conversion and agrees that "the fundamental pathological change which is present in every case [of hysteria] . . . lies in an abnormal excitability of the nervous system."[41] But he regards Oppenheim's statements about the instability of molecules and abnormal excitability as too vague. Breuer uses his physiological model of hysteria to offer a simple and elegant alternative explanation for the ease with which psychic disturbances generate somatic abnormalities in these patients. He argues that those areas of the nervous system which normally remain unaffected by psychic activity are protected by high resistances, comparable to resistances in an electric circuit, which prevent cerebral excitation from flowing into these pathways. In the pathogenesis of hysteria, high levels of excitation are developed which do not have access to normal outlets. These high levels of excitation merely overcome standard resistances and flow into the normally insulated pathways—yielding somatic abnormalities such as spastic paralyses, contractures, and so on.

A possible third factor in Breuer's excursion into physiological theorizing was the publication in 1894 of a book by Sigmund Exner entitled *Entwurf zu einer physiologische Erklärung der psychische Erscheinungen.* The work offered a comprehensive physiological exposition of normal mental functions and was widely regarded as a major achievement in psychophysiological theorizing. Breuer, who was a close friend of Exner's as well as his family physician, cites *Entwurf* on several occasions in his theoretical chapter. It seems quite possible that the publication of Exner's book served as an additional inspiration to Breuer's own physiological speculations.

Freud was dissatisfied with Breuer's theoretical chapter; he wrote in a letter to a friend: "The book with Breuer will include . . . a chapter by him—from which I dissociate myself."[42] Freud's disapproval was, of course, due in large part to Breuer's emphasis of the hypnoid theory and his relegation of the defense concept to a secondary position. But Freud was undoubtedly unhappy with Breuer's physiological speculations as well. His own perception of the significance to be accorded to the abreaction theory and the concept of quotas of affect is presented in "The Neuro-Psychoses of Defence," and is in sharp contrast to Breuer's physiological discussion:

> I should like, finally, to dwell for a moment on the working hypothesis which I have made use of in this exposition of the neuroses of defence. I refer to the concept that in mental functions something is to be distinguished—a quota of affect or sum of excitation—which possesses all the characteristics of a quantity (though we have no means of measuring it), which is capable of increase, diminution, displacement and discharge, and which is spread over the memory-traces of ideas somewhat as an electric charge is spread over the surface of a body.
>
> This hypothesis, which, incidentally, already underlies our theory of "abreaction" in our "Preliminary Communication," can be applied in the same sense as physicists apply the hypothesis of a flow of electric fluid. It is provisionally

justified by its utility in co-ordinating and explaining a great variety of psychical states.[43]

There is no mention of nervous system activities or neurodynamic energy. Similarly, in *Studies on Hysteria*, the sections written by Freud contain no physiological speculations. This includes his chapter on psychotherapy, in which he thoroughly reviews his theory of hysteria.

Freud's theoretical discussions in the psychotherapy chapter deal primarily with the defense model. But he remarks that, since resistance during therapy is an integral part of defense hysteria, the apparent absence of resistance in the case of Anna O. obliges him to acknowledge the existence of hypnoid hysterias as well: "I regard this distinction [i.e., the absence of resistance in Anna O.'s self-therapy, as opposed to its invariable presence in hysterias due to defense] as so important that, on the strength of it, I willingly adhere to this hypothesis of there being a hypnoid hysteria." Freud notes, however, that he has never personally come across any genuine cases of hypnoid hysteria. On the contrary:

> Any [apparent case of hypnoid hysteria] that I took in hand has turned into a defence hysteria. It is not, indeed, that I have never had to do with symptoms which demonstrably arose during dissociated states of consciousness and were obliged for that reason to remain excluded from the ego. This was sometimes so in my cases as well; but I was able to show afterwards that the so-called hypnoid state owed its separation to the fact that in it a psychical group had come into effect which had previously been split off by defence. In short, I am unable to suppress a suspicion that somewhere or other the roots of hypnoid and defence hysteria come together, and that the primary factor is defence. But I can say nothing about this.[44]

Freud thus accords the hypnoid theory much the same status as Breuer ascribes to the defense concept. Each insists in *Studies of Hysteria* that, while the other's formula possesses some validity, his own model is the more fundamental one and the one which is the key to the pathogenesis of hysteria.

But by the time *Studies on Hysteria* appeared in print (1895), this controversy with Breuer was really no longer an issue of immediate concern to Freud. He was by then fully convinced that his defense theory did indeed provide a correct explanation for the genesis of those hysterical phenomena which could be traced to psychological factors, and he was now more concerned with investigating the nature of the experiences, the psychic traumas, that trigger the defense process. The clinical experiences which had inspired Freud to develop the defense theory—clinical experiences related to patients he had begun to see late in 1892—had also led him to accord critical significance to sexual life and to sexual events in the pathogenesis of hysteria, for he observed that the ideas which his patients sought strenuously to repress, and which provoked substantial resistance in therapy, were almost invariably of a sexual nature. Freud was now most concerned with defining more exactly the role of sexuality in the pathogenesis of hysteria and other neuroses.

6. Sexuality and the Etiology of the Neuroses

Sexuality and Hysteria

The special vulnerability to hysteria of unmarried girls, the often blatantly erotic nature of the bodily contortions that are typically a part of acute hysterical attacks, and the consistent presence of hyperesthesia of the genital regions, together with other genital symptoms, in hysterical patients were characteristics of hysteria that had repeatedly been noted by physicians studying the disease. Consequently, they had traditionally accorded a central role in the genesis of hysteria both to organic abnormalities of the genitalia and to peculiarities of sexual life—particularly abstinence. These views were still prevalent in the nineteenth century.

Commenting on the importance traditionally attributed to genital abnormalities, Paul Briquet noted in *Traité de l'Hystérie* (1859) that "from the most remote period of antiquity to the present day, doctors . . . have arrived at the conclusion that [hysteria] depends directly on the genital organs."[1] In particular, they generally believed that hysteria is essentially a disease of women and that disturbances of the uterus are the primary factors. Indeed, the term *hysteria* was derived from the Greek word for uterus (ὑστέρα). In the nineteenth century, physicians writing on hysteria tended to attach increasing importance to disturbances of genital organs other than the uterus, but the general emphasis on genital pathology changed little.

The reinterpretation of hysteria as a functional disorder of the nervous system, or *neurosis,* was typically viewed as complementing rather than contradicting this emphasis on organic genital disease. Those writers who approved of the general concept of functional nervous system abnormalities—that is, abnormalities involving dynamic changes in

119

the nervous system but no anatomical lesions—argued that such disorders might be secondary to some localized, nonneural illness: a diseased organ might induce physiological changes in the nerves innervating the organ, and these functional changes would be "reflected" throughout the rest of the nervous system, thus establishing a neurosis. Hysteria was now seen as one of these "reflex neuroses", emanating specifically from genital disorders. The Viennese neurologist Moriz Benedikt, for example, while arguing that the essence of hysteria lies in "an excessively labile irritability of the nervous system," also insisted that diseased genital organs are of primary significance and that "gynecological examination and management . . . is of absolute importance."[2]

This view of hysteria and the entire concept of reflex neuroses received very little attention from pathoanatomically oriented psychiatrists, who were, of course, largely critical of the notion of functional nervous system abnormalities. But the reflex neurosis concept was not limited to maverick neurologists such as Benedikt. On the contrary, it enjoyed extensive popularity in general medicine and in specialties other than neuropsychiatry. The question of how different organ systems might induce reflex neuroses became, in fact, a popular theme in various specialties—with gastroenterologists speaking of "gastric neuroses" due to diseases of the stomach, otolaryngologists studying "nasal neuroses," and so on. Among gynecologists, the reflex neurosis view of hysteria was widely advocated.[3]

Although this theory of the pathogenesis of hysteria has little in common with Breuer and Freud's psychological models, it did receive some endorsement from Breuer in *Studies on Hysteria:*

> It seems to me . . . that the old "reflex theory" of [hysterical] symptoms . . . should not be completely rejected. The vomiting, which of course accompanies the dilatation of the uterus in pregnancy, may, where there is abnormal excitability, quite well be set going in a reflex manner by trivial uterine stimuli, or perhaps even by the periodic changes in size of the ovaries. We are acquainted with so many remote effects resulting from organic changes, so many strange instances of "referred pain," that we cannot reject the possibility that a host of nervous symptoms which are sometimes determined psychically may in other cases be remote effects of reflex action.[4]

Freud expressed some enthusiasm for his friend Wilhelm Fliess's work on reflex neuroses, but he otherwise displayed little interest in the concept. Fliess, a Berlin physician with a practice predominantly in otolaryngology, published several works on nasal reflex neuroses, that is, neuroses presumably due to nasal disorders—a theme which appeared frequently in the otolaryngology literature during this period.[5] Freud wrote of one of these papers, which he reviewed for Fliess prior to its presentation at a medical convention: "I shall only say that I like it very much, and that I do not think the congress will produce anything more important."[6] He states in another letter to Fliess, "I . . . entirely agree with you that the nasal reflex neurosis is one of the commonest disorders."[7] But his enthusiasm seems to have been motivated largely by friendship, for in the same letters Freud criticizes another author for attempting to explain a neurosis in terms of nonneural anatomical changes rather than concentrating on physiological changes within the nervous system.

Freud does suggest on several occasions that illnesses not directly involving the nervous system may contribute to the development of hysterical symptoms, but the reflex neurosis concept appears rarely in his papers and does not seem to have significantly influenced his thinking. In particular, genital disorders play no role in his theory of hysteria.

Like genital abnormalities, sexual continence was also traditionally regarded as an important factor in the genesis of hysteria. Again quoting Paul Briquet: "From the most remote times, philosophy and medicine have viewed continence as the principal and even as the sole cause of hysteria."[8] The roles traditionally accorded to sexual continence and to genital abnormalities were intimately related. It was thought that coitus is necessary to preserve the normal function of the genitalia, and that abstinence induces in the genitals pathological changes which subsequently lead to hysteria.[9]

But in the nineteenth century, many authors who believed in the etiological importance of abnormal sexual behavior, particularly continence, emphasized the emotional impact of such behavior rather than its effects on the genitalia. Benedikt, for example, discusses genital disorders and abnormal sexual behavior as two separate and distinct pathogenic elements. After speaking of the significance of genital disturbances, he states:

> Abnormalities of sexual life constitute a further important etiological factor for the pathology of hysteria. The control of sexual excitation among nuns, and frequent excitement without suitable satisfaction in harems, are fruitful sources of severe hysteria. Excitement without satisfaction among

> wives whose husbands are libidinous but impotent, . . . and a
> relatively excessive desire and overexcitation . . . of the sex-
> ual drive, frequently engender hysterical neuroses.[10]

Robert Carter, an English physician who subsequently specialized in ophthalmic surgery, expressed what had by midcentury become a common view among physicians when he stressed the importance of irregularities in sexual life as a source of hysteria but insisted that their significance is psychological and that efforts to associate hysteria and genital disorders are misguided. Carter states in his book, *On the Pathology and Treatment of Hysteria* (1853):

> The effect of emotion in producing hysteria has long been a
> matter of common observation . . . [At] the onset of this in-
> quiry, we are . . . compelled to investigate the power of the
> sexual passion, as compared with that of feelings more gen-
> erally acknowledged . . . For while the advance of civilization
> and the everincreasing complications of social intercourse
> tend to call forth new feelings, and by their means to throw
> amativeness somewhat into the shade, as one powerful emo-
> tion among many others, still its absolute intensity is in no
> way lessened, and from the modern necessity for its entire
> concealment, it is likely to produce hysteria in a larger num-
> ber of the women subject to its influence, than it would do if
> the state of society permitted its free expression. It may,
> therefore, be inferred, as a matter of reasoning, that the
> sexual emotions are those most concerned in the production
> of the disease.[11]

Carter rejected the notion that continence might cause its ill effects by inducing genital disorders; moreover, he condemned the routine performance of a gynecological examination in the evaluation of hysterical patients, arguing that vaginal manipulation merely exacerbates the unsatisfied passions which initiate the neurosis.

Whatever the mode of operation attributed to it, sexual abstinence continued throughout the century to be regarded as a major source of hysteria. The popularity of this belief is illustrated in a comment by John Hughlings Jackson. In a paper published in 1878, Jackson insists that a certain form of aphasia cannot be caused by anatomical lesions. He wishes to argue that those who display this type of aphasia are in fact hysterics, whose illness is due to some functional abnormality. Jackson makes his point this way: "Let us state the facts. The patients are nearly always boys or unmarried women. The bearing of this is obvious."[12] Jackson expects his reader to immediately identify boys and unmarried women—or sexual continence— with hysteria.

In contrast to the popular association of hysteria with sexual life, Freud initially took the exceptional view that sexual matters play no special role in the disease. His position reflected that of Charcot, who insisted that heredity was overwhelmingly the most important etiological factor in hysteria. Charcot's theory of heredity was, in turn, shaped primarily by the concept of hereditary degeneration which had been developed by Benedict-Augustin Morel and Valentin Magnan to explain a wide range of psychiatric disorders, and which exerted such an extensive influence in French psychiatry during this period. In addition, Paul Briquet in 1858 had thoroughly reviewed those theories which emphasized either sexual continence or genital disorders as the source of hysteria and had rejected both theses on the basis of counterarguments drawn from his clinical experience. Charcot spoke highly of Briquet's book, and Freud cites some of Briquet's arguments against the sexual and genital theories.

While emphasizing heredity, and categorically rejecting any etiological role for genital disorders, Freud does, in his earliest papers, concede some significance to sexual behavior. His views in this regard are summarized in an 1888 article on hysteria:

> The aetiology of the *status hystericus* is to be looked for entirely in heredity. . . . Compared with the factor of heredity all other factors take second place and play the part of incidental causes, the importance of which is as a rule overrated in practice. . . . As regards what is often asserted to be the preponderant influence of abnormalities in the sexual sphere upon the development of hysteria, it must be said that its importance is as a rule over-estimated. In the first place, hysteria is found in sexually immature girls and boys, just as, too, the neurosis with all its characteristics also occurs in the male sex, though a great deal more rarely. . . . Furthermore, hysteria has been observed in women with a complete lack of genitalia, and every physician will have seen a number of cases of hysteria in women whose genitals exhibited no anatomical changes at all, just as, on the contrary, the majority of women with diseases of the sexual organs do not suffer from hysteria. It must, however, be admitted that [behavioral] conditions related . . . to sexual life play a great

> part in the aetiology of hysteria (as of all neuroses), and they
> do so on account of the high psychical significance of this
> function especially in the female sex.[13]

Freud's acknowledgment of the special significance of sexual behavior
appears, however, to have been more a concession to standard views
than a matter of conviction. Sexual behavior is not mentioned in his
work on hysteria over the next four years, and he writes in *Studies on
Hysteria:*

> When I began to analyse . . . Frau Emmy von N. [1889], the
> expectation of a sexual neurosis being the basis of hysteria
> was fairly remote from my mind. I had come fresh from the
> school of Charcot, and I regarded the linking of hysteria
> with the topic of sexuality as a sort of insult—just as the
> women patients themselves do.[14]

Indeed, there are no references to sexual factors in his notes on Frau
Emmy von N.

Freud's views were shared by those neuropsychiatrists who had
similarly adopted French concepts concerning the hereditary basis of
psychopathology. Richard von Krafft-Ebing, professor of psychiatry at
Vienna from 1889, argued that sexuality plays a role in generating
neuroses only in people with the proper hereditary predisposition:

> In both lay and medical circles, the view is often held that an
> unsatisfied sexual drive, particularly among females, is the
> source of neuroses and even psychoses. . . . The influence of
> sexual abstinence is dependent in its effects on the personal-
> ity of the individual and the intensity of the drive. . . . One
> can separate people into those with normal characteristics
> and sexual needs and those with a neuropathic constitution,
> which often includes an abnormally strong sexual need. Ab-
> stinence, among the first group, will never be accompanied
> by dangers for nervous and psychic life.[15]

Other German neuropsychiatrists expressed comparable views on the
relative importance of heredity and sexuality, in part because such
formulations offered an easy compromise between the evidence in favor of the importance of sexual life and counterevidence indicating
that sexuality plays no special role. But, despite their general emphasis
on hereditary predisposition, these writers, including Krafft-Ebing, still
devote relatively more attention to sexual life than can be found in
Freud's work between 1886 and 1892.

Freud does refer once more to the importance of sexual life in some papers written late in 1892. In the second draft of the "Preliminary Communication," he considers the role of psychic traumas in inducing splits in consciousness, and he argues: "Sexual life is especially well suited to provide the content [of such traumas] owing to the very great contrast it presents to the rest of the personality and to its ideas being impossible to react to."[16] It is difficult to say whether such comments are primarily a reflection of Freud's recent clinical experience or are merely once again a concession to standard views. At any rate, the theme is not developed further, and Freud did not at this time regard the suppressed trauma in hysteria as typically sexual. On the contrary, he believed that these suppressed ideas were of no special sort and had only their unpleasant affects in common, and that they were pathogenic only in people suffering from a predisposing "tendency towards the dissociation of consciousness."

A greater emphasis on sexual life came only with the development of the defense theory (1894). The theory of defense—with its insistence on the special, peculiarly distressful, nature of the repressed idea—was inspired by patients' acknowledgments of efforts at suppression and, more importantly, by Freud's recognition of the phenomenon of resistance. But the memories which his patients acknowledged suppressing, and which instigated resistance in therapy, were typically sexual. This observation finally led Freud to accord a special significance to traumatic sexual ideas.

The cases of Elisabeth von R. and Lucy R., both of whom began therapy about the end of 1892, were among the earliest in which Freud achieved some insight into resistance, and both analyses primarily involved the uncovering of repressed erotic thoughts. For Elisabeth von R., the repressed ideas elicited in therapy, after the overcoming of much resistance, primarily concerned erotic thoughts and memories involving two men, one a family friend, the other her brother-in-law. In the case of Lucy R., who worked as a governess and whose major symptom entailed the persistent and disturbing sensation of peculiar odors, the repressed material uncovered in therapy and linked to her symptoms, again after much resistance, concerned erotic thoughts relating to her employer. It seems probable that Freud's reevaluation of the role of sexuality in hysteria emanated from his work with these patients in the early months of 1893. In his paper "The Neuro-Psychoses of Defence," in which he introduces the defense concept, Freud cites both cases to illustrate the special importance of sexual life:

In females incompatible ideas . . . arise chiefly on the soil of
sexual experience and sensation; and the patients can recollect as precisely as could be desired their efforts at defence,
their intention of "pushing the thing away," of not thinking
of it, of suppressing it. I will give some examples, which I
could easily multiply from my own observation: the case of a
girl [Elisabeth von R.], who blamed herself because, while
she was nursing her sick father, she had thought about a
young man [the family friend] who had made a slight erotic
impression on her; the case of a governess [Lucy R.] who
had fallen in love with her employer and had resolved to
drive this inclination out of her mind because it seemed to
her incompatible with her pride; and so on.[17]

In the same paper, Freud argues that obsessions, like hysteria, are
based upon defense and the repression of distressing ideas, and he
insists that the repressed ideas of obsessional neurosis are also invariably of a sexual nature:

In all the cases I have analysed it was the subject's *sexual life*
that had given rise to a distressing affect of precisely the
same quality as that attaching to his obsession. Theoretically,
it is not impossible that this affect should sometimes arise in
other fields; I can only report that so far I have not come
across any other origin. Moreover, it is easy to see that it is
precisely sexual life which brings with it the most copious
occasions for the emergence of incompatible ideas.[18]

In a paper which appeared some months later, "Obsessions and Phobias" (January, 1895), Freud gives sketches of numerous case histories
involving obsessions. The repressed memories in these cases are consistently sexual.

The new emphasis on sexuality is reflected in the preface to *Studies
on Hysteria,* where the authors state that "sexuality seems to play a
principal part in the pathogenesis of hysteria as a source of psychical
traumas and as a motive for 'defence.' "[19] Freud and Breuer remark
that they have had to omit their best evidence for this thesis, because
the relevant material could not be presented without giving clues to the
identity of the patients and thereby betraying professional confidence.
Nevertheless, the more recent of the five cases reported in the book—
Lucy R., Katharina, and Elisabeth von R.—all involve a history of repressed sexual memories. Moreover, Freud notes of his earlier case,

Emmy von N., that he was not aware of the significance of sexuality at the time of her therapy, but that a review of his notes suggests that sexual factors did in fact play a major role in generating her illness.

Breuer had not undertaken the care of any hysterical patients since Anna O., and in her case he had accorded no role to sexual factors. But he was apparently impressed by Freud's clinical experiences, for in *Studies on Hysteria* he joins Freud in insisting on the special importance of sexuality. He maintains, of course, that hypnoid states are more relevant to the pathogenesis of hysteria than defense and repression, and he therefore does not accept Freud's emphasis on the repression of sexual memories. But he offers alternative explanations for the particular significance of sexuality. He suggests that erotic raptures make one more susceptible to hypnoid states, and he argues that unreleased sexual excitation results in greater quantities of affect being available for conversion into somatic hysterical symptoms. Finally, he agrees that, insofar as defense is a factor, it is sexual ideas which trigger defense and repression. Breuer remarks that sexuality is not the exclusive source of hysterical phenomena, but he notes: "It is perhaps worth while insisting again and again that the sexual factor is by far the most important and the most productive of pathological results."[20]

Neurasthenia

Freud's new emphasis on the role of sexual experiences in the development of hysteria and obsessional neurosis led him, around this time, to an increasing interest in still another neurosis, neurasthenia, which he had previously largely ignored. Neurasthenia was the subject of an extensive literature during this period and was commonly discussed in works dealing with hysteria. It had previously been ignored by Freud primarily because he believed that psychological factors played no role in its pathogenesis and that the disease was not responsive to psychotherapy. But neurasthenia was widely thought to be caused by various sexual practices, and Freud now began to study the syndrome with the hope of constructing a general theory of the neuroses encompassing all neurotic syndromes and based on their origins in sexual life.

The term *neurasthenia* was coined by the American physician George Beard, who was also the first to clearly delineate this neurosis. Beginning with an 1869 paper entitled "Neurasthenia, or Nervous Exhaustion," Beard argued in numerous books and articles that neurasthenia is a well-defined and widespread clinical entity characterized by general physical and mental debility. It is, in Beard's view, a functional abnormality of the nervous system involving a pathological decrease in nervous energy. Beard suggested that neurasthenia is precipitated by all those activities which lead to overexertion and exhaustion, and he put particular emphasis on the increased pace and heavy demands of modern life.[21]

Beard's work received extensive attention in Europe, where neurasthenia became the subject of a large literature. Bibliographies by Paul Moebius (1894) and by Franz Müller (1893) list several hundred books and papers on the syndrome, dating mostly from the 1880s and early 1890s.[22] Moebius notes that earlier writers had also spoken of nervous weakness but had generated little interest in the concept. In Moebius's view, the special impact of Beard's work can be attributed to his coinage of the term neurasthenia and his clear delineation and excellent description of the syndrome. Another factor, according to Moebius, was that up until recently "the new medicine bore a predominantly anatomical-pathological character. To recognize anatomical changes in disease processes . . . that alone appeared worthy of scientific physicians. Since the so-called 'functional' disorders promised little or no yield in this respect, everyone turned away from them."[23] Krafft-Ebing also suggests that the sudden interest in nervous weakness and the tremendous reception accorded Beard's work was due in large part to the decline of the pathoanatomical emphasis.[24]

Some authors insisted that there is no clear distinction between hysteria and neurasthenia. But most writers, including Moebius, Charcot, Krafft-Ebing, and the most influential psychiatric nosographer of the period, Emil Kraepelin, agreed with Beard's thesis that they are two separable syndromes. Charcot, for example, while noting that patients often suffer from both hysteria and neurasthenia, asserted that the diseases can also be found separately and that the clinical picture of neurasthenia is quite different from that of hysteria. According to Charcot, neurasthenia is marked by its own stigmata—headaches, back pain, loss of intellectual acuity, general physical debility, gastrointestinal disturbances—as well as a myriad of variable symptoms, but it does not exhibit the acute convulsive attacks or the standard chronic symptoms of hysteria.[25]

Numerous factors were invoked in accounting for the etiology of neurasthenia. Beard implicated all forms of overwork; in addition, he saw neurasthenia as a peculiarly American malady, stemming from the particular strain of American working habits. While this notion of the special vulnerability of Americans gained only limited endorsement in

Europe, European authors did widely accept Beard's argument that mental and physical overexertion, and the demands of modern civilization, play an important role in generating the syndrome. However, Continental psychiatrists also emphasized other causal factors, especially heredity and abnormalities of sexual life. Perhaps the most common position on the origins of neurasthenia was the eclectic view illustrated in an early article by Wilhelm Erb (1878):

> It is especially people from neuropathically disposed families who form a major contingent of those suffering from this disease; from families in which psychoses, hysteria, hypochondria, and other neuroses are common. . . .
>
> Of . . . direct causes, I can from my experience designate three special categories as particularly significant:
>
> Mental overexertion can often . . . lead to neurasthenia: very exacting professions, and difficult mental work, especially when it involves working at nights. Worry and excitement are similarly effective, as are strong emotions and passions . . . in predisposed persons.
>
> Sexual excess is a much more important and more frequent cause of the illness: Onanism, begun at an early age and lasting for a long time; and excessive coitus—I have repeatedly seen otherwise healthy men who, after severe sexual excesses, presented the entire clinical picture of neurasthenia. . . .
>
> To a more limited degree, it appears that physical overexertion can also be effective. . . .
>
> It has yet to be established whether there are still other sources for the disorder; but it is probable that severe, debilitating disease, poor nutrition, and other factors lowering the efficiency of the nervous system, can be effective in this direction.[26]

The influence of heredity was asserted by most authors, and some, especially Charcot, considered it as by far the most significant factor. Yet even at the Salpetrière, heredity was not believed to be as important for neurasthenia as it was for hysteria. Paul Blocq, a senior staff physician at the Salpetrière, maintained that a hereditary nervous predisposition may be absent in neurasthenia, and that consequently other etiological factors play a greater role in this disease than they do in most neuropathological syndromes.[27]

Among these other factors, peculiarities of sexual life—particularly masturbation and the practice of coitus interruptus—received the most attention. This was due in part to the fact that sexual symptoms—such as impotence or premature ejaculation—held an important place in what was perceived as the standard clinical picture of neurasthenia, and some writers simply regarded these symptoms as clues to the source of the entire illness. Other organ systems were also associated with major neurasthenic symptoms and similarly inspired theories about the origin of the disease. At the Salpetrière, for example, greater attention was paid to gastrointestinal symptoms—including dyspepsia, nausea, and flatulence—than to genital complaints; and various theories were proposed which viewed neurasthenia as a reflex neurosis derived from some gastrointestinal abnormality. But the sexual symptoms were especially common and were very often the ones most disturbing to the patient, and they therefore demanded the physician's particular attention. A number of physicians proposed the existence of various subtypes of neurasthenia, based on variations in the dominant symptoms among different groups of patients. Among those subtypes, sexual neurasthenia—neurasthenia with predominantly sexual symptoms—is the category most often noted and discussed in the literature. The prominence of sexual symptoms naturally inspired theories attributing a special role to sexual practices in the pathogenesis of the disease.

Theories focusing on the pathogenic role of sexual habits may also have been inspired by the role popularly accorded to sexual factors in the etiology of hysteria—a disease closely linked with neurasthenia by most writers. In addition, there was a general belief at the time that genital functions exert a special influence on the nervous system. Krafft-Ebing wrote in *Psychopathia Sexualis* that "since the generative organs stand in important . . . connection with the entire nervous system, and especially with its psychical and somatic functions, it is easy to understand the frequency of general neuroses and psychoses arising in sexual (functional or organic) disturbances."[28] Other writers pointed to the emotional and intellectual changes which accompany puberty, castration, menstruation, and diseases of the sexual organs as illustration of the peculiarly intimate relationship between sexual functions and the nervous system. Popular concepts concerning this relationship were yet another factor inspiring theories that stressed sexual habits as the cause of neurasthenia.

The role to be ascribed to sexual habits, particularly masturbation, in the etiology of neurasthenia was the subject of considerable debate. Valentin Magnan, at that time the major exponent of the concept of hereditary degeneration, suggested that masturbation is itself the product of an hereditary taint and, rather than being a cause of neurasthenia, it is merely an early sign of a predisposition that will lead to neurasthenia. This view was endorsed by Otto Binswanger, professor of psychiatry and director of the psychiatric clinic at Jena.[29] It was mentioned by numerous other German authors as well, but generally with less enthusiasm.

Krafft-Ebing agreed that hereditary disposition is the main factor, but he nevertheless insisted that masturbation plays a major role in a large percentage of cases, particularly those cases which display prominent sexual symptoms such as impotence or premature ejaculation. In *Psychopathia Sexualis,* he refers to men who, "as a result of abusus veneris, or more particularly of masturbation, suffer from neurasthenia sexualis."[30] Leopold Loewenfeld was a Munich neurologist whose publications on the neuroses were widely read and frequently cited, and whom Freud described as "a man whose judgement undoubtedly carries great weight with the medical public."[31] Loewenfeld devotes a chapter of his text *Die Nervösen Störungen sexuelle Ursprungen* to onanism. He lists nine authors "who have generally acknowledged the development of . . . neurasthenia as a consequence of onanism," and he concludes that "in a great, very great percentage of neurasthenics, whom we come across daily, onanism figures among the causal factors."[32] The views of Loewenfeld and Krafft-Ebing on the pathogenic role of masturbation typify those most often found in the German literature on neurasthenia.

Coitus interruptus is also mentioned by Krafft-Ebing and Loewenfeld as an etiological factor in neurasthenia, but is regarded as of considerably less importance in this regard than masturbation. Krafft-Ebing, however, argues that coitus interruptus does have significant ill effects for women—presumably because it involves sexual arousal without sufficient satisfaction—and that it is an important cause of neurasthenia among women. This view concurred with that of numerous gynecologists. There was in fact a large gynecological literature on the neuropathological consequences of coitus interruptus, with neurasthenia receiving particular attention.[33]

Most neurologists either accorded coitus interruptus the minor role advocated by Loewenfeld or endorsed Krafft-Ebing's remarks on its special significance for women. Some writers, however, insisted that it is actually a major source of neurasthenia for men as well as women. Albert Eulenberg, a neurologist on the faculty of the University of Berlin, published an article entitled "Über coitus reservatus als Ursache sexualer Neurasthenie bei Männern," in which he maintained that coitus interruptus is "an undoubtedly frequent, and ever more frequent, cause of sexual neurasthenia among men."[34] Alexander Peyer, a Zurich physician, published the most thoroughly documented cases of neurasthenia derived from coitus interruptus and is the source most often cited in the neurological literature on the subject. Peyer, in *Der unvollständige Beischlaf und seine Folgen beim Männlichen Geschlechte* (1890), writes:

> The various causes of sexual neurasthenia are generally known: they are sexual excesses in every form—such as masturbation in youths and, later, intemperance in coitus—as well as chronic diseases of the urethra secondary to gonorrhea, etc. We have, however, still another cause for the origin of the above disease; [a cause] which in a certain age group is as frequent as all the others put together. . . . I mean coitus incompletus, reservatus, or interruptus.[35]

Peyer goes on to describe the cases of fourteen men, all otherwise healthy and with no history of neurological disease or hereditary predisposition, who allegedly developed neurasthenia as a result of practicing coitus interruptus.

Whether they stressed masturbation or coitus interruptus as the source of neurasthenia, these writers thought their theories justified not merely because they were consistently able to elicit histories of such practices from their patients, but also because their theories seemed to account for the prominence of impotence and premature ejaculation among the symptoms of neurasthenia. In addition, such theories were in harmony with the role popularly accorded to sexual behavior in the etiology of hysteria, and were also in accord with the popularly recognized effects of genital abnormalities and other genital changes— changes associated, for example, with puberty, or menopause—on the nervous system.

Freud's earliest work contains occasional comments on neurasthenia, but he did not show any special interest in the syndrome prior to 1893. He mentioned neurasthenia on several occasions in 1886 and 1887, but he produced no papers or even substantial passages on the subject during these years, and his few references to the syndrome cannot be compared to his extensive work on hysteria.

In January, 1887, Freud published a short review of a book on neurasthenia. He also mentioned the disease in some of his correspondence from this period. In two letters to his fiancée from Paris, Freud speaks of a possible neuropathic taint in his family and states that he and a sister display a "tendency towards neurasthenia." In a letter to Breuer, he suggests that military service is a good cure for neurasthenia—a notion actually proposed in the book he had reviewed. Finally, in several letters to Wilhelm Fliess dating from the end of 1887 and early 1888, Freud discusses a patient who seemed to be suffering from neurasthenia.[36] But there is nothing more on the subject during 1886 and 1887. Moreover, except for some comments in his paper "Hysteria" (1888)—where he repeats Charcot's views on the need for distinguishing between neurasthenia and hysteria, and on their frequent appearance in the same patient—neurasthenia is rarely mentioned by Freud prior to the end of 1892.

Freud's lack of any particular interest in neurasthenia does require some explanation in view of the fact that the syndrome was considered the most important neurosis aside from hysteria and was constantly being discussed with and compared to hysteria. But Freud's attitude can be accounted for without great difficulty. His concern with hysteria centered primarily on those symptoms of the disease that could be traced to psychological causes and on the cure of these symptoms through psychotherapy. Initially, he was more preoccupied with Charcot's interpretation of hysteria as a dynamic or functional nervous system abnormality and with the radical departure from his own pathoanatomical training which this interpretation represented. In later years he continued to insist that psychological formulas cannot offer a comprehensive explanation of hysteria and that a physiological explanation of various aspects of the disease, if presently impossible, must ultimately be sought. But his efforts—inspired primarily by Charcot and Breuer—were directed particularly towards the further elucidation of psychological models and the further development of psychotherapeutic methods. We have seen, for example, that from 1889 to 1891 Freud's only publications relating to the neuroses were on hypnosis and hypnotic therapy for psychogenic symptoms. If Freud regarded the understanding of hysteria as incomplete without a physiological formula, it is nevertheless clear that he was quite happy to concentrate his own efforts on pursuing those insights into the disease which psychology obviously offered.

But psychological factors were popularly accorded no significant role in the pathogenesis of neurasthenia, and it was generally believed that neurasthenia was not amenable to psychotherapy. Charcot suggested that shock or trauma can induce neurasthenia as well as hysteria and that this is probably why the two syndromes so often appear together. But he insisted that, while in hysteria shock works by inducing a hypnotic state and rendering the patient vulnerable to autosuggestions and to psychogenic symptoms, in neurasthenia the shock has a direct effect on the nervous system and induces physiological changes without any mediating psychical mechanism. Similarly, those writers who believed in the etiological significance for neurasthenia of mental and physical overwork uniformly agreed that such overwork induces its ill effects directly on the nervous system. No psychic mechanisms were postulated. If emotions such as worry and anxiety were assigned a role in pathogenesis, they were regarded as simply placing an additional strain on nervous energy.

Pathogenic sexual habits were also believed to work their ill effects without the mediation of psychological factors. The most common formula was that masturbation (or coitus interruptus) leads to physical changes in the genitalia and these changes in turn induce neurasthenia as a reflex neurosis. Others argued that these sexual habits directly affect the nervous system—that masturbation in young boys, for example, is pathogenic because the nervous system has not yet developed to the degree that it can cope with frequent sexual excitement. Krafft-Ebing did admit that the ill effects of masturbation are in part psychological. He suggested that, in boys who have read or heard about the dangers of masturbation, the practice could create fears and anxieties which would then be a factor in generating neurasthenia. Loewenfeld offered similar comments. But both authors regarded this psychological mechanism as a minor, additional pathogenic factor and both emphasized the purely physiological effects of onanism. The psychological model was not, in general, very popular.

This broad consensus—that psychological factors were of very limited importance for the pathogenesis of neurasthenia—was reinforced by the apparent resistance of neurasthenia to psychotherapy. Hypnotic suggestion, which was particularly useful in coping with psychogenic problems, seemed to have no impact on neurasthenia. A comment by Paul Blocq reflects the view of the Salpetrière hypnotists: "There is no example more conclusive than that of neurasthenia to show the limits of hypnosis from a therapeutic point of view."[37] Even Hippolyte Bernheim, who was most sanguine with regard to the therapeutic potential of hypnosis, acknowledged its virtual uselessness in neurasthenia.

Freud agreed that neurasthenia is not a psychogenic abnormality, and he continued to endorse this view in later years. In 1894 he wrote of the syndrome: "There is no ground at all to assume a *psychical* mechanism";[38] and in *Studies on Hysteria:* "I found that neurasthenia presented a monotonous clinical picture in which . . . a 'psychical mechanism' played no part."[39] With regard to treatment of the syndrome, Freud was undoubtedly aware of the general lack of success with hypnotic therapy, and this probably helped to shape his opinion that no psychological factors are involved in the genesis of the disease. Since his interests in hysteria were specifically directed towards the elucidation of its psychological causes and the psychotherapeutic resolution of its symptoms, it is easy to see why his enthusiasm concerning investigations of hysteria did not extend to neurasthenia as well.

When Freud did finally turn his attention to neurasthenia, he did so because of his reevaluation of the role of sexuality in hysteria. Freud's new conviction that sexual trauma is the source of both hysteria and obsessional neurosis, and his awareness that sexual behavior was widely accorded a major role in the etiology of neurasthenia, suggested the possibility that a general theory of the neuroses might be formulated based upon their origins in sexuality. His subsequent work on neurasthenia was concerned essentially with its sexual etiology and was inspired by his interest in developing this general sexual theory of the neuroses. Freud's correspondence to Fliess includes numerous drafts dealing with neurasthenia, and the first of these ("Draft A") is devoted almost entirely to the sexual origin of the syndrome. Freud explains some time later, in *Studies on Hysteria* (1895):

> Starting out from Breuer's method, I found myself engaged in a consideration of the aetiology and mechanism of the neuroses. . . . In the first place I was obliged to recognize that, in so far as one can speak of determining causes which lead to the *acquisition* of neuroses, their aetiology is to be looked for in *sexual* factors. There followed the discovery that different sexual factors, in the most general sense, produce different pictures of neurotic disorders. And it then became possible, in the degree to which this relation was confirmed, to venture on using aetiology for the purpose of characterizing the neuroses.[40]

Freud's recognition of the special role of sexuality in hysteria coincided with his discovery of resistance and his development of the defense theory, for he consistently found that it was sexual ideas and memories which inspired resistance and defense. The cases of Fraulein Elisabeth von R. and Miss Lucy R., which were among the first to display clearly the phenomenon of resistance and to suggest the special significance of sexuality, were begun late in 1892. But the "Preliminary Communication," written with Breuer probably in December, 1892, predates the defense model and does not yet acknowledge the unique importance of sexual factors. I therefore suggested in the previous section that the new emphasis on sexuality emerged early in 1893. However, the first of the drafts on neurasthenia which Freud sent to Fliess has been tentatively dated the end of 1892 by the editors of the Fliess correspondence. There is thus an apparent inconsistency between the new interest in neurasthenia, and especially its sexual etiology, expressed in the draft to Fliess and, at the same time, the absence of any exceptional concern with sexuality in the "Preliminary Communication." The probable solution is that Freud's current clinical work had, before the end of 1892, already indicated that some special role must be accorded sexuality in the etiology of the neuroses, but he was as yet not sure exactly how extensive that role might be. He was therefore unprepared to ascribe any exceptional significance to sexuality in a published work, such as the "Preliminary Communication." But these early indications of the special importance of sexuality in hysteria had already sufficed to turn his attention to neurasthenia and to inspire the Fliess draft.

At any rate, the end of 1892 marked the beginning of Freud's increased interest in neurasthenia and the start of his search for a general theory of the neuroses based on their sexual etiology.

Toward a General Theory of the Neuroses

In his earliest drafts on neurasthenia, Freud also discusses "anxiety neurosis," which he describes as a separate syndrome, distinct from neurasthenia. In contrast to this view, anxiety was generally regarded as simply a symptom of neurasthenia, and indeed it had received considerable attention in the context of neurasthenic symptomatology. There were occasional works which dealt solely with anxiety, such as two articles by the German psychiatrist Ewald Hecker: "Über larvirte und abortive Angstzustände bei Neurasthenie" (1893), and "Zur Behandlung der neurasthenischen Angstzustände" (1892).[41] These papers were cited by Freud on several occasions. But, as can be seen from the titles, Hecker did not attempt to separate anxiety and related symptoms from neurasthenia.

Charcot suggested that some symptoms generally associated with anxiety, particularly phobias, ought to be regarded not as symptoms of neurasthenia, but as the product of a hereditary abnormality which also predisposes one to neurasthenia. Leopold Loewenfeld stated that, having noted the sharp distinction between neurasthenics in whom anxiety played no special role and those cases in which anxiety predominated, he had at one time considered a formula such as that proposed by Charcot. But neither Charcot nor Loewenfeld viewed anxiety as representing a separate syndrome distinct from neurasthenia.

Freud, on the other hand, argues that the symptoms which he would associate with anxiety neurosis—general irritability; oversensitiveness to noise; physical symptoms such as excessive perspiring, tremors, ravenous hunger, diarrhea, vertigo—are more often found in combination with one another than in connection with the standard symptoms—headaches, fatigue, back pain—of neurasthenia. In addition, anxiety is found in association with hysteria as well as neurasthenia, and is not exclusively bound to the latter. But Freud's major justification for labelling anxiety a separate neurosis is his belief that he can establish an etiology for anxiety states different from that of neurasthenia. Neurasthenia, in Freud's view, is essentially the result of masturbation, while anxiety states are the product of inadequate sexual gratification—most notably, the lack of gratification which, for women, accompanies coitus interruptus.

This etiological formula is already suggested in a draft by Freud dated February, 1893 ("Draft B").[42] Freud writes of neurasthenia in males: "Its source is masturbation, the frequency of which runs completely parallel with the frequency of male neurasthenia." He is at this point still uncertain about the basis for the syndrome in women. With regard to anxiety neurosis, he states: "There is no question but that it is acquired . . . through coitus interruptus." Both masturbation and coitus interruptus were, of course, widely acknowledged to be major causes of neurasthenia. Their elevation in Freud's theory to the status of exclusive causes was prompted in large part by analogy with the apparently exclusive role played by sexual life in the etiology of hysteria. The delineation of two separate neuroses, with one being induced by masturbation and the other by coitus interruptus, was similarly prompted to a considerable degree by theoretical considerations. Freud insisted that masturbation, which involves overindulgence and repeated gratification, could not have the same effect as coitus interruptus and related practices, which apparently involve insufficient gratification. Also, Freud believed that habitual masturbation entails overexertion and that this could account for the mental and physical exhaustion characteristic of neurasthenia, while coitus interruptus leads to an accumulation of unreleased excitation and could explain the aimless overactivity that typifies anxiety states. But if these speculative considerations served to suggest the etiological formula, that formula was, in Freud's view, fully justified by the clinical evidence. Freud argues, for example, that he has been able consistently to establish a history of coitus interruptus in patients who exhibit symptoms such as those described in Ewald Hecker's papers on anxiety, and the letters and drafts he sent to Fliess contain numerous references to case histories which fit his etiological scheme. One such reference appears in a letter dated October 6, 1893: "Woman, age 41, children, 16, 14, 11, 7. Nervous disorder for the last 12 years; well during pregnancy; subsequent recurrence; not made worse by the last pregnancy. Attacks of giddiness with feeling of weakness, agoraphobia, *anxious* expectation, no sign of neurasthenia, little hysteria. Aetiology [of coitus interruptus] confirmed. A case of simple [anxiety neurosis]".[43]

In January, 1895, Freud published an article entitled "On the Grounds for Detaching a Particular Syndrome from Neurasthenia under the Description 'Anxiety Neurosis'." This was his first publication dealing principally with neurasthenia and anxiety. Freud summarizes his position in the introduction: "Although Hecker recognizes certain symptoms as equivalents or rudiments of an anxiety attack, he does not separate them from the domain of neurasthenia, as I propose to do. But this is evidently due to his not having taken into account the differences between the etiological determinants in the two cases.[44]

Freud does not maintain in this paper that coitus interruptus is the exclusive source of anxiety neurosis. He suggests that some cases may be due solely to heredity, and he lists several additional factors from sexual life, such as continence, marriage to an impotent male, and increased sexual drive during the climacteric, which might induce the disease. Finally, he states that "anxiety neurosis also arises . . . as a result of the factor of overwork and exhaustion." But Freud still presents coitus interruptus as the predominant factor, and he believes that the other "sexual noxae"—the other potentially pathogenic sexual factors—share with coitus interruptus the common disease-producing aspect of insufficient sexual gratification. Freud argues further that, in those cases where anxiety neurosis is the result of exhaustion, exhaustion induces the disease by means of some debilitating physiological effect on sexual functioning comparable to that caused by the sexual noxae. In another paper, he writes that, when heredity is the source of anxiety symptoms, the hereditary stigma involves that same abnormality of the vita sexualis which in other cases is induced by sexual noxae or exhaustion. Freud's comments on the effects of heredity and exhaustion are rather obscure. But he did not, at any rate, regard these two factors as the source of very many cases of anxiety. He states in his paper that "[the] sexual aetiology of anxiety neurosis can be demonstrated with . . . overwhelming frequency."[45]

A rebuttal to Freud's thesis, written by Leopold Loewenfeld, was printed in the *Münchener Medicinische Wochenschrift* in March, 1895, two months after the appearance of the anxiety neurosis article. Loewenfeld writes:

> Freud was apparently led to the assertion of his anxiety neurosis less by the nature of the anxiety symptoms than by certain views on their etiology. In his view, the etiology of acquired anxiety neurosis ought to be distinguished from that of neurasthenia. The deleterious factors which lead to anxiety neurosis belong, according to Freud, exclusively to sexual life (primarily Congress. interrupt.; also, abstinence, and unsatisfied arousal). . . .
>
> My own observations also indicate that anomalies of sexual life are of great significance for the development of [anxiety symptoms]. What I must dispute is simply the regularity and specificity of the sexual etiology which Freud assumes for . . . anxiety states.[46]

Loewenfeld gives examples of patients in whom anxiety states were triggered by psychic shock or other factors, without the accompaniment of pathogenic sexual practices or recent changes in sexual behavior.

Freud, in turn, responded with a second article, "A Reply to Criticism of My Paper on Anxiety Neurosis," which appeared in July, 1895. He acknowledges that the assertion of a specific sexual etiology for anxiety is his main justification for detaching anxiety neurosis from neurasthenia, but he insists that his etiological formula is valid and has been clinically substantiated. With regard to Loewenfeld's argument that some cases of anxiety are due to psychic shocks and other nonsexual factors, Freud notes that he has also seen numerous cases in which anxiety states followed traumas of this sort. But, Freud continues, it would be wrong "to accept [Loewenfeld's] post hoc ergo propter hoc conclusion straight away." Psychic shocks and other emotional upsets are, he insists, simply "stock" factors which can lead to various illnesses and which result in anxiety neurosis only among people who are predisposed to that neurosis through abnormalities of sexual life: "If the same specific cause can be shown to exist in the aetiology of all, or the great majority, of cases of anxiety neurosis, our view of the matter need not be shaken by the fact that the illness does not break out until one or other stock factor, such as emotion, has come into operation."[47] Freud draws an analogy to the situation in people suffering from gout: the symptoms of gout may first emerge or may worsen following trauma to a limb, but that trauma can hardly be regarded as the cause of the disease.

Loewenfeld had also suggested that Freud pays insufficient attention to the role of heredity. But Freud replies that heredity is in most cases a nonspecific factor which may render someone particularly susceptible to neuroses, or influence the intensity of a neurotic disorder, but which cannot by itself induce a particular neurosis. This can come about solely through "the specific etiological factor arising from sexual life."

Freud acknowledges in the paper that his etiological formula for anxiety is part of a general theory asserting the sexual basis of all neuroses. He also states that his designation of coitus interruptus and related noxae as the source of anxiety, and masturbation as the source of neurasthenia, reflects a corollary to this general theory—a belief that a different sexual pattern is associated with each neurotic syndrome: "A further assertion which my observations forced me to make was to the effect that the various sexual noxae are not to be found in the aetiology of every neurosis indifferently, but that unmistakable special relationships hold between particular noxae and particular neuroses."[48]

With regard to the means by which sexual noxae induce neurotic disorders, Freud believed that different mechanisms are at work in each of the neuroses. For hysteria and obsessions he had, of course, developed his psychological defense model. Neurasthenia, on the other hand, he perceived as involving a physiological mechanism, with no psychic components. This was the standard view among writers on neurasthenia, and it is repeatedly asserted by Freud. It seemed justified on several counts, including the apparent absence of psychogenic symptoms and the unresponsiveness to psychotherapy. But Freud did not accept the common notion that neurasthenia is a reflex neurosis, resulting from some genital abnormality which is, in turn, the immediate consequence of masturbation. He argued, on the contrary, that masturbation works its effects directly upon the nervous system. In a letter to Fliess, Freud criticizes Alexander Peyer for postulating anatomical changes in the genitals as the key factor in neurasthenia instead of looking for direct changes in the nervous system.[49]

Freud gave only a few indications of what this direct neurophysiological effect of masturbation might involve. He envisioned the sexual drive as being based ultimately on a nervous excitation, produced by the action of the genitals on the nerves innervating them. According to

Freud, when this "somatic sexual excitation" reaches a certain level, it elicits psychosexual responses and sexual behavior which, in turn, are designed to reduce the level of excitation. Freud suggests that masturbation, which typically involves persistent indulgence, prevents the normal accumulation of "somatic sexual excitation." Presumably, all the symptoms of weakness and exhaustion which characterize neurasthenia merely reflect this neurodynamic impoverishment.

The notion that neurasthenia involves a decrease in nervous energy or excitation was almost universally accepted. There was considerable difference of opinion, however, on how this energy depletion is brought about. Beard's concept was simply one of overutilization: the normal nervous energy reserve is depleted by overwork and exceptional exertion. Freud's model is also based on the concept of overutilization and merely adapts the basic hypothesis of a decrease in nervous energy to his theory of an exclusively sexual etiology.

The pathogenesis of anxiety neurosis presented more of a problem for Freud, and he was uncertain for some time as to whether the process is a psychological or purely physiological one. The etiological importance of particular types of sexual behavior suggested a process comparable to that of neurasthenia; in addition, anxiety symptoms very frequently appeared in conjunction with neurasthenia. But anxiety was also common among hysterics and a psychic mechanism seemed equally plausible. In "Draft B" (February, 1893), Freud appears to prefer a psychological explanation. He suggests that anxiety accompanies the practice of coitus interruptus and is due to fears of pregnancy. However, he changes his position in November, 1893, and states that an exclusively physiological explanation is required.

It is the physiological mechanism that receives Freud's final endorsement. In an undated draft ("Draft E") which was apparently written in the summer of 1894, Freud offers several explanations for his decision. But these lack very much force, and it is probable that the major factor in his choice of an exclusively physiological mechanism was the analogy with neurasthenia, based upon their common source in specific types of sexual behavior. Freud suggests in "Draft E" that the basis for anxiety is an accumulation of somatic sexual excitation. This notion is repeated in his first paper on anxiety neurosis (January, 1895), and serves to integrate the etiological roles of abstinence, coitus interruptus, marriage to an impotent male, and other situations involving inadequate sexual gratification. All of these sexual problems, according to Freud, are pathological because they do not allow a sufficient release of somatic sexual tension. This formula is, in effect, the converse of that proposed for neurasthenia, and Freud contrasts the two syndromes in these terms, speaking of the one as an "accumulation of excitation" and the other as an "impoverishment of excitation."

But Freud notes that patients suffering from anxiety neurosis do not display any great sexual desire, despite their lack of gratification: "In whole sets of cases anxiety neurosis is accompanied by a most noticeable decrease of sexual libido or *psychical desire,* so that on being told that their complaint results from "insufficient satisfaction," patients regularly reply that that is impossible, for precisely now all sexual need has become extinguished in them." Freud concludes that in these patients the accumulated excitation is prevented from exerting its normal effect on the psyche, and instead of increased libido one gets a transformation or conversion of the excitation into the physical symptoms of anxiety (such as rapid pulse, hyperventilation, and intestinal irritability): "The mechanism of anxiety neurosis is to be looked for in a deflection of somatic excitation from the psychical sphere, and in a consequent abnormal employment of that excitation."[50]

In "Draft E," Freud considers the question of why this deflection occurs. He offers various explanations, depending upon the particular type of sexual behavior which is generating the syndrome. But, in his first published paper on anxiety neurosis (January, 1895), Freud notes that all the sexual practices leading to anxiety involve insufficient gratification, and he suggests simply that the somatic excitation is "deflected into other paths, which hold out greater promise of discharge."[51] In any case, there is an obvious analogy with Freud's model for hysteria and obsessions. In all of these syndromes, normal reactions are resisted or otherwise prevented and symptoms merely reflect an alternative, abnormal utilization of excitation. The essential distinction, for Freud, is that in anxiety it is somatic excitation which is converted or transformed, while in hysteria and obsessions the excitation is psychological.

Neurasthenia, anxiety, hysteria, and obsessions are the four major syndromes around which Freud hoped to construct his general theory of the neuroses. He regarded them as conforming to two general models. Hysteria and obsessions, the neuropsychoses of defense, are based upon memories of past sexual occurrences and involve disease processes which are to a large degree psychological. Neurasthenia and anxiety, on the other hand, are based upon current abnormalities of sexual life and are brought about through purely physiological processes. During this period, Freud often refers to the latter two syndromes collectively as "the simple neuroses," "the sexual neuroses," or merely "the neuroses," in contradistinction to the neuropsychoses. From 1897 onward Freud usually labels them "current neuroses" (*aktuelle Neurose* or *Aktualneurose*), emphasizing their dependence on current sexual practices as opposed to the dependence of neuropsychoses on memories of past sexual experiences.[52]

Freud tried to fit other neuropsychiatric abnormalities into these two general models of neuropsychoses and simple neuroses. In his paper "The Neuro-Psychoses of Defence" (1894), he includes "hallucinatory confusion" among those syndromes which are based on a defense against incompatible memories. In hallucinatory confusion, he suggests, an idea and its affect are both repressed and the ego behaves as if the events related to the memory had never occurred. He offers the example of a girl who repressed the memory of her lover's departure and continually hallucinated his presence. Hallucinatory confusion is, however, mentioned only rarely by Freud in subsequent papers.

In January, 1895, Freud sent a draft on paranoia to Fliess ("Draft H") and stated that "now it is in fact the case that paranoia in its classical form is a *pathological mode of defence*, like hysteria, obsessional neuroses and hallucinatory confusion."[53] The presumed mechanism for paranoia is that the affect associated with a repressed sexual idea— affect such as a feeling of guilt or self-reproach—is transposed or projected from the ego to the external world; so that, for example, self-reproaches are replaced by a belief that one is being accused by others. Paranoia is usually included among the neuropsychoses of defense in Freud's publications during the last years of the century.

In "The Neuro-Psychoses of Defence," Freud suggests that phobias closely resemble obsessions and involve the same sort of mechanism. The affect of a repressed sexual idea is transposed and attached to another idea, which is thereby rendered the object of the phobia. Freud changed his view some months later and stated that "the mechanism of phobias is entirely different from that of obsessions."[54] Phobias, he now asserts, are merely a part of anxiety neurosis. This notion is repeated in a lecture given in January, 1895.[55] But, in the first paper on anxiety neurosis, also dated January, 1895, Freud distinguishes two different types of phobias. One type is based on the repression of an idea and is indeed comparable to obsessions. In the other type, the phobias of anxiety neurosis, "the affect does not originate in a repressed idea, [and is] . . . *not further reducible by psychological analysis, nor amenable to psychotherapy [italics in original]*."[56] Freud suggests that the mechanism of this second type of phobia is, like that of other anxiety neurosis symptoms, purely physiological.[57]

In a draft on melancholia ("Draft G"), which has been tentatively dated January, 1895, Freud interprets melancholia as a neurosis resulting from the loss of "psychic sexual excitation." This in turn may be due to an insufficiency of somatic sexual excitation (neurasthenic melancholia), a diversion of somatic sexual excitation away from the psychic sphere (anxious melancholia), or simply an endogenous impoverishment of somatic sexual excitation (melancholia proper). This model is not very firmly endorsed and Freud elsewhere suggests alternative explanations, often relating melancholia more closely to the neuropsychoses.[58]

Freud's discussions of these various clinical entities—hallucinatory confusion, paranoia, phobias, and melancholia— typically conveyed considerable doubt and reservations; and he never felt as secure in these explanations as he did in his interpretations of hysteria, obsessions, neurasthenia, and anxiety. Consequently, these last four syndromes remained the key syndromes in his search for a general theory of the neuroses.

Heredity and Sexuality

With his recognition of the role of sexual factors in the etiology of the neuroses, Freud no longer accorded heredity the overwhelming significance that he had earlier ascribed to it. Heredity, nevertheless, continued to play a part in his etiological models. In his first paper on anxiety neurosis (January, 1895), he states: "In some cases of anxiety neurosis no aetiology at all is to be discovered. It is worth noting that in such cases there is seldom any difficulty in establishing evidence of a grave hereditary taint."[59] This formula is clearly a device to account for those situations in which Freud was unable to establish his sexual etiology, and he regarded such cases as rare. But heredity was seen as a factor in other patients as well. In the second anxiety neurosis paper (July, 1895), Freud speaks of heredity as a precondition which is present in many cases. He defines preconditions as those factors which generally cannot cause a disease by themselves, but without which the "specific causes" would often have no pathological effect. Heredity, Freud maintains, is not as important as writers such as Loewenfeld would insist; the major cause of both anxiety neurosis and neurasthenia is the specific sexual practice. This view is justified, according to Freud, by the fact that the sexual element can nearly always be established, whereas indications of an hereditary taint are frequently absent. In addition, pathological heredity is a nonspecific factor which can predis-

pose one to various neuroses—as can be seen by the presence of different neuroses in the same family. It is the nature of the sexual element
that determines in each case which neurosis does, in fact, develop. But
Freud maintains that "hereditary disposition is the most important precondition for anxiety neurosis."

The notion of hereditary precondition in anxiety neurosis, and in
neurasthenia as well, solved two important problems for Freud: it accounted for familial patterns in the disease, and it explained why there
is no exact correspondence between the pursuit of a particular sexual
practice and the presence or the severity of the illness—why, for example, someone who practiced coitus interruptus for five years might
remain unaffected while someone else might be ill after two years. But
Freud was generally satisfied that his specific sexual noxae—coitus interruptus, masturbation, and so forth—were sufficiently detrimental in
themselves to cause these neuroses, and he did not feel obliged to
regard heredity as a necessary complement to sexual factors in his
etiological formula. Also, he believed that he could most often establish
a relationship between the intensity and duration of sexual noxae and
the severity of the response. As a result, although heredity is consistently regarded as a precondition, Freud felt free to concentrate his
attention on the sexual elements in the disease, and he did not believe
that the role assigned to heredity represented an obstacle to his construction of a sexual theory of the neurosis.

But the situation was quite different with hysteria and obsessions.
The sexual experiences which, in Freud's clinical cases, appeared responsible for prompting repression and defense often seemed quite
innocuous and inadequate to elicit such severe responses, and it appeared to Freud as though predisposition must play an essential and
indispensable role:

> In some cases, no doubt, we are concerned with experiences
> which must be regarded as severe traumas—an attempted
> rape, perhaps. . . . But in other cases the experiences are
> astonishingly trivial. In one of my women patients it turned
> out that her neurosis was based on the experience of a boy
> of her acquaintance stroking her hand tenderly and, at
> another time, pressing his knee against her dress as they sat
> side by side at table, while his expression let her see that he
> was doing something forbidden. . . . If serious and trifling
> events alike . . . are to be recognized as the ultimate traumas
> of hysteria, then we may be tempted to hazard the explana-

tion that hysterics are peculiarly constituted creatures—probably on account of some hereditary disposition.[60]

In *Studies on Hysteria* (1895), which appeared about the same time as the anxiety neurosis papers, Freud supports this view that some predisposition, most often hereditary, must be involved in hysteria. He describes Frau Emmy von N., for example, as "undoubtedly a personality with a severe neuropathic heredity. It seems likely that there can be no hysteria apart from a disposition of this kind."[61] Freud and Breuer both criticize Pierre Janet's theory on the part played by heredity in hysteria, and most of their remarks on heredity in *Studies On Hysteria* pertain to this critique. But Freud disagrees with specific aspects of Janet's thesis, not with the general notion that hereditary disposition is a key factor in the disease.

Janet's views on the role of heredity, like those of Charcot, were derived in large part from the concepts of hereditary degeneration which had been propounded by Morel and Magnan and which exerted such an extensive influence in French neuropsychiatry at this time. But Janet differed from Charcot by putting particular emphasis on the degeneration aspect and insisting that hysterical patients display a distinct impairment of mental faculties. This idea of degeneration was itself quite popular at the Salpetrière. In 1886 Alfred Binet and Charles Féré wrote with regard to diseases of psychogenic origin:

> It should be added that these diseases, produced by means of the imagination, are not merely influenced by a local disturbance; the subject who allows himself to be dominated by this idea of disease must be peculiarly excitable and open to suggestion; he must be endowed with a condition of congenital psychical weakness which is frequently found in conjunction with more or less strongly marked neuropathic manifestations.[62]

Jules Janet, in a paper entitled "L'hystérie et l'hypnotisme, d'après la théorie de la double personnalité" (1888), argued that all people possess unconscious as well as conscious personalities. What distinguishes hysterics is that in these people the unconscious personality is capable of breaking through the primary ego and exerting exceptional influence over behavior, thereby generating hysterical symptoms. The basic abnormality in hysteria is the weakness of the primary ego which allows the unconscious to wield this pathological influence.[63] Pierre Janet, proceeding in part from his brother's observations, endorses the notion that there exists, in hysteria, a basic weakness of the primary ego. But in his view this weakness is the source of secondary personalities. He argues that in hysteria the primary ego is incapable of properly absorbing and integrating all the experiences to which it is exposed, and that consequently there are formed dissociated, unconscious groups of ideas, leading independent psychic existences. This, according to Janet, is the basis for the peculiar split in consciousness which characterizes hysteria:

> The [splitting] of the personality is . . . the immediate consequence of this weakness of psychological synthesis. The latter allows psychological phenomena to subsist, but does not unite them to the idea of the personality. We may represent to ourselves . . . subconscious acts, as secondary groupings, as accessory systematizations of those neglected psychological phenomena.[64]

The weakness of the primary personality, its inability to assimilate adequately sensations and perceptions, is in Janet's view a consequence of hereditary degeneration.

Freud and Breuer's criticism of this theory is directed essentially at Janet's concept of degenerative mental weakness. Janet maintains that hysterical patients are necessarily weakminded, but Freud and Breuer both argue that many of their patients have been extremely gifted people who possessed exceptional mental abilities. They suggest that the mental incapacity so frequently displayed by hysterical patients is a result of their illness rather than the cause of it. But their argument is not aimed at denying the importance of hereditary predisposition. The distinction can be seen in Freud's comments on Frau Emmy von N.: "To describe such a woman as a 'degenerate' would be to distort the meaning of the word out of all recognition. . . . I must confess . . . that I can see no sign in Frau von N.'s history of the 'psychical inefficiency' to which Janet attributes the genesis of hysteria."[65] But he nevertheless asserts that Frau von N. suffered from a "severe neuropathic heredity," and he notes that "we should do well to distinguish between the concepts of 'disposition' and 'degeneracy'."

Freud did not, of course, subscribe fully to the emphasis on hereditary predisposition prevalent at the Salpetrière. He insisted that defense and the repression of sexual memories are the major factors in the etiological equation, and he argued that some patients give no history of an hereditary taint and display no abnormalities prior to the occurrence of the sexual trauma. But, because so many of the traumatic experiences uncovered in therapy were of a trivial nature, he still felt obliged to regard some sort of predisposition as a key factor in all cases. One consequence of this was a somewhat pessimistic prognosis. Catharsis, Freud maintained, could uncover repressed sexual memories, but it could not cope with the patient's disposition to hysteria and therefore could not prevent new repressions and new symptoms: "There is [an] obstacle in the way of the effectiveness of the cathartic method. . . . It cannot affect the underlying causes of hysteria: thus it cannot prevent fresh symptoms from taking the place of the ones which had been got rid of."[66] The attribution of an important role to predisposition in hysteria and obsessions also had the effect of hindering Freud's attempts to develop a general theory of the neuroses. Since he felt unable to relegate predisposition to the essentially ancillary role he had assigned it with regard to neurasthenia and anxiety, he was stymied in his efforts to characterize each of the neuroses as essentially the result of specific sexual factors.

But Freud's views on the role of heredity in the genesis of hysteria and obsessions changed radically with his development of the theory of infantile sexual traumas.

Freud refers in "Draft A"(tentatively dated December, 1892) to "sexual traumas before the age of understanding," and he also makes some other early references to infantile sexual trauma. However, while his clinical work was uncovering histories of such experiences in some of his neurotic patients, Freud did not for some time accord these experiences any etiological role beyond that ascribed to sexual traumas generally. But his evaluation of these infantile occurrences changed dramatically in the latter part of 1895, presumably in response to more thorough therapeutic analyses, deeper probing of his patients' repressed material, and, consequently, more consistent revelations of infantile sexual experiences. Freud wrote to Fliess on October 8, 1895: "Note that among other things I suspect the following: that hysteria is conditioned by a primary sexual experience (before puberty) accompanied by revulsion and fright; and that obsessional neurosis is conditioned by the same accompanied by pleasure." A week later he was more confident of the new formula: "Have I revealed the great clinical secret to you, either in writing or by word of mouth? Hysteria is the consequence of a presexual *sexual shock*. Obsessional neurosis is the consequence of presexual *sexual pleasure* later transformed into guilt. . . . 'Presexual' means before puberty."[67]

This new concept led to a major revision of Freud's etiological model. For unlike those later sexual traumas which Freud, in his more superficial analyses, had regarded as the ultimate source of hysterical and obsessional symptoms, these infantile events were uniformly of a substantial nature: seductions, assaults, repeated episodes of genital play and manipulation. They seemed, in Freud's view, to be well suited for inducing neuroses, much as coitus interruptus and masturbation seemed sufficiently deleterious to account for anxiety and neurasthenia. He therefore no longer felt obliged to postulate some predisposing factor as a necessary complement to sexual trauma in the generation of hysteria and obsessions. Heredity could now be relegated to the same secondary role in the neuropsychoses as it had been assigned in neurasthenia and anxiety.

One immediate result is a change in Freud's prognosis for hysteria and obsessions. Since the repressed infantile trauma now seemed the essential etiological factor, and since this could be resolved through catharsis, the outlook now appeared brighter. Freud wrote to Fliess on October 16, 1895: "I am practically sure I have solved the riddle of hysteria and obsessional neurosis with the formula of infantile sexual shock and sexual pleasure, and I am just as sure that both neuroses are radically curable now."[68]

Freud still believed that postpubertal sexual experiences, most often trivial in themselves, play a major role in generating hysterical and obsessional symptoms, but he now insisted that these experiences are rendered pathogenic because of their association with a primary, infantile trauma—and not because of some separate predispositional factor. Freud wrote some months later:

> All the events subsequent to puberty to which an influence must be attributed upon the development of the hysterical neurosis and upon the formation of its symptoms are in fact only concurrent causes—*"agents provocateurs"* as Charcot used to say, though for him nervous heredity occupied the place which I claim for the precocious sexual experience. . . .
> Analysis demonstrates in an irrefutable fashion that they enjoy a pathogenic influence for hysteria only owing to their faculty for awakening the unconscious psychical trace of the childhood event. It is also thanks to their connection with the primary pathogenic impression, and inspired by it, that their memories will become unconscious in their turn and will be able to assist in the growth of a psychical activity withdrawn from the power of conscious functions.[69]

Heredity is still cited by Freud as a factor in the etiology of hysteria and obsessions, but its significance is drastically reduced. It now serves only to resolve the two ancillary problems mentioned in connection with neurasthenia and anxiety: it helps to explain familial patterns in the disease and it accounts for why there is no exact correspondence between exposure to infantile sexual trauma and subsequent development of a neurosis—why, for example, a sexual assault in infancy might lead to severe illness in one person and leave another relatively unscarred. But, even with regard to these problems, Freud viewed heredity as playing only a limited role. He believed that there is, in fact, a generally straightforward correspondence between the intensity and duration of infantile sexual experiences and the later development of hysteria or obsessional neurosis. He also maintained that his emphasis on infantile sexual experiences provided an alternative explanation for familial patterns in the neuroses:

> I will ask you to consider . . . the special frequency with which sexual relations in childhood occur precisely between brothers and sisters and cousins, as a result of their opportunities for being together so often; supposing, then, ten or fifteen years later several members of the younger generation of the family are found to be ill, might not this appearance of a family neurosis naturally lead to the false supposition that a hereditary disposition is present where there is only a *pseudo-heredity*.[70]

In another paper, Freud discusses a case in which a brother, a sister, and a cousin all were neurotic, giving the appearance of an hereditary abnormality. But it was known in the family that the cousin had been sexually assaulted as a child by a servant, and analysis of the brother revealed that he had been seduced by his cousin and had later initiated his sister into sexual play. These relationships, Freud insists, were the actual source of their illnesses.[71]

In the stories of infantile sexual trauma revealed by Freud's female patients during analysis, it was most often the father who was named as seducer—a point which Freud chose to omit from his publications during this period, but which is mentioned in his correspondence to Fliess. This again offered, in Freud's view, an explanation for why neuroses were so frequently associated with familial patterns of illness. If hysterical women are the victims of incestuous fathers, then one could expect as a rule to see the combination of eccentric, disturbed father and hysterical daughter—a combination which in all probability would be wrongly interpreted as evidence of an hereditary taint.

Freud alluded to his new theory on the etiology of the neuropsychoses in a lecture delivered October 26, 1895.[72] He presented the theory more fully in two papers which appeared in 1896: "Further Remarks on the Neuro-Psychoses of Defence" (May, 1896) and "The Etiology of Hysteria" (May—June, 1896). The only etiological distinction between obsessional neurosis and hysteria, in Freud's view, is that the former involves an active, pleasurable childhood encounter, while hysteria is the result of a passive, either indifferent or somewhat unpleasant, experience. Freud believed that the patient suffering from obsessions had initially been the victim of a sexual assault, and that this had resulted in a premature sexual awakening and had subsequently led to his induction of another child into sexual play. But it is specifically the latter experience, according to Freud, which accounts for the child's later obsessional neurosis. This distinction, between passive experiences as the source of hysteria and active, pleasurable ones as the origin of obsessions, appeared to be the pattern revealed by his analysis of hysterical and obsessional patients. In addition, obsessional neurosis seemed particularly to involve feelings of personal inadequacy, self-reproach and guilt, and Freud interpreted this as a transposition of feelings associated with the repressed memory of the patient's childhood assault on another child. Finally, this formula appeared, in Freud's view, to explain why hysterical patients were usually women, while those suffering from obsessions were more often men.

By associating hysteria and obsessions with infantile sexual traumas, and relegating heredity to an ancillary role, Freud was finally able to designate a specific sexual factor as the primary cause of each of his major neuroses. He presents his general theory in another 1896 paper, "Heredity and the Etiology of the Neuroses." The paper, published in French in the *Revue neurologique,* begins:

> I am addressing in particular the disciples of J.M. Charcot, in order to put forward some objections to the aetiological theory of the neuroses which was handed on to us by our teacher.
>
> The role attributed in that theory to nervous heredity is well known: it is the sole true and indispensable cause of neurotic affections. . . .
>
> I have long entertained doubts on this subject, but I have had to wait to find corroborative facts in my daily experience as a doctor.

Freud acknowledges that heredity may play a predisposing role, but he insists that the essential cause of each of the neuroses is some sexual factor:

> I shall maintain . . . that each of the major neuroses which I
> have enumerated [hysteria, obsessions, neurasthenia, anxiety
> neurosis] has as its immediate cause . . . functional pathologi-
> cal modifications [which] *have as their common source the sub-
> ject's sexual life, whether they lie in a disorder of his contemporary
> sexual life or in important events in his past life.*
>   This, to tell the truth, is no new, unheard-of proposi-
> tion. Sexual disorders have always been admitted among the
> causes of nervous illness, but they have been subordinated to
> heredity and co-ordinated with the other *agents provocateurs*
> [italics in original]; their aetiological influence has been re-
> stricted to a limited number of observed cases. . . . What
> gives its distinctive character to my line of approach is that I
> elevate these sexual influences to the rank of specific causes,
> that I recognize their action in every case of neurosis, and
> finally that I trace a regular parallelism, a proof of a special
> aetiological relation between the nature of the sexual in-
> fluence and the pathological species of the neurosis.[73]

The designation of a specific factor from sexual life as the major
cause of each of the neuroses not only led to a devaluing of heredity,
but also prompted Freud to embark on a comprehensive explication of
the neuroses based on their sexual sources. However, as neurasthenia
and anxiety neurosis seemed explicable only in physiological terms,
Freud concluded that a comprehensive theory would likewise have to
be physiological. This led him, in late 1895, to an uncharacteristic excursion into physiological speculation.

7. Freud's "Project for a Scientific Psychology"

Toward Speculations on a Physiology of Mind

In the latter part of 1895, Freud devoted considerable effort to developing physiological explanations for psychological phenomena. He had, of course, consistently eschewed such models in his studies of hypnosis and hysteria, and his only previous excursion into the physiology of psychological phenomena (or psychophysiology) was some remarks on the speech apparatus in *On Aphasia*. Freud's reversal of this earlier tendency to avoid what he had characterized as futile speculation was prompted primarily by his work on neurasthenia and anxiety neurosis and his attempt to construct a general theory of the neuroses.

Freud did not wish to limit his theory of the neuroses solely to etiological considerations, to the argument that different sexual factors were the specific cause of each of these syndromes. He hoped to develop also a unified theory of the pathological processes—the intermediate steps—by which the various sexual noxae produce neurotic symptoms. But the pathology of neurasthenia and anxiety, according to Freud, involved only physiological mechanisms and could be explained only in physiological terms. This suggested that any general theory of pathological processes would also have to be in physiological terms, and that therefore his psychological models for hysteria and obsessions would have to be translated into neurodynamics. He had argued that anxiety and neurasthenia involve, respectively, excesses and depletions of "somatic sexual excitation"; the construction of an integrated theory seemed to require that hysteria and obsessions similarly be explained as manifestations of somatic sexual excitation.

Freud's search for a general pathology of the neuroses, and his

153

excursions into psychophysiological theorizing, were spurred on by a number of clinical observations. In particular, Freud's clinical experience indicated that hysteria most often appears in combination with neurasthenia or anxiety neurosis, especially the latter:

> The neuroses which commonly occur are mostly to be described as "mixed." Neurasthenia and anxiety neuroses are easily found in pure forms as well, especially in young people. Pure forms of hysteria and obsessional neurosis are rare; as a rule these two neuroses are combined with anxiety neurosis. . . . As regards hysteria, . . . it follows that that disorder can scarcely be segregated from the nexus of the sexual neuroses [i.e., neurasthenia and anxiety] for the purposes of study, that as a rule it represents only a single side, only one aspect, of a complicated case of neurosis, and that it is only in marginal cases that it can be found and treated in isolation.[1]

This suggested to Freud that the changes in somatic sexual excitation which supposedly underlie neurasthenia and anxiety neurosis might indeed be of fundamental significance for the pathogenesis of hysteria. During the months preceding Freud's development of the theory of infantile sexual traumas (first mentioned in October, 1895), when he was still struggling to explain how apparently innocuous sexual encounters could lead to hysteria, it appeared that physiological changes brought on by the sexual neuroses might serve as an essential predisposing factor. But, even after he had formulated the thesis that hysterical and obsessional patients had invariably suffered significant infantile sexual traumas, and that these traumas were the major source of their illness, he continued to believe that the somatic effects of an accompanying neurasthenia or anxiety neurosis might play an important role in the neuropsychoses.

Freud had, of course, argued earlier that there were elements in the pathogenesis of hysteria which could not be elucidated by psychology and which required neurodynamic explanations, and yet he had not previously attempted to formulate physiological models. But this was in part because, while he had maintained that psychology alone could not offer a complete understanding of hysteria, he had consistently believed that the major pathogenic mechanism in hysteria—the means by which a psychic trauma leads to hysterical symptoms—can be explained in psychological terms. Physiology might be required to account for the origin of hysterical stigmata, or to account for the "capacity for conversion"—the tendency to convert affect into somatic hysterical symptoms—which Freud regarded as distinguishing hysteria from obsessions; but defense and repression, as well as Freud's earlier formulas for the pathogenic mechanism underlying hysterical symptoms, had seemed amenable to purely psychological discussions. In contrast, the current questions concerning the role of physiology in hysteria and related neuroses—the questions generated by the presence of "simple neuroses," particularly anxiety, in virtually all hysterical patients—explicitly challenged Freud's concept of repression and suggested that purely psychological models of repression would not suffice after all. Anxiety neurosis, according to Freud, involves an accumulation of somatic sexual excitation. The disease develops when the excitation is deflected away from the psychic sphere and converted into anxiety symptoms. Freud, in "Draft E" (written probably in the summer of 1894), offered various explanations of why this deflection occurs, relating it to the specific sexual patterns which accounted for the patient's inadequate sexual release and his accumulation of excitation. In the first paper on anxiety neurosis (January, 1895), he states simply that all the sexual patterns which lead to anxiety neurosis involve inadequate gratification, and the accumulated sexual excitation is merely deflected into pathways which offer a greater chance of discharge. The analogy with defense and repression in hysteria and obsessional neurosis is obvious. Defense and repression in the neuropsychoses are also supposedly a means for diverting excitation away from normal outlets and into pathways where release can be more easily achieved. Freud points out the analogy in his correspondence with Fliess, and he uses the term *defense* in accounting for the deflection of excitation in some patients suffering from anxiety neurosis. The major distinction, according to Freud, is that in the neuropsychoses it is psychological excitation which is accumulated and deflected, whereas in anxiety neurosis it is somatic excitation. But having observed, as stated in *Studies on Hysteria*, that almost all of his hysterical patients give histories of very limited sexual release and display symptoms of anxiety, Freud concluded that perhaps the accumulation of somatic sexual excitation in these patients was a factor in their hysterical defense and repression.

This possibility was particularly attractive as it would help to resolve one of the major difficulties in Freud's theory of the neuropsychoses. Freud had so far been unable to account for why sexual traumas were so uniquely pernicious. With his development of the theory of infantile sexual trauma in the fall of 1895, he believed that he had finally discovered etiological factors sufficiently deleterious to cause the subsequent illness; but he was still unable to explain why other forms of psychic trauma—a falling-out with a friend, for example—could not similarly cause repression and hysteria. Freud acknowledged that sociological factors, especially contemporary morality, had lent a special significance to sexuality. But such factors, in Freud's view, could hardly have rendered a unique status to sexual trauma. It appeared to Freud that the explanation must lie in the realm of somatic sexual functions, and the presence of anxiety neurosis in most cases of hysteria reinforced this view. Freud speculates in a draft sent to Fliess in January, 1896 ("Draft K"):

> We shall be plunged deep into psychological riddles if we enquire into the origin of the unpleasure [that is, the discomfort generated by incompatible ideas] which seems to be released by premature sexual stimulation and without which, after all, a repression cannot be explained. The most plausible answer will appeal to the fact that shame and morality are the repressing forces. . . . I fear, nevertheless, that this explanation will not stand up to deeper testing. . . . In my opinion there must be an independent source for the release of unpleasure in sexual life: once that source is present, it can activate sensations of disgust, lend force to morality, and so on. I hold to the model of anxiety neurosis in adults, where a quantity deriving from sexual life similarly causes a disturbance in the psychical sphere, though [had it not been for the frustration of normal sexual outlets] it would ordinarily have found another use in the sexual process. So long as there is no correct theory of the sexual process, the question of the origin of the unpleasure operating in repression remains unanswered.[2]

Assigning a crucial role to somatic sexual excitation in the development of unpleasure and in the emergence of hysterical defense and repression seemed to offer a possible resolution of the difficulty.

Freud's model for anxiety neurosis also provided a further motivation for his psychophysiological speculations. During the period when he was writing the "Preliminary Communication" (published January, 1893), Freud regarded the hysteric's suppression of disturbing memories as merely instances of that normal psychic inhibition which is constantly being employed to cope with distracting or bothersome ideas. The pathological element, in Freud's view, was the failure of inhibition in hysterical patients. This occurred because of a "tendency towards the splitting of consciousness," which allowed the disturbing idea to avoid inhibition by the primary consciousness and to exert an abnormal influence on thought and behavior. When, during the subsequent year, Freud formulated his defense theory, his view of the relationship between hysterical repression and normal inhibition changed radically. With his recognition that the memories involved in generating hysterical symptoms are of an exceptionally disturbing and threatening nature, Freud declared that the reaction of the ego to such memories has little in common with normal inhibition. He now regarded repression as a distinct and wholly pathological process, and he viewed the symptoms of hysteria, particularly somatic conversions, as following directly from the mere act of repression. But, with the development of his model for anxiety neurosis, the distinction between repression and inhibition was blurred. Anxiety neurosis was believed by Freud to be caused by inadequate sexual gratification and to involve a process, very much like hysterical defense and repression, whereby sexual excitation is deflected from the psychic sphere and converted into somatic symptoms. But the diversion of sexual excitation away from the psyche during periods when gratification is unavailable would seem to be a standard function of psychic inhibition. Directing one's thoughts away from drives which cannot be immediately fulfilled is indeed a normal, everyday process. Is anxiety neurosis then simply the pathological result of continuous, prolonged inhibition? This view was untenable if Freud wished to maintain that conversion is the result of a unique pathological process; and yet it seemed impossible to argue that anxiety neurosis involves a mechanism distinctly different from normal inhibition. Freud hoped that a clarification of the relationship between anxiety and hysteria would resolve the dilemma and reestablish the distinction between repression and inhibition.

These problems generated by Freud's studies of the simple neuroses—in particular, the problems of defining the relationship of repression to somatic sexual excitation and differentiating repression from inhibition—were the major inspiration for Freud's excursion into psychophysiology during 1895. Freud redefined defense to include both inhibition (normal defense) and repression (pathological defense), and he wrote of his psychophysiological speculations: "All I was trying to do was to explain defense."[3]

The "Project for a Scientific Psychology," the surviving draft of Freud's physiological theorizing, was written in September and October, 1895, and consists of three sections. The first is concerned primarily with establishing the physiological foundations for normal psychic inhibition. The discussion also encompasses the normal dispostion of exogenous excitation (that is, excitation derived from the impingement of external stimuli on the organism) and the normal utilization of endogenous excitation (excitation generated by one's own organic processes and related to innate drives, such as those for food, oxygen, and sexual satisfaction). Freud's second chapter is devoted to a neurodynamic explanation of repression and the pathogenesis of hysteria. It is here that he tries to establish the distinction between repression and inhibition. He also considers the physiological basis for the almost invariable presence of simple neuroses in hysterical patients, and for the peculiar pathogenicity of sexual trauma.

In the third and final section, Freud extends his neurophysiological model to encompass normal psychic processes such as thought and cognition. The section is for the most part concerned with elucidating further the mechanism of normal inhibition and with demonstrating how this inhibitory process lies at the foundation of all mental functioning.

Freud's earliest mention of his new concern with psychophysiological speculations appears in a letter to Fliess dated April 27, 1895, three months after the publication of his first paper on anxiety neurosis and about six weeks after his completion of the final section of *Studies on Hysteria*. There are comments on the progress of his speculations in several subsequent letters. On August 6, he writes that "I believe I have found my way to the understanding of pathological defence [i.e., repression], and with it to the understanding of many important psychological processes." A few days later he is more pessimistic.[4] But in any case, none of his notes on psychophysiology from these months has survived and it is impossible to judge how his thinking actually progressed during this period.

In early September, according to Ernest Jones, Freud went to Berlin to visit Fliess and was so inspired by their conversations that he began to write the "Project" on the train home.[5] Freud does report in a letter dated September 23: "In the train I started writing a short account of the $\phi\psi\Omega$ [used as symbols in the "Project"] for you to criticise, and I am now continuing it in my free time and in the intervals between the acts of my . . . practice."[6] But the decision to develop his physiological models in a lengthy manuscript was not simply the result of conversations with Fliess. Freud's formulation of the theory of infantile sexual traumas, during the weeks following his visit, was undoubtedly a more important factor in the writing of the "Project." Freud's first letter to Fliess announcing the infantile trauma theory is dated October 8, but the theory is central to his discussion of psychopathology in the second section of the "Project," probably written a week or two earlier. The concept of infantile sexual traumas was significant for the "Project" because it suggested new approaches to the problems of the distinction between repression and inhibition and the relation of repression to somatic sexual excitation. In most psychic traumas, the experience itself is considerably more distressing than its recollection. Freud, in the wake of his formulation of the infantile trauma theory, suggests that, in the case of infantile sexual abuse, the reverse is true. The child, whose sexuality is as yet undeveloped, will tolerate with little discomposure experiences whose memory, following puberty and the awakening of sexuality, will involve significantly greater distress. Freud proposes that this peculiar arrangement, in which the memory is more disturbing than the event, is the factor which induces pathological, rather than normal, defense (that is, repression rather than inhibition). He also maintains that it is specifically the generation of quantities of somatic sexual excitation at puberty which alters the psyche's response to infantile sexual memories. These notions are the basis for Freud's discussion of hysteria in the "Project."

The surviving manuscript was completed during the first week of October, 1895. The third section is headed with the date October 5, and Freud sent the work, in two notebooks, to Fliess on October 8. Freud spoke in an accompanying letter of another notebook, which dealt further with repression, but this has not survived. The only additional material relating to the psychophysiological speculations of the "Project" appears in a letter to Fliess written New Year's Day, 1896, in which Freud offers several pages of revisions to his basic neurodynamic model.[7]

Some Basic Concepts

The psychophysiological theories of the "Project" are based upon standard contemporary notions of brain function, particularly upon concepts concerning the reflex nature of cerebral activity and the importance of cerebral inhibitory phenomena. Freud's speculations resemble to some degree the neurodynamic model formulated by Breuer in *Studies on Hysteria,* as well as the much more detailed and comprehensive theories developed by Sigmund Exner in his *Entwurf zu einer physiologischen Erklärung der psychischen Erscheinungen* (1894). But psychophysiological treatises were quite popular during this period and were written by numerous neuropsychiatrists, physiologists, and psychologists throughout Europe, and these treatises typically proceed from the same principles as the "Project" and involve models similar to Freud's. Freud was undoubtedly familiar with many such works—he states at the beginning of the "Project" that "similar experiments are now frequent"[8]—and there is little basis for attributing any special importance to the speculations of his Viennese colleagues in the shaping of his theories.

Freud begins by introducing the concept of a quantity of nervous excitation, or Q.[9] The quantification of nervous excitation is justified, in Freud's view, by clinical observations. Cases of hysteria and obsessional neurosis, he argues, clearly demonstrate a proportionality between the intensity of pathogenic traumas—the "stimuli" which induce the neuroses—and the magnitude of subsequent symptoms; and this proportionality suggests that one can speak of quantities of stimulus and response. Such observations were the basis for Freud's earlier quantification of psychic excitation, and he is now simply translating the earlier, psychological model into physiological terms. The same clinical considerations had also led Freud to formulate his principle of constancy, the concept that the organism strives to release excess excitation and to maintain its sum of excitation at a constant level, and this too is now given a neurodynamic interpretation. Freud proposes as a first principle that nerves tend to divest themselves of Q.

Physiologists studying nervous system reflexes had also consistently observed a proportionality between stimulus and response. The physiologist Charles Richet wrote, for example: "In a simple reflex movement [such as that of a decapitated frog], all conditions being otherwise equal in the irritability of the nervous conductors, the nerve centers and the muscles, the reflex reaction is directly proportional to the intensity of the excitant."[10] Such observations had similarly suggested that nervous excitation can be quantified and that there exists a tendency to rid the nervous system of excitation. Consequently, the concept of quantities of excitation, and the notion that nervous excitation is maintained at a constant level, were common elements in neurophysiological speculations during the latter part of the nineteenth century.

Freud integrated his theory of nervous excitation with the neuronal theory of nervous system structure. The term *nerve-cell* as used in the second half of the nineteenth century referred only to the neural cell-body; the relationship of the cell-body to various appendages, particularly to axons, was the subject of considerable controversy. However, in 1886 Wilhelm His presented the results of microscopic studies demonstrating the embryonic development of the axon out of the cell-body, and subsequent investigations reinforced the view that the cell-body and

its appendages comprise a single cellular unit. In 1891 Wilhelm Waldeyer published a review article dealing with the evidence in favor of this
view, and he coined the term *neurone* to designate the neural cellular
unit.[11] Freud utilizes the neurone theory in the "Project":

> The nervous system consists of distinct and similarly con-
> structed neurones, which have contact with one another
> through the medium of a foreign substance, which terminate
> upon one another as they do upon portions of foreign tissue
> [e.g., muscle tissue], [and] in which certain lines of conduc-
> tion are laid down in so far as they [i.e., the neurones] re-
> ceive [excitations] through cell-processes and [give them off]
> through an axis-cylinder [i.e., axon].[12]

According to Freud, neurones can be charged, or "cathected,"[13]
with a quantity of excitation. In keeping with the principle of inertia—
the neurodynamic equivalent of the constancy principle—a neurone
would tend to divest itself of such cathexes, and this suggests to Freud
the concept of a current of Q, passing into the neurone through its
cell-processes and out through its axon. However, the observation that
stimuli do not always elicit immediate responses indicates that Q is
often retained within the system. This leads Freud to the hypothesis of
"contact-barriers."

Freud suggests that retention of Q within a neurone is the result of
neuronal resistances to the passage of Q-currents. These resistances, he
believes, are located at the points of contact between neurones; and he
therefore labels them contact-barriers. But the resistance offered by a
contact-barrier can be modified, and such modifications are, according
to Freud, the physiological basis of both learning and memory. The
passage of Q across a barrier has the effect of lowering the resistance at
that barrier to the subsequent passage of additional Q, and as a result a
subsequent Q can pass more easily: "The process of conduction itself
will create . . . an improved conductive capacity for subsequent conduction."[14] This facilitation of Q-currents constitutes the physiology of
learning: for example, on initially learning to ride a bicycle, the enlist-
ing of the proper neural pathways required to coordinate all the movements necessary for bike-riding (i.e., the passing of Q-currents across
the proper neuronal barriers) would be slow and difficult. With practice, which in effect entails repeated excitation of the same pathways,
the passage of Q-currents across the proper contact barriers would be
facilitated by repeated use, the proper movements would occur more
easily, and the task would thus be "learned." Relative degrees of facili-

tation of different barriers determine the direction of a Q-current and are the basis of memory: again using bike-riding as an example—upon one's returning to riding after the skill had once been learned, Q-currents triggered by the new attempt to ride are most likely to pass in the direction of facilitated pathways established by previous learning, rather than along relatively unfacilitated collateral pathways; so that the proper, coordinated movements required for riding are, in effect, "remembered." Facilitation is proportional to the magnitude of the Q which passes across a barrier, and to the frequency with which Q-currents pass across; consequently, learning and memory are proportional to the magnitude of a stimulus and to the degree of repetition of the stimulus.

The term *Bahnung* (translated "facilitation") was coined by Sigmund Exner in an 1884 article entitled "Zur Kenntniss von der Wechselwirkung der Erregungen in Centralnervensystems" in which Exner states that "the discharge of an initial cortical excitation facilitates a second discharge."[15] But this concept of facilitation, and the belief that facilitation constitutes the physiological basis of learning, had been standard notions for much of the century. The everyday observation that a response can be executed more easily once it has been practiced or has become habitual was typically interpreted as indicating that the neural pathway involved has been facilitated by repetition. Physiological experiments on reaction time reinforced this view. Remarks by the French psychologist Hippolyte Taine, in a book highly praised by Freud (*De L'Intelligence* [1864]), reflect the common opinion:

> The more often a pathway has been used in the past by [nerve] currents, the better is the chance that a subsequent current will follow the same path. . . . In this way we come to execute our learned movements, after a shorter or longer learning period, wholly automatically—our walking, running, swimming, and riding, the handling of a weapon, a tool, or a musical instrument.[16]

The notion that the pattern of interneural facilitations forms the basis of memory was not quite as popular. Virtually all authors agreed that memory must involve some physical changes at the neuronal level, but more weight was usually given to changes within the neurones than to alterations in intercellular connections. However, the latter factor was generally accorded some role in memory, and there were a number of authors who regarded interneural facilitations as the essential element. Theodule Ribot, professor of psychology at the College de

France and a close associate of the Salpetrière researchers, wrote in 1882 that memory involves two physiological conditions: (1) a particular modification impressed upon the nervous elements, and (2) an association, a specific connection established between a given number of elements.[17] Later, Ribot emphasized the second condition—the establishment of dynamic affinities between neurones—as the major factor.

Freud's discussion of memory leads to his distinguishing between two different types of neurones. He argues in the "Project" that, while memory and learning involve the modification of neuronal contact-barriers, "perception," or receptivity to sensation, seems to entail a responsiveness on the part of the organism which remains unchanged over time and therefore seems to require that there be another class of neurones which is not altered by each new excitation. This was also a common notion, and Freud speaks of "the current distinction between 'perceptual cells' and 'mnemic cells.'" Freud suggests that the perceptual neurones are characterized by permanently facilitated contact-barriers. The difference between perceptual and mnemic neurones need not, in Freud's view, be regarded as innate. Since perceptual cells receive their stimulation directly from the external world, while mnemic cells have only internal connections, the perceptual cells may be exposed to excitations of a much greater magnitude than those encountered by mnemic cells, and these large Qs may simply wipe out the contact-barriers of the perceptual neurones. Freud labels the memory cells ψ neurones, and the perceptual cells ϕ neurones.

Freud also introduces a third type of nerve cell, the ω neurones, which he associates with consciousness. Freud first suggests that these ω neurones receive their excitation via memory, or ψ, cells, but in a letter to Fliess dated January, 1896, he revises this scheme and proposes that the ω neurones are in fact excited directly by perceptual cells. In any case, Freud consistently defines the location of the various cell types within the nervous system in terms of their positions relative to each other and devotes very little attention to identifying specific anatomical locations for these cell types. Perceptual, or ϕ, neurones are, of course, associated with peripheral sensory nerves; and Freud states that "we will provisionally regard the ψ system as identified with the grey matter of the brain."[18] He also implies that those ψ neurones which receive exogenous excitation (excitation from outside the body), via the ϕ system, are located in the more superficial cellular strata of the cerebral grey matter, while ψ cells receiving endogenous excitation are found in the deeper strata. But there is no further discussion of cerebral localization, and there is no mention of cerebral centers such as those considered in Exner's book and in Theodor Meynert's psychophysiological speculations. This is in keeping with Freud's consistent skepticism regarding the localization of psychic functions in specific areas of the brain.

Freud's principle of inertia—the neurophysiological equivalent of his constancy principle—states that the system strives to divest itself of quantities of excitation, or Q. In discussing the ω neurones, the neurones associated with consciousness, Freud considers the sensations of pleasure and unpleasure (*Unlust*):

> Since we have certain knowledge of a trend in psychical life towards *avoiding unpleasure,* we are tempted to identify that trend with the primary trend towards inertia. In that case *unpleasure* would have to be regarded as coinciding with a raising of the level of [Q]. . . . It would be the ω sensation when there is an increase of [Q]. . . . Pleasure would be the sensation of discharge [of Q].[19]

The concept of unpleasure is distinguished from that of pain (*Schmerz*). Pain is conceived by Freud as a physical phenomenon brought about by the introduction of large quantities of exogenous excitation into the system, with an exact correspondence between the magnitude of the exogenous Qs and the degree of pain. Unpleasure is the subjective, conscious sensation of any increase of Q, and would therefore comprise part of the subjective response to pain. The association of pain and unpleasure with large quantities of excitation was supported by the observation that any exogenous stimulus, if magnified sufficiently, is accompanied by pain.

The idea that pleasure is connected with the release of accumulated excitation was, once again, a common notion during this period. In a paper written many years after the "Project," Freud cites statements by Gustav Fechner, dating from 1873, which equate pleasure with nervous system stability and unpleasure with instability. Many writers, proceeding from the interpretation of all behavior in terms of reflexes, suggested that pleasure is simply the sensation of an adequate response to stimuli, while unpleasure accompanies situations in which no sufficient response occurs. For example, Wilhelm Griesinger observed:

> As soon as one experiences [a stimulus], one also has motion; as soon as one has an idea, there is also exertion. The free execution of this conversion is perceived as satisfaction. . . .

> [A] feeling of well-being, of pleasure, is attached to the
> act. . . . Disturbances [of this translation of stimuli into ac-
> tion] result in psychic unpleasure, spiritual pain.[20]

But Freud notes in the "Project" that, while the release of excitation
and the resolution of unpleasure is the primary function of the nervous
system, the system is continually obliged to accommodate prolonged
increases in excitation. In particular, the excitation generated by endogenous biological needs, such as hunger, must be retained until
sufficient quantities have accumulated to enable the organism to carry
out that specific action—the acquiring of food, for example— necessary
to satisfy the need:

> The nervous system receives stimuli from the somatic ele-
> ment itself—endogenous stimuli—which have equally to be
> discharged. These have their origin in the cells of the body
> and give rise to the major needs: hunger, respiration, sexual-
> ity. . . . [These] only cease subject to particular conditions,
> which must be realized in the external world. (Cf., for in-
> stance, the need for nourishment.) In order to accomplish
> such an action (which deserves to be named "specific"), an
> effort is required which is independent of endogenous [Q]
> and in general greater, since the individual is being sub-
> jected to conditions which may be described as *the exigencies
> of life*. In consequence, the nervous system is obliged to aban-
> don its original trend to inertia. . . . It must put up with
> [accumulating] a store of [Q] sufficient to meet the demand
> for a specific action.[21]

Endogenous excitation, according to Freud's model, is received by ψ ,
or mnemic neurones. It was Freud's consideration of this need for
accumulating excitation that had led him to postulate the existence of
contact-barriers—which serve to retain Q—between these mnemic
neurones.

The Ego and the Satisfaction of Biological Needs

Freud suggests that in the newborn the accumulation of endogenous excitation in ψ yields only emotional responses, such as crying.
This, of course, cannot in itself satisfy the biological need generating
the Q; but it will often lead to satisfaction, as in the case of a hungry
infant whose crying leads to his being fed. According to Freud, such an
experience of satisfaction will be accompanied by perception of the

objects serving as instruments of this experience, and by perception of the infant's own movements involved in the execution of the specific action needed to grasp that object. Consequently, associations will eventually be established in ψ among the mnemic image of the objects, the mnemic image of the infant's movements, and the memory of the biological need. Freud explains the neurodynamics of association in the following way:

> Hitherto we have learnt to know of ψ neurones being influenced through φ [the perceptual neurones] and through endogenous paths of conduction; but the different ψ neurones were cut off from one another by contact-barriers with strong resistances. Now there is a basic law of *association by simultaneity* . . . which is the foundation of all links between the ψ neurones. . . . Cathexis of a ψ neurone, α , passes over to another, β , if α and β have at some time been simultaneously cathected. . . . Thus a contact-barrier has been facilitated through the simultaneous cathexis α – β . It follows in the terms of our theory that a [Q] passes more easily from a neurone to a cathected neurone than to an uncathected one. . . .
>
> . . . A [Q] in neurone α will go not only in the direction of the barrier which is best facilitated, but also in the direction of the barrier which is cathected from the further side [i.e., where the adjacent neurone is also cathected]. . . . Thus, as a result of the experience of satisfaction, a facilitation comes about between two mnemic images [i.e., the image of the satisfying object and the image of the movements necessary to grasp the object] and the [neurones receiving endogenous excitation] which are cathected in the state of urgency.[22]

Association psychology—that approach to psychology which attempts to explain mental functioning in terms of the association of ideas—was a standard foundation for psychophysiological speculation during the nineteenth century, and the notion that associations are based upon the facilitation of pathways connecting nervous elements was a constant fixture of such speculations. The equation of association and neural facilitation can be found in David Hartley's fundamental work on the psychology of association (1749).[23] While theories of nervous structure and function changed radically during the following century and a half, the basic concept remained unchanged. Herbert

Spencer's statement in *The Principles of Psychology* (1855) is representative: "The psychical relationship between two [ideas] answers to the physical relation between two disturbed portions of grey matter, which are put in such direct or indirect communication that some discharge takes place between them."[24]

Freud suggests that, as a consequence of the associations established by early experiences of satisfaction, a subsequent accumulation of endogenous excitation will result in a flow of Q across the facilitated pathways into the mnemic image of the desired object. The infant will then hallucinate the object. Excitation will also flow into the mnemic image of the child's movements during the experience of satisfaction, and he might carry out these movements in response to the hallucination. This will, of course, fail to yield any satisfaction and will result only in disappointment. The infant must therefore develop a means for avoiding such behavior and for restricting the performance of the specific action to occasions when the desired object is actually present and experiences of satisfaction can actually be obtained.

Freud proposes that the constant reception of endogenous Q into ψ leads to the persistent presence of a body of cathected neurones in ψ. Some of these neurones are permanently cathected, while others have only a temporary charge. In Freud's speculative scheme, this body of cathected neurones is the physiological basis of the ego. The ego works to prevent the hallucination of desired objects and to achieve true experiences of satisfaction. It does this via a mechanism, "which is described generally as inhibition."[25] Freud has already argued that when two adjoining neurones are cathected there occurs a facilitation of the contact-barrier lying between them. According to this model, a current of Q which would ordinarily pass from neurone A to neurone B can be deflected to a third neurone, C, if C is a cathected neurone lying next to A (C is labelled a "side-cathexis"). In this way the current from A to B would be inhibited. The network of cathected neurones which comprise the ego serve, in Freud's view, as an instrument for such deflections, or inhibitions.

In the case of an accumulation of endogenous Q, the ego deflects that current which would otherwise flow to the mnemic image of the desired object and yield a hallucination. This prevention of hallucinations means that the desired object will be consciously perceived only when it is actually present. The representation of the perceived object in ω (the neurones underlying consciousness) will then be able to serve as a criterion for the reality of the object and for the appropriateness of the specific action:

If there is inhibition by a cathected ego, the indications of ω discharge become quite generally *indications of reality*, which ψ learns . . . to make use of. If, when an *indication of reality* of this kind emerges, the ego is in a state of [increased endogenous Q], it will allow discharge towards the specific action [which will grasp the desired object and yield satisfaction].[26]

Those situations in which there is no inhibition by the ego, and accumulated Q is permitted to generate hallucinations, are labelled "psychical primary processes" by Freud. In contrast, processes which are mediated by the inhibitory activity of the ego are called "psychical secondary processes". Primary processes are viewed by Freud as reflex phenomena, while the ego is seen as preventing reflex responses that might result in inappropriate behavior. This model conforms with the popular theory which regarded reflexes as constituting the basis of nervous system activity and viewed the inhibition of reflexes as the key to higher brain functions. The various psychophysiological explications of hypnosis discussed in chapter 4 were based upon the same theory. They all argue that, in a normal state of consciousness, higher cerebral activity prevents reflex responses to suggestions, but that, in hypnosis, this higher cerebral activity is depressed and the reflex execution of suggestions is consequently able to occur.

This concept of brain function was based on both physiological and psychological observations. The literature refers repeatedly, for example, to experiments with frogs which demonstrated that decapitation is followed by an enhancement of reflex activity. Such experiments were generally interpreted as indicating that the brain normally serves to inhibit reflexes. Psychological observations seemed to confirm this view. It was noted that one can, by an "effort of will," inhibit reflex responses. A frequently cited example is the dental patient who is able, by an "act of will," to control the squirming and withdrawing which would be his normal reflex response to the pain of treatment. Thought processes were seen as following the same pattern. The literature often refers to the example of verbal insults: a straightforward reflex response would be counterinsults or blows; but one can, through the intervention of higher mental processes, inhibit such automatic responses. The psychology of verbal suggestions, which elicit automatic responses only when one is no longer in full control of his mental faculties, offered further support for the reflex-inhibition concept.

Some writers, proceeding essentially from psychological evidence, presented the theory of reflexes and inhibitions in purely psychological terms. But there were several important factors which encouraged the development of psychophysiological formulations. First, of course, there was the analogy between the psychological and physiological phenomena, and this was interpreted by many as indicating that the psychological phenomena were merely a particular expression of general, physiological principles. In addition, many of the psychological observations dealt with phenomena which could not be separated from physiology. An example is the case of the dental patient: since responsiveness to pain is as much a function of physiological as of psychological factors, it appeared that a strictly psychological discussion would not suffice. Finally, it was noted that thought processes can be altered by purely physiological intervention. One can, for example, be reduced to a state in which one responds in a more reflex manner to insults, or to verbal suggestions, merely by drinking too much alcohol. This too was interpreted by some observers as indicating that psychological reflexes and inhibitions ought to be explained in physiological terms.

The label *ego*, used by Freud, was employed by numerous authors to designate inhibitory cerebral activity, although a more usual term was *will*. Theodule Ribot, in his book *Les Maladies de la Volonté*, notes that the will was popularly believed to initiate as well as inhibit movements. He argues, however, that "if one admits, with all contemporary physiologists, that the reflex is the base and type of all action," then it is specifically the inhibition of actions which must be accounted for; and therefore the will ought properly to be regarded as an instrument of inhibition.[27]

Since reflex behavior was thought to involve the automatic discharge of excitation along established pathways, the will, or ego, was commonly conceived as operating by diverting excitation away from these pathways. Thus, Freud's view of the neurodynamics of ego inhibition was widely shared.

Freud associates psychical primary processes—the reflex response to accumulated endogenous excitation—with infantile behavior; further, he regards the development of the inhibitory activity of the ego, and the emergence of psychical secondary processes, as characterizing maturation. Once again we are dealing with a popular concept. Karl Wernicke, in an 1874 paper, refers to several German authors holding similar views:

> According to Brücke and Lotze [Rudolph Lotze, professor of philosophy at Göttingen from 1844, and author of numerous books on psychophysiology] movements must be

separated into primary and secondary. The primary are the reflexive, which long precede consciousness in children; from these the child collects movement-images, which it utilizes in the conscious and voluntarily executed secondary movements.[28]

This is not exactly Freud's model. Freud does not distinguish between primary and secondary processes as, respectively, unconscious and conscious. Also, he regards both types of processes as utilizing learned motor images. Even more remote from Freud's thinking is Wernicke's attempt to interpret primary and secondary movements as involving separate parts of the brain—a thesis described by Wernicke as combining "the results of the physiological and philosophical deductions [of] Brücke and Lotze with conclusions [concerning the separate locations of conscious and unconscious cerebral activity] derived by Meynert from anatomical facts."[29] Yet there is indeed a close resemblance between Brücke and Lotze's formulation and Freud's model.

But, in view of the popularity of such formulations, which are found in numerous English and French works as well as in the German literature, it would be misleading to regard Freud's ideas as derived specifically from his teacher Brücke or from any other particular source. To observers who were oriented towards interpreting behavior in terms of reflexes and inhibitions, this view of infantile development was suggested by various phenomena. It was supported by everyday psychological observations, such as the observation, in child development, of a progressive capacity to suppress reflex responses to biological needs and a progressive ability to tolerate the pressure of these needs until conditions permit gratification. Physiological phenomena also suggested a pattern of development progressing from the dominance of primitive reflexes to the emergence of more complex forms of behavior. It was noted, for example, that newborn infants demonstrate numerous reflexes which are completely suppressed as new connections with the brain are established (through myelination). It was also known that anencephalic babies display normal neonatal behavior, indicating further that development involves the progressive assumption of control by the cortex over primitive patterns of reflex functioning.

Theodule Ribot, proceeding from both physiological and psychological observations, maintains in *Maladies de la Volonté* that

the newborn is, as described by Virchow, "a spinal animal." His activity is purely reflex; it is characterized by such a profusion of movements that the work of education will consist for a long time of suppressing or restraining the greatest number. . . .

Desire marks an ascending step from the reflex state to the voluntary state.

Ribot's use of *desire* resembles Freud's concept of primary processes:

We understand by desire the most elementary forms of the affective life. . . . Physiologically, they do not differ from reflexes of a complex order. . . . Their tendency to translate themselves into acts is immediate and irresistible, like that of the reflexes. In the natural state, and insofar as it is pure of alloy, desire tends to satisfy itself immediately. This is its law, it is inscribed in the organism. Small infants . . . furnish excellent examples. In the adult, desire is no longer in a natural state. Education, habit, reflection mutilate it or inhibit it.[30]

Other Ego Functions

The ego, according to Freud's model, does considerably more than simply prevent hallucinations and inhibit reflex responses to endogenous excitation. In the third section of the "Project," and in part of the first section, Freud discusses the psychophysiology of complex mental activities, and he regards these activities as further manifestations of ego function.

Experiences of satisfaction occur, in Freud's view, when there is first an "indication of reality" concerning a desired object—that is, a conscious perception of the object's actual presence—and the ego then permits a full Q discharge in the direction of the motor responses needed to grasp the object. Freud suggests that the ego also plays a role in arranging for the occurrence of particular indications of reality. When there is a perception which bears some resemblance to the desired object but does not coincide sufficiently to allow a full Q discharge and an experience of satisfaction—when, for example, there is a partial perception of the object, or a perception of the object at a distance— then a small Q current passes from the cathected neurones of the ego to the mnemic neurones which received the excitation of the perception. The latter neurones (group A) discharge the cathexis coming from the ego in the direction of facilitated pathways, and these pathways lead to a variety of mnemic images—associations of group A— including images of motor activity. The current from the ego to group

A acts in effect as a test current, which under optimal conditions leads to the cathexis of motor images whose execution in movements will so maneuver one's body as to yield an adequate perception of the desired object. This process is aided by a simultaneous small cathexis, by the ego, of the mnemic image of the desired object (group B). The simultaneous cathexes of groups A and B serve to facilitate connecting pathways. Freud offers the following example:

> Let us suppose, for instance, that the mnemic image wished for [by a child] is the image of the mother's breast and a front view of its nipple. . . . In the child's memory there is an experience, made by chance in the course of sucking, that with a particular head-movement the front image turns into the side image. The side image which is now seen leads to the [image of the] head-movement; an experiment shows that its counterpart must be carried out, and the perception of the front view is achieved.[31]

In this procedure, the ego began by, in effect, comparing and distinguishing between the perceived object and the desired object, and Freud refers to this ego work as the prototype of "judging." The process by which the ego cathects the facilitated pathways associated with the perceived object is regarded by Freud as the prototype of "thought." Freud does not fully explain the neurodynamics of these processes, nor does he explain the dynamics of various related mental processes alluded to in his discussion. But he argues that biological considerations, the necessity for satisfying physical needs, indicate that there must exist neural mechanisms resembling those which he proposes.

Freud writes in the "Project" that "the aim and end of all thought-processes is . . . to bring about a *state of identity*, the [converging] of a cathexis [Q], emanating from outside [i.e., a perception], into a neurone cathected from the ego [i.e., the mnemic image of a desired object]."[32] This suggests that, in Freud's view, all thought, however abstract and sophisticated, is ultimately geared to satisfying biological needs. Indeed, Freud explicitly asserts that "thought has a practical aim and a biologically established end."

The cathexis of perceptual images by the ego is not limited to those perceptions which bear some resemblance to desired objects. Freud suggests that the demand for satisfying biological needs requires that all perceptions attract some Q current from the ego, since the ego has no way of distinguishing, a priori, which perceptions might lead ultimately to an experience of satisfaction. This establishment of a Q current from the ego to the neurones of a perceptual image is viewed by Freud as the process of "attention." Attention is triggered by the indications of reality reaching the mnemic system (ψ) from the ω neurones (the neurones associated with consciousness). The dynamics of this process, the actual mechanism by which a current is established from ω to ψ , is acknowledged by Freud to be rather obscure.

If attention were not directed at a perception, the peripheral ψ neurones excited by the perception would contain only the Q received from the external stimulus via ϕ (the perceptual neurones). This excitation would be discharged according to established facilitations, but the process would be a limited one because of the smallness of Q: "This passage [of excitation] would probably soon come to an end, since the Q divides up and forthwith, in some near-by neurone, becomes too small to flow any further." When there is attention—that is, the establishment of a Q current from the ego—this additional Q furnished by the ego enables the thought process to be carried further: "It is certain that more and remoter neurones are cathected now than when there is a merely associative process without attention."[33] Even if this does not lead to an experience of satisfaction, the process still has biological value since new facilitations are developed which might be useful in transforming some future perception into an experience of satisfaction.

The thought process, as described by Freud, is dependent on the ability of the ego to generate small Q currents. Freud argues that the currents must be small because the ego cannot afford to deplete the stores of excitation needed for the execution of specific actions. In addition, large Q currents would simply overwhelm neural pathways in the manner of primary processes, would yield inappropriate reflex actions, and would render thought impossible. Freud suggests, however, that an explanation is required for how the highly cathected neurones of the ego are able to produce small currents. The explanation which he offers introduces a new concept, that of "bound states." The inhibitory power of the ego has been attributed to side-cathexes established by the cathected neurones which comprise the ego. These side-cathexes draw Q away from its passage along facilitated pathways. Freud now argues that the mutual side-cathexes of the ego neurones serve in effect to retain, or bind, excitation within the ego. As a result, currents emanating from the ego are, under ordinary circumstances, necessarily small. Freud concludes: "This bound state, which combines high cathexis with small current, would . . . characterize processes of thought mechanically."[34]

Freud's psychophysiology of higher mental processes once more resembles the speculations of numerous contemporary writers. Particularly popular was the notion that attention involves an expenditure of excitation by the ego (or will) and results in the facilitation of certain cerebral pathways related to current perceptions. This theme is developed extensively by Sigmund Exner in his *Entwurf zu einer physiologischen Erklärung der psychischen Erscheinungen* (1894), which contains a chapter on attention. Similar views are presented, for example, by the English physicians Henry Maudsley (*The Physiology of Mind* [1876]) and William Carpenter (*Principles of Mental Physiology* [1874]).[35] Attention was usually discussed in the context of inhibition, and it was argued that those pathways not facilitated by attention are, in effect, inhibited. This was Exner's approach, and was indeed the standard approach to the subject. But this line of thought is not pursued by Freud.

Freud bases his discussion of complex mental functions upon the premise that all mental activity is ultimately reducible to the quest for satisfaction of biological needs. This too was a common theme in contemporary psychology. Theodule Ribot, in *Psychologie des Sentiments* (1896), endorses this theory of mind and refers to numerous other nineteenth-century writers who presented similar views. Emphasis on the satisfaction of biological needs as the key to mental activity was prompted particularly by evolution theory. Evolutionary considerations indicated that complex mental functions must have developed out of primitive processes, and that these primitive processes were necessarily closely related to the basic requirements of the organism. Evolution also indicated that complex functions are essentially mechanisms for more efficiently procuring desired objects. Observations of infantile development reinforced this view. It was noted that the responsiveness of the infant is almost exclusively related to the demands of his physiological needs, and that more sophisticated functions emerge as variations of primitive mechanisms for attaining satisfaction. In Ribot's words:

> Let one consider . . . the myriads of animals who are only a bundle of needs for whom all psychology consists in finding food, in defending themselves, in propagating themselves: their senses (and many are reduced to only one) are tools, gross instruments, teleological arms in the service of their needs. . . . In man, is fetal life, or even that of the first months much different? Does it not consist almost entirely of needs, satisfied or not, and, consequently, of pleasures and pains. From the purely physiological point of view, cognition

[i.e., thought processes generally] appears not as a mistress, but as a servant [to biological needs].[36]

Freud suggests that development of the inhibitory processes of the ego can be understood in terms of the avoidance of unpleasure. Experiences of satisfaction are, of course, accompanied by a release of accumulated Q and a sensation of pleasure, and the ego mechanisms for achieving experiences of satisfaction therefore fit the description of serving to avoid unpleasure. But Freud argues that the ego works to avoid unpleasure in other ways as well.

Freud notes that if the mnemic image of a painful event is recathected—perhaps in a process of association triggered by some new experience—the memory of the painful event is accompanied by unpleasure. This presents a problem for Freud's model, since unpleasure indicates an increase in Q and it is not clear where, in the case of remembering, the additional Q comes from. An explanation is offered involving a new class of neurones:

> There must be "secretory" neurones which, when they are excited, cause the generation in the interior of the body of something which operates as a stimulus upon the endogenous paths of conduction to ψ –neurones which thus influence the production of endogenous [Q], and accordingly do not discharge [Q] but supply it in roundabout ways. We call these [secretory] neurones "key neurones."[37]

Freud proposes that these key neurones are excited when there is an exceptionally large Q in ψ. As painful experiences by definition involve the intrusion of a large Q into ψ, such experiences must, according to Freud's model, invariably be accompanied by the excitation of key neurones. This means that facilitations are invariably established between key neurones and the mnemic image of painful events. As a result, recathexis of such mnemic images leads to the excitation of key neurones, the development of new quotients of endogenous Q, and the generation of unpleasure.

But the ego can work to prevent this unpleasure, by inhibiting the passage of excitation from the mnemic image to the key neurones: "Let us suppose that A is a [painful] mnemic image and B a key neurone. . . . Then, if A is awakened . . . unpleasure would be released. . . . With an inhibitory action from [the ego] the release of unpleasure will turn out very slight and the nervous system will be spared the development and discharge of Q."[38] Freud suggests that ego inhibition of this sort has biological advantages. In an actual painful experience, the sensation of unpleasure and the reflex discharge of accumulated Q, perhaps in the form of some self-protective maneuver, would be appropriate. But when a painful experience is merely remembered, the development of unpleasure and the subsequent discharge of Q can be detrimental. Even when a painful experience actually reoccurs, a limited response might be desirable. Therefore an ego side-cathexis of appropriate magnitude, moderating key neurone excitation, might be advantageous. Indications of reality—excitations triggered by conscious perceptions in ω —enable the ego to distinguish between actual experiences and mere recathected memories.

This mechanism for avoiding the release of unpleasure is discussed in the first section of the "Project." It is considered again, although with a somewhat different emphasis, in section three. Freud has now introduced the concept of bound energy; and he suggests that the mnemic image of a painful idea gradually becomes bound to the ego, so that upon recathexis of the image only a limited amount of excitation is discharged from it. Freud does not refer again to the concept of "key neurones," but he offers no alternative explanation for how a recathected memory might release unpleasure.

Freud also proposes an additional ego mechanism for avoiding the unpleasure released upon recathexis of a painful memory. If, in the course of a process of thought, the test current emanating from the ego cathects the neurones of a painful mnemic image, the release of unpleasure which is triggered leads to a deflection of the Q current and a redirection of the thought process. Consequently, the thought pathway which is finally facilitated will circumvent the painful memory, and a subsequent recathexis of the same line of thought will similarly avoid that memory.

The avoidance of unpleasure is referred to in the "Project" as "defense." Freud introduces the term "primary defense," but its usage is rather ambiguous. Occasionally, "primary defense" would seem to denote only defense via primary processes—that is, the situation in which a painful perception, or the cathexis of a painful memory, results in a substantial accumulation of Q and sensation of unpleasure and immediately triggers a reflex discharge of Q. (A discharge in response to pain, whether brought about by a primary process or mediated by the ego, might take the form of some self-protective action; this would conform to the contemporary biological concept of defense as self-conserving responses to environmental, particularly predatory, threats.) However, in most references to "primary defense," the term clearly embraces Freud's two ego devices for dealing with unpleasure—the binding of painful memories to the ego, and the circumventing of such memories. Freud also speaks of "normal defense," which again refers to his two ego mechanisms. In the second section of the "Project," where the pathology of hysteria is considered, hysteria is regarded as involving "pathological defense," as distinguished from the primary or normal type.

The Pathogenesis of Hysteria

Section two of the "Project" is entitled "Psychopathology," and Freud probably intended to discuss all the neuroses, or at least all the neuropsychoses (hysteria, obsessions, and perhaps paranoia) in this section. But this plan was not completed. There is a heading A, "Psychopathology of Hysteria," but no corresponding B; and only hysteria is actually considered in the manuscript.

The first and third sections of the "Project," which are concerned primarily with the neurodynamics of normal ego activity, are largely a reworking of standard contemporary views. Freud's discussion in section two is an attempt to explain hysteria in terms of these popular concepts of psychophysiology.

Freud begins by considering what he calls "hysterical compulsions":

> Every observer of hysteria is struck in the first place by the fact that hysterical patients are subject to a *compulsion* which is exercised by *excessively intense ideas*. An idea will, for instance, emerge in consciousness with particular frequency without the passage [of events] justifying it; or the arousing of this idea will be accompanied by psychical consequences that are unintelligible. The emergence of the excessively intense idea brings with it consequences which, on the one hand, cannot be suppressed and, on the other hand, cannot be understood—release of affect, motor innervations, impediments.[39]

While "excessively intense ideas," or "idées fixes" as they were usually designated, received considerable attention in the hysteria literature, Freud had not placed any special emphasis on them in his previous discussions of hysterical symptoms. On the contrary, he had consistently emphasized the somatic symptoms of the disease. In his early papers, during the years following his contact with Charcot, he argued that hysterical symptoms frequently have an ideational source—a view consistent with Charcot's model, which interpreted hysterical symptoms as the result of suggestions occurring during autohypnotic states. But Freud regarded the underlying pathogenic ideas as most often unconscious, and he believed that their clinical manifestations were essentially somatic. Freud's emphasis on somatic symptoms became even greater upon his development of the defense theory, largely because he then believed that such symptoms are specifically characteristic of hysteria and serve to distinguish hysteria from other defense neuroses. Freud argued that repression yields hysteria only in people who possess a "capacity for conversion" which facilitates the conversion into somatic symptoms of affect derived from repressed ideas. Freud's clinical discussions during this period reveal that he believed that such somatic symptoms have a psychological rationale and do not simply entail some random expenditure of affect. But, again, he regarded the ideas underlying somatic abnormalities in hysteria as typically unconscious.

Freud emphasizes mental symptoms, or "excessively intense ideas," in the "Project" because he wishes to discuss hysterical symptoms as the consequence of abnormal thought processes. Since compulsive ideas obviously entail some sort of peculiar thinking, they provide greater evidence for such processes than do somatic symptoms—for which the ideational basis, being generally unconscious, has to be inferred—and can therefore serve as a more secure foundation for his discussion. (An example of an idée fixe, or compulsive hysterical idea, would be Anna O.'s insistence, during one period of her illness, that she tell Breuer a daily Hans Christian Andersen–type story.)

Freud notes that excessively intense ideas occur normally, but he argues that in hysteria they are of a special nature. In normal situations such ideas can be accounted for in terms of "strong and justifiable motives." But in hysteria the compulsive ideas are typically unintelligible and apparently absurd. Analysis, however, offers an explanation of hysterical compulsion. Freud gives the following example:

> Before the analysis, A is an excessively intense idea, which forces its way into consciousness too often, and each time gives rise to weeping. The subject does not know why he weeps at A; he regards it as absurd but cannot prevent it.
>
> After the analysis, it has been discovered that there is an idea B, which justifiably gives rise to weeping and which justifiably recurs frequently. . . . The effect of B is not absurd; it is intelligible to the subject. . . .
>
> B stands in a particular relation to A.
>
> For there has been an occurrence which consisted of

> B+A. A was an incidental circumstance; B was appropriate
> for producing the lasting effect. The reproduction of this
> event in memory has now taken a form of such a kind that it
> is as though A had stepped into B's place. A has become a
> substitute, a *symbol* for B.[40]

Symbol formation also occurs normally. But normally one is aware of
the relationship between the symbol and that which it symbolizes: "The
knight who fights for his lady's glove knows . . . that the glove owes its
importance to the lady." In hysteria, however, B is repressed from
consciousness and the patient does not know the connection between A
and B. The fact that A is actually an unconscious substitute for a
repressed idea explains why the special role of A in mental life appears
so unintelligible prior to analysis.

Freud argues that repression is a constant factor in neuropsychotic
symptom formation and is undoubtedly the key to the development of
hysterical compulsions. He notes that, once the repressed idea is uncovered, a compulsion is not merely explained but is also resolved.

Freud goes on to observe that it is invariably distressful ideas, ideas
associated with unpleasure, that are repressed. This suggests to him
that repression might be related to the normal defense mechanisms of
the ego for dealing with painful memories. In particular, Freud has
proposed in section one of the "Project"—where he discusses "normal
defense"—that, if a current of thought emanating from the ego comes
across a mnemic image which releases unpleasure, the thought is immediately diverted and channeled in another direction. The analogy
between this mechanism and hysterical repression is supported by the
observation that repressed ideas, even after being brought into consciousness, often remain unintegrated and excluded from thought processes. For example, a patient who acknowledges the occurrence of a
previously repressed event may still isolate that event in his consciousness and refuse to acknowledge its psychological importance or its
significance for his illness. A resistance must be overcome before the
memory can fully enter into normal trains of thought.

But the outcome of hysterical repression clearly differs from that
of normal defense. Memories which trigger normal defense are never
so thoroughly eliminated from consciousness that they cannot be
aroused by a fresh perception. In hysteria, however, perceptions which
ought to stir the repressed memory arouse instead some symbol of it,
such as an hysterical compulsive idea. Further, in normal defense the
ego works by inhibiting the passage of excitation to and from the

mnemic image. In hysteria, the compulsive idea, the symbol of the repressed material, is typically associated with considerable unpleasure and it seems as though a full quota of Q has been reflexly diverted from the repressed idea to its symbol—a pattern more closely resembling primary processes than ego functions.

Freud considers the possibility that the "pathological defense" of hysteria is simply the response of the psyche to exceptionally distressing ideas. But he notes that the repressed memories are invariably sexual, and he asserts: "it is quite impossible to suppose that distressing sexual affects so greatly exceed all other unpleasurable affects in intensity. It must be another characteristic of sexual ideas that can [account for repression, or pathological defense]."[41] Most of section two of the "Project" is devoted to establishing what this special characteristic of sexual ideas is and demonstrating how it works to bring about repression.

In the ensuing discussion, Freud presents his new theory that the basic pathogenic factor in hysteria is a sexual trauma during childhood. But he notes that the illness does not emerge at the time of this trauma. On the contrary, it is only at some point after puberty that hysteria develops, triggered by an event reminiscent of the childhood sexual experience. Freud offers the example of a woman suffering from an hysterical compulsion of "not being able to go into shops alone." Analysis revealed that when she was eight years old she was sexually assaulted on two occasions by a shopkeeper whose store she had entered alone. However, her hysteria did not begin at this time. Her symptom emerged only some years later; during therapy she associated its onset with a related, but comparatively innocuous, incident which occurred when she was twelve.

But, in Freud's view, repression—the pathological defense mechanism whereby a large quota of Q is reflexly diverted from an unpleasant idea to some symbol of that idea—leads immediately to hysterical symptoms, with the symptoms being the symbols of the repressed material. He therefore concludes that the observed delay in symptom formation in hysteria must be due to a delay in the repression of the primary childhood trauma. Freud accounts for this by suggesting that the unpleasure which characterizes the recollection of the event and triggers the repression did not accompany the actual occurrence of the event. This strange circumstance, in which the memory generates more unpleasure than the experience itself, is related by Freud to the fact that puberty has intervened between event and reminiscence.

Freud does not dwell on the problem of how puberty manages to transform a neutral experience into a recollection charged with unpleasure, but the "Project" does indicate the type of psychophysiological process he had in mind. Freud regarded sexual excitation as being based ultimately on the discharge of sexual toxins, presumably by the genitalia. These toxins stimulate the nervous pathways leading from the genitals, thereby generating somatic sexual excitation. A sexually arousing experience would operate by triggering the nerves which travel to the toxin-producing cells, inducing the discharge of toxin and the development of somatic sexual excitation. This model is comparable to Freud's scheme concerning unpleasant experiences and key neurones. Freud had suggested that the recathexis of a painful memory leads to excitation of certain secretory, or key, neurones which "cause the generation in the interior of the body of something which operates upon the endogenous paths of conduction to ψ ." As a result, large quantities of Q are generated and there is a sensation of unpleasure. Freud, in fact, refers to the analogy between the mechanisms of unpleasure and of sexuality in his discussion of key neurones: "Support is lent to this puzzling but indispensible hypothesis [of key neurones] by what happens in the case of sexual release."[42]

Freud maintains that the infantile sexual experiences which underlie hysteria are not, in general, overtly painful. He suggests that they are typically neutral, and sometimes even pleasurable. Consequently, these experiences would not lead to the facilitation of pathways between their mnemic image and key neurones; and their recollection would not yield unpleasure via such pathways. There can also be no facilitation of pathways between the mnemic image of these childhood events and sexual secretory cells, as the latter are not developed until puberty. Therefore, these experiences, and their recollection prior to puberty, are not accompanied by sexual excitation.

However, once the sexual secretory cells are functioning, any subsequent remembering of the childhood trauma does elicit sexual excitation. Such recollections are usually not long in coming, and can be expected to occur shortly after the onset of puberty. But exposure to large quantities of sexual excitation is not typical at this age, and the child has not yet developed the psychological mechanisms needed to cope with this excitation. Freud has argued earlier, in drafts sent to Fliess, that the inability to deal with quantities of somatic sexual excitation is the basis of anxiety neurosis, and he now suggests that anxiety is generated in the present situation. Freud writes of the patient who had been assaulted by a shopkeeper: "The memory [at age twelve] aroused what it was certainly not able to at the time [of the assault], a *sexual release*, which was transfomed into anxiety."[43] But accumulations of excitation also cause unpleasure, particularly when there is difficulty in discharging the excitation. This is the source of the unpleasure which, upon postpubertal recollection of the childhood experience, induces defense.

An explanation is still required for why it is specifically pathological defense, or repression, which is induced. Freud proposes that pathological defense is generated by the mere circumstance of a neutral experience becoming a painful memory. According to Freud, such a circumstance arises rarely, and is in fact a rather unique characteristic of prepubertal sexual experiences. Consequently, his theory would account for the exclusive role of infantile sexual trauma in the pathogenesis of hysteria. The last passages of the section are concerned with the neurodynamics of pathological defense. Freud suggests that, in order for normal defense to develop, attention must be directed to the first release of unpleasure by a painful experience. If attention is present, some of the excitation which underlies the sensation of unpleasure will be absorbed by the ego, and will be applied to the construction of side-cathexes to inhibit the passage of further Q currents to and from the painful mnemic image. A recathexis of the image might again release unpleasure, but less will be released than on the first occasion. Moreover, the ego can easily strengthen its side-cathexes until defense reaches an adequate level. However, the ego is guided in its direction of attention—that is, in its discharge of small test currents—primarily by indications of reality, indications of the actual presence of objects, from ω, the neurones underlying consciousness. As a result, attention is directed particularly towards perceptions. Therefore, in situations where the initial release of unpleasure is triggered by a memory rather than by a perception, the unpleasure is not accompanied by ego attention and normal defense never begins to develop. The result is pathological defense or repression: unpleasure is generated with every recathexis of the memory; and, in the absence of ego defense mechanisms, the quota of Q underlying the unpleasure is discharged by a reflex primary process—perhaps being diverted to another mnemic image which becomes the symbol of the painful idea.

In this discussion Freud has proposed solutions for all those problems which had motivated his excursion into psychophysiology. He establishes a distinction between repression and inhibition, or pathological and normal defense, and he offers an explanation for why only infantile sexual traumas can induce hysteria. Further, the accumulation of somatic sexual excitation is assigned a crucial role in repression, thus enabling Freud to explain why hysterical patients are so often found to suffer from anxiety neurosis as well. Finally, the significance which he attributes to somatic sexual excitation in hysteria points towards a general theory of the neuroses based upon the role of somatic sexual excitation in each of the neurotic syndromes.

But Freud has obviously presented hypotheses for which neurophysiology offered very little justification. By proceeding from basic principles, he apparently hoped to establish that his proposals were at least neurodynamically sound; but the attempt at a rigorous approach is abandoned by section two, and there is little to demonstrate the feasibility of his models. On the contrary, there are numerous internal inconsistencies. For several months after writing the "Project," Freud was alternately doubtful and optimistic about the prospect of resolving these difficulties and constructing a plausible physiological explanation of repression. In the letter which accompanied the manuscript (October 8, 1895), Freud wrote to Fliess that "the mechanical explanation is not coming off." But then, on October 20, he informed Fliess:

> One strenuous night last week . . . the barriers suddenly lifted, the veils dropped, and it was possible to see from the details of neurosis all the way to the very conditioning of consciousness. Everything fell into place. . . . The three systems of neurones, the "free" and "bound" states of quantity, the primary and secondary processes, . . . the two biological rules of attention and defence, . . . the state of the psychosexual group, the sexual determination of repression, . . . the whole thing held together, and still does . . . .
>
> If I had waited a fortnight before setting it all down for you it would have been so much clearer.[44]

Some weeks later the doubts once more emerged, and Freud wrote of his intention to put aside his psychophysiological speculations. But on January 1, 1896, he sent Fliess several pages of revisions to the "Project," dealing with the relative positions of ω and ψ neurones within the nervous system.[45]

It appears, however, that shortly after this last letter Freud's misgivings about his speculations finally led him to abandon his pursuit of a physiology of repression. He perhaps continued to work sporadically on the formulations of the "Project" for a few months longer; there are comments in his correspondence from 1896 which, although ambiguous, seem to refer to such work. But there is no further explicit mention of the "Project" or its psychophysiological theories.

8. Beyond the Seduction Theory

Following his abandonment of the "Project," Freud once again emphasized psychological interpretations of neurotic phenomena. As in his earliest papers on hysteria, he coupled this emphasis on psychology with a continued insistence upon the ultimate need for physiological explanations of some aspects of the neuroses; in particular, he now maintained that a comprehensive theory of the neuroses could not be formulated without a greater understanding of sexual physiology. However, he continued to focus his own efforts on his psychological explanations of the neuroses, and, over the next decade (1896–1905), he greatly modified and elaborated these explanations. Most importantly, he discarded the seduction theory, developed new concepts regarding childhood sexuality, and radically revised his views on the psychological mechanisms of symptom formation in the neuroses.

The Ongoing Physiological Dimension: Sexual Physiology and the Concept of "Sexual Toxins"

After the "Project," Freud's further references to the need for physiological insights into certain aspects of the neuroses usually touched upon questions of sexual physiology. Those problems which had served as motivation for the "Project" still remained unsolved, and Freud continued to believe that only sexual physiology could provide the solutions. He still viewed neurasthenia and anxiety neurosis as involving abnormalities in the disposition of somatic sexual excitation. Also, he still deduced, from the clinical similarities among the various neuroses and from the frequent combination of neuroses in individual patients, that somatic sexual excitation must also play a central role in the psychoneuroses.* He therefore continued to believe that a physiology of somatic sexual excitation would ultimately be required for a comprehensive understanding of these diseases. Most importantly, Freud continued to maintain that only such a physiology could explain how puberty is able to change a neutral or even pleasurable experience into an unpleasant memory, thereby leading to repression. Freud wrote in "Draft K" (January 1, 1896): "So long as there is no correct theory of the sexual process, the question of the origin of the unpleasure operating in repression remains unanswered."[1]

Freud subsequently suggested that the body's production of chemical substances related to sexual functioning, or "sexual toxins," is the key to the physiology of sexual processes, and he argued repeatedly that these toxins are also the key to a physiology of the neuroses.

Theories relating neurological and psychiatric abnormalities to the operation of endogenous "toxins" were quite common during the latter part of the nineteenth century—a trend noted by Freud in a book review written in 1895, where he refers to the "hitherto popular [hypotheses] that [certain nervous diseases] involve a toxification."[2] Toxins, both foreign and endogenous, were commonly identified as the cause of disease processes throughout medicine at this time, and the general popularity of such theories was undoubtedly an important factor in shaping the views of neuropsychiatrists. But probably the major inspiration for such theories in neuropsychiatry was observations of the neurological and psychiatric changes caused by intoxicants such as alcohol, hashish, and opiates. The similarities between the effects of these drugs and the symptoms of various neuropsychiatric disorders strongly suggested to observers that the latter might be the result of some autointoxication. A particularly common view was that endogenous toxins, or "autointoxicants," are the residue of normal metabolic processes, and that they become pathogenic when they are allowed to accumulate, either because of improper excretion or because of overproduction. For example, many writers attributed neurasthenia to overexertion, and they frequently proposed that this overwork leads to neuroses by inducing excessive metabolic activity in muscles and nerves, which in turn causes an excess production of either muscular or neural metabolic residues. According to this thesis, the accumulated metabolic prod-

---

*The term *psychoneuroses,* designating hysteria, obsessions, and related neuroses, was first used by Freud in the "Project." By the end of 1896, *psychoneuroses* had replaced the earlier term *neuro-psychoses.*

ucts hinder normal nervous system functioning and in this way induce the symptoms of neurasthenia.

The popularity of these theories of autointoxification is indicated by the extensive contemporary literature on urinalysis as a tool for research into neuropsychiatric disorders. It was hoped that abnormalities in the excretion of metabolic residues would be discovered in the urine of neuropsychiatric patients, thereby yielding insight into the chemical processes underlying their diseases.

The various discussions of neurosis- and psychosis-inducing toxins in the neuropsychiatric literature did not typically attribute any special importance to sexuality or identify sexual toxins as the cause of disease processes. Nevertheless, these theories probably exerted some influence on Freud's views concerning the role of sexual toxins in the neuroses. Freud did, at any rate, appeal to the similarities between neurotic symptoms and the symptoms of narcotic intoxication to support his toxicological interpretation of the neuroses.

A more important factor, however, in shaping Freud's notions about sexual toxins was contemporary work in endocrinology, particularly work on thyroid function and Graves' disease. Some writers on Graves' disease—while noting, of course, standard signs and symptoms such as exophthalmia and other ophthalmic abnormalities, thyroid goiter, excessive perspiration, rapid pulse, and elevated metabolic rate—had paid particular attention to neurological and psychological changes and had suggested that the disease is essentially a nervous system abnormality. Autopsies yielded no pathoanatomical changes in the nervous system, but it was proposed that the syndrome is a neurosis—that is, a disease involving abnormal nervous function without anatomical changes. The nervousness, irritability, and emotional lability found in Graves' disease appeared to resemble hysterical symptoms, and this similarity was cited in support of the neurosis theory. Charcot and his coworkers at the Salpetrière seem to have been the major proponents of this view. But in 1887 this thesis was challenged by Paul Moebius, a Leipzig neurologist, in a paper which was among the earliest to suggest that Graves' disease is actually caused by pathological changes in the thyroid. In a second article, appearing in 1891, Moebius developed his thyroid theory further and offered a lengthy rebuttal of the neurosis formula. He was willing to concede that Graves' disease seemed to strike people with "unstable nervous systems" and is found primarily in "neuropathic families," but he insisted that it could be understood only in terms of abnormalities of the thyroid.[3]

Surgical removal of goitrous thyroids had been practiced for some years, and it had in many cases produced a syndrome that was recognized as a form of a naturally occurring disease first described in 1874 and labelled *myxedema* in 1878. The surgical production of myxedema soon served to establish the view that the naturally occurring disease must be caused by thyroid insufficiency. A decade later, Moebius constructed his argument concerning the role of the thyroid in Graves' disease on the basis of the clinical parallels between Graves' disease and myxedema:

> If one compares [Graves'] disease with myxedema, then one finds a number of coinciding points. Both diseases are chronic, as a rule feverless, lead to cachexia [i.e., wasting], are usually fatal, affect mostly middle-aged women. The thyroid is diseased in both, heart activity is changed, psychic behavior suffers, and disturbances are displayed in the skin.

But, Moebius continued:

> On the other hand, the picture of myxedema is in a certain sense the opposite of [Graves'] disease. In one the thyroid is enlarged, in the other shrunken; in one a quickening, in the other a slowing of heart activity, . . . in one increased mental excitement and nervous irritability, in the other apathy and slowness.[4]

Moebius concluded that, since myxedema is due to a loss of thyroid function, Graves' disease must involve overactivity of the thyroid, and he appears to have been the first to offer this theory. In his second paper Moebius cited additional evidence for this view, including recent indications that surgical removal of the thyroid can induce amelioration of Graves' disease.

There was, at this time, no very clear notion of what exactly the thyroid does. But during the 1880s numerous experiments were undertaken involving the implantation of thyroid substance and the injection of thyroid extracts, both in animals whose thyroids had been surgically removed and in humans suffering from myxedema, and the success of these experiments in resolving the symptoms of thyroid insufficiency was enough to popularize the notion that normal thyroid activity must be based on chemicals secreted by the gland. Many who endorsed Moebius's views therefore interpreted the symptoms of Graves' disease as toxicological effects caused by excessive secretion of thyroid toxins.

Moebius had written extensively on hysteria and his work was highly regarded by Freud, who at one point refers to him as "the best mind among the neurologists." Freud first cites Moebius's work on Graves' disease in his translation of Charcot's *Tuesday Lectures* (1892–1894). In a footnote to a case presentation of a patient suffering from the disease, Freud criticizes Charcot for his overemphasis of heredity:

> [Charcot's] over-estimation of the part played by the factor of heredity may also explain the fact that, in dealing with Graves' disease, Charcot does not mention the organ in whose changes, as weighty indications tell us, we must look for the true cause of the affection. I refer, of course, to the thyroid gland and . . . I may mention Moebius's excellent paper on Graves' disease in the *Deutsche Zeitschrift für Nervenheilkunde*, 1, (1891).[5]

When, in 1894 and 1895, Freud began tracing the pathogenesis of his four major neuroses—neurasthenia, anxiety neurosis, hysteria, and obsessional neurosis—to sexual experiences and the disposition of somatic sexual excitation, rather than to hereditary factors, the role of thyroid toxins in Graves' disease appeared to provide a useful prototype for a physiology of the neuroses. It was, of course, well known during this period that various organs, including the genitals, produce secretions which profoundly influence sexuality, so that there was considerable basis for hypothesizing the existence of toxins responsible for generating somatic sexual excitation. The secretory function of the testes had been postulated by authors for over a century, and beginning in 1849 numerous experiments offered support for this view. Physiologists noted, for example, that if an animal is castrated and its testes implanted in some other part of the body, normal sexual development might still occur—indicating that the operative factor is a chemical substance secreted by the organ.

Organs other than the genitals were also identified as producing toxins which influence sexual life. By 1886, the syndrome of acromegaly had been clearly associated with abnormalities of pituitary secretion, and the absence of menstruation, loss of libido, and atrophy of the gonads which accompany the disease were interpreted as indicating that pituitary toxins play a vital role in sexual development. Thyroid enlargement during puberty, menstruation, and pregnancy had been observed for centuries, and the thyroid had frequently been related to the female genitalia. When experiments suggested that the thyroid operates primarily as a secretory organ, many physicians assumed that its secretions must play a role in sexual physiology. This view was reinforced by the observation that women suffering from myxedema dis-

play prolonged and excessive menstrual bleeding, and that cretinism—
a syndrome which had for some years been associated with myxedema
and had similarly been ascribed to thyroid insufficiency—is accompanied by retarded sexual development. There was thus extensive material suggesting the plausibility of a toxicological theory of sexual excitation.[6] But Graves' disease provided, in addition, an example of toxins
actually causing symptoms which resemble those of the neuroses (e.g.,
nervousness, irritability, emotional lability). It therefore, in Freud's
view, supplied the strongest evidence that the pathogenesis of the neuroses might be traced to the activity of toxins.

In a discussion of anxiety written in April, 1896, Freud remarks:
"I have always regarded anxiety neurosis, and the neuroses generally,
as primarily toxic states, and I have often thought of the similarity of
the symptoms in anxiety neurosis and [Graves'] disease."[7] During the
next ten years, he repeatedly cites thyroid function and Graves' disease as models when arguing that a comprehensive explanation of the
neuroses must take into account the physiology of sexual toxins.

Freud's exchanges with his friend Wilhelm Fliess also influenced
his views on sexual toxins. The theories associating neuroses with somatic sexual excitation were developed independently of Fliess, and the
connection between somatic sexual excitation and sexual toxins was also
made independently. In his correspondence with Fliess, Freud refers
repeatedly to the toxicological approach as his own idea. However,
Fliess also constructed theories concerning sexual toxins and his work
contributed several important details to Freud's model. Further, Fliess's
work served to convince Freud of the correctness of his own toxicological interpretations, and Freud on several occasions expressed the hope
that Fliess's contributions might finally render a physiology of the neuroses feasible. In March, 1896, he wrote to Fliess: "I think I am just
beginning to understand the anxiety neurosis now; . . . it is a toxic state
the physiological foundation for which is an organic process. It is to be
hoped that the unknown organ (the thyroid or whatever it may be) will
not remain unknown to you for long." And several months later:
"Chemical factors, etc.—perhaps you may supply me with solid ground
on which I shall be able to give up explaining things psychologically
and start finding a firm basis in physiology!"[8]

Fliess's theories concerning sexual toxins appear in a book entitled
Die Beziehungen zwischen Nase und weiblichen Geschlechtsorganen, published
in 1897.[9] In earlier papers Fliess had presented clinical evidence that
nasal abnormalities can be the source of reflex neuroses; that is, such
abnormalities can cause physiological changes in the nerves innervating

the nose, and these changes can then be reflected throughout the nervous system. This notion had received considerable attention in the otolaryngology literature of the period. But concepts of reflex neuroses, including interpretations of hysteria and neurasthenia as reflex neuroses, were most often associated with genital abnormalities, and Fliess had therefore considered the possibility of a special relationship between the nose and the genitals. He had cited phenomena such as the swelling of the nasal turbinates (bony protuberances in the nose) during menstruation, and cases in which menstruation is accompanied by nose bleeds, as evidence of such a relationship.[10] In his 1897 book Fliess again argues for this connection between the nose and the genitals, but he now discusses links between the genitals and other organ systems as well.

Fliess maintains that a large number of both normal and pathological processes demonstrate cyclic patterns, and that in menstruating women these cycles coincide with the menstrual cycle. He concludes that cyclic changes, based upon factors which are particularly related to sexual life, play a dominant role in all of human physiology. Fliess supports his argument with numerous case histories of cyclic diseases. He proposes that there are two basic cycles, one characteristic of females and the other of males. Both types are found in everyone, but one type dominates according to one's sex. Fliess further insists that these cyclic patterns are present through childhood and do not simply emerge with sexual maturity. He suggests that in childhood they play an important role in determining patterns of growth.

These cycles, according to Fliess, are based upon periodically secreted toxins. He notes, as evidence for the plausibility of this theory, that several secretory organs are known to produce toxins which have widespread physiological effects and bear a special relationship to sexuality. Fliess discusses the pituitary gland and the sexual symptoms of acromegaly, and he also mentions links between sexuality and the thyroid, including sexual changes in myxedema and Graves' disease.

Several syndromes are cited by Fliess as offering particular evidence for the existence and the physiological importance of periodic sexual toxins, and here Fliess draws extensively on Freud's work. In a discussion of anxiety, for example, Fliess refers to the anxiety which accompanies various intoxications—such as acute nicotine poisoning or colchicine poisoning—as evidence that anxiety is caused by the action of toxins. But he points out that Freud has succeeded in tracing anxiety to somatic sexual excitation. Finally, Fliess argues that anxiety generally occurs in cycles. (He notes parenthetically that

Freud had been challenged by Leopold Loewenfeld to reconcile this widely acknowledged cyclic pattern with Freud's theory of the sexual etiology of anxiety neurosis.)[11] Fliess concludes that there is thus impressive evidence for the role of periodic sexual toxins in the generation of anxiety.

Fliess also discusses migraine headaches. Migraines had been the topic of numerous exchanges between Fliess and Freud.[12] Freud's approach was to relate the headaches to sexual excitation, with a pathogenesis analogous to that of anxiety neurosis. In a draft on migraines, which he sent to Fliess probably in early 1895 ("Draft I"), he offered various observations linking the headaches with sexuality: they are rare in children and in the elderly, they coincide with menstruation in many women, they typically cease during pregnancy. He also noted that they occur periodically. Freud concluded: "This would seem to show that migraine is a toxic effect produced by the sexual stimulating substance when this cannot find sufficient discharge."[13] Fliess, in connecting migraines with his concept of periodic sexual toxins, presents essentially the same arguments as Freud developed in his draft.

Freud read the manuscript of Fliess's book in March, 1896, and believed that his friend was making important progress towards a comprehensive theory of sexual toxins. He attempted to utilize Fliess's concept of periodicity on numerous occasions during the next few years. Freud was particularly enthusiastic about Fliess's notion of bisexuality, his assertion that both male and female toxins are present in everyone; this concept became part of Freud's own theory of sexual toxins.

The influence of Fliess's models can be seen, for example, in a letter written by Freud in December, 1896: "I cannot suppress a suspicion that the distinction between neurasthenia and anxiety neuroses, which I detected clinically, is connected with the existence of the two [male and female periodic] substances."[14]

Remarks concerning sexual toxins are found throughout Freud's work during the decade after his writing of the "Project." But, while he continually returned to the subject of sexual toxins and regarded it as potentially crucial to a comprehensive understanding of the neuroses, Freud never actually attempted to formulate a theory of sexual physiology and its role in the neuroses. He continued to regard such physiological theorizing as far too speculative to yield very fruitful results in the foreseeable future, and he persisted instead in concentrating his efforts on modifying and elaborating his psychological interpretations of the neuroses.

Freud's Clinical Explanation of the Neuroses

In several letters written late in 1895, when he was still struggling with the physiological theories of the "Project," Freud contrasts his difficulties in developing a physiological explanation of the neuroses with his apparent success in formulating a valid and comprehensive "clinical explanation." He was referring primarily to his theory that the key factor in obsessions and hysteria is some sexual trauma which occurs during childhood and is subsequently repressed. Freud believed that his clinical experience had firmly established this theory, and that it was secure despite whatever difficulties he might have in elucidating the physiological mechanism of repression:"I have bundled the [psychophysiological] drafts into a drawer. . . . But the clinical explanation of hysteria still stands; it is beautiful and simple, and perhaps I shall pull myself together and write it down for you soon." Elsewhere, upon acknowledging the inadequacy of his physiological models, he remarks: "Perhaps in the end I may have to learn to content myself with the clinical explanation of the neuroses."[15]

As Freud abandoned his efforts to construct comprehensive physiological theories, he concentrated increasingly on elaborating this clinical explanation. In particular, he devoted his attention to clarifying the relationship between the patients' infantile sexual traumas and their subsequent neurotic symptoms.

When Freud first formulated his theory of infantile sexual encounters in 1895, he distinguished between the etiology of hysteria and obsessions by suggesting that the former is the consequence of a passive, either indifferent or painful, childhood event and the latter the result of an active, pleasurable experience. Freud believed that the patient suffering from obsessions had initially been the passive victim of a sexual assault, and that this had resulted in a premature sexual awakening and had subsequently led to his induction of another child into sexual play. But he insisted that it is specifically the latter experience which accounts for the child's later obsessional neurosis. This distinction between the causes of obsessions and hysteria appeared to be the pattern displayed in his analysis of neurotic patients. In addition, the etiology assigned to obsessions seemed to offer some insight into the source of specific obsessional symptoms. Feelings of personal inadequacy and guilt were among the most prominent symptoms displayed by Freud's obsessional patients, and he interpreted these symptoms as an echo of emotions associated with the patients' repressed memories of their childhood sexual assaults on other children.

In the "Project," Freud proposed that repression occurs only when the memory of an event generates more unpleasure than the event itself. He insisted that this can happen solely in the case of infantile sexual experiences: because of the peculiar somatic and psychological changes which accompany puberty, an infantile sexual encounter that was only slightly unpleasant, or neutral, or even enjoyable, might nevertheless generate extensive unpleasure when remembered later. Although he failed in his attempt to develop a physiological explanation for this phenomenon, Freud nevertheless continued to endorse the model, and the formulation is repeated on numerous occasions in the year following his writing of the "Project." With regard to obsessions, Freud maintains that the unpleasure which develops after puberty and triggers repression manifests itself primarily in the form of self-reproaches for childhood aggressiveness. He suggests that the sense of worthlessness and guilt which characterizes the syndrome is a transformation of these feelings of self-reproach.

This interpretation of the relationship between pathogenic event and subsequent symptoms in obsessional neurosis is much more straightforward than any such relationship that Freud could define between the source and the symptoms of hysteria, and he remarks on several occasions that the clinical course of obsessions presents a clearer picture to him than does that of hysteria. Consequently, in his various discussions of the neuropsychoses (or psychoneuroses) during this period, he refers primarily to obsessional neuroses to illustrate the mechanisms of symptom formation. The most important of these discussions are contained in a draft sent to Fliess on New Year's Day, 1896 (Draft K), and in a paper submitted for publication in February, 1896, entitled "Further Remarks on the Neuro-Psychoses of Defence."

In both "Draft K" and "Further Remarks on the Neuro-Psychoses of Defence," Freud's references to obsessional neurosis appear in the context of a new general model of symptom formation. Freud argued in the "Project" that the repression of pathogenic infantile experiences begins very shortly after puberty. He maintained that some new event which reminds one of the childhood encounter invariably occurs without much delay following the onset of puberty, and that this recollection of the infantile experience releases unpleasure and induces repression. But Freud also observed that the full clinical picture of hysteria generally emerges only some years after puberty. Therefore, Freud subsequently distinguished between two separate periods of repression: one—beginning in puberty and following upon the initial repression of the pathogenic memory—during which there are no symptoms or only comparatively minor ones; and another period comprising the time of manifest neurosis. Prior to his development of the defense concept, Freud had viewed hysterical symptoms as the expression of ideas which are constantly being inhibited by normal people, and he had spoken of hysteria as involving the "failure" of inhibition. With the formulation of the defense theory, he insisted instead that the ideas repressed in hysteria are of a special nature, exceptionally distressing to the ego; he argued that, even though these ideas manifest themselves as hysterical symptoms, the fact that the ideas per se remain unconscious ought to be interpreted as the "success" of repression. Now, however, Freud refers to the time between the initial repression of the infantile experience and the outbreak of serious neurosis as the period of successful repression, and he perceives the development of significant illness as marking the "return of the repressed." At this point the ego can no longer effectively prevent all expression of the repressed material, and a compromise emerges whereby the ideas remain unconscious but gain symbolic expression in the form of symptoms. In "Draft K," Freud offers the following sketch of the natural history of a psychoneurosis:

> The course taken by the illness in neuroses of repression is in general always the same: (1) The [childhood] sexual experience (or series of experiences) which is traumatic and premature and is to be repressed. (2) Its repression on some later occasion [following puberty] which arouses a memory of it; at the same time the formation of a [generally benign] primary symptom. (3) A stage of successful defence, which is equivalent to health except for the existence of the primary symptom. (4) The stage in which the repressed ideas return, and in which, during the struggle between them and the ego, new symptoms are formed which are those of the illness proper.[16]

Obsessional neurosis provides the major illustration of this pathological process. In "Further Remarks on the Neuro-Psychoses of Defence" (1896), Freud offers his sketch of an obsessional neurosis: "In a first period . . . the events occur which contain the germ of the later neurosis . . . . This period is brought to a close by the advent of sexual 'maturation.' . . . A self-reproach now becomes attached to the memory of [the infantile] pleasurable actions." This is followed by repression and the formation of the relatively innocuous primary symptom:

> Conscientiousness, shame and self-distrust are symptoms of this kind, with which the third period begins—the period of *apparent* health, but actually, of successful defence.

The next period, that of the illness, is characterized by
the *return of the repressed memories.* . . . The re-activated memories, however, and the self-reproaches formed from them
never re-emerge into consciousness unchanged: what become conscious as obsessional ideas and affects, and take the
place of the pathogenic memories so far as conscious life is
concerned, are structures in the nature of a *compromise* between the repressed ideas and the repressing ones.[17]

Two types of obsessional symptoms are generated in this way. The
first type, obsessional ideas, involves a distorted consciousness of the
infantile memory: major aspects of the memory are replaced by contemporary material of a nonsexual nature, and this altered recollection
becomes the obsessive idea. A second type of symptom involves the
representation in consciousness of the repressed affect—the self-
reproach—rather than the repressed memory. Again there is a distortion, and some other unpleasant affect such as shame or anxiety is
substituted for self-reproach. Freud insists that psychoanalysis is capable of tracing these obsessional ideas and affects back to their repressed
infantile source and of demonstrating that it is this source which lends
the obsessions their pathological intensity.

Freud also discusses a further set of symptoms, derived from the
ego's effort to fend off those caused by the return of the repressed.
Symptoms such as compulsive behavior, or obsessional brooding on
abstract and suprasensual thoughts, are interpreted by Freud as reflecting the ego's attempt to turn attention away from the patient's basic
obsessional ideas and affects. This new class of symptoms is labelled
"secondary defense."

Freud's discussion of obsessive neurosis in "Further Remarks on
the Neuro-Psychoses of Defence" contains, by way of illustration, an
explication of a patient's history. The case is that of an eleven-year-old
boy who developed a complex ritual around going to bed:

He did not go to sleep until he had told his mother in the
minutest detail all the experiences he had had during the
day; there must be no bits of paper or other rubbish on the
carpet in his bedroom in the evening; his bed had to be
pushed right up against the wall, three chairs had to be
placed in front of it, and the pillows had to lie in a particular way. In order to go to sleep he was obliged first to kick
both his legs out a certain number of times and then lie on
his side.

Freud traced the obsessive ritual to the boy's sexual encounters with a servant girl several years before the onset of his symptoms. The ritual had emerged, according to Freud, only at some point after a recent experience had aroused the memory of the childhood sexual encounters. Freud goes on:

> The meaning of the ceremonial was easy to guess and was established point by point by psycho-analysis. The chairs were placed in front of the bed and the bed pushed against the wall in order that nobody else should be able to get at the bed; the pillows were arranged in a particular way so that they should be differently arranged from how they were on [the evening of his major childhood sexual encounter]; the movements with his legs were to kick away the person who was lying on him; sleeping on his side was because in the scene he had been lying on his back; his circumstantial confession to his mother was because . . . he had been silent to his mother about this and other sexual experiences; and, finally, the reason for his keeping his bedroom floor clean was that neglect to do so had been the chief reproach that he had so far had to hear from his mother.[18]

In his explication of this and other cases of obsessive neurosis, Freud felt confident that he could account for virtually all the symptoms of the syndrome, and he regarded his discussion of obsessive neurosis as offering substantial support for his general theory of symptom formation in the psychoneuroses. Freud considered the clinical course of hysteria and paranoia in the context of the same general scheme, but he was unable to offer an explanation of these diseases as comprehensive as that formulated for obsessions. In particular, he could propose no clear-cut relationship between the pathogenic experience and the subsequent symptoms in these diseases. With regard to hysteria, its characterization as the consequence of a passive, unpleasant, infantile sexual encounter did yield some insight into symptomatology: many of the psychological symptoms of hysteria seemed to reflect an aversion to sexuality, and Freud could explain this as the patient's response to the repressed infantile trauma. But the most prominent and characteristic hysterical symptoms were, in Freud's view, the somatic conversions; and the distinction between hysteria and obsessions in terms of passive and active childhood sexual encounters suggested no explanation for why repression in the former case should specifically lead to somatic symptoms. Freud had earlier proposed that hysteria occurs only in people who possess an innate "capacity for conversion," but that was at a time when he could find no difference in the pathogenic events leading to obsessions and hysteria. He had now, he believed, succeeded in defining some distinction between the causes of the two diseases; he expected that further clarification of the special etiology of hysteria should finally provide an explanation for hysterical conversions.

Freud's attempts to resolve this difficulty focused primarily on a formula emphasizing the child's age at the time of his pathogenic sexual encounter. He had maintained that the sexual aggressiveness which figures in the development of obsessional neurosis must emerge comparatively late in childhood and must be preceded by a passive encounter that serves to awaken the child's sexual curiosity prematurely. This thesis had suggested to him the possibility that the passive sexual experiences which figure in the genesis of neuroses, including those which lead to hysteria, uniformly occur at an earlier age than the aggressive experiences which lead to obsessions. Freud subsequently proposed that if one could associate the pathogenic event in hysteria with an age when the child's mental faculties had not yet fully developed, and when he would typically offer a physical response to all stimuli, then the somatic conversions of hysteria might be explained as stemming from the characteristics of the organism at the time of the pathogenic event.

Freud presented his theory of infantile sexual traumas in three papers published in the spring of 1896: "Heredity and the Etiology of the Neuroses," "Further Remarks on the Neuro-Psychoses of Defence" (both completed in February, 1896), and "The Etiology of Hysteria" (delivered as a lecture in April and submitted for publication a month later). All three offer the view that hysteria is the consequence of a passive encounter, while obsessions evolve from infantile sexual aggressiveness. But the latter two papers suggest that the child's age at the time of the pathogenic event is also a factor in determining which neurosis develops.

In the following months, Freud attributed increasing importance to age. In a letter to Fliess dated May 30, 1896, he divides childhood into three periods during which neurosis-inducing experiences might take place: the first lasting up to age four, the second from age four to eight, and a third beginning sometime between ages eight and ten and lasting until the onset of puberty. Freud proposes that encounters which lead to hysteria belong to the first phase, those which yield obsessional neurosis occur during the second phase, and experiences which produce paranoia fall within the final phase. He also suggests that, because of the child's limited mental development up to age four, memories dating from the first period are not translated into verbal images. As a result, "the arousal of a ... sexual scene [from this period] leads, not to psychical consequences, but to *conversion*." This approach to the problem of hysterical conversions is developed further in another letter written in December, 1896.[19]

Freud's clinical explanation of the neuroses argued essentially that the psychoneuroses are derived from infantile sexual experiences and that the nature of these experiences determines which particular neurotic symptoms subsequently emerge. By linking the emergence of hysterical conversion symptoms with the stage of the patient's mental development at the time of his or her infantile sexual encounters, Freud appeared to be taking a major step towards completing his clinical explanation. But there were other difficulties, related both to the sexual etiology of the neuroses and the relationship between etiology and symptoms, which soon led to further revisions in his models.

Fantasies

In several letters written to Fliess during the spring of 1897, Freud introduced the concept of *fantasies* into his theory of the neuroses. He remarked that the analysis of neurotic patients uncovers repressed imaginings, or fantasies, and he suggested that these are inspired by childhood sexual experiences and are constructed for the purpose of blocking the memory of those experiences: "Phantasies are psychical facades constructed in order to bar the way to [the infantile] memories. Phantasies at the same time serve the trend towards refining the memories, towards sublimating them."[20] Having been confronted with patients' fantasies—with repressed ideas that were clearly not a straightforward recollection of the patients' actual experiences—Freud proposed an explanation that fitted with his current theory. He concluded that the fantasies must be an imaginary reworking of childhood sexual experiences, and, by analogy with symptom formation, he suggested that this reworking probably occurs in the interest of repression. He maintained further that repressed fantasies are formulated, like symptoms, as a compromise between the pathogenic memory and the repressing ego.

But the concept of fantasies presented a direct challenge to the theory of infantile sexual traumas. Freud could discern no clear way of distinguishing whether the repressed material elicited in therapy was fantasy or memory, so that the truth of the seduction stories reported by his patients seemed called into question. Yet, Freud continued to endorse the seduction theory. One reason was that in several cases the stories of seduction told by his patients had been corroborated by others who were involved. In addition, similar stories were continually being reported by new patients, and Freud found them convincing. In a letter written on April 28, 1897—in the midst of his early discussions of fantasies—Freud tells of a patient who had that morning informed him that "her supposedly otherwise highminded and respectable father regularly took her to bed when she was from eight to twelve and misused her." Freud's response was to assume that "similar and worse things must have happened in her [earlier] childhood."[21]

In his correspondence dealing with neurotic fantasies, Freud also discusses the role of sexual "impulses" in neuroses: "The psychical structures which, in hysteria, are affected by repression are not in reality memories ... but *impulses* which arise from the primal scenes [i.e., from the pathogenic sexual experiences].[22] This new emphasis on impulses emerged largely from a consideration of the distinction between the pathogenesis of perversions and that of neuroses. Perverse sexual practices were traced by many authors to infantile sexual traumas of the type Freud associated with neuroses, and Freud was therefore concerned with defining in what way the pathogenic processes differed for the two groups of syndromes. He initially proposed that the distinction lay in whether or not the memory of the trauma subsequently arouses unpleasure and is repressed. But the key factor in perversions appeared to be the persistence of abnormal impulses triggered by the infantile sexual experience. This suggested to Freud that, in cases where neuroses develop, repression must be directed primarily against these abnormal impulses rather than against simply the memory of the traumatic event. Furthermore, Freud believed he could invariably discern such perverse sexual impulses amid the repressed material uncovered in his analyses of neurotic patients.

But Freud's exploration of the relationship between perversions and neuroses dates from December, 1896, and yet it was only in his letters on fantasies, written some months later, that he explicitly shifted his emphasis from repressed memories to repressed impulses. I believe it likely that his discussion of impulses in these letters was intended primarily to counter the challenge to the seduction theory posed by fantasies. Freud asserts in the correspondence that perverse impulses are easily discerned in neurotic patients, and he assumed, along with a great number of his contemporaries, that such impulses must be due to some unusual sexual experience in childhood. There is therefore an implication that, even if one questions a patient's stories of childhood seduction, the presence of these perverse impulses indicates that some such event must have occurred.

The only example of infantile impulses mentioned by Freud is a desire for the death of the parent of the same sex: "Hostile impulses against parents (a wish that they should die) are also an integral constituent of neuroses . . . . It seems as though this death-wish is directed in sons against their father and in daughters against their mother."[23] Freud clearly intimates that these death-wishes are due to sexual jealousy and a desire for sexual contact with the surviving parent. Most of the seduction stories told to him by neurotic patients involved a girl's seduction by her father. Again, there is an implication that, even if one questions the veracity of such "memories," the presence of perverse impulses such as these death-wishes provides substantial proof that some comparable sexual experience, sufficiently traumatic to arouse these impulses, must in fact have occurred.

Freud continued to support the seduction theory during the next several months. But, in a letter written to Fliess in September, 1897, he abruptly changed his position and stated that "I no longer believe in my *neurotica*."[24] Freud cited four reasons for the rejection of his theory: (1) he was continually disappointed in his attempts to bring analyses to a satisfactory conclusion, an indication that he did not yet have the real key; (2) he could not accept the implication that so many fathers were guilty of sexually abusing their children; (3) he had discovered that there is no way to distinguish between truth and fiction among the repressed ideas brought to light by analysis; (4) he noted that even in the worst psychoses (that is, situations in which there is extensive failure of the ego's efforts at repression) unconscious memories never fully succeed in overcoming the ego's resistance, and it therefore seemed doubtful that in treatment one might have overcome all resistances and reached the actual secrets of childhood experiences.

Three of these reasons could have been cited months earlier, while the fourth bears no relation to any comments previously made by Freud and is not pursued in subsequent discussions, so that there is no clear indication of why rejection of the seduction theory came at this particular time. One could suppose that the therapeutic disappointments, the unlikely seduction stories, and the challenge posed by the discovery of fantasies had simply generated a cumulative effect at this point. But it is more probable that Freud's self-analysis, begun in the preceding weeks, was the determining factor.[25]

Freud undertook his self-analysis both to resolve what he perceived as neurotic traits in his own behavior and to test at first hand the correctness of his theories and clinical methods. The analysis consisted primarily of the examination of dreams. In his earliest case history of a neurotic patient (Emmy von N.), Freud had already tended to view the content of the patient's dreams as symptoms of her neurosis. He now believed that symptoms are to be traced to repressed memories of childhood events, and he takes the same approach in his explication of dreams.

Freud stated some years later that he undertook this self-analysis in response to his father's death in October, 1896, but he did not begin intensive work on the analysis until the following summer. The discovery of neurotic fantasies during the spring of 1897 probably served to encourage his efforts at dream interpretation. The concept of neurotic fantasies was derived from the observation that a large number of repressed ideas are formed, like neurotic symptoms, by means of a compromise between repressed memories and the repressing ego. Freud had for some time believed that the ideas found in his patients' dreams are constructed in the same way, and consequently the discovery of neurotic fantasies served to reinforce his views on the nature of dreams and on their importance as manifestations of repressed material.

Freud's self-analysis uncovered repressed ideas and impulses comparable to those revealed in his analyses of neurotic patients. In particular, he came across those hostile impulses directed against one's father which he had previously regarded as evidence that some traumatic sexual experience must have occurred in childhood. Yet he could not recall such experiences, nor did he believe that they had in fact taken place. Conversations with his mother, in which he attempted to uncover the events underlying the repressed material revealed by his self-analysis, apparently supported his belief that seductions of the type he had postulated for his patients had never occurred in his own case.

This was probably the major factor in his rejection of the seduction theory. In listing his reasons for rejecting the theory, Freud makes an oblique reference to his self-analysis. He states that he could not accept the implication that "in every case the father, not excluding my own, had to be blamed as a pervert." The mention of his father indicates that Freud had uncovered in his self-analysis repressed ideas which he had previously traced to paternal abuse. The fact that he could find no evidence of such abuse in his own case apparently helped to convince him that the seduction theory was untenable.

Freud did uncover memories of some less dramatic sexual episodes, involving the woman who was his nurse. He does not give many details about these episodes, but he states that "she was my teacher in sexual matters." Freud seems to have regarded these events as the true source of his neurotic traits—rather than those traumatic sexual encounters, usually involving the child's father, which he had previously postulated. He states in a letter to Fliess that his nurse was the source of his troubles rather than his father.

However, the encounters involving his nurse could not account for the hostile feelings directed against his father, and he could not discover any unusual event that might have induced such feelings. Freud recalled that he had once, at about age two, seen his mother nude. In the absence of any other explanation, he concluded that this must have served to arouse sexual impulses and to generate jealousy of his father. But such an episode seemed rather commonplace. Freud therefore speculated that infantile sexual attraction to one's mother and jealousy of the father is probably a universal phenomenon. These impulses, he suggested in a letter to Fliess, emerge in early childhood and are later repressed in the normal course of development:

> I have found, in my own case too, falling in love with the
> mother and jealousy of the father, and I now regard it as a
> universal event of early childhood. . . . If that is so, we can
> understand the riveting power of *Oedipus Rex*, in spite of all
> the objections raised by reason against its presupposition of
> destiny; . . . the Greek legend seizes on a compulsion which
> everyone recognizes because he feels its existence within
> himself. Each member of the audience was once, in germ
> and in phantasy, just such an Oedipus, and each one recoils
> in horror from the dream-fulfillment here transplanted into
> reality, with the whole quota of repression which separates
> his infantile state from his present one.[26]

The ideas and impulses which were revealed by Freud's self-analysis, and which he had previously traced to childhood seductions, are thus either ascribed to less dramatic experiences involving his nurse or regarded as normal and associated with commonplace occurrences. Freud still believed that Oedipal impulses are abnormally intense in children destined to develop serious neuroses and that these excessively intense impulses must be triggered by unusual childhood events involving the children's parents. But, since the situation in such children was now regarded as a variation on a normal phenomenon, it appeared plausible that these pathogenic events might as a rule be comparatively minor childhood experiences rather than the seductions which Freud had previously postulated. These less dramatic sexual encounters consequently replace seductions in Freud's formulas concerning the pathogenesis of neuroses. With his recognition of Oedipal impulses as normal phenomena and his shift of emphasis from seductions to less spectacular sexual encounters, Freud now suggests that pathogenesis in the psychoneuroses involves an interaction between sexual experiences and normal infantile sexual impulses.

In the context of the seduction theory, fantasies had been viewed as a reworking of infantile sexual memories for the purpose of more effectively repressing these memories. Now, however, patients' seduction stories are recognized as themselves generally fantasies, and these stories are perceived as more than a reworking of actual events: they are an erotic embellishment of events. A reevaluation of the nature of fantasies seemed therefore to be required. According to Freud's new model of pathogenesis, psychoneuroses are based upon a normal impulse being intensified by a childhood experience. Freud now maintains that fantasies are simply psychic manifestations of these pathologically intense impulses. He argues, for example, that seduction stories are the product of abnormally intense Oedipal impulses.

Fantasies are still believed to reflect infantile memories in the sense that, if repressed fantasies are uncovered and analyzed, they can lead to the recollection of relevant childhood events. But Freud now characterizes them, not simply as a reworking of memories, but as an imagined gratification of pathological impulses.

Freud also suggests that neurotic fantasies are not formed until puberty. This view stemmed from a belief that the fantasies uncovered in therapy display a sexual sophistication beyond that of childhood, and that they also contain memories dating from a later age. Freud wrote to Fliess in January, 1899, that "phantasies are products of later periods and are projected back from the then present on to the earliest childhood." The same notion is expressed in "Screen Memories" (1899). In an essay written in 1905, he states that fantasies are "mostly produced during the years of puberty."[27]

With rejection of the seduction theory, and modification of the roles accorded impulses and fantasies, a new clinical explanation of the psychoneuroses emerged: psychoneuroses are due to pathologically intense variants of normal infantile sexual impulses. The pathological impulses are eventually repressed, but reemerge briefly with the sexual awakening of puberty. At this time, neurotic fantasies are generated. Both impulses and fantasies then undergo a period of successful repression. Normal sexual impulses are also repressed to some degree, because of their associations with the pathological material. At some later date, there is a "return of the repressed" in the form of symptoms.

The new emphasis on impulses, and on fantasies as the derivative of impulses, also led to a redefinition of neurotic symptoms. Numerous authors had noted the erotic nature of hysterical attacks and had suggested that these attacks are manifestations of erotic drives; Freud, influenced in part by these observations, had proposed on several occasions that symptoms reflect desires. The characterization of repressed ideas as based on sexual impulses gave a new significance to this concept. The "return of the repressed" is now viewed as an effort to enact repressed fantasies and to satisfy infantile impulses. The compromise between repressed ideas and a repressing ego is now seen as a compromise between a sexual impulse and one's misgivings and feelings of guilt concerning that impulse. This model is utilized by Freud in, for example, his explication of Dora's symptoms in "Fragment of an Analysis of a Case of Hysteria" (most of which was written in 1901, although not published until 1905). One of Dora's symptoms was an hysterical cough. In the course of therapy Freud uncovered intense Oedipal impulses together with repressed fantasies of the patient's father engaged in oral-genital play, and he interpreted Dora's cough as the disguised expression of these impulses and fantasies.[28] In the *Three Essays on the Theory of Sexuality* (1905), Freud offered the general principle that, in neuroses, "the symptoms constitute the sexual activity of the patient."[29]

Infantile Sexuality

Freud's rejection of the seduction theory is usually regarded as the starting point for his development of a theory of infantile sexuality. According to this view, the realization that his patients' seduction stories were actually fantasies suggested to Freud that there must be infantile sexual drives which generate these fantasies, and this was his introduction to infantile sexuality. Freud's own remarks in his essay "On the History of the Psycho-Analytic Movement" (1914) encouraged this interpretation of the evolution of his ideas:

> Influenced by Charcot's view of the traumatic origin of hysteria, one was readily inclined to accept as true and aetiologically significant the statements made by patients in which they ascribed their symptoms to . . . sexual experiences in the first years of childhood—to put it bluntly, to seduction. When this aetiology broke down under the weight of its own

improbability and contradiction in definitely ascertainable circumstances, the result was helpless bewilderment. Analysis had led back to these infantile sexual traumas by the right path, and yet they were not true. . . . [But] if hysterical subjects trace back their symptoms to traumas that are fictitious, then the new fact which emerges is precisely that they create such scenes in *phantasy,* and this psychical reality requires to be taken into account alongside practical reality. This reflection was soon followed by the discovery that these phantasies were intended to cover up the autoerotic activity of the first years of childhood. . . . And now, from behind the phantasies, the whole range of a child's sexual life came to light.[30]

But the concept of infantile erotogenic zones, which is a central element in Freud's theory of infantile sexuality, had actually been introduced in the context of the seduction model. This indicates that distinctions are required between those aspects of Freud's sexual theory which antedate his recognition of seduction stories as fantasies, and those aspects which were formulated in response to that discovery.

Infantile erotogenic zones were first mentioned by Freud in his discussion of the distinction between the pathogenesis of perversions and that of neuroses. Perversions were widely regarded as emanating from infantile sexual traumas of the sort which Freud associated with the psychoneuroses.[31] Indeed, shortly after formulating his seduction theory, Freud stated in "Draft K" (January, 1896): "Here a subsidiary problem branches off: how does it come about that under analogous conditions, perversion or simple immorality emerges instead of neuroses?"[32] Freud did not at that time attempt to resolve the problem, but he returned to the question in a letter written the following December. Freud suggested that sometimes the memory of an infantile sexual trauma releases pleasure rather than unpleasure upon being recollected following sexual development. One then gets compulsion and perversion instead of repression and neurosis. He proposed that the choice between pleasure and unpleasure is determined in part by the child's basic nature, and he tried to relate this to Fliess's theory of bisexuality:

> In order to account for why the outcome [of premature sexual experience] is sometimes perversion and sometimes neurosis, I avail myself of the bisexuality of all human beings. In a purely male being there would be a surplus of male release at

the [transitional points in sexual development], . . . that is, pleasure would be generated and consequently perversion; in purely female beings there would be a surplus of unpleasurable substance at these times.[33]

In a given case, the emergence of perversion or neurosis would be decided by the relative quantities of male and female toxins released.

But Freud also pointed to another factor in the choice between perversion and neurosis by introducing the concept of abandoned erotogenic zones. He argued that sexual excitation in childhood is associated with many areas of the body which later play no role in sexuality, and he indicated that the sexual abandonment of these zones due to normal physiological changes accounts in part for why later recollection of childhood experiences causes unpleasure and induces repression. (Freud did not elaborate. But he regarded the anus as one of these infantile erotogenic zones and believed that childhood experiences which involve excessive anal stimulation generate sexual excitation. His thesis is that the explanation for why such experiences appear in retrospect to be disgusting and unpleasant, and why memories of them are repressed, lies in part in the physiologically determined abandonment of the anus as an erotogenic area.) Freud further implied that the development of perversions occurs when some primitive facet of infantile sexuality fails to lose its erotogenic nature, and he stated this view explicitly in a letter written in January, 1897. (Freud believed, for example, that, in the event of a childhood anal erotic experience, if the anal area should subsequently retain its erotogenic nature, then anal perversions will ensue instead of neuroses.)

The key factor in perversions was, in Freud's view, the persistence of sexual impulses aroused by the childhood event. This soon suggested to Freud that the essential point in neuroses must be repression of these abnormal impulses, rather than repression of merely the memory of the childhood trauma. But he continued to believe that repression occurs only in the wake of abandonment of the erotogenic zones involved in the childhood experience.

The thesis relating perversions and neuroses to infantile erotogenic zones was developed more explicitly in a letter written in November, 1897, several months after Freud's rejection of the seduction theory:

I have often suspected that something organic played a part in repression; I was able once before to tell you that it was a question of the abandonment of former sexual zones. . . .
Now, the zones which no longer produce a release of sexual-

ity in normal and mature human beings must be the regions of the anus and of the mouth and throat. . . . In animals these sexual zones continue in force; . . . if this persists in human beings too, perversion results.[34]

Perversion also occurs, according to Freud, when childhood sexual traumas affect only those regions which normally persist as sexual zones in maturity. But, when strictly infantile zones are excited by such traumas, then, if these zones are later abandoned in the normal way, repression and neurosis will follow.

The concept of erotogenic zones is not original. Krafft-Ebing, for example, wrote in *Psychopathia Sexualis* (1886):

> Under pathological conditions, . . . other portions of the body . . . about the mammae and genitals may attain the significance of "erogenous" zones. . . .
>
> . . . In man, physiologically, the only "erogenous" zone is the glans penis, and, perhaps, the skin of the external genitals.
>   Under pathological conditions the anus may become an "erogenous" area: . . . anal auto-masturbation . . . passive pederasty.[35]

Krafft-Ebing did not interpret these abnormal zones in terms of a failure to abandon infantile sexual areas. But elsewhere he referred to the normal abandonment of the clitoris as an erogenous zone in favor of the vagina and cervix uteri—a notion which was later developed at length by Freud.

The term *erogenous zone* used by Krafft-Ebing had been coined by the Parisian neurologist Ernst Chambard in his doctoral thesis (1881). Chambard, who was affiliated with the Salpetrière, wrote his thesis on hypnosis in hysterical patients, and he introduced the term in the context of a discussion of hysterical symptomatology. The designation *hysterogenic zone* was widely used at this time to denote areas of the body whose stimulation was often found to set off hysterical attacks. The most commonly noted of these zones was the region of the abdomen over the ovaries, and physicians frequently cited this fact, together with the erotic nature of many hysterical attacks, as evidence of the sexual etiology of hysteria. Chambard introduced *erogenous zone* as a variation on *hysterogenic zone,* while discussing attack-inducing areas in a patient whose attacks were particularly erotic and who was also nymphomaniacal.[36]

Freud's emphasis was, of course, quite specifically on infantile erotogenic zones—that is, on areas of the body whose stimulation in infancy is accompanied by intense sensual pleasure and whose sensual significance is later subsumed to that of the genitalia. Consequently, the work of Krafft-Ebing and Chambard was, in general, more relevant to the question of terminology than to that of concepts. But one can also cite writers who preceded Freud in developing concepts of infantile sexual areas. The Berlin neurologist Albert Moll, for example, spoke of a primitive instinct of "contrectation"—a desire for skin contact. According to Moll, whose work is mentioned by Freud in his correspondence, this primitive impulse emerges quite early in life and only gradually, in the course of development, becomes somewhat delimited to specific sexual areas of the body and associated with other sexual aims.[37]

Numerous authors had interpreted sucking as an infantile sexual phenomenon, and Freud wrote that "no observer has felt any doubt as to the sexual nature of this activity." A Hungarian pediatrician, S. Lindner, in an article entitled "Das Saugen an den Fingern, Lippen, etc. bei den Kindern (Ludeln)" (1879), pointed to instances in which sucking is accompanied by masturbation as evidence of the sexual nature of the former. Lindner, who was later cited by Freud, reported the case of a two-year-old girl who would suck on one hand while rubbing her clitoris with the other. When he interfered with the masturbating, the child protested, "Leave me alone, otherwise I can't suck."[38] Wilhelm Fliess, in his 1897 book, also regarded sucking as a form of infantile sexuality. Fliess suggested that children display periodic variations in their sucking habits, and he interpreted this as evidence for the operation of periodically secreted sexual toxins.

Freud stated that his own notion of abandoned sexual zones was linked to consideration of changes in the sexual significance of olfactory sensations, and many of his early remarks on infantile erotogenic zones are concerned with the sexual role of smells in children and animals. Connections between olfactory functions, sexuality, and neuroses were of particular interest to Fliess and were undoubtedly the subject of many exchanges between Fliess and Freud. These exchanges likely provided another important source for Freud's theories of infantile sexual areas.

In the wake of his rejection of the seduction theory, Freud altered his views on infantile sexuality. The most significant change was his recognition that the normal display of sexual impulses in early infancy is substantially greater than he had previously believed. When he had first introduced the notion of abandoned erotogenic zones, Freud was aware of numerous manifestations of sexuality among children. However, he regarded infantile sexuality as something more potential than actual and viewed its persistent expression as pathological. This was also the view most commonly expressed in the contemporary medical literature. Masturbation in infancy was mentioned frequently in the literature, and sucking and other childhood practices were often interpreted as sexual behavior. But it was generally assumed that in a normal child one finds very little masturbatory or other sexual play after the first few years of life, and that the sexual activity which does occur is of a purely reflex, mechanical nature, unaccompanied by psychosexual phenomena.

Krafft-Ebing, in *Psychopathia Sexualis,* wrote that many physicians are familiar with manifestations of sexuality in very young children, and he reported several cases of infantile masturbation. He also suggested that such behavior may occur in normal children. But he insisted that when there is a regular pattern of overt sexual activity through childhood, and particularly when this activity involves psychosexual pleasure, then it "may always be regarded as an accompanying symptom of a neuropsychopathic constitutional condition.[39]

There were a few authors, particularly pediatricians, who regarded overt sexuality in childhood as not necessarily abnormal. Freud later cites a paper to this effect by the Viennese physician Wilhelm Stekel, entitled "Coitus im Kindesalter" (1895).[40] But this view was exceptional. Most writers, especially neuropsychiatrists, agreed with Krafft-Ebing.

When a child did exhibit prominent sexual activity, his behavior was usually ascribed to an hereditary neuropathic abnormality. Another explanation was that the child had been seduced by an adult or older child and this experience had triggered an abnormally precocious sexual awakening. Freud initially shared the view that aggressive sexuality in childhood was exceptional and required an explanation. It was largely for this reason that, when he proposed the theory of infantile sexual traumas and associated obsessional neurosis with a pleasurable sexual encounter initiated by the patient, he insisted that the patient must have previously been the passive victim of an assault which had served to awaken prematurely his sexual curiosity. Similarly, Freud at first interpreted his infantile erotogenic zones as potential sources of sexual excitation which are not normally aroused to any great degree. He regarded the emergence of impulses related to these zones as necessarily the consequence of some unusual experience, and as leading to perversions and to neuroses.

With his recognition of the universality of infantile Oedipal impulses and his rejection of the seduction theory (1897), Freud shifted to the view that there normally exists a complex psychosexual life during early childhood and that sexuality is normally given significant expression during this period of development. He asserted further that there are aspects of infantile sexuality other than those related to the stimulation of erotogenic zones. In *Three Essays on the Theory of Sexuality* (1905), in which he first published his new concepts of infantile sexuality, Freud suggests that sexual excitation accompanies muscular exertion, intense emotional states, intellectual work, and other situations. He also considers the phenomena of exhibitionism and voyeurism in children. Freud writes, for example, of the relationship between sexuality and emotional states:

> It is easy to establish, whether by contemporary observation or by subsequent research, that all comparatively intense affective processes, including even terrifying ones, trench upon sexuality. . . . For quite often in such circumstances a stimulus may be felt which urges the child to touch his genitals, or something may take place akin to a nocturnal emission with all its bewildering consequences.[41]

Freud continued to regard erotogenic zones as the major factor in infantile sexuality, but he considered these additional elements as also important—both for an understanding of the child and for insight into the etiology of later psychiatric abnormalities.

However, despite these various changes in Freud's views on infantile sexuality, the essential aspects of the model developed in 1896 (when he still endorsed the seduction concept) are preserved in the new theory. Childhood sexuality is still perceived as existing, at least after the first few years of life, primarily in a latent form, with only limited overt expression, and more prominent sexual behavior is considered pathological. Further, perversions and neuroses are still traced to an inappropriate awakening of this latent infantile sexuality. Finally, perversions continue to be interpreted as involving the persistence into maturity of infantile sexual patterns, while neuroses are linked to the abandonment and repression of this type of sexuality.

Developing his thesis further, Freud writes in *Three Essays on the Theory of Sexuality*:

> It [seems] to us . . . that children bring germs of sexual activity with them into the world, that they already enjoy sexual satisfaction when they begin to take nourishment and that they persistently seek to repeat the experience in the familiar

activity of "thumb-sucking." The sexual activity of children, however, does not, it [appears], develop *pari passu* with their other functions, but, after a short period of efflorescence . . . enters upon the so-called period of latency.[42]

The latency period is marked, in Freud's view, by the repression of infantile forms of sexuality, an occurrence which is crucial for normal sexual development. (The meaning of *repression* has now changed somewhat. It now refers to the normal abandonment of infantile eroto-genic zones due to physiological changes, as well as to the suppression of primitive sexual impulses such as voyeurism or exhibitionism or those impulses related to the stimulation of infantile erotogenic zones. Freud at this point makes no sharp distinction between erotogenic zones on the one hand and impulses on the other, and his use of terms such as "instincts" or "sexual components" seems to encompass both.) When sexuality reemerges at puberty the various erotogenic zones and other primitive elements of sexual life are subordinated to the primacy of the genital zone, and the autoerotic, masturbatory sexual activity of infancy is exchanged for a sexuality oriented towards some object. This is the course of normal development. But it occasionally happens that some components of infantile sexuality are unusually intense and are not fully sublimated during the period of latency. These components may then persist into puberty and become a part of the individual's sexual life as an adult—thereby yielding perversions. Or they may at some point bow to an exceptional effort at repression, in which case perversion is replaced by a psychoneurosis. Neurosis occurs because repression in these instances is of only limited effectiveness and the perversion is able to find expression in the form of neurotic symptoms. For example, oral eroticism is, according to Freud, a normal manifesta-tion of infantile sexuality. In the course of normal development the oral zone loses its erotogenic aspect and oral erotic impulses are re-pressed. If, however, such impulses become overly intense during in-fancy, perhaps by overstimulation, then normal repression does not occur. In some instances, the oral zone will maintain its erotogenic nature and oral perversions will ensue, while in other cases an abnor-mally intense oral eroticism will bow to an exceptional but only partially successful effort at repression and will reemerge in later life in the form of neurotic symptoms. Freud summarizes this model in passages written in 1905: "I showed [in the *Three Essays*] that *perversions* corre-spond to disturbances . . . owing to the overpowering and compulsive development of certain of the component [sexual] instincts." But:

> A different result is brought about if in the course of devel-
> opment some of the components which are of excessive
> strength . . . are submitted to the process of repression
> (which, it must be insisted, is not equivalent to their being
> abolished). If this happens, the excitations concerned con-
> tinue to be generated as before; but they are prevented . . .
> from attaining their aim and are diverted into numerous
> other channels till they find their way to expression as
> symptoms.[43]

(Freud believed that the question of why exceptionally strong infantile
instincts generate perversions in some cases and are repressed in others
would have to be answered in terms of innate physiological factors,
since instincts are invariably based upon some physical element—such
as an erotogenic zone—whose abandonment or retention depends on
physiological processes.)

Freud's views on both the general structure of infantile sexuality
and the pathogenic mechanism for perversions and neuroses, as found
in this model, differ little from the views expressed in 1896.

The major innovation in *Three Essays on the Theory of Sexuality* is, of
course, Freud's effort to develop a detailed understanding of normal
infantile sexuality, and his concern with this problem stems ultimately
from his recognition of the universality of infantile Oedipal impulses
and his consequent appreciation of the scope and magnitude of normal
infantile sexual phenomena. But Freud's interest in the details of childhood sexuality developed only gradually in the wake of his generalization concerning Oedipal impulses and his rejection of the seduction
theory. This interest actually emerged only when Freud had begun
once again to emphasize innate factors as the key to the etiology of
hysteria.

In 1896, Freud believed that the unusually intense primitive impulses which figure in pathogenesis are caused entirely by extraordinary childhood sexual experiences. A theory of normal development—
in particular, a recognition of infantile erotogenic zones—was important only for explaining why the memory of the key childhood event,
and the impulses stimulated by the event, later elicit unpleasure and
repression. The subsequent recognition of Oedipal impulses as normal
phenomena, together with the shift in emphasis from seductions to less
spectacular sexual encounters, suggested that pathogenesis in the psychoneuroses must be explained in terms of an interaction between
sexual experiences and normal infantile sexual impulses. This indi-

cated a need for a greater understanding of these normal impulses and helped to turn Freud's attention towards a more detailed consideration of the various manifestations of infantile sexuality. But, in the months immediately following rejection of the seduction theory, Freud continued to believe that infantile experiences were the primary factors in pathogenesis, and he continued to place the major emphasis on these experiences. In his discussion of erotogenic zones dated November, 1897, Freud assumes that symptoms involving primitive erotic areas can be explained wholly in terms of the peculiar details of a pathogenic sexual experience, and little is said of the normal expression of these zones. In an article published in January and February, 1898, "Sexuality in the Etiology of the Neuroses," the emphasis is still on the infantile experiences which initiate the process leading to neuroses, and again little is said of normal infantile sexuality.[44]

However, with rejection of the seduction theory, the sexual encounters which Freud now associated with neuroses were not only less dramatic; they were also less exceptional. Indeed, they hardly differed from what might be expected to occur in the course of every infancy. Consequently, Freud was soon obliged to consider the problem of why such experiences can apparently lead to neuroses in some people and leave others unscathed. The solution seemed to lie in the realm of innate differences in sexual development, and Freud later wrote that "accidental influences derived from experience having thus receded into the background, the factors of constitution and heredity necessarily gained the upper hand once more."[45] This emphasis on innate characteristics served to increase Freud's interest in the normal pattern of infantile sexuality.

In the context of the seduction theory, a repressed oral fixation, for example, would be attributed to some oral-sexual experience, and nothing would have to be known about infantile sexuality beyond the fact that oral eroticism is one of its components. But, in terms of the new theory stressing innate factors, Freud thought that the production of an oral fixation could be comprehended only if one had adequate knowledge of the normal vicissitudes of oral eroticism during the early years of childhood. A satisfactory theory of the neuroses therefore seemed to require more detailed delineation of the various components of infantile sexuality and of their prominence at different stages in early childhood.

But Freud believed that infantile sexual development could be explained only in terms of sexual physiology. Consequently, with the shift in emphasis from childhood experiences to innate developmental factors, physiology, in Freud's view, took on still more significance with regard to prospects for a comprehensive explanation of the neuroses.

The Status of Physiology After 1897

In papers written after his rejection of the seduction theory, Freud continued to insist repeatedly that infantile sexuality is based upon physiological processes and that these processes play a crucial role in the etiology of the neuroses. He notes on several occasions that too little is known about sexual physiology to formulate a satisfactory theory of the mechanisms of the neuroses, but he retains his earlier view that sexual physiology is controlled by chemical factors. In a case history of a hysterical patient ("Fragment of an Analysis of a Case of Hysteria"), written initially in 1901 and published in 1905, Freud maintains:

> It is the therapeutic technique alone that is purely psychological; the theory does not by any means fail to point out that neuroses have an organic basis—though it is true that it does not look for that basis in any pathological anatomical changes, and provisionally substitutes the conception of organic functions for the chemical changes which we should expect to find but which we are at present unable to apprehend.[46]

Freud presents some tentative notions regarding a physiology of sexuality in his *Three Essays on the Theory of Sexuality*: if an erotogenic zone is stimulated or some other type of sexual arousal occurs, a substance decomposes to yield a chemical toxin and this toxin acts on the nervous system to produce somatic sexual excitation. This is essentially a restatement of his earlier views, and Freud again cites the sexual effects of known toxins—particularly thyroid toxins—in support of the chemical model.

Freud implies that the abandonment of infantile sexual elements in the normal course of development involves a progressive loss of the ability to generate sexual toxins by previously effective forms of stimulation. Childhood sexual impulses are directed toward eliciting somatic sexual excitation, primarily by manipulation of erotogenic zones; consequently, when the various forms of stimulation no longer generate sexual toxins, the relevant impulses are also repressed. Freud refers on several occasions to the role of psychological factors—such as shame and disgust—in bringing about that repression of primitive sexual impulses that occurs during the latter part of childhood (the "latency period"). But he insists that these psychological elements are secondary to physiological processes:

> It is during this period of total or only partial latency that
> are built up the mental forces which are later to impede the
> course of the sexual instinct and, like dams, restrict its flow—
> disgust, feelings of shame and the claims of aesthetic and
> moral ideas. One gets an impression from civilized children
> that the construction of these dams is a product of educa-
> tion, and no doubt education has much to do with it. But in
> reality this development is organically determined and fixed
> by heredity.[47]

Freud maintains that the repression of sexual ideas and impulses in the
neuroses is also secondary to this physiological repression of infantile
sexual elements: " 'Defence' in the purely psychological sense has been
replaced by organic 'sexual repression'."[48]

Freud had argued since 1896 that pathological situations occur
when components of infantile sexuality are unusually intense and defy
normal repression. (Either they are partially repressed and find expression in the form of neurotic symptoms, or they are not repressed at all
and simply persist as perversions.) With rejection of the seduction theory, Freud continued to believe that childhood experiences can play a
role in abnormally arousing and intensifying a particular infantile sexual component, but he now insisted that there must be some innate
physiological abnormality contributing to pathogenesis. In the *Three
Essays on the Theory of Sexuality,* he declares that he can say little about
what the cause of this innate abnormality might be; but he notes that
the fathers of many of his patients suffered from syphilis before marriage, and he suggests that perhaps parental syphilis has a significant
hereditary effect on the development of psychoneuroses. This view is
repeated in his "Fragment of an Analysis", and the entire question of
heredity, which Freud had tried to minimize when he was formulating
the seduction theory, once more becomes an issue. Freud does not
attempt to speculate on how syphilis or some other hereditary factor
might influence sexual physiology and lead to neuroses, but the new
interest in heredity and the references to syphilis demonstrate how
rejection of the seduction theory was accompanied by intensified conviction of the need for physiological explanations.

For an explanation of why overdeveloped infantile sexual components lead in some cases to neuroses and in others to perversions,
Freud appealed to the concept of physiological bisexuality. The notion
that everyone possesses the physiological potential to develop characteristics of both sexes, and that everyone is therefore basically bisexual,

can be found frequently in late nineteenth-century medical texts. It was suggested by the recognition of normal sexual homologies—such as a recognition of the clitoris as a vestigial penis—and also by evolutionary theory and observation of the bisexuality of simple animals. In addition, the concept of bisexuality offered an explanation for the occasional occurrence of congenital hermaphroditism; such hermaphroditism was simply attributed to an abnormal balance of male and female factors. The development of secondary sexual characteristics proper to the opposite sex which occurs after castration, and in the wake of various disease processes, lent further support to theories of physiological bisexuality.

The concept of bisexuality received extensive attention in the neuropsychiatric literature in connection with explanations of sexual inversion (homosexuality). Numerous writers attempted to explain inversion as the consequence of a congenital disturbance in the ratio of male and female somatic sexual factors. Others argued that inversion can often be traced to traumatic sexual experiences in childhood. But those in favor of the congenital, physiological explanation pointed out that histories of childhood trauma can be elicited in only a small percentage of inverts, and that, furthermore, many people are exposed to the same types of experiences in childhood without becoming inverts. A major difficulty confronting the bisexuality theory was the observation that there is no correlation between inversion and hermaphroditism. However, various solutions were offered to this problem. Krafft-Ebing, for example, suggested that the sexual apparatus consists of genital, spinal, and cerebral components. The absence of hermaphroditism merely indicates a normal male-female equilibrium in the genital component, but there might still be an abnormality in the spinal or cerebral sphere. He attributed inversion to an improper balance between male and female cerebral sexual centers.[49]

Those who supported physiological explanations of inversion could have spoken of physiological bisexuality in inverts without postulating such a bisexuality in normal people as well. But the belief in a universal bisexuality was so well established in medicine that most writers, including Krafft-Ebing, interpreted the physiological abnormality of inversion as involving an aberration of a normal phenomenon. Freud notes in the Three Essays on the Theory of Sexuality that "the majority of authors who derive inversion from bisexuality bring forward that factor not only in the case of inverts, but also for all those who have grown up to be normal, and . . . , as a logical consequence, they regard inversion as the result of a disturbance in development."[50]

Freud's own notion of physiological bisexuality was based on Fliess's concept of two periodically elicited sexual toxins, one associated with male development and the other connected with female development. Both toxins, according to Fliess, are found in every individual, but in each case the toxin proper to one's sex dominates. By the end of 1896, Freud was applying Fliess's formula to explaining how infantile sexual traumas can in some cases cause perversions and in others neuroses. Freud had observed that the repressed sexual ideas uncovered in his analyses often involved perversions. He concluded that, following an infantile trauma, there is a conflict of two forces, one favoring the emergence of a perversion and the other favoring its repression. He noted that the majority of hysterics are women, and he believed that women are more likely to repress sexual material than are men. Freud therefore associated repression with Fliess's female factor and perversion with Fliess's male factor. He suggested that during periods of sexual transition, such as puberty, the recollection of childhood sexual traumas causes secretion of sexual toxins, and pleasure or unpleasure is elicited according to the relative strength of, respectively, male and female toxins. If it is predominantly pleasure which is elicited, perversions occur; if unpleasure is generated, repression and neuroses supervene.

When he proposed this formula associating perversions and neuroses with male and female toxins, Freud also suggested that the choice of perversion or neurosis depends upon whether or not the childhood sexual encounter involves erotogenic zones which are later abandoned or repressed. When Freud began to emphasize the role of "impulses," he restated this thesis to the effect that the key factor in pathogenesis is abnormally intense sexual impulses and these impulses either persist or are repressed according to whether the relevant somatic elements of infantile sexuality—such as infantile erotogenic zones—persist or are repressed. But this left open the question of what causes an abnormally stimulated or excited sexual element to be repressed. Freud later indicated that this is again determined by the relative strength of male and female factors, with the female aspect being responsible for repression. The persistence of infantile impulses during the latency period is most prominently manifested as autoerotic masturbatory activity, and in *Three Essays* Freud characterizes this masturbation as masculine and its cessation as feminine: "So far as the auto-erotic and masturbatory manifestations of sexuality are concerned, we might lay it down that the sexuality of little girls is of a wholly masculine character."[51] In his "Fragment of an Analysis," he regards his patient's repression of masturbatory behavior as "the boundary between two phases of her sexual life, of which the first was masculine in character, and the second feminine."[52]

Freud does offer a tentative explanation for why the repression of intense infantile impulses is associated with femininity. He argues that in women infantile autoeroticism primarily involves clitoral masturbation. But at puberty the clitoris is abandoned as an erotogenic zone in favor of the vagina, and consequently intense infantile impulses will tend to disappear. In men, the major erotogenic zone of childhood remains the center of sexuality in adulthood, and there is therefore a greater likelihood of infantile impulses persisting:

> When erotogenic susceptibility to stimulation has been successfully transferred by a woman from the clitoris to the vaginal orifice, it implies that she has adopted a new leading zone for the purposes of her later sexual activity. A man, on the other hand, retains his leading zone unchanged from childhood. The fact that women change their leading erotogenic zone in this way, together with the wave of repression at puberty, which, as it were, puts aside their childish masculinity, are the chief determinants of the greater proneness of women to neurosis and especially to hysteria. These determinants, therefore, are intimately related to the essence of femininity.[53]

But Freud continues to insist that a full understanding of the feminine and masculine forces at work in shaping neuroses and perversions must be derived from a greater understanding of physiological bisexuality—in particular, from a greater understanding of Fliess's sexual toxins. Freud wrote to Fliess in 1898: "I seized eagerly on your notion of bisexuality, which I regard as the most significant for my subject since that of defence." And in 1901:

> My next book, so far as I can see, will be called "Bisexuality in Man"; . . . I shall need a long and serious discussion with you. The idea itself is yours. . . . So perhaps I shall have to borrow still more from you. . . . This would mean an expansion of the anatomical-biological part, which in my hands alone would be very meagre.[54]

In addition to questions concerning normal infantile sexual processes and questions regarding masculine and feminine responses to perverse impulses, rejection of the seduction theory also generated other problems which seemed to demand physiological solutions. For example, it was once again unclear what determines which particular neurosis develops in response to a pathogenic situation. With the deemphasis of sexual traumas following abandonment of the seduction theory, earlier solutions correlating different neuroses with different types of sexual trauma, or with the age at which the trauma occurred, no longer appeared valid. Freud resolved the problem by returning to his earlier concept of a physiological "capacity for conversion": under pathological conditions, hysteria develops in those people who possess a neurophysiological capacity for converting psychic excitation into somatic symptoms; in those without such a capacity, some other neurosis emerges. Now, however, Freud uses the term "somatic compliance" instead of "capacity for conversion."[55]

But the key issues remained those related to sexual physiology. This is true not only for the psychoneuroses, but for the simple neuroses—neurasthenia and anxiety neurosis—as well. Freud continued to associate neurasthenia with a deficiency of somatic sexual excitation and anxiety neurosis with a displacement of somatic sexual excitation away from its normal paths of expression. All the neuroses, he believed, could be comprehensively explained only with a greater understanding of sexual physiology. Freud wrote in 1905:

> If we are prepared to take into account what has been learnt from psycho-analysis, we can say that the essence of [the neuroses] lies in disturbances of the sexual processes, the processes which determine in the organism the formation and utilization of sexual libido. It is scarcely possible to avoid picturing these processes as being in the last resort of a chemical nature; so that in what are termed the [simple] neuroses we may recognize the *somatic* effects of disturbances of the sexual metabolism, and in the psychoneuroses the *psychical* effects of those disturbances as well. The similarity of the neuroses to the phenomena of intoxication and abstinence after the use of certain alkaloids, as well as to Graves' disease . . . is forced upon our notice clinically.[56]

Nevertheless, Freud's major efforts continued to be directed towards developing psychological interpretations of the neuroses, and he still believed that, given the present state of knowledge, it would be futile to focus on physiological models.

9. *The Interpretation of Dreams*

Freud did not publish his new theories concerning infantile sexuality, repression, and the pathogenesis of psychoneuroses—the theories he developed following his rejection of the seduction formula—until 1905, in his *Three Essays on the Theory of Sexuality*. But he presented his explanation of neurotic symptom formation, his interpretation of symptoms as a compromise between repressed material and a repressing ego, in several works published during the preceding few years. The most important of these was *The Interpretation of Dreams* (1899), in which Freud discusses the psychology of dreams as a paradigm for the psychological processes involved in the formation of neurotic symptoms.

Dreams and Neuroses

The irrational and often incoherent nature of dreams, and their hallucinatory quality—the confusion of dream and reality—had always suggested to observers a kinship between dreams and mental disorders, and comparisons of psychiatric disturbances to dreams were in all ages a prominent fixture in works dealing with mental illness. In the nineteenth century, insanity was commonly interpreted as proceeding from a loss of those higher, integrative forms of mental functioning—designated as *ego,* or, more often, as *will*—which normally control and direct thought; and dreams were widely regarded as involving a similar process, with the ego or will being temporarily suspended during sleep. Those writers who identified higher mental functions with specific areas of the brain and wished to associate mental illness with disturbances of these brain areas placed particular emphasis on the analogy with dreams. Meynert, for example, insisted that several neuropsychiatric syndromes are caused by a pathological decrease in blood flow to the cortex and a relative increase in flow to subcortical centers, and he referred to dreams in support of this thesis. Meynert argues that sleep, since it is accompanied by a drop in blood pressure, must itself involve a transient decrease in perfusion of the cortex and relative increase in perfusion of subcortical areas, which are located closer to the heart. This, he insists, is the major change in brain physiology during sleep and the primary factor in conditioning the brain for dreaming. Consequently the similarity between dreams and mental illness provides, in Meynert's view, evidence that various psychiatric disturbances are caused by comparable changes in cerebral perfusion.[1]

In addition to drawing analogies between the nature of dreams and that of mental disturbances, neuropsychiatrists also spoke of dreams as important symptoms of mental disease. It is in this context that Freud first refers to dreams. In the earliest of his case histories of hysterical patients, that of Emmy von N., Freud recorded the content of Emmy's dreams as symptomatic of her illness. During the years which followed, he treated hysterical symptoms according to Breuer's cathartic method, tracing them to the traumatic events which supposedly initiated the difficulty. He attempted to deal with the contents of dreams in the same manner. Freud wrote later that

> it was in the course of [applying Breuer's method] that I came upon dream interpretation. My patients were pledged to communicate to me every idea or thought that occurred to them in connection with some particular subject; amongst other things they told me their dreams and so taught me that a dream can be inserted into the psychical chain that has to be traced backwards in the memory from a pathological idea. It was then only a short step to treating the dream itself as a symptom and to applying to dreams the method of interpretation that had been worked out for symptoms.[2]

Freud's interest in dreams had actually emerged much earlier and had, in fact, predated the beginning of his studies in the neuroses. During the 1880s, for example, he discussed dreams on numerous occasions in his correspondence with his fiancée.[3] But his perception of the significance of dreams as neurotic symptoms served to intensify this early interest.

Freud's observations in his correspondence with Martha Bernays deal primarily with his own dreams, and, following the development of his clinical interest in the subject, Freud devoted increased attention to his own dreams. A few months after the publication of *Studies on Hysteria,* on the night of July 23–24, 1895, he had a dream which he subsequently regarded as a turning point in his investigations of the neuroses. In attempting to analyze what he later labelled his "dream of Irma's Injection" by uncovering the events which had motivated it, Freud decided that the dream was based upon a desire to exonerate himself from responsibility for a patient's continued ill health and to vindicate his approach to the neuroses. He later wrote: "The dream acquitted me of the responsibility for Irma's condition by showing that it was due to other factors—it produced a whole series of reasons. The dream represented a particular state of affairs as I should have wished it to be. *Thus its content was the fulfilment of a wish and its motive was a wish* [italics in original]."[4] Freud insisted on several occasions that this marked his initial recognition of dreams as wish-fulfillments. In a letter to Fliess written in June, 1900,[5] he asks:

> Do you suppose that some day a marble tablet will be placed on the house, inscribed with these words:

> In this house on July 24th, 1895,
> the Secret of Dreams was revealed to
> Dr. Sigmund Freud

This last comment, as well as others in the Fliess correspondence, indicate that Freud believed he was the first to regard dreams as wish-fulfillments. But, in *The Interpretation of Dreams,* he acknowledged that various writers, including Wilhelm Griesinger, had earlier associated dreams with the fulfillment of wishes. Freud did insist, however, that he was the first to generalize this concept and to propose that all dreams are of this nature.[6]

Freud's earliest statements on dreams as wish-fulfillments appear in the "Project" (September and October, 1895), and follow his discussion of primary and secondary psychic processes. According to Freud, primary processes refer to situations in which, following an accumulation of endogenous Q, Q is allowed to flow unchecked into the mnemic image of the desired object. The object is then hallucinated, and movements may be executed to grasp the hallucination and to release the accumulated excitation. Such primary processes, Freud insists, are characteristic of infantile mentation. In the course of development, the child learns to avoid hallucinations and to store quantities of Q until a desired object is actually present and satisfaction can actually be achieved. In terms of neuromechanics, this is brought about by the emergence of a system of cathected neurones which constitute the physiological foundation of the ego and which, by means of side-cathexes, prevent the free flow of Q into mnemic images of desired objects. But Freud then suggests that dreaming involves hallucinated wish-fulfillments and is a persistent form of primary process.

This characterization of dreams fit neatly into contemporary notions of mental functioning. Freud's distinction between primary and secondary processes converged with the widely held concept that primitive forms of behavior, controlled by the lower parts of the nervous system, involve straightforward reflex responses to both external stimuli and internal instinctual drives, and that forms of behavior which emerge later in the course of development, and which are under the control of higher cerebral centers, involve the inhibition of simple reflexes and the emergence of more sophisticated responses to stimuli. Furthermore, the neuropsychiatric literature commonly associated sleep and dreams with the temporary loss of higher mental functions and with a reversion to more primitive psychological patterns. Freud reiterates in the "Project" the popular notion that the ego is temporarily suspended during sleep, and he asserts that this is "the precondition of psychical primary processes." This convergence of his formula with standard ideas concerning sleep and mental processes undoubtedly served to encourage Freud's pursuit of the wish-fulfillment theory.

Dreams were most often mentioned by neuropsychiatrists in the context of analogies with mental disturbances, and those writers who preceded Freud with notions of dreams as wish-fulfillments also drew analogies with mental illness. Griesinger, for example, states in his text *Mental Pathology and Therapeutics:*

> To the individual who is distressed by bodily and mental troubles, the dream realises what reality has refused—happiness and fortune. The starving Trenck [Friedrich Freiherr von Trenck, an eighteenth-century autobiographer], during his imprisonment, often dreamed of rich repasts; the beggar dreams that he is wealthy, the person who has lost by death some dear friend fondly dreams of the most intimate and lasting reunion. So also in mental disease . . . bright ideas of fortune, greatness, eminence, riches, etc.; stand out— and . . . the [initial] mental misery changes voluntarily to the mirth of the maniac. Thus we see clearly how supposed possession and imaginary realisation of good things and wishes, the denial or destruction of which furnished a . . . cause of

the disease, constitute commonly the chief subjects of the delirium of insanity.[7]

Freud, in his references to dreams in the "Project," says relatively little concerning analogies between dreams and neuroses. He does state that "the pathological mechanisms which are revealed in the psychoneuroses by the most careful analysis have the greatest similarity to dream-processes," and he notes a few specific similarities.[8] He maintains, for example, that hysterical symptoms are symbols of a repressed pathogenic memory, and he observes that symbol formation is also characteristic of dreams—a parallel which had been drawn by Breuer and Freud in the "Preliminary Communication" (1893). This leads to the proposal that neurotic symptoms are, like dreams, primary processes. But Freud at this time was concerned more with exploring the significance of his patients' dreams as neurotic symptoms than with enumerating parallels between dreams in general and neuroses. The realization that dreams can be approached as symptoms in neurotic patients did suggest to Freud that perhaps dreams in normal people might also be interpreted as manifestations of material excluded from consciousness, and this is the basis for those comparisons between dreams and symptoms which he does draw. But analogies between the two phenomena are not developed to any significant degree in the "Project."

However, in the years after his writing of the "Project," Freud was led by several factors to accord a greater importance to analogies between dreams and neuroses. One such factor was his increasing interest in the details of symptom formation. When writing the "Project," Freud's views on symptom formation did not go very far beyond the notion that symptoms reflect an expenditure of quantities of excitation which, because of repression, are not allowed their normal outlet. There are occasional further comments on the relationship between symptoms and the underlying repressed ideas, such as his observations about symptoms being symbols of the repressed, but these themes were not pursued. With abandonment of the "Project" and concentration on his clinical explanation of the neuroses, Freud placed a new emphasis on the dynamics of symptom formation. In particular, he developed the notion of "the return of the repressed" and the concept of symptoms as compromises between repressed memories and the repressing ego, and he attempted to demonstrate how the specific symptoms of psychoneuroses emerge from this compromise. It soon occurred to Freud that dreams, which are also based upon material excluded from consciousness, might also involve a compromise between this unconscious material and the ego. Consequently, along with his new emphasis on the processes of symptom formation, he displays a new interest in dreams as a model for these processes. In a letter to Fliess written in May, 1896, Freud suggests: "One species of psychical disturbance arises if the power of the [repressed material] increases; another if the force of the thought-inhibition relaxes. (. . . —dreams as a prototype) [*sic*]."[9]

The discovery of neurotic fantasies was another factor which contributed to Freud's increasing concern with comparisons of dreams and neuroses. In correspondence written during the spring of 1896, Freud asserts that the repressed ideas uncovered in analysis consist largely of fantasies which are formulated, like symptoms, by means of a compromise between repressed memories and the ego. These fantasies seemed to Freud to closely resemble dreams, and their discovery reinforced Freud's views on the nature of patients' dreams and on the importance of their dreams as clinical material. But the discovery of neurotic fantasies also reinforced Freud's views on the structure of dreams in general—those of healthy people as well as those of people suffering from neuroses—and lent additional significance to the exploration of dreams as a source of information regarding neurotic processes. In the letters dealing with fantasies, Freud repeatedly compares them to dreams. He also informs Fliess at this time: "I have felt impelled to start writing about dreams."[10]

Freud's observation—also during the spring of 1897—that repression is directed primarily against impulses aroused by infantile experiences, rather than against simply the memory of such experiences, served as additional encouragement to comparisons between dreams and neuroses. There were, at this time, several precedents for viewing neurotic symptoms, like dreams, as wish-fulfillments. Griesinger, for example, had interpreted the deliria of insanity as wish-fulfillment, and this concept received wide endorsement. Freud implicitly applies the concept in his first paper on the neuropsychoses of defense (1894), when he associates hallucinatory delusions with the complete repression of unpleasant events and circumstances.[11] In discussing the neuroses, writers commonly attributed hysteria to lack of sexual gratification and interpreted hysterical convulsions as erotic raptures prompted by the organism's desire to satisfy unfulfilled drives. But, prior to 1897, Freud made no explicit attempt to apply the notion of wish-fulfillment to neurotic symptoms. However, with the new emphasis on repressed sexual impulses, it appeared to Freud that the return of the repressed must involve the reemergence of these impulses and that symptoms must involve their partial expression. This finally suggested to Freud in May, 1897, that symptoms, as well as dreams, may be perceived as wish-fulfillments: "The first motive for the construction of symptoms is . . . libido. Thus symptoms, like dreams, are *the fulfilment of a wish*."[12] When, in the ensuing months, neurotic fantasies were reinterpreted as not merely a reworking of repressed memories in the interest of defense, but as an imagined gratification of repressed libidinal impulses, Freud speculated that symptoms might be in part an acting out of these fantasies. This strengthened his conceptualization of symptoms as wish-fulfillments.

Freud subsequently viewed symptoms as a compromise between libidinous impulses and the ego's feelings of guilt and desires for self-punishment triggered by these impulses, and he proposed that symptoms are actually wish-fulfilling with respect to both the underlying sexual impulses and the desire for self-punishment. In later correspondence, he illustrates this thesis:

> A symptom arises where the repressed and the repressing thought can come together in the wish-fulfilment. A symptom is the wish-fulfilment of the repressing thought when, for instance, it is a punishment, a self-punishment, the final replacement of self-gratification. . . .
>
> This key opens many doors. Do you know, for instance, why X.Y. suffers from hysterical vomiting? Because in phantasy she is pregnant, because she is so insatiable that she cannot put up with not having a baby by her last phantasy-lover. . . . But she must vomit too, because in that case she will be starved and emaciated, and will lose her beauty and no longer be attractive to anyone. Thus the sense of the symptom is a contradictory pair of wish-fulfilments.[13]

The interpretation of symptoms as wish-fulfillments added, of course, a major new facet to the analogy between dreams and neuroses.

During the summer and fall of 1897, Freud became increasingly skeptical of the seduction theory. But he believed that, whatever his uncertainty concerning the origin of pathological impulses, his theories regarding the construction and significance of symptoms remained valid. He now viewed dreams primarily as a prototype of symptom construction, and he remarked: "The most assured thing seems to me to be the explanation of dreams." In the letter announcing rejection of the seduction theory, he notes: "The dreams still stand secure."[14]

An additional aspect to the analogy between dreams and neuroses emerged following Freud's rejection of the seduction theory. In discussions of dreams prior to this time, Freud assumed that dreams, like neuroses, are based upon material excluded from consciousness, and he believed that in neurotics this material consists essentially of the repressed ideas which are also generating the patients' symptoms. In particular, he believed that the dreams of neurotics are based upon memories of infantile sexual traumas. But he could define no specific source for dream material in normal people. In some early discussions, including comments in *Studies on Hysteria,* Freud endorsed the often-proposed concept that dreams are constructed around ideas from the preceding day that were insufficiently thought out at the time of their occurrence—with the dream serving, in effect, to complete unfinished trains of thought. However, the analysis of patients' dreams revealed that material from the preceding day is used primarily for disguising those repressed ideas and impulses which are the true basis of their dreams. This suggested to Freud that in normal people there must also be some more profound source for dreams. He had always maintained that people normally inhibit and suppress ideas which are painful or which they would rather forget, and it occurred to him that these might be the ideas motivating their dreams. But, since normal people had presumably not experienced sexual traumas in infancy, Freud was unable to delineate a specific source for the dreams of normal people analogous to that defined for neurotics.

With rejection of the seduction theory, Freud attributes greater importance to normal infantile sexual impulses and ascribes the pathogenesis of neuroses to an intensification of these impulses. He proposes that in both the normal and the pathological situation the various manifestations of infantile sexuality are generally inhibited in later childhood, and he redefines repression to denote this abandonment of infantile sexual components. Neuroses emerge, according to the new theory, because the repression of abnormally intense infantile impulses is only partially effective and such impulses eventually find expression in the form of neurotic symptoms. But the new emphasis on normal infantile sexuality, and on its repression during the latency period, suggested to Freud that the dreams of normal people, like those of neurotics, might be based upon repressed sexual impulses. His self-analysis, in which he was able to trace various dreams to repressed Oedipal impulses, reinforced this view. During the next few years, Freud does not explicitly insist that dreams are invariably generated by repressed infantile sexual impulses. On the contrary, he states in *The Interpretation of Dreams:*

> The theory of the psychoneuroses asserts as an indisputable and invariable fact that only sexual wishful impulses from infancy, which have undergone repression . . . during the developmental period of childhood, are capable of being revived during *later* developmental periods . . . and are thus able to furnish the motive force for the formation of psychoneurotic symptoms of every kind. . . . I will leave it an open question whether these sexual and infantile factors are equally required in the theory of dreams.[15]

But he does insist in *The Interpretation of Dreams* that all dreams have infantile sources, and he implies in another section that they can generally be expected to also have sexual sources.

The Interpretation of Dreams, written between 1897 and 1899, was not intended simply as a monograph on dreams, related to but distinct from Freud's work on the neuroses. On the contrary, Freud's continued delineation of new similarities between dreams and neuroses lent, in his view, constantly increasing value to dream analysis as illustrative of neurotic processes, and his primary aim in the book is to discuss dreams as a prototype of these processes. Freud states in the preface:

> Psychological investigation shows that the dream is the first member of a class of abnormal psychical phenomena of which further members, such as hysterical phobias, obsessions and delusions, are found for practical reasons to be a matter of concern to physicians. As will be seen in the sequel, dreams can make no such claim to practical importance; but their theoretical value as a paradigm is on the other hand proportionally greater. Anyone who has failed to explain the origin of dream-images can scarcely hope to understand phobias, obsessions or delusions or to bring a therapeutic influence to bear on them.[16]

Freud's objectives in writing *The Interpretation of Dreams* must be viewed in the context of the peculiar nature of his clinical procedure. On the basis of his analyses of neurotic patients, Freud developed a theory of the natural history of neuroses and theories of normal mental processes and of childhood sexual development. He was convinced that his clinical experiences with the psychoanalytic method provided overwhelming evidence for these theories. But no one else practiced psychoanalysis, and Freud's experiences with the method were not substantiated by any other observers. Prior to 1897, during the period when his theories were based on the supposition that neuroses evolve from repressed traumatic encounters, this situation presented only limited difficulties. Freud then anticipated that the repeated discovery of repressed traumas such as infantile seductions, traumas which could no doubt often be independently substantiated and were obviously well-suited to serve as pathogenic events, would eventually suffice to demonstrate the correctness of his theories. But the revised formulas which emerged following rejection of the seduction theory, and which no longer postulated some uniform type of experience as the source of neuroses, did not offer any hope of such straightforward confirmation. The fact that Freud alone practiced psychoanalysis now became particularly problematic: a more detailed presentation of his clinical evidence was now required if his theories were to be established; yet, because no one shared his analytic procedure, citation of evidence tied exclusively to this method would carry only limited weight. Freud was consequently obliged to develop other evidence in support of his conclusions.

Freud's approach was to demonstrate how his formulas are capable of providing comprehensive explanations for familiar phenomena not directly related to the neuroses and to use such demonstrations as the major evidence for the correctness of his theories. For example, he supports his theory of infantile sexuality primarily by arguing that it offers the best explanation for the development of perversions. In his *Three Essays on the Theory of Sexuality,* the first essay is devoted entirely to perversions (the second is on infantile sexuality, and the third is concerned with the changes which occur at puberty). Freud reviews the extensive literature on the subject—which was divided between works emphasizing innate factors as the source of perversions and others stressing the role of abnormal childhood experiences—and he cites evidence for and against both views. He then introduces his own formula as a compromise between the two schools: he suggests that there is an innate tendency towards sexual perversions in everyone and that this tendency manifests itself in infantile sexual impulses. Infantile sexuality is generally repressed in later childhood, but in some cases early infantile impulses become overly intense—either because of innate overdevelopment or because of their overstimulation due to exceptional childhood experiences—and they may then avoid repression and yield perversions in later life. Freud insists that this theory accounts for all the observations upon which the earlier formulas were based, while it resolves the objections to the earlier formulas. In addition, it offers an explanation for common infantile activities such as sucking, and it indicates why perversions are so common and are so easily induced. Further, it accounts for why behavior such as kissing, which bears no direct relation to sexual intercourse, can nevertheless be found universally to play a subsidiary role in normal sexual activity; such behavior, in Freud's view, merely represents the vestiges of oral and other infantile sexual drives. These are the major arguments presented by Freud in defense of his theory of sexuality, and evidence derived from his analyses of neurotic patients is introduced only tangentially. The thesis that neuroses are based upon the repression of overly intense infantile sexual impulses is stated only in the concluding summary.

Freud similarly chose to introduce his theory of neurotic symptom formation by demonstrating how the theory offers a convincing explanation for familiar phenomena. There were, in fact, a variety of phenomena which he thought useful for this purpose. He believed that slips of the tongue, forgetting, bungled actions, and related types of behavior can all best be explained in terms of an interaction between repressed ideas and a repressing ego; he developed this theme in *The Psychopathology of Everyday Life,* begun in 1900 and published in 1901. In *Jokes and Their Relation to the Unconscious,* which was completed in 1905, Freud argues that jokes are constructed in the same manner, and he attempts to demonstrate that this view offers the greatest insight into the nature of humor. But Freud believed that dreams are the best material for introducing the psychic processes involved in neuroses. He had, of course, devoted more attention to dreams than to these other phenomena. Also, there was an extensive psychological and psychiatric literature on dreams; as in his discussion of perversion in the *Three Essays on the Theory of Sexuality,* Freud could show how his own formula incorporates differing theories, reconciles seemingly contradictory views, and accounts for the observations which had inspired these various interpretations. For example, numerous writers had noted the prominence in dreams of childhood events and had therefore emphasized the role of childhood memories in dream construction. Others insisted that dreams are based primarily on the experiences of the preceding day. Freud argues in *The Interpretation of Dreams* that the ultimate sources of dreams are repressed infantile ideas, but he insists that events of the preceding day also play an important role, both by arousing these repressed ideas and by providing material with which the infantile thoughts are partially disguised in dreams. Thus, both theories and both types of observation are accounted for. Chapter 1 of *The Interpretation of Dreams* is devoted to a review of the literature, and Freud asserts in a later chapter: "We have . . . been able to find a place in our structure for the most various and contradictory findings of earlier writers, thanks to the novelty of our theory of dreams, which combines them, as it were, into a higher unity."[17]

Freud was not very satisfied with this device of presenting his theory of neurotic processes by first demonstrating how the theory can serve to explain other phenomena. He believed that the analysis of neurotic patients provides by far the strongest evidence for his theory and that no discussions of dreams or jokes could be quite as convincing. Consequently, although Freud states in *The Interpretation of Dreams* that "it is my intention to make use of my present elucidation of dreams as a preliminary step towards solving the more difficult problems of the psychology of the neuroses," he subsequently felt obliged to refer to his analyses of neurotic patients to support various points concerning dream interpretaion.[18] Later in the book he notes:

> Though my own line of approach to the subject of dreams was determined by my previous work on the psychology of the neuroses, I had not intended to make use of the latter as a basis of reference in the present work. Nevertheless I am constantly being driven to do so, instead of proceeding as I should have wished, in the contrary direction and using dreams as a means of approach to the psychology of the neuroses.[19]

But, in view of the fact that he alone practiced analysis and his clinical material could therefore not be expected to receive general acceptance, Freud continued to believe that discussions of jokes, parapraxes (a word coined to translate *fehlleistungen,* Freud's collective term for slips of the tongue, forgetting, etc.), and especially dreams were the best means for introducing his theory. He remarks in his "Fragment of an Analysis," written in 1901 and published in 1905:

> It was not without good reasons that in the year 1900 I gave precedence to a laborious and exhaustive study of dreams (*The Interpretation of Dreams*) over the publications upon the psychology of the neuroses which I had in view. And incidentally, I was able to judge from its reception with what an inadequate degree of comprehension such efforts are met by other specialists at the present time. In this instance there was no validity in the objection that [his assertions could not be tested and checked]. For every one can submit his own dreams to analytic examination, and the technique of inter-

preting dreams may be easily learnt from the instructions
and examples which I have given. I must once more insist,
just as I did at that time, that a thorough investigation of the
problems of dreams is an indispensable prerequisite for any
comprehension of the mental processes in hysteria and the
other psychoneuroses.[20]

Freud clearly perceived his publication of *The Interpretation of Dreams* not
merely as an offshoot of his studies of neuroses, but as a necessary
prologue to additional efforts to win acceptance of his neurosis theories.

Psychic Processes in The Interpretation of Dreams

Freud devotes the first chapter of *The Interpretation of Dreams* to a
review of the previous literature on the subject. In the next chapter he
offers his analysis of his "Dream of Irma's Injection," the dream to
which he traced his initial recognition of wish-fullfillment in dreams.
He then presents his thesis that in fact all dreams entail the fulfillment
of wishes. Freud acknowledges that, on the one hand, many other
writers have also noted wish-fulfillment in dreams, and, on the other
hand, his generalization of this observation might seem highly dubious
in view of the painful and unpleasant nature of so many dreams. But
he asserts that, as in his "Dream of Irma's Injection," wish-fulfillment
concerns the "latent content," the hidden meaning of the dream, and
any unpleasantness associated with the "manifest content" does not
negate his principle:

> We must make a contrast between the *manifest* and the *latent*
> content of dreams. There is no question that there are
> dreams whose manifest content is of the most distressing
> kind. But has anyone tried to interpret such dreams? to re-
> veal the latent thoughts behind them? If not, then the . . .
> objections raised against my theory will not hold water: it still
> remains possible that distressing dreams . . . when they have
> been interpreted, may turn out to be fulfillments of wishes.[21]

Freud supports his thesis by analyzing several unpleasant dreams and
demonstrating their hidden, wish-fulfilling significance. One example is
the dream of a patient whose sister's older son had died some years
earlier:

> The patient, who was a young girl, began thus: " . . . Last
> night, then, I dreamt that *I saw Karl* [the dead boy's younger

brother] *lying before me dead. He was lying in his little coffin with his hands folded and with candles all round—in fact just like little Otto* [the dead boy], *whose death was such a blow to me* [italics in original]."

The patient, who was familiar with Freud's dream theory, insisted that such a circumstance could hardly represent her wishes. But Freud then goes on:

> After reflecting a little I was able to give her the correct interpretation of the dream, which she afterwards confirmed. . . .
> The girl had early been left an orphan and had been brought up in the house of a much older sister. Among the friends who visited at the house was a man who made a lasting impression on her heart. . . . After [a] breach the man ceased to visit the house; . . . [the patient] did not succeed, however, in freeing herself from her attachment to her sister's friend. . . . Whenever it was announced that the object of her affection, who was by profession a literary man, was to give a lecture anywhere, she was invariably in the audience; . . . I remembered that she had told me the day before that the Professor was going to a particular concert and that she intended to go to it as well so as to enjoy a glimpse of him once more. That had been on the day before the dream, and the concert was to take place on the day on which she told me the dream. It was therefore easy for me to construct the correct interpretation, and I asked her whether she could think of anything that happened after little Otto's death. She answered at once: "Of course; the Professor came to see us again after a long absence, and I saw him once more beside little Otto's coffin." This was exactly what I had expected, and I interpreted the dream in this way: "If now the other boy were to die, the same thing would happen. You would spend the day with your sister and the Professor would be certain to come to offer his condolences, so that you would see him again under the same conditions as the other time. The dream means no more than your wish to see him once more, a wish which you are inwardly struggling against. I know you have a ticket for to-day's concert in your pocket. Your dream was a dream of impatience: it anticipated the glimpse you are to have of him to-day by a few hours."[22]

Freud suggests that, in cases such as this where wish-fulfillment is unrecognizable, the distortion of the latent content is deliberate and is designed to suppress the latent material and to keep it from becoming conscious. He illustrates the point with further dream analyses, in which he demonstrates that the latent material involves thoughts and wishes which the dreamer would prefer to deny and repress. Freud concludes that "a dream is a (disguised) fulfillment of a (suppressed or repressed) wish."[23]

Freud later considers the source of these latent wishes. He notes that the more thoroughly he analyzes dreams, the more often he comes across ideas dating from early childhood, and that this is true even of dreams which initially seemed to be instigated by wishes stemming from a later period. He therefore offers the hypothesis that dreams invariably have childhood sources. Freud suggests that, in those cases in which wishes from a later period can also be detected, the dreams actually involve fulfillment of a succession of wishes, with the ultimate source being a wish stemming from childhood. This thesis is again illustrated by sample analyses. Freud discusses, for example, a series of his own dreams in which he imagined himself journeying to Rome. Although he had travelled in Italy a number of times, he had never been to Rome; the dreams fulfilled his repeatedly frustrated desire to visit the city. But analysis revealed that childhood wishes also lay behind these dreams:

> Hannibal, who I had come to resemble in [the respect of having travelled to Italy without reaching Rome], had been the favourite hero of my later school days. Like so many boys of that age, I had sympathized in the Punic Wars not with the Romans but with the Carthaginians. And when in the higher classes I began to understand for the first time what it meant to belong to an alien race, and anti-semitic feelings among the other boys warned me that I must take up a definite position, the figure of the semitic general rose still higher in my esteem. To my youthful mind Hannibal and Rome symbolized the conflict between the tenacity of Jewry and the organization of the Catholic church. And the increasing importance of the effects of the anti-semitic movement upon our emotional life helped to fix the thoughts and feelings of those early days. Thus the wish to go to Rome had become in my dream-life a cloak and symbol for a number of other passionate wishes [stemming from childhood].[24]

In another chapter Freud considers the mechanisms by which the latent content which serves to instigate a dream is reworked and transcribed into manifest content. One mechanism is condensation: the latent content generally involves a wealth of material, and this material is expressed briefly and succinctly in the dream. A second factor is displacement: a change of emphasis occurs with transcription, and those elements which stand out in a dream as the most significant components of the manifest content are not those which represent the most important elements of the latent content. Another mechanism, closely related to displacement, is one that Freud calls "considerations of representability." Dreams are comprised essentially of visual hallucinations, and the aspects of the latent content which receive particular emphasis in the manifest content are those which are most amenable to pictorial representation. Finally, Freud speaks of "secondary revision." Condensation, displacement, and considerations of representability, when applied to the latent content, yield a collection of disconnected images; the psyche, as in all instances when it is confronted with apparently nonsensical material, attempts to impose some intelligible structure on these images. This "secondary revision," according to Freud, accounts for why dreams so often appear superficially to be logical and reasonable. Freud's discussion of these various mechanisms, and his demonstrations of how they work to transcribe latent content into manifest content, serve to lend credence to his thesis that dreams involve the disguised expression of repressed thoughts.

Freud subsequently argues that this process of transcription reflects the ego's efforts to keep the latent content of dreams from becoming conscious, and he speaks frequently of censorship of latent content by the ego. But he also perceives transcription as nevertheless yielding a limited conscious expression of the repressed material and as therefore involving a partial evasion of censorship. Freud finally suggests that this interaction between the underlying wish and censorship by the ego, the two factors involved in dream construction, can be fully understood only in the context of a more general theory of mental processes. The final chapter of the book is devoted to considering dreams in relation to a general psychology.

Freud suggests that the mental apparatus consists of several distinct psychic systems, including a perceptual system and a number of different memory systems organized according to different patterns of association and recall. He appeals to the study of dreams as evidence that there are, in addition, two systems related to modes or processes of thinking—one system associated with the wishes which inspire dreams, and the other responsible for the censorship of these wishes. Freud insists that his delineation of these various systems has no anatomical significance, and in the entire discussion he makes no reference to anatomical or physiological principles. The apparatus is described solely in psychological terms. But Freud does propose that these different systems should be viewed as located along a reflex pathway, with the perceptual system located, of course, at the sensory end of the pathway. The system of thinking associated with dream censorship must, according to Freud, be the same agency which controls thought during waking life and which is responsible for voluntary, conscious actions. He therefore places this system at the motor end of the apparatus, and he labels it "the Preconscious" to indicate that excitation of this system (by, for example, some new sensation) can lead immediately to a consciousness of relevant thoughts provided only that the excitation is intense enough to attract attention. The system which supplies the latent content of dreams is labelled "the Unconscious" and is perceived by Freud as situated before the Preconscious in the sensory-motor reflex pathway. Excitation of the Unconscious can lead to a consciousness of relevant thoughts only after these thoughts have passed through the Preconscious and submitted to censorship by the latter. Freud in later years refers to this conceptualization of the mental apparatus as his topographical model.

The absence of hallucinatory wish-fulfillment from normal waking life is attributed by Freud to the effectiveness of Preconscious censorship in the waking state. Wish-fulfilling dreams occur during sleep in part because of a lowering of the censorship barrier. Freud maintains, in addition, that dream hallucinations involve a retrogressive flow of excitation from the Unconscious to the perceptual system, and he suggests that sleep, which cuts off the normal flow of excitation from peripheral sense organs to the perceptual system, renders this retrogressive movement possible. This concept appeared also in the "Project" and was in fact a common notion in contemporary literature on psychic processes. Almost all authors discussed psychic excitation as proceeding in a reflex pattern from sensation to perception and ultimately to some movement, and hallucinations, in the context of this model, seemed necessarily to involve a retrogression of excitation. The English physician Henry Maudsley, for example, writes in *The Physiology of Mind* (1876): "As [an] idea is excited into activity by the impression on the senses, so it may in turn react backwards upon the sensory centers giving rise even under certain circumstances to illusions and hallucinations."[25]

According to Freud's model, the censorship of the Preconscious is only partially relaxed in sleep and it is for this reason that the Unconscious wishes which motivate dreams rarely become fully conscious. Instead, latent content is reworked and obscured beneath manifest content, under pressure of the remaining censorship. However, the dream's disguised fulfillment of the Unconscious wish still constitutes a partial evasion of the weakened censorship. Dreams are therefore regarded by Freud as a compromise between the Preconscious and the Unconscious.

In discussing the source of the infantile Unconscious wishes which motivate dreams, Freud introduces concepts from the "Project" concerning the dream process and the development of mental functions. He remarks that the psychic apparatus strives to divest itself of accumulations of excitation, but that endogenous excitation associated with biological needs can only be released through specific actions. (The excitation related to hunger, for example, can be effectively discharged only through the act of eating.) The newborn child quickly becomes familiar with the objective situations under which such excitations can be discharged; but, initially, when excitation reaccumulates, the infant simply hallucinates the desired object and attempts to grasp the hallucination. This, of course, yields no satisfaction and the child subsequently develops thought processes which inhibit such hallucinations and enable him to manipulate his environment so as to gain actual access to desired objects. Consequently, wish-fulfilling hallucinations cease to play a role in waking life. Freud proposes, however, that the hallucinatory fulfillment of infantile wishes in dreams is a reemergence of this primitive form of mental functioning:

> Thought is after all nothing but a substitute for a hallucinatory wish. . . . Dreams . . . have merely preserved for us in that respect a sample of the psychical apparatus's primary method of working, a method which was abandoned as being inefficient. What once dominated waking life, while the mind was still young and incompetent, seems now to have been banished into the night. . . . *Dreaming is a piece of infantile mental life that has been superseded* [italics in original].[26]

Preconscious censorship of Unconscious wishes, whether in waking or sleep, is seen by Freud as reflecting the mature psyche's effort to inhibit infantile hallucinatory wish-fulfillment.

It is clear, however, from Freud's discussion in the earlier chapters of the book, that he perceives dreams as entailing not merely a reversion to a primitive style of mentation, but also reversion to a mode of mental functioning which is primitive in content as well as in style. Freud's distinction between Unconscious and Preconscious in the topographical model is designed to accommodate this distinction in content as well as style. The topographical model can be traced to a letter written to Fliess in December, 1896. Freud at that time still endorsed the seduction theory, and in the letter he developed an earlier proposal that the type of neurosis to evolve from a sexual trauma is determined by the child's age at the time of the trauma. He was most concerned with accounting for why hysterical symptoms take the specific form of somatic conversions, and he hoped that the correlation of different neuroses with different ages of pathogenesis might offer an explanation. Freud began by discussing the nature of memory. He suggested that one's mnemic images are each present in several different "registrations" within the psychical apparatus and that these various registrations represent different levels of psychic organization, which emerge successively during early development. Freud compared this model with that proposed for the speech apparatus in his book on aphasia. He had then argued that word images within the speech apparatus are similarly arranged in several different modes of organization, ranging from the primitive modes developed during early childhood to the more sophisticated patterns which emerge with maturity. His major point in the aphasia discussion was that the most sophisticated patterns generally dominate behavior and that under pathological conditions, when there is damage to the speech apparatus, these complex and more delicate patterns of organization are the first to be lost. The apparatus then reverts to a comparatively simpler form of verbal expression.

Freud, in his letter to Fliess (December, 1896), tentatively distinguishes three registrations for memory:

> Wz [*Wahrnehmungszeichen* (indication of perception)] is the first registration of the perceptions; it is quite incapable of consciousness, and arranged according to associations by simultaneity.
>
> Ub (*Unbewusstsein* [unconsciousness]) is the second registration, arranged according to other (perhaps causal) relations. *Ub* traces would perhaps correspond to conceptual memories; equally inaccessible to consciousness.
>
> Vb (*Vorbewusstsein* [preconsciousness]) is the third transcription, attached to word-presentations and corresponding to our official ego.[27]

Freud suggested that there are specific ages in childhood during which a new type of registration is developed, and that at this time the mnemic images existing in more primitive registrations are transcribed into this new type. He also offered a chart correlating the pathogenesis of hysteria, obsessions, and paranoia with different periods of child hood, and he indicated that the ages of memory transcription correspond to the borderline ages between the various periods of pathogenesis. For example, the pathogenesis of hysteria is associated with the period up to four years of age, that of obsessive neurosis is connected with years four to eight, and age four is regarded as a time of memory transcription, when the Ub registration first develops and memories from the more primitive Wz are transcribed into the Ub. Freud then interpreted repression as a failure of transcription. Repression occurs in situations where transcription would release unpleasure, specifically when the memory of a sexual encounter would, upon transcription, generate greater unpleasure than accompanied the original event. In such cases, the memory of the event persists solely in its primitive registration. This model entailed a new explanation of psychoneurotic symptoms. As Freud wrote in the letter to Fliess: "If a later transcript is lacking, . . . excitation is dealt with in accordance with the psychological laws in force in the earlier psychical period and along the paths open at that time."[28] The implication with respect to hysterical conversions was that, since prior to four years of age the response to excitation is typically some motor activity, excitation of a repressed memory dating from that period will naturally yield a motor response (i.e., a conversion symptom).

With rejection of the seduction theory in 1897, Freud disgarded his thesis relating the different neuroses to differences in the patient's age at the time of pathogenesis, and in his subsequent discussions of the neuroses, he made no further reference to the concept of memory registrations. But this concept, with some modification, seemed particularly useful for a tentative psychology of dreams.

It was generally accepted at this time that infantile behavior involves reflex responses to biological needs and is characterized by an intolerance of delays in satisfaction, and Freud's interpretation of infantile development as proceeding from hallucinatory wish-fulfillments to an inhibition of such hallucinations and an increased facility in arranging for real satisfaction was consistent with these popular notions. Freud's analogy between wish-fulfillment in dreams and infantile processes, first mentioned in the "Project," followed from this conceptualization of infantile development and received further support from the common belief that sleep involves a reversion to primitive modes of thought. This element of Freud's dream psychology was therefore in accord with standard views and, having demonstrated in the early chapters of *The Interpretation of Dreams* that dreams are indeed wish-fulfillments, Freud perceived no difficulty in reintroducing the analogy to infantile processes. But Freud had also argued in the earlier part of the book that dreams stem specifically from infantile wishes—a refinement of his dream theory which had evolved only in the preceding few years—and consequently his psychology of dreams now had to account for a reversion to infancy in content as well as in form. He therefore revived his earlier concept of memory registrations and postulated a psychic system, the Unconscious, which preserves both the infantile mode of operation and the specific contents of infantile thoughts; in addition, he suggested that the more mature psychic system, the Preconscious, suppresses the primitive content together with the primitive form. With a weakening of Preconscious censorship, infantile thoughts and infantile process reemerge. (Freud maintains in his topographical model that the Unconscious and Preconscious systems are separate from the memory apparatus, but he clearly indicates that they have particular affinities with separate groups of memories.)

In the last chapter of *The Interpretation of Dreams,* Freud also discusses the utility of dreams. He remarked earlier that in all dreams a wish to sleep is among the instigating wishes, and he believed that dreams generally fulfill this wish and work to preserve sleep. The common situation in which some disturbing stimulus, instead of arousing a sleeper, is simply absorbed into a dream, is interpreted as evidence that dreams work effectively to maintain sleep. Freud now suggests that dreams also serve to prevent the adverse expenditure of excitation by the Unconscious and the Preconscious. He proposes that Unconscious wishes are constantly accumulating quotas of excitation and that the Preconscious is obliged to expend excitation in order to control the Unconscious and keep it from discharging its cathexes in fruitless activity. This is particularly problematic during sleep when Preconscious excitation is somewhat depleted. But since activity cannot be so easily aroused in sleep, a partial expenditure of Unconscious excitation can be permitted without adverse effect. The dream compromise allows this harmless release of Unconscious excitation and enables the Preconscious to conserve some of the excitation that would be expended if it were obliged to fully suppress the dream wish:

> It was indeed to be expected that dreaming, even though it
> may originally have been a process without a useful purpose,
> would have procured itself some function in the interplay of
> mental forces. And we can now see what that function is.
> Dreaming has taken on the task of bringing back under con
> trol of the preconscious the excitation in the [Unconscious]
> which has been left free; in so doing, it discharges the
> [Unconscious] excitation, serves it as a safety valve and at the
> same time preserves . . . sleep.[29]

Freud indicates repeatedly in *The Interpretation of Dreams* that his
psychology of dreams provides a paradigm for neurotic processes. He
suggests that neurotic symptoms are also an expression of repressed
infantile wishes and that they are formed, like dreams, by means of a
compromise between the Unconscious wish and the Preconscious censorship. Further, he insists that, as in dreams, this compromise is designed to allow a limited outlet to Unconscious excitation while maintaining sufficient Preconscious control to prevent more adverse behavior:

> Even where psychical health is perfect, the subjugation of
> the [Unconscious] by the [Preconscious] is not complete; the
> measure of suppression indicates the degree of our psychical
> normality. Neurotic symptoms show that the two systems are
> in conflict with each other; they are the products of a com-
> promise which brings the conflict to an end for the time
> being. On the one hand, they allow the [Unconscious] an
> outlet for the discharge of its excitation, and provide it with
> a kind of sally-port, while, on the other hand, they make it
> possible for the [Preconscious] to control the [Unconscious]
> to some extent.[30]

But most of Freud's references to the neuroses in *The Interpretation
of Dreams* are observations from patient analyses introduced to support
his dream psychology. For example, in defending against possible arguments that his dream interpretations are arbitrary, he writes: "We
might also point out . . . that our procedure in interpreting dreams is
identical with the procedure by which we resolve hysterical symptoms;
and there the correctness of our method is warranted by the . . . disappearance of the symptoms."[31] Insofar as Freud intended to establish a
dream theory which could then be used as evidence for the correctness
of his theory of the neuroses and for the validity of his clinical method,
this appeal to analytic material in support of the dream theory tends, of

course, to reduce his argument to a circular one. But, although Freud expresses his regrets about this use of his clinical observations and recognizes that he thereby confuses his argument, he apparently felt that such references do not completely compromise that argument. Freud believed that material from his analyses of neurotics offered some of the best evidence for his dream theory—and it was for this reason that he cited such material—but he seems nevertheless to have felt that his other evidence in support of the dream theory went a long way of itself towards establishing the validity of the theory. For example, while the cures achieved in analysis were, in his view, a strong indication that his interpretations were not arbitrary, he regarded other indications—including the thoroughness with which his interpretations were capable of accounting for all the various elements of a dream—as also providing substantial evidence for the veracity of his explanations. The fact that his theory was able to account for virtually all the observations about dreams cited in the literature, and was able to incorporate virtually all of the earlier dream theories propounded on the basis of these observations, provided, in Freud's view, particularly strong support for his own formula. After expressing his discontent at having made such frequent use of material drawn from his work in the neuroses, Freud writes:

> In my dissatisfaction at this state of things, I am glad to
> pause for a little over another consideration which seems to
> put a higher value on my efforts. I found myself faced by a
> topic on which, as has been shown in my first chapter, the
> opinions of the authorities were characterized by the sharp-
> est contradictions. My treatment of the problems of dreams
> has found room for the majority of these contradictory
> views.[32]

But, while Freud apparently believed that he had indeed succeeded in establishing this dream psychology on its own merits, and that he could now use the dream theory to support his formulas for the neuroses, he also believed that the psychology derived from his study of dreams required some modification before it could actually be applied to the neuroses. Freud's cursory remarks on the weaknesses and strengths of his arguments appear at the beginning of section E of the final chapter, and sections E and F—the last two of the book—are devoted to some revisions of his psychology.

In the dream psychology the expression of suppressed Unconscious wishes was associated with a weakening of the Preconscious during sleep, and Freud is now particularly concerned with establishing that sleep is not a prerequisite for the penetration of Unconscious material into consciousness. He is also interested in making the point that not all infantile wishes, but only a specific group, serve as the basis of dreams and neuroses.

Freud had asserted earlier that when thoughts related to recent experiences help to generate a dream, they do so by arousing a related infantile wish. He also maintained that when these recent thoughts appear, in a distorted form, as part of the dream material, the elements which appear in the dream have merely been appropriated by the Preconscious censorship to disguise the underlying infantile wish. For example, one of Freud's dreams of Rome was inspired in part by an engraving of the city which he had seen the previous day in a patient's home, and the scene in the print appeared in the dream as a view glimpsed by Freud from the window of a train. According to Freud's earlier remarks, this appearance in the dream, in distorted form, of the previous day's experience simply reflects the Preconscious's selection of elements from recent memory for use in camouflaging the infantile wish which provided the ultimate stimulation for the dream. Now, however, Freud insists that another explanation is required for how it comes about that recent thoughts which serve to inspire a dream are then represented in the dream in such a distorted form. In developing his explanation, Freud reintroduces concepts of psychic functioning presented earlier in the "Project." He suggests that new ideas typically receive a small cathexis of excitation from the Preconscious and that this excitation is then transmitted along associative pathways, thereby establishing a train of thought. (Unless exceptional amounts of excitation are involved, these trains of thought usually remain unconscious.) Alternatively, an idea may simply be ignored by the Preconscious, or it may initially receive a Preconscious cathexis and its cathexis may be withdrawn at some point; in these cases, the trains of thought stemming from these ideas remain undeveloped. But there are also cases in which an idea that has been ignored, or whose Preconscious cathexis has been withdrawn, arouses an Unconscious wish and is then cathected by the Unconscious. Indeed, Freud maintains that it is sometimes these Unconscious associations which account for why the idea is ignored by the Preconscious. In any case, such ideas then draw on their Unconscious cathexes to establish trains of thought. But when this occurs, the thought patterns which emerge are not patterns associated with normal Preconscious functioning; on the contrary, they conform to the peculiar mode of functioning of the Unconscious. This mode of functioning, as now perceived by Freud, encompasses not only regression to hallucinations, but also those processes of condensation, displacement, and so forth, which were mentioned earlier as the mechanisms by which latent content was reworked and distorted in dreams. Freud now asserts that, when recent thoughts appear in dreams, they appear in such a distorted form because, due to their association with the underlying Unconscious wish, they have been cathected by the Unconscious and submitted to Unconscious processes. He thereby revises his earlier model which attributed dream distortion simply to the influence of Preconscious censorship.

This discussion yields a new conceptualization of the Unconscious. In the dream psychology, the Unconscious was characterized as involving not merely a particular mode of psychic functioning but also a particular body of material—the infantile wishes—to which this Unconscious mode of functioning was applied. Now, however, Freud has detached the primitive Unconscious thought pattern from the primitive ideas and has insisted that this pattern may also be applied to later material in those instances where the later thoughts bear some special relation to infantile wishes. The terms "primary process" and "secondary process"—which convey the notion of two different modes of functioning detached from any specific body of material—are now introduced for the first time in the book to designate the operations of the Unconscious and Preconscious systems.[33] Freud maintains further that the submission of recent thoughts to Unconscious processes occurs during the waking state and is not dependent on sleep. Sleep, he asserts, simply gives these reworked thoughts an exceptional opportunity for conscious expression. Later, citing slips of the tongue and jokes as examples, Freud notes that thoughts submitted to Unconscious processes occasionally find expression in the waking state as well. He subsequently insists that neurotic symptoms are formed in the same manner:

> We discover by analysing the symptom . . . that . . . normal thoughts have been submitted to abnormal treatment: *they have been transformed into the symptom by means of condensation and the formation of compromises, by way of superficial associations and in disregard of contradictions, and also, it may be, along the path of* [retrogression] [italics in original].[34]

Freud next attempts to delineate a specific group of infantile wishes as the source of dreams, neurotic symptoms, and other manifestations of Unconscious activity. He had argued in the dream psychology that dreams are caused by "suppressed or repressed" infantile wishes, but he had indicated then that suppression or repression referred merely to the Preconscious's efforts to prevent hallucinatory fulfillment of infantile wishes and that all infantile wishes are submitted to the same sort of inhibition. He now revises this view.

Freud once more discusses how infants, in their efforts to divest themselves of accumulated excitation, will initially hallucinate objects which they have learned to associate with satisfaction, and he reviews how, in the course of development, a secondary process emerges which inhibits these hallucinations and works more efficiently to achieve experiences of satisfaction. Now, however, introducing additional notions from the "Project," he goes into greater detail about the operation of this secondary process. Freud suggests that, in seeking the release of accumulated excitation, the Preconscious proceeds by utilizing small cathexes to test various paths of thought and movement, with the balance of excitation left in reserve until a pathway leading to adequate satisfaction is available: "When once the second system has concluded its exploratory thought-activity, it releases the inhibition and damming-up of the excitations and allows them to discharge themselves in movement."[35] Freud then considers how the operation of this secondary process relates to the general tendency to avoid unpleasure. He earlier associated the accumulation of excitation with unpleasure and the tendency to discharge such accumulations with a tendency to avoid unpleasure. He now notes, more specifically, that unpleasure is also aroused if the memory of a painful event is recathected, and he suggests that consequently there is a tendency to avoid recathecting these memories. Freud maintains, however, that, in pursuing its search for experiences of satisfaction, the Preconscious must have access to all memories; he concludes that the Preconscious, with its sophisticated inhibitory mechanisms, develops a means for inhibiting the release of unpleasure upon recathexis of a painful memory.

But this mechanism occasionally fails. Freud asserts that the primitive wishful impulses which emerged prior to development of the Preconscious continue to provide the basic motivation for all thought and behavior in later life, and that the Preconscious merely works to divert and direct these impulses but does not have full control over them. Among these primitive impulses, there are some which are no longer associated with affects of pleasure, but are instead connected with unpleasure because of a clash with more mature aims and impulses. (Although it is not stated explicitly, it is clear that Freud has in mind primitive sexual impulses.) When some new train of thought arouses such impulses, by recalling an infantile memory related to them, the Preconscious is incapable of controlling the resulting unpleasure and responds by simply avoiding further cathexis of the relevant thoughts. Freud suggests that it is specifically these thoughts, associated with now unpleasurable infantile impulses and consequently abandoned by the Preconscious, which are subject to primary processes and figure in dreams, neurotic symptoms, jokes and related phenomena. He thereby defines a special group of infantile wishes as the source of these phenomena.

Freud now defines *repression* as applying specifically to thoughts connected with these particular infantile wishes: "The unpleasure principle takes control and causes the [Preconscious] to turn away from the transference thoughts [i.e., the current thoughts which arouse an unpleasurable Unconscious impulse]. They are left to themselves—'repressed.' "[36] Repression is in this way implicitly differentiated from the Preconscious's general "inhibition" or "suppression" of all primitive impulses. Freud does not pursue this distinction further, but in a later footnote he writes that "I have omitted to state whether I attribute different meanings to the words 'suppressed' and 'repressed'. It should have been clear, however, that the latter lays more stress than the former upon the fact of attachment to the unconscious."[37]

There is little attempt in *The Interpretation of Dreams* to identify the primitive impulses which are initially pleasant and later become unpleasurable. Freud does say that the existence of such impulses is indicated by the observation that "disgust emerges in childhood after having been absent to begin with."[38] He also notes that in the psychoneuroses these impulses invariably prove to be sexual ones. But they were not defined further until the *Three Essays on the Theory of Sexuality* (1905).

Physiology and Psychology in Freud's Early Theories: Concluding Remarks

To those observers who construe the "Project" as evidence of Freud's preference for physiological explanations of neurotic phenomena, the shift in *The Interpretation of Dreams* to an explanation of the neuroses in terms of analogies to normal psychological processes marks Freud's shift from a physiological to a more strictly psychological approach. This is the view taken, for example, by Ernst Kris.[39] It is supported by the observation that various principles of mental functioning—such as the principle of constancy and the concepts of primary and secondary processes—are interpreted physiologically in the "Project" and then presented as psychological concepts in *The Interpretation of Dreams*. But the "Project" was written primarily to establish a clear distinction between repression and normal psychic inhibition, and to elucidate how puberty could convert a neutral or pleasant infantile experience into an unpleasant and repressed memory. A physiological approach was taken because Freud's work in the preceding few months indicated that these problems could best be resolved in physiological terms, not because he at that time had some general preference for physiological explanations. From his earliest work on the neuroses, nine years prior to his writing of the "Project," Freud had consistently condemned efforts to develop physiological models of the neuroses as fruitless speculation; and it was only when he was confronted by these particular problems, which appeared insoluble in purely psychological terms, that he resorted to physiological interpretations. When, in the ensuing months, it became clear that his physiology was indeed too speculative to offer satisfactory solutions to these problems, Freud simply put this approach aside and returned to his earlier emphasis on psychological discussions of his clinical observations.

Some writers, including Siegfried Bernfeld, have insisted that the principles of mental functioning which are defined in physiological terms in the "Project" and in psychological terms in *The Interpretation of Dreams* and later works—principles such as that of primary and secondary processes—were originally derived by Freud from contemporary neurophysiology.[40] This would suggest that, even if my thesis is correct and Freud did consistently emphasize psychological interpretations of neurotic phenomena, physiology nevertheless played a significant role in shaping his later theoretical models. A few authors have carried this argument even further and have insisted that Freud's neurosis theories and dream theories were based entirely upon neurophysiology. Peter Amacher writes in *Freud's Neurological Education and Its Influence on Psychoanalytic Theory:* "[Freud's] dream theory was essentially a logical application to dreams of the [neurological] principles he had learned, not a synthesis resting on extensive subjective or clinical observations."[41] Amacher's argument is endorsed by others, including Robert Holt and Raymond Fancher. Fancher, in "The Neurological Origin of Freud's Dream Theory," also insists that the entire dream theory was formulated on the basis of neurophysiological considerations.[42] In addition, Robert Holt calls for a total restructuring of psychoanalytic models on the grounds that present models are founded primarily on an outmoded physiology and therefore must themselves be outmoded.[43]

The extreme position taken by Amacher, Fancher, and Holt can be challenged by a number of objections. The essence of Freud's psychology of dreams and neuroses is the notion of a conflict between two psychic systems, and these writers ignore the fact that there was throughout the nineteenth century a well-established psychological tra-dition—based largely upon the psychology of Herbart and quite inde-pendent of physiology—which emphasized a conflict between psychic entities. Freud had read widely in this psychology and it undoubtedly exerted an important influence on his models. The concept of splits in consciousness, which played such a prominent role in psychologies of hypnosis during the nineteenth century, was a further source for Freud's theories of multiple psychic systems. Also, there is an ancient and widespread philosophical distinction between "appetites" on the one hand and the psychic forces which control and inhibit these appe-tites on the other; once Freud had identified sexual ideas and impulses as the key to neuroses, this tradition provided an additional source for his formulations concerning psychic systems in conflict.

Most importantly, Amacher and the others, in their overemphasis of physiology, completely ignore the role of Freud's clinical experi-ence in shaping his theoretical models. Even if one assumes that all of Freud's formulations are based upon earlier psychological or physio-logical theories, it is impossible to understand his choices among these theories—why he utilized some elements and rejected others—with-out considering his clinical experiences. For example, in attempting to account for Freud's emphasis on sexuality in his theories of the neu-roses, one might note that throughout the nineteenth century writers had consistently stressed sexual factors when discussing the etiology of hysteria. But Freud was quite familiar with this literature in 1886, and yet from 1886 to 1894 he rejected sexual theories and insisted that hysteria is primarily hereditary. Consequently, merely citing the ear-lier literature on hysteria and sexuality does not yield very much insight into why Freud ultimately endorsed the sexual emphasis. This can be understood only in the context of Freud's clinical work from 1892 to 1894 and the consistent reappearance of sexual themes in his patients' stories. Similarly, although one can cite numerous theories of intrapsychic conflict which may have influenced Freud, Freud's choice of theory, and the changes in his theory during the course of his early work on the neuroses, cannot be understood without con-sidering his clinical experiences. Freud initially interpreted the sup-pression of pathogenic memories as a manifestation of normal psychic inhibition, and he associated hysterical symptom formation with a fail-ure of inhibition. Later, he insisted that the suppression of pathogenic memories is a special response to particularly painful ideas and in-volves a process distinct from normal inhibition. The shift in models can only be understood in the context of Freud's clinical work in 1893 and 1894 and, in particular, his recognition of patients' resistance to therapy.

But, while Freud's theories of psychic conflict were shaped primarily by his clinical experiences and by the formulations of contemporary psychology, and while physiology played a very small part in the development of these theories, this does not fully resolve the problem of physiological influences on Freud's thought. One must still respond to Bernfeld's argument that neurophysiology provided those principles of mental functioning—such as the principle of constancy—to which Freud appealed in the "Project" and in *The Interpretation of Dreams* when attempting to imbed his concept of psychic conflict into a general psychology of mental processes. However, this argument can also be rebutted. The principles of mental functioning utilized by Freud were indeed quite popular in contemporary physiology. But they were derived mainly from behavioral observations, and the physiologists had in large part merely translated the behavioral material into the language of their science. Further, these concepts appear repeatedly in the psychological literature of the time and were most often perceived simply as psychological principles. They were expressed in physiological terms in the "Project" because Freud was then concerned with constructing a physiological model, but they were in no sense intrinsically tied to physiology.

The most important of these basic concepts, those which play a major role in Freud's psychology, are: the quantification of excitation, together with the principle of constancy—the concept that the system strives to divest itself of accumulations of excitation; the distinction of two separate modes of psychic functioning; and the thesis that under certain conditions the organism reverts to the more primitive of these modes of functioning. Freud had written of the quantification of excitation and the principle of constancy in 1892, several years before his writing of the "Project," and one discovers by considering his early work that he based his formulation of these concepts upon behavioral observations and that he originally interpreted the concepts in psychological terms. The idea of a quota of excitation, which is conveyed into the organism by a stimulus and which then has to be discharged, was suggested to Freud by his observation of a proportionality between the degree of emotional shock associated with a traumatic experience and the intensity of subsequent neurotic symptoms. In addition, he noted that it is common usage to speak of affective psychic states as forces which must be expended. In the "Preliminary Communication" (1893), he and Breuer cite expressions such as "to cry oneself out" and to "blow off steam" as epitomizing this common notion of the need to release accumulated psychic excitation. Also, Freud was well versed in a psychological literature which, without reference to physiology, dealt extensively with the organism's tendency to react automatically and in a measured way to stimuli. Finally, Freud makes no reference to any physiological sources for his concepts and, with the exception of the "Project," consistently discusses these concepts in purely psychological terms. It is true that Freud's quantification of excitation and principle of constancy converged with physiological notions concerning reflexes and the proportionality between stimulus and response, but, since Freud's own formulation was originally a psychological one based on behavioral phenomena, one is hardly justified in labelling his concepts neurophysiological in origin.

The two other major concepts utilized by Freud in formulating his general psychology were both quite popular at this time and were also derived in large part from psychological observations and commonly perceived simply as psychological principles. It is therefore again incorrect to regard them as associated primarily or fundamentally with physiology. The concept of two modes of psychic functioning—one related to infantile behavior and involving reflex-like responses to excitation and attempts at immediate satisfaction of biological needs, and another emerging during later development and involving the inhibition of infantile behavior and a more circumspect and efficient search for satisfaction—was inspired by innumerable psychological phenomena. It was repeatedly noted, for example, that young children demand immediate relief from the pressure of biological needs and display a very low tolerance of delays in satisfaction; development was perceived as yielding an increased ability to tolerate such delays and to cope more effectively with stimuli. Texts on psychology commonly defined the will as a faculty which emerges relatively late in the course of development and works to control and inhibit primitive reflex responses to stimulation, and such formulas were usually independent of physiological considerations.

The concept that one reverts under certain conditions to primitive modes of behavior was indeed expressed in physiological terms by numerous authors—such as John Hughlings Jackson, whose discussion of aphasia as involving a reversion to primitive forms of language usage was cited by Freud in his work on aphasia. But various types of abnormal behavior were commonly interpreted as a return to infantile patterns without any reference to physiology. The pugnacity and loss of social restraint which emerges with alcoholic intoxication, for example, were widely regarded as an abandonment of inhibitions associated with education and intellectual development and as a reversion to infantile modes of behavior, an interpretation most often independent of any physiological assumptions. Insanity, particularly mania, was traditionally viewed in the same way, as a loss of inhibition and a release of primitive and infantile drives, and this formula too was typically offered without reference to physiology.

But while the theory of mental processes offered in *The Interpretation of Dreams* was based essentially on psychological considerations and presented in psychological terms, Freud does indicate in the work that physiological explanations will ultimately be needed if a comprehensive theory of mental functioning in the neuroses is to be formulated. He notes that those developmental changes which cause certain infantile impulses to become unpleasurable are bound up with physical development (an oblique reference to somatic sexual development), and he implies that they are therefore not explicable in psychological terms. In addition, the development of excitation upon recathexis of unpleasurable ideas involves, in Freud's view, some secretory process—a thesis related to his speculations on the endocrine sources of sexual excitation; consequently this too requires physiological elucidation. Finally, he suggests that even the basic modes of operation of the psychic apparatus will be fully understood only when they are explained in physiological terms by the physiology of the future.

10. Epilogue

In the thirty-four years from his publication of the *Three Essays on the Theory of Sexuality* in 1905 to his death in 1939, Freud continued to revise and expand upon the various components of his psychology: his concepts of childhood sexuality and normal sexual development; his theories of the sexual etiology of neuroses and other forms of mental illness; his psychology of normal and pathological mental processes and their foundation in distinct and competing psychic systems; and his therapeutic formulas for the treatment and resolution of neuroses. Of the twenty-three volumes in the *Standard Edition* of Freud's complete psychological works, fifteen consist of works written during this later period. These later papers contain, of course, substantial and important modifications of Freud's theories. An example is his shift from the topographical model, with its delineation of the Unconscious and the Preconscious as the two psychic systems which shape and determine mental functioning, to the "structural model" and its definition of the Ego and the Id—whose relation is more complex than simply a distinction between censored and primitive on the one hand and uncensored and more mature on the other—as the two psychic systems governing mentation. But virtually all of the theoretical models formulated during this later period can easily be recognized as variations on theories, concepts, and themes first developed by Freud during the initial nineteen years of his study of the neuroses (1886–1905).

It is clear from quite early in Freud's work that he perceived his psychology as having significance for issues far beyond the realm of neuropsychiatry and mental illness. Nor did he see its wider significance as limited to the explanation of such psychic phenomena as dreams, jokes, and slips of the tongue. Rather, he viewed his psychology as potentially all-encompassing, potentially capable of offering explanations for all psychic phenomena. In his initial reference to the Oedipus legend, when first noting the apparent universality of childhood jealousy towards the parent of the same sex, Freud invokes the legend, not in the context of selecting a label for the phenomenon he has discovered, but in the context of offering an explanation for what he calls the "riveting power" of Sophocles' play; in the years after 1905 Freud increasingly sought to derive from his psychological models a psychology of art and literature, a psychology of religion, a psychology of history.

But even in these endeavors Freud did not really wander very far from the medical tradition of his period. In the decades after Darwin's publication of *The Origin of Species* (1859), it was widely assumed by both neuropsychiatrists and nonmedical psychologists that all aspects of mental functioning had developed out of primitive processes geared to the satisfaction of biological needs and had evolved as devices for more effectively achieving that satisfaction. From this perspective, observers commonly concluded that the ultimate motivation for all mental functioning continues to be the gratification of biological drives and that a psychology based on this premise ought to be capable of accounting not only for all psychological phenomena, but for all social and cultural phenomena as well. Freud was far from unique among psychiatrists and psychologists in his attempts to offer such an accounting.

Moreover, Freud, throughout his later career, perceived his excursions into the realms of social and cultural history as intimately bound to his study of psychopathology. These excursions were not merely applications of his theory of normal psychodynamics, they were equally attempts to cast light on the social and cultural dimensions of what he viewed as pathological psychic processes. Here, too, his course was consistent with the practice of his colleagues. Works on neurasthenia, for example, more often than not touched on the deleterious aspects of modern civilization and the social and cultural ramifications of neurasthenia. Studies of psychosexual pathology, such as Krafft-Ebing's books, typically digressed into historical and biographical analyses and social commentary. Freud, in his own digressions into cultural and social history and commentary, repeatedly returns to questions concerning psychopathology. Moreover, these digressions were imbedded in a corpus which continued to be dominated by writings dealing more strictly with issues of pathology.

While Freud's discussions of art, religion, and social history may appear superficially to take him rather far afield from issues related to the neuroses, it is quite obvious from his other works that he was in many respects peculiarly tenacious in focusing his attention on the syndromes that he had chosen as his particular area of investigation. For example, while he often touches upon the question of the relative weight to be given to physiology and psychology in accounting for neurotic phenomena, Freud—unlike many of his colleagues, such as Meynert, Brücke, Sigmund Exner, Auguste Forel, who speculated extensively on the relationship of mind to brain—never digressed into speculations of this sort outside of the "Project," and he did so in the "Project" only in the context of trying to resolve specific problems confronting his theory of the neuroses. It might seem somewhat peculiar that, having decided from his first studies of the neuroses that psychology offered the most accessible insights into hysteria and related syndromes and that psychotherapy offered the most promising therapeutic approach to these syndromes, Freud should have been concerned at all with this question of the weight to be accorded to physiology and should have continued to return to it even after abandoning the "Project"; indeed, he continued to do so until the end of his career. But, particularly after his recognition of the importance of infantile sexuality, when he came to view pathogenesis in the psychoneuroses as involving the interaction of childhood experiences with innate disposition, Freud in large part regarded the issue of physiology versus psychology as essentially equivalent to the issue of innate disposition versus environmental trauma, and the relative weight to be accorded these two factors has traditionally been a pertinent question not only throughout psychiatry, but throughout all of medicine. It is a question that has been raised with regard to most medical syndromes and is never really answered in any absolute sense, but typically tends to fade away once an adequate therapeutic approach to a syndrome is found. For example, the role of innate disposition versus environment in the etiology of chronic tuberculosis was the subject of much debate and contention through most of the nineteenth century, until the tubercle bacillus was recognized as the causative agent of chronic tuberculosis. This discovery did not really resolve the issue as one could still argue that, since observations show that there is no simple correlation between exposure to the bacillus and contraction of the disease, innate factors may still play a role in determining one's susceptibility to the disease. But tracing the disease to the tubercle bacillus established the path by which effective intervention was most likely to be achieved and thereby rendered the debate between disposition and environment, for practical purposes, a less pressing issue. The debate then largely ceased. The issue of heredity versus environment remains most alive with regard to illnesses for which a comprehensive therapeutic approach is still most remote—such as schizophrenia or cancer. Freud's ongoing concern with the question of disposition versus environment, or physiology versus psychology, in the neuroses is at least to some degree a measure of his ongoing dissatisfaction with his method of therapeutic intervention for these illnesses.

My analysis of the development of Freud's psychology is, of course, an "internal" analysis—an analysis which perceives Freud's work as best understood in the context of its relationship to late nineteenth-century neurology, psychiatry, and nonmedical psychology. I have said little about the impact of "external" factors, social and cultural factors, on Freud's theories, and, insofar as external factors can be distinguished from internal ones, I certainly believe that the impact of the former in the shaping of Freud's basic models was quite minor. But this is not a reflection of some general bias on my part concerning how the history of science ought to be approached or can best be understood. It is, rather, a reflection of what was clearly Freud's own perception of and approach to the task he had undertaken. Freud chose as his major professional endeavor the investigation of a subject widely regarded by his colleagues to be a most important and as yet unresolved question—the pathogenesis of hysteria and related neuroses; he devoted himself to resolving this question in a fashion that took account not only of his own observations but of the observations and theories of his colleagues. He chose to work essentially within his profession and to have the parameters of his theorizing defined by the conceptual schemes of his profession. A dissection of Freud's models into a list of basic concepts would yield relatively few such concepts which could not be found in some form in the work of earlier neuropsychiatrists or psychologists. What was revolutionary in Freud's work was the fact that, by substantially modifying and integrating current concepts, he molded them into a more comprehensive and more elegant theory covering a wide range of both normal and pathological phenomena.

One can ask to what degree social and cultural factors played a role in rendering Freud's chosen problem, the pathogenesis of neuroses, such a live issue in neuropsychiatry. But, as I demonstrated in chapters 2 and 3, the attention accorded the neuroses in the last decades of the nineteenth century can easily be accounted for by developments within psychiatry. As the pathoanatomical approach, which dominated academic psychiatry through much of the nineteenth century, succeeded in eliminating more and more syndromes from the list of pathological enigmas, it left behind on that list syndromes which were obviously less amenable to anatomical investigation. Consequently, these latter syndromes—among which hysteria and related neuroses had always been quite prominent—received increasing attention both from those who still hoped to discover underlying anatomical lesions and from those who sought to develop alternative pathological models. Freud joined the latter camp and devoted his career to pursuing an alternative model.

This is not, of course, to deny that there are nuances in Freud's theories that reflect social and cultural influences rather than the influence of contemporary medical thought or of his own clinical experience. One can note, for example, at various points in Freud's writing a definite pessimism regarding the ego's capacity to harness antisocial and potentially destructive primitive impulses, and this pessimism reflects at least in part the impact of contemporary social and political events such as the rise of political anti-Semitism in Austria. Such influences are particularly notable in Freud's writings on the psychology of art, religion, and social history. But, since so many of Freud's basic concepts were drawn from contemporary medicine and psychology, a search for substantial social and cultural impact on the shaping of these concepts really requires that one begin by looking back to the time when the concepts first entered medical thought in the form later encountered by Freud. A study of social and cultural determinants of the concepts of an unconscious and of intrapsychic conflict, for example, would be most fruitful if it were to focus on the early and middle decades of the nineteenth century and the emerging prominence of these concepts in psychiatry, rather than focusing on fin-de-siècle Vienna.

In my presentation of the development of Freud's theories, I have also eschewed any psychohistorical or psychobiographical observations. The aspect of Freud's personality perhaps most relevant to his work on the neuroses, an aspect that can easily be inferred from his work and is explicitly recognized by him in some of his correspondence, was his determination to do some exceptional, hopefully revolutionary, piece of research and to gain prominence for his achievement. Freud, from the beginning of his medical career, consciously sought out an issue in medicine whose pursuit might lead to some revolutionary achievement. His experiments with cocaine beginning in 1884 were, for example, an early endeavor in which he invested such ambitions. When, during his stay in Paris in 1885, he heard Charcot assert that the work of anatomical psychiatry was essentially complete and that an understanding of hysteria would offer the key to the alternative theories of pathology that must now be pursued, Freud could hardly disregard the message. Attention was focused on hysteria, the subject was ripe for new insights, and any major contribution would likely be recognized. Freud, after some rather tentative and sporadic early work on the syndrome, eventually devoted himself almost exclusively to the investigation of the neuroses. Once having done so, he directed his efforts particularly towards the elaboration of broad, elegant general formulas—again reflecting his desire to achieve some revolutionary theoretical breakthrough.

But what was most important with regard to Freud's ultimate achievement is that he strove to pursue these formulas qua scientist: using recognized concepts as the basis for his theorizing, modifying these concepts in light of his clinical experience, remaining receptive in an impressive way to experiences which contradicted his current formulas. (His ultimate abandonment of the seduction theory, despite having devoted several years and much energy to the theory and having repeatedly proclaimed it and defended it in print, is an example of this receptivity.) It is Freud's course as a scientist that I have attempted to chart in the foregoing work.

Notes, Bibliography, Index

Notes

1. Introduction

1. Ola Andersson, *Studies in the Prehistory of Psychoanalysis* (Stockholm, 1962), p. 149.

2. Ernst Kris, "The Significance of Freud's Earliest Discoveries," *International Journal of Psychoanalysis* 31 (1950): 108–16. Also Kris's introduction to Freud's *The Origins of Psycho-Analysis*, Eric Mosbacher and James Strachey, ed. Marie Bonaparte, Anna Freud, and Ernst Kris (London, 1954).

3. Siegfried Bernfeld, "Freud's Earliest Theories and the School of Helmholtz," *Psychoanalytic Quarterly* 13 (1944): 341–62.

4. Peter Amacher, *Freud's Neurological Education and Its Influence on Psychoanalytic Theory*, Psychological Issues, vol. 4, no. 4 (New York, 1965).

5. Raymond Fancher, "The Neurological Origin of Freud's Dream Theory," *Journal of the History of the Behavioral Sciences* 7 (1971): 59–74; Robert R. Holt, "Freud's Biological Assumptions," in *Psychoanalysis and Current Biological Thought*, ed. Norman S. Greenfield and William C. Lewis (Madison, Wisconsin, 1965), pp. 93–121.

6. Holt, ibid.; also Holt's comments in Arnold H. Modell, "The Concept of Psychic Energy," *Journal of the American Psychoanalytic Association* 11 (1963): 605ff.

7. Amacher's failure to appreciate the significance of Freud's clinical experience is noted by Stanley W. Jackson in his review of Amacher's book: *Journal of the History of Medicine*, 1966, pp. 202–03.

8. Discussions of the critical reception accorded Freud's early work appear in J. H. Schultz, "Psychoanalyse. Die Breuer-Freudschen Lehren, ihre Entwicklung and Aufnahme," *Zeitschrift für angewandte Psychologie* 2 (1909): 440–97; Ilse Bry and Alfred H. Rifkin, "Freud and the History of Ideas; Primary Sources, 1886–1910," *Science and Psychoanalysis* (New York, 1962), 5:6–36; and Hannah Decker, "The Medical Reception of Psychoanalysis in Germany, 1894–1907: Three Brief Studies," *Bulletin of the History of Medicine* 45

(1971); 461–81. Some of this material is also reviewed in Henri Ellenberger, *The Discovery of the Unconscious* (New York, 1970), pp. 771–72, 783–84, 792–93.

9. Quoted by Ernest Jones, *The Life and Work of Sigmund Freud*, 3 vols. (New York, 1953), 3:203.

2. Pathoanatomical Psychiatry

1. Jose Maria Lopez Pinero and Jose Maria Morales Meseguer, *Neurosis y Psicoterapia* (Madrid, 1970).

2. For example, Erwin Ackerknecht, *A Short History of Psychiatry*, tr. Sulammith Wolff (New York, 1959).

3. Jeanne Pièrre Falret, *Des maladies mentales et des asiles d'alienes* (Paris, 1864), p. vi.

4. Cited in Ackerknecht, *Medicine at the Paris Hospital: 1794–1848* (Baltimore, 1967), p. 55.

5. R. T. H. Laennec, "Anatomie Pathologique," in *Dictionnaire des sciences medicales* (Paris, 1812), 2:47.

6. Falret, p. v.

7. G. W. Henry, "Organic Mental Diseases," in Gregory Zilboorg and G. W. Henry, *A History of Medical Psychology* (New York, 1941), pp. 526–57.

8. Ackerknecht, *Short History*, p. 66.

9. Benedict-Augustin Morel, "Des caractères de l'hérédité dans les maladies nerveuses," *Archives Générales de Médecine* 14 (1859): 257–83.

10. See discussion of Magnan's work in Georges Genil-Perrin, "L'idée de dégénérescence en médecine mental" (Thesis, Paris Faculty of Medicine, 1913), pp. 88ff.

11. Falret, p. lxvi.

12. In the preface to the 1861 edition of his text, Griesinger had written:

> In the Universities our specialty is still far too much ignored, and clinical instruction especially is as yet nowhere conducted and acknowledged in a degree corresponding to the importance of the subject. I have done my part. In Tübingen, for upwards of ten years, I regularly delivered lectures upon medical psychology, in conjunction with my principal subject, and, as often as opportunity offered, admitted cases of mental disease into my clinique, making them, like any other disease, the subjects of clinical instruction and discussion. The advantage of this is so apparent that I live in the hope that very soon the establishment of regular psychological cliniques will become general. It is through these that the proper idea, the purely medical, of mental disease, conjoined, however, with a knowledge of the morbid mental symptoms, can first receive that general extension, so very desirable, whereby mere asylum managers can no longer call themselves medical psychologists. (*Mental Pathology and Therapeutics*, 2d German ed., tr. C. Lockhart Robert-

son and James Rutherford, facsimile of the English edition of 1867 [London, 1965], p. viii).

13. Ibid., pp. 1, 4.

14. Ibid., p. 408.

15. Ibid., p. 413.

16. Ibid., pp. 207–08.

17. Ibid., p. 164.

18. Ibid., pp. 39–40, 42–43.

19. Knud Faber, *Nosography* (New York, 1930), pp. 55–56.

20. Carl August Wunderlich, *Wien und Paris: Ein Beitrag zur Geschichte und Beurtheilung der gegenwärtigen heilkunde in Deutschland und Frankreich* (Stuttgart, 1841).

21. Rudolph Virchow, *Cellular Pathology*, tr. Frank Chance (Philadelphia, 1863).

22. Faber, pp. 56–57.

23. Erna Lesky, *Die Wiener medizinische Schule* (Cologne, 1965), pp. 373–74, 380.

24. Meynert's views on the proper path for psychiatry appear in the manuscript of a petition he submitted to the Vienna medical faculty in 1868. The petition requests that the subject of his teaching be expanded from "the structure and function of the brain and spinal cord with relation to their pathology" to "psychiatry based on the structure, function and pathology of the central nervous system." The manuscript and related material have been published by Otto Marx, "Psychiatry on a Neuropathological Basis: Th. Meynert's Application for the Extension of His Venia Legendi," *Clio Medica* 6 (1971): 139–58.

25. Theodor Meynert, *Psychiatry,* tr. Bernard Sachs, facsimile of the 1885 edition (New York, 1968), p. 143.

26. Meynert, "Zum Verstandnis der functionellen Nervenkrankheiten," *Wiener medizinische Blätter,* 1882, p. 518.

27. Meynert, "Der Bau der Gross-Hirnrinde und seine ortlichen Verschiedenheiten, nebst einem pathologisch-anatomischen Corollarium," (Neuwied and Leipzig, 1868), p. 34.

28. Meynert, "Ueber Zwangsvorstellungen," *Wiener klinische Wochenschrift,* 1888, p. 110.

29. Ibid., p. 111.

30. Meynert, "Der Bau der Gross-Hirnrinde," p. 6.

31. Meynert, "Zum Verstandnis"; Meynert, "Ueber functionelle Nervenkrankheiten," *Anzeiger der K.K. Gesellschaft der Aerzte in Wien* (1883), pp. 158–61; Meynert, "Ueber Zwangsvorstellungen"; and Meynert, "On the Collaboration of Parts of the Brain," (1890), in *Some Papers on the Cerebral Cortex*, tr. Gerhard von Bonin (Springfield, Ill., 1960).

32. Meynert, "Zum Verstandnis," and "Ueber Nervenkrankheiten."

33. Meynert, "Der Bau der Gross-Hirnrinde," p. 5.

34. Carl Westphal, "Nekrolog" for Wilhelm Griesinger, *Archiv für Psychiatrie und Nervenkrankheiten* 1 (1869): 765–66.

35. Westphal, *Gesammelte Abhandlungen*, ed. A. Westphal (Berlin, 1892), 2:557.

36. Ibid., p. 571.

37. From James W. Papez on Gudden, in Webb Haymaker and Frances Schiller, eds., *The Founders of Neurology* (Springfield, Ill., 1970), pp. 45ff.

38. Auguste Forel, *Out of My Life*, tr. Bernard Miall (New York, 1937).

39. Ibid., p. 110.

40. Webb Haymaker, "Paul Flechsig," in Haymaker and Schiller, *Founders of Neurology*, pp. 24–27.

41. Ibid.

42. Paul Flechsig, *Der körperliche Grundlagen der Geistesstörungen* (Leipzig, 1882), pp. 11–12.

43. Carl Wernicke, *Lehrbuch der Gehirnkrankheiten für Aertze und Studirende*, 3 vols. (Kassel und Berlin, 1881), 1: Vorwort.

44. Ibid., 2:iii–iv.

45. Kurt Goldstein, "Carl Wernicke," in Haymaker and Schiller, *Founders of Neurology*, pp. 531–35.

46. Freud, "Abstracts of the Scientific Writings of Dr. Sigmund Freud" (1897), from *The Standard Edition of the Complete Psychological Works of Sigmund Freud*, tr. and ed. James Strachey, assisted by Alix Strachey and Alan Tyson, 24 vols. (London, 1953–1966) (hereafter cited as *Standard Edition*), 3:227–56.

47. Siegfried Bernfeld, "Sigmund Freud, M.D., 1882–1885," *International Journal of Psychoanalysis* 32 (1951): 204–17. Documents relating to Freud's nomination and appointment to the post of Privatdocent have been published by Josef and Renée Gicklhorn, *Sigmund Freud's akademische Laufbahn* (Vienna, 1960).

48. Freud, "An Autobiographical Study" (1925), *Standard Edition* 20:11.

49. Cited by Freud in a letter to Martha Bernays, 29 May 1884, in *Letters of Sigmund Freud*, tr. Tania and James Stern, ed. Ernst Freud (London, 1970), p. 126.

50. Freud, "Autobiographical Study," p. 12.

51. Freud to Martha Bernays, 17 May and 31 March 1885, *Letters*, pp. 156–57, 151.

52. Freud, "Report on My Studies in Paris and Berlin" (1886), *Standard Edition* 1: 5–15.

53. Ibid., p. 10.

54. Meynert was then director of a clinic which was part of the national asylum system. It was at this point that, through Rokitansky, he acquired the directorship of the newly established psychiatric clinic at the Vienna General Hospital, (Erna Lesky, *Die Wiener medizinische Schule*, p. 380).

55. Emil Kraepelin, *Der Richtungen der Psychiatrischen Forschung* (Leipzig, 1887), p. 6.

56. Ibid., pp. 7–8.

57. Krafft-Ebing replaced the recently deceased Max Leidesdorf, who had shared Meynert's pathoanatomical emphasis. He assumed Leidesdorf's positions as member of the faculty and head of a second psychiatric teaching clinic, located in the national asylum. When Meynert died in 1892, Krafft-Ebing moved up to Meynert's post as professor of psychiatry and chief of the psychiatric teaching clinic of the Vienna General Hospital.

58. Richard von Krafft-Ebing, "Die Entwicklung und Bedeutung der Psychiatrie als klinischer Wissenschaft," *Wiener klinische Wochenschrift* (1889), p. 817.

59. Krafft-Ebing, *Lehrbuch der Psychiatrie auf klinische Grundlage* (Stuttgart, 1879), 2:11–12.

60. A number of observers, most notably Ola Andersson, have suggested that this recognition of a need for alternative nonanatomical explanations of particular syndromes was inspired by concurrent advances in neurophysiology. Andersson, speaking of the search by some psychiatrists for new, nonanatomical models of pathology, writes: "This change was in keeping with the general trend in medical research and technology under the impact of the rapid development of physiology during the latter part of the nineteenth century" (*Prehistory of Psychoanalysis*, p. 69). This thesis is not, however, supported by the literature of the period. It is true that some authors, in an effort to account for syndromes which did not seem to involve anatomical lesions, attempted to explain the patient's symptoms in terms of physiological alterations in the nervous system. But the neurophysiological concepts to which they appealed were not new to psychiatry and did not inspire the change in models. On the contrary, the same concepts of nervous system functioning can be found in earlier works by anatomically oriented psychiatrists. Theodor Meynert, for example, had for a number of years made extensive use of virtually all the neurophysiological principles invoked by those attempting to construct new, nonanatomical formulas. Meynert, however, viewed the physiology simply as an adjunct to pathological anatomy, as a device for explaining—by reference to the physiology of sensation, motor coordination, reflexes, etc.—how the underlying anatomical lesion interferes with normal functioning to generate clinical symptoms. The change, therefore, is not in the incorporation of new physiological concepts, but in rejection of the anatomical premise.

61. Paul Flechsig, *Der körperliche Grundlagen*, p. 12.

62. Robert Thomsen and Hermann Oppenheim, "Ueber das Vorkommen and die Bedeutung der sensorischen Anästhesie bei Erkrankungen des zentralen Nervensystems," *Archiv für Psychiatrie* 15 (1884). Also Oppenheim in "Verhandlungen ärztlicher Gesellschaften," *Berliner klinische Wochenschrift* (1884), p. 725.

63. Carl Westphal, in "Berliner medicinische Gesellschaft," *Berliner klinische Wochenschrift* (1879), p. 125.

64. Oppenheim, *Die traumatischen Neurosen* (Berlin, 1889), pp. 1, 123.

65. Ibid., p. 5.

3. Charcot, Freud, and the Physiological Model of Hysteria

1. Jean Martin Charcot, *Lectures on Localization in Diseases of the Brain,* tr. E. P. Fowler (New York, 1878), preface.

2. Ackerknecht, *A Short History of Psychiatry,* p. 73.

3. E.g., Charcot, *Lectures on Localization;* Charcot, *Lectures on the Pathological Anatomy of the Nervous System,* tr. Cornelius Comegys (Cincinnati, 1881); Charcot, *Lectures on the Localization of Cerebral and Spinal Diseases,* tr. W. B. Hadden (London, 1883).

4. E.g., Moriz Benedikt, *Elektrotherapie* (Vienna, 1868), p.41; Moriz Rosenthal, *Klinik der Nervenkrankheiten,* 2d ed. (Stuttgart, 1875), p. 464.

5. Charcot, *Clinical Lectures on Diseases of the Nervous System,* tr. Thomas Savill (London, 1889), pp. 9, 12–13.

6. Ibid., p. 18.

7. Ibid., p. 85ff.

8. Ibid., pp. 281, 288.

9. Freud, "Preface to the Translation of Bernheim's *De la Suggestion*" (1888), *Standard Edition* 1:77.

10. Ibid.

11. Charcot, *Clinical Lectures,* p. 302.

12. Ibid., p. 305.

13. William Cullen, *First Lines in the Practice of Physic,* 2 vols. (Edinburgh, 1802), 2:65–66.

14. M. H. Romberg, *Diseases of the Nervous System,* tr. Edward Sieveking (London, 1853), p. xiii.

15. E.g., Benjamin Brodie, *The Works of Sir Benjamin Brodie,* ed. Charles Hawkins, 3 vols. (London, 1865), p. 665.

16. James Braid, *Neurypnology* (London, 1843), p. 15.

17. Cited in Richard Hunter and Ida Macalpine, *Three Hundred Years of Psychiatry: 1535–1860.* (London, 1963), pp. 906–07.

18. See, in particular, Henri Ellenberger, "The Evolution of Depth Psychology," in *Historic Derivations of Modern Psychiatry,* ed. Iago Galdston (New York, 1967), pp. 159–84; also, Ellenberger, *Discovery of the Unconscious.*

19. Benedikt, *Elektrotherapie,* p. 418.

20. Lesky, *Die Wiener medizinische Schule,* p. 393.

21. Ibid., p. 150.

22. Charcot, *Clinical Lectures,* p. 13.

23. Lopez Pinero and Morales Meseguer also suggest that Charcot's functional theory of hysteria had a special impact because of his status as a pathological anatomist (*Neurosis y Psicoterapia,* p. 330).

24. There has been considerable discussion as to the source of Charcot's interest in hypnosis. G. Guillain (*J. M. Charcot: 1825–1893,* Paris, 1955) asserts that Charcot was familiar with the work of numerous early writers on hypnotism, and Guillain lists about eight of these authors. Pierre Janet suggests that

several other writers were most responsible for Charcot's concern with hypnotism. (Relevant citations from Guillain and Janet are in A. R. G. Owen, *Hysteria, Hypnosis, and Healing: The Work of J. M. Charcot* (London, 1971), pp. 182–83). But, with regard to Guillain's argument, the mere listing of works with which Charcot was familiar does not prove very much, as virtually every physician had some acquaintance with the literature on hypnosis. More importantly, none of the authors cited by Janet or Guillain held views on hypnosis which can compare with Richet's in terms of their approximation to Charcot's own views. Richet and Charcot both insisted that the hypnotic state is a neurosis, involving physiological changes in the nervous system, and that it is clinically comparable to other neuroses; further, both authors maintained that hypnotism is of potential value in the therapy of other neuroses, particularly hysteria. This similarity of ideas, as well as the close collaboration between Charcot and Richet, suggest that Richet's work was indeed of particular importance for Charcot. It is significant that Hippolyte Bernheim, whose own views on hypnotism were developed in opposition to those of Richet and Charcot, said of Richet: "This author has had the merit of having called the attention of the medical world to the phenomena of hypnotism" (Hippolyte Bernheim, *Suggestive Therapeutics,* French ed. of 1887, tr. Christian Herder [Westport, Conn., 1957], p. 120). Also, Charcot's protégé Alfred Binet wrote that "after 1870, M. Richet was the first investigator to reinaugurate the study of hypnotism" (Alfred Binet, *On Double Consciousness* [Chicago, 1890], p. 9).

25. Charles Richet, "Du Somnambulisme Provoqué," *Journale de l'Anatomie et de le Physiologie Normales et Pathologiques* 11 (1875): 348–78.

26. Charcot, "Sur les divers états nerveux determinés par l'hypnotisation chez les hystériques," *Comptes Rendues des Séances de l'Académie des Sciences* 94 (1882): 403–05.

27. Cited by Ellenberger, *Discovery of the Unconscious,* p. 750.

28. Freud, "Charcot" (1893), *Standard Edition* 3:11–23.

29. Oppenheim, *Die traumatischen Neurosen,* p. 124.

30. Paul Moebius, "Ueber den Begriff der Hysterie," *Centralblatt für Nervenheilkunde* 11 (1888): 66–71.

31. Joseph Delboeuf, *Le magnetisme animal* (Paris, 1889), p. 11.

32. Henri Ellenberger, for example, speaks of the leisure enjoyed by certain classes and of the "theatricality" which characterized these groups: "It has often been asked why hysteria was so frequent in the 1880's and so rapidly declined after 1900. One plausible explanation is that it was in accord with the theatrical and affected way of life of that period" (*Discovery of the Unconscious,* p. 256).

33. The psychiatrist Konrad Rieger stated in 1929 that he would now label differently many of the patients whom, in the 1880s and 1890s, he characterized as hysterics. Cited by Ackerknecht, *Short History of Psychiatry,* p. 79n.

34. Freud, "Report," p. 5.

35. Ibid., pp. 8–9.

36. Freud to Martha Bernays, 24 November 1885, *Letters,* p. 196.

37. Freud, "Report," pp. 10–11.

38. Reviews of Freud's lecture "On Male Hysteria" can be found in: *Allgemeine Wiener medizinische Zeitung* 31 (1886): 506–07: *Anzeiger der K.K. Gesellschaft der Aertze in Wien,* no.25 (1886), pp. 149–51; *Münchener Medicinische Wochenschrift* 33 (1886): 768; *Wiener medizinische Blätter* 9 (1886): 1292–93; *Wiener medizinische Presse* 27 (1886): 1407–09; *Wiener medizinische Wochenschrift* 36 (1886): 1445–47.

39. Review in *Wiener medizinische Blätter,* p. 1293.

40. Rosenthal, *Klinik,* p. 464.

41. Rosenthal, "Untersuchungen und Beobachtungen über Hysterie," *Wiener medizinische Presse* 20 (1879): 569–72, 604–07, 633–36, 670–72, 737–41, 801–05; Rosenthal, "Untersuchungen und Beobachtungen über Hysterie und Transfert," *Archiv für Psychiatrie* 12 (1882): 201–31; Rosenthal, "Zur Charakteristik der Hysterie," *Allgemeine Wiener medizinische Zeitung,* 1887, pp. 571–72, 584–85.

42. Freud, "Hysteria" (1888), *Standard Edition* 1:41–57.

43. Max Leidesdorf, *Lehrbuch der psychischen Krankheiten* (Erlangen, 1865), p. 239. See also Erna Lesky, *Die Wiener medizinische Schule,* pp. 184f.

44. Charcot regarded traumatic neurosis—that cluster of symptoms, including paralysis, pain, and sensory abnormalities, which was often found to follow upon accidents, most notably railway accidents, but which could not be accounted for by the victims' discernible physical injuries—as simply a form of hysteria. But Hermann Oppenheim insisted that it is a distinct syndrome. Henri Ellenberger, in *The Discovery of the Unconscious* (pp. 437–41), argues that this was the major point of disagreement between Charcot and German neuropsychiatrists, including the Viennese. But Meynert, in this paper, clearly associates traumatic neurosis with hysteria (p. 500). The important distinction for Meynert is between hysteria, or traumatic neurosis, on the one hand, and common paralysis, with clear-cut anatomical lesions, on the other; and he is concerned only with establishing, in opposition to Charcot, the pathoanatomical basis of the former. (Meynert did believe that some patients classified as hysterics were mere simulators, and he distinguished this group from the sufferers of "real" hysteria or traumatic neurosis.)

45. Meynert, "Beitrag zum Verständniss der traumatischen Neurose," *Wiener klinische Wochenschrift,* 1889, p. 498.

46. Ibid., p. 501.

47. Charcot, *Poliklinische Vorträge: Schuljahr 1887/1888,* tr. (of vol. 1 of Charcot's *Leçons du Mardi*) by Sigmund Freud (Leipzig and Vienna, 1892), p. 100n.

48. Meynert, "Ueber Zwangsvorstellungen," pp. 139–40. Also, Meynert, "Ueber kunstliche Störungen des psychischen Gleichgewichtes," in his *Sammlung von Populär-Wissenschaftlichen Vorträgen über den Bau und die Leistungen des Gehirns* (Vienna and Leipzig, 1892), pp. 233–53.

49. Meynert, "Ueber hypnotische Erscheinungen," *Wiener klinische Wochenschrift,* 1888, p. 451.

50. Ibid., p. 495.

51. Meynert, "Beitrag," p. 501.

52. Freud, "Hysteria," p. 41.

53. Freud, section III of "Some Points for a Comparative Study of Organic and Hysterical Paralyses" (1893), *Standard Edition* 1:160–72. The article was published in 1893, but this section was probably written in 1888. See editor's note, pp. 157–59.

54. In his article "Hysteria," Freud explicitly rejects the notion of hysterical symptoms being caused by vascular constriction and ischemia, because "a vascular spasm is from its nature an organic [i.e., anatomical] change, the effect of which is determined by anatomical conditions," and such a model is therefore ruled out by the "ignorance of anatomy" exhibited by hysterical symptoms.

55. Bernheim, *Suggestive Therapeutics,* p. 183.

56. Ibid., p. viii.

57. Freud, "Preface to Bernheim," pp. 77–78.

58. Ibid., pp. 79–80.

59. Ibid., pp. 82–83.

4. Psychology Versus Physiology in Freud's Hysteria and Hypnosis Papers, 1886–1894

1. Freud, "Observation of a Severe Case of Hemi-Anaesthesia in a Hysterical Male" (1886), *Standard Edition* 1:25–31.

2. Freud, "Hysteria," p. 42.

3. Ibid., p. 41.

4. These were Freud's only publications related to his work on the neuroses for the three years, 1889–1891.

5. Freud, "Hypnosis" (1891), *Standard Edition* 1:106.

6. A review of two unpublished lectures on hypnosis and suggestion, given by Freud in April and May, 1892, before the Wiener medizinischen Klub, appeared in the *Internationale klinische Rundschau,* 1892, p. 814.

7. Freud, "Review of Auguste Forel's *Hypnotism*" (1889), *Standard Edition* 1:100.

8. Bernfeld, "Freud's Earliest Theories"; Amacher, *Freud's Neurological Education*; Kris, "Significance of Freud's Earliest Discoveries."

9. Oppenheim, "Thätsachliches und Hypothetisches über das Wesen der Hysterie," *Berliner klinische Wochenschrift,* 1890, pp. 553–56.

10. Moebius, "Thätsachliches und Hypothetisches über das Wesen der Hysterie," *Neurologische Beiträge,* 2 vols. (Leipzig, 1894) 1:20–24.

11. Freud, in Freud and Josef Breuer, *Studies on Hysteria* (1895), *Standard Edition* 2:65.

12. Rudolph Heidenhain, *Der sogenannte thierische Magnetismus* (Leipzig, 1880), p. 35.

13. Wilhelm Wundt, "Hypnotismus und Suggestion," *Philosophische Studien* 8:1–85.

14. Danilewsky, "Die Hemmungen der Reflex- und Willkürbewegungen, Beiträge zur Lehre vom thierischen Hypnotismus," *Archiv für der gesammte Physiologie* 24 (1881): 489–525.

15. Albert Moll, *Der Hypnotismus*, (Berlin, 1889), p. 156.

16. Forel, *Der Hypnotismus*, 2d ed. (Stuttgart, 1891), pp. 1–19.

17. Freud, "Review of Forel," p. 101.

18. Freud, "Preface to Bernheim," p. 84.

19. Freud, "Review of Forel," p. 96.

20. Heidenhain, *Der sogenannte thierische Magnetismus*, p. 35.

21. Amacher, *Freud's Neurological Education*.

22. Thomas Laycock, "On the Reflex Function of the Brain," *British and Foreign Medical Review* 19 (1845); 298ff.

23. Theodule Ribot, *Les Maladies de la Volonté* (Paris, 1883), pp. 14–15.

24. Ribot, *Diseases of Memory* (London, 1882), p. 78.

25. Ribot, *Les Maladies de la Volonté*, p. 136.

26. Hack Tuke, "Imperative Ideas," *Brain*, 1894, pp. 192–94.

27. Wernicke, *Der Aphasische Symptomencomplex* (Breslau, 1874).

28. Ibid., p. 1.

29. The only exception to this usage has been in citations from Meynert, where *functional* is given a purely nosological meaning. Since the pathoanatomical psychiatrists generally did not recognize "dynamic" pathology, *functional*, like *neurosis*, was often reduced by these psychiatrists to a merely nosological expression.

30. Cf. Ludwig Binswanger, "Freud und die Verfassung der klinische Psychiatrie," *Schweizerisches Archiv fur Neurologie und Psychiatrie* 37 (1936): 177–99; Bernfeld, "Freud's Earliest Theories"; Kris, "Significance of Freud's Earliest Discoveries"; Erwin Stengel, "A Re-evaluation of Freud's Book *On Aphasia,*" *International Journal of Psychoanalysis* 35 (1954): 85–89; Richard Schoenwald, "A Turning Point in Freud's Life: *Zur Auffassung der Aphasien,*" *Osiris* 11 (1954): 119–26; Rainier Spehlmann, *Sigmund Freuds neurologische Schriften* (Berlin, 1953).

31. Freud, "Report," p. 12.

32. Freud, "Aphasie," in A. Villaret's *Handwörterbuch der gesammten Medizin* (Stuttgart, 1888), pp. 88–90.

33. John Hughlings Jackson, in an article cited by Freud, similarly makes the point that aphasia in hysteria takes forms different from those found in aphasias caused by known anatomical diseases. His explanation, like Freud's, is that the hysterical patients are not in fact suffering from local brain lesions. ("On Affections of Speech from Diseases of the Brain, Part I," in *Selected Writings of John Hughlings Jackson,* ed. James Taylor, 2 vols. [New York, 1958] 1:155–70.)

34. Freud, "Comparative Study," p. 167.

35. Freud, *On Aphasia* (1891), tr. Erwin Stengel (New York, 1953), p. 29.

36. Ibid., p. 87.

37. Laycock, "On the Reflex Function of the Brain"; Laycock, *Mind and Brain* (New York, 1869).

38. Jackson, "On Affections of Speech, Part III," *Selected Writings* 1:184–204.

39. Jones, *Sigmund Freud* 1:223.

40. For a resumé of Breuer's contributions to physiology, see Paul F. Cranefield, "Josef Breuer," in *The Dictionary of Scientific Biography,* ed. Charles C. Gillispie (New York, 1971), 3:445–50.

41. Breuer, "Autobiography of Josef Breuer," ed. and tr. C. P. Oberdorf, *International Journal of Psychoanalysis* 34 (1953): 64–67.

42. Breuer, in *Studies on Hysteria,* pp. 21–47.

43. Ibid., p. 25.

44. Ibid., p. 34.

45. Ibid., p. 35.

46. This is Anna O.'s history as presented in *Studies on Hysteria.* Henri Ellenberger, drawing upon notes written by Breuer in 1882 (as yet unpublished), as well as upon a sanatorium report of the same year, has presented additional information concerning Anna's illness ("The Story of 'Anna O.': A Critical Review with New Data," *Journal of the History of the Behavioral Sciences,* 1972, pp. 267–80).

47. Freud, *Letters,* p. 56.

48. Freud, "Autobiographical Study," pp. 19–20.

49. Breuer, letter published in Ackerknecht, "Josef Breuer über seinen Anteil an der Psychoanalysis," *Gesnerus* 14 (1957): 169–71. Quotation is from Paul F. Cranefield's translation of the letter ("Josef Breuer's Evaluation of His Contribution to Psychoanalysis," *International Journal of Psychoanalysis* 39 [1958]: 319–22).

50. Freud, in *Studies on Hysteria,* pp. 48, 105n.

51. See Freud's statement on his technique; ibid., p. 53. Ola Andersson (*Prehistory of Psychoanalysis,* pp. 89–90) also makes the point that Freud continued to emphasize hypnotic suggestion for some time after his first references to Breuer's method.

52. Freud, "Review of Forel," p. 100.

53. Breuer and Freud, "On the Psychical Mechanism of Hysterical Phenomena: Preliminary Communication" (1893), *Standard Edition* 2: 3–17 (hereafter cited as "Preliminary Communication").

54. Ibid., p. 17.

55. Ibid., pp. 5–6.

56. Ibid., p. 6.

57. Ibid., p. 17.

58. Freud, "Comparative Study," pp. 169–72.

59. Criticism of Herbart's neglect of physiology can be found, for example, in the work of Friedrich Beneke. Beneke's response to Herbart is discussed in G. S. Brett, *History of Psychology,* ed. R. S. Peters (Cambridge, Mass., 1965).

60. James Strachey implies that Freud later acknowledged Gustav Fechner's psychophysics as the source of the constancy principle (*Standard Edition* 1:296n.), but this is not so. In his paper "Beyond the Pleasure Principle," published in 1920 (*Standard Edition* 18:7–64), Freud presents the pleasure principle as calling for the maintenance of psychic energy at a specific level, thus paralleling the constancy theory. Further he states that

> we cannot . . . remain indifferent to the discovery that an investigator of such penetration as G. T. Fechner held a view on the subject of pleasure and unpleasure which coincides in all essentials with the one that has been forced upon us by psychoanalytic work. Fechner's statement . . . reads as follows: "In so far as conscious impulses always have some relation to pleasure and unpleasure, pleasure and unpleasure too can be regarded as having a psychophysical relation to conditions of stability and instability. . . . According to this hypothesis, every psycho-physical motion rising above the threshold of consciousness is attended by pleasure in proportion as, beyond a certain limit, it approximates to complete stability, and is attended by unpleasure in proportion as, beyond a certain limit, it deviates from complete stability."
> . . . The tendency which we . . . attribute to the mental apparatus is subsumed as a special case under Fechner's principle of the "tendency to stability," to which he has brought the feelings of pleasure and unpleasure into relation (ibid., 18:8–9).

But Freud does not say that Fechner was the source of the constancy theory; and there is no evidence that Freud knew Fechner's work in 1892. Further, Fechner is talking specifically of "drives" as the psychic expression of the stability principle, with the satisfaction of an instinctual drive paralleling the restoration of stability; and Freud's thinking on hysteria in 1892 was still far removed from notions of drives and the pleasure principle.

At any rate, Fechner's principles also have little to do with neurophysiology. They merely express the philosophical thesis that the psyche and the organism exhibit the same "tendency to stability" as the inorganic universe. (The passage cited by Freud is from Fechner, *Einige Ideen zur Schöpfungs-und Entwicklungsgeschichte der Organismus* [Leipzig, 1873], p. 94.)

61. Freud, "On the Psychical Mechanism of Hysterical Phenomena" (1893), *Standard Edition* 3:27–39.

62. Freud, "Preface and Footnotes to the Translation of Charcot's *Lecons du Mardi de la Salpetrière, 1887–8*" (1892–1894), *Standard Edition* 1:137.

63. Freud, "Comparative Study," pp. 171–72.

64. Breuer and Freud, "Preliminary Communication," pp. 7–8n.

65. Adolph Strümpell, "Ueber die traumatischen Neurosen," *Berliner Klinik* 3 (1888): 1–29; and *Ueber die Entstehung und die Heilung von Krankheiten durch Vorstellungen* (Erlangen, 1888).

66. Breuer and Freud, "Preliminary Communication," p. 8n.

67. Moriz Benedikt, "Aus der Pariser Kongresszeit. Erinnerungen und Beobachtungen," *Internationale klinische Rundschau*, 1889, pp. 1531–33, 1573–76, 1611–14, 1657–59, 1699–1703, 1858–60. The theme of pathological secrets was further developed by Moriz Benedikt in "Second Life. Das Seelen-Binnenleben des gesunden und kranken Menschen," *Wiener Klinik*, 1894, pp. 127–38.

68. Freud, "The Neuro-Psychoses of Defence" (1894), *Standard Edition* 3:50.

5. Freud's Theory of Defense

1. Breuer and Freud, "Preliminary Communication," p. 10.

2. Ibid., p. 11.

3. Freud, "Preface and Footnotes to Charcot," p. 138.

4. Freud, "A Successful Case of Treatment by Hypnotism" (1892–1893), *Standard Edition* 1:117–28.

5. Breuer and Freud, "Preliminary Communication," p. 12.

6. Richet, "Du Somnambulisme Provoqué," p. 362.

7. Étienne Azam, *Hypnotisme, Double Conscience et Alterations de la Personnalité* (Paris, 1887).

8. Jules Janet, "Le hystérie et l'hypnotisme, d'après la théorie de la double personnalité," *Revue Scientifique* 41 (1888): 616–23.

9. Binet, *On Double Consciousness;* Binet, *Alterations of Personality,* tr. Helen Green Baldwin (London, 1896).

10. Pierre Janet, *The Mental State of Hystericals,* tr. Caroline Rollin Corson (New York and London, 1901), p. 495.

11. Krafft-Ebing, *An Experimental Study in the Domain of Hypnotism,* tr. Charles G. Chaddock (New York, 1889).

12. Binet, *Alterations of Personality,* p. 78.

13. Pierre Janet, *Mental State of Hystericals,* pp. 514–15.

14. Freud, "The Neuro-Psychoses of Defence," p. 46. Freud also refers to a third group of cases, labelled "retention hysteria," in which the failure of normal abreaction does not actually seem to involve a division of consciousness. This new class of cases is mentioned only rarely in subsequent papers, and the concept is not developed to any significant degree.

15. Ibid., p. 47.

16. Ibid.

17. Freud, in Freud and Breuer, *Studies on Hysteria,* p. 268.

18. Ibid.

19. Ibid., p. 154.

20. Freud, "Draft E," undated, "Extracts from the Fliess Correspondence," *Standard Edition* 1:193; "Draft N," enclosed with letter dated 31 May 1897, ibid., p. 257. Freud interpreted paranoia as a mode of defense on numerous

occasions. The earliest of these discussions is "Draft H," dated 24 January 1895, ibid., pp. 206–12.

21. Freud, "The Neuro-Psychoses of Defence," p. 51.

22. Luise von Karpinska, "Ueber die psychologischen Grundlagen des Freudismus," *International Zeitschrift für ärztliche Psychoanalyse* 2 (1914): 305ff; Maria Dorer, *Historische Grundlagen der Psychoanalyse* (Leipzig, 1932).

23. Johann Friedrich Herbart, *A Textbook in Psychology,* tr. Margaret K. Smith (New York, 1891), p. 159.

24. From "Geschichte der Wiener Universität von 1848 bis 1898," published by the academic senate of the Vienna University, Vienna, 1898. Cited by Dorer, *Historische Grundlagen,* p. 114.

25. See Jones, *Sigmund Freud* 1:374.

26. Gustav Adolf Lindner, *Manual of Empirical Psychology as an Inductive Science,* tr. Charles DeGarmo (Boston, 1889).

27. Dorer, *Historische Grundlagen,* p. 113.

28. Andersson, *Prehistory of Psychoanalysis,* p. 224.

29. Heinrich Obersteiner, "Experimental Researches in Attention," *Brain,* 1879, pp. 443, 442.

30. Ibid., pp. 453, 452.

31. Griesinger, *Mental Pathology and Therapeutics,* pp. 48–49.

32. Ibid., p. 44.

33. Breuer, in Freud and Breuer, *Studies on Hysteria,* pp. 216, 235–36.

34. Freud, "The Neuro-Psychoses of Defence," p. 52.

35. Breuer, in Freud and Breuer, *Studies on Hysteria,* pp. 218–19, 248.

36. Ibid., p. 193.

37. Ibid., p. 197.

38. John Hughlings Jackson, "On Affections of Speech, Part II," *Selected Writings* 1:171–83.

39. Breuer, in Freud and Breuer, *Studies on Hysteria,* p. 200.

40. Freud, "The Neuro-Psychoses of Defence," p. 51.

41. Breuer, in Freud and Breuer, *Studies on Hysteria,* p. 191.

42. Freud to Fliess, 22 June 1894, *Origins,* p. 95.

43. Freud, "The Neuro-Psychoses of Defence," pp. 60–61.

44. Freud, in Freud and Breuer, *Studies on Hysteria,* p. 286.

6. Sexuality and the Etiology of the Neuroses

1. Paul Briquet, *Traité clinique et thérapeutique de l'Hystérie* (Paris, 1859), p. 8.

2. Benedikt, *Elektrotherapie,* p. 423.

3. Cf., August Rheinstadter, "Ueber weibliche Nervosität, *Volkmann's Sammlung klinischer Vorträge, Gynäkologie* 56:1493–1510. The Munich neurologist Leopold Loewenfeld noted in 1894 that "most gynecologists, and perhaps doctors generally, maintain the view that the origin of by far the great majority

of functional nervous diseases in women lies in the region of the genital organs" (Loewenfeld, *Pathologie und Therapie der Neurasthenie und Hysterie* [Wiesbaden, 1894] p. 70).

4. Breuer, in Freud and Breuer, *Studies on Hysteria*, p. 242.

5. Wilhelm Fliess, "Die nasale Reflexneurose," *Verhandlungen des Kongresses für innere Medizin* (Wiesbaden, 1893), pp. 384–94; Fliess, *Neue Beitrage zur Klinik und Therapie der nasale Reflexneurose* (Leipzig and Vienna, 1893).

6. Freud, "Draft C", undated, *Origins*, pp. 73–75.

7. Freud to Fliess, 30 May 1893, *Origins*, p. 73.

8. Briquet, *Traité*, p. 126.

9. See, for example, Alois Valenta, "Ueber den sogennanten Coitus Reservatus als eine Hauptursache der chronischen Metritus und den weiblichen Nervosität," *Memorabilien: Monatshefte für rationelle praktische Aerzte* 25 (1880): 481–85.

10. Benedikt, *Elektrotherapie*, p. 423.

11. Robert Brudenell Carter, *On the Pathology and Treatment of Hysteria* (London, 1853), pp. 34–35.

12. Jackson, "On Affections of Speech, Part I," p. 170.

13. Freud, "Hysteria," pp. 50–51.

14. Freud, in Freud and Breuer, *Studies on Hysteria*, pp. 259–60.

15. Krafft-Ebing, "Ueber Nervösen und Psychosen durch sexuelle Abstinenz," *Jahrbuch für Psychiatrie* 8 (1889): 1–6.

16. Freud, "Sketches for the 'Preliminary Communication'" (1892), *Standard Edition* 1:147–54.

17. Freud, "The Neuro-Psychoses of Defence," pp. 47–48.

18. Ibid., p. 52.

19. Freud and Breuer, *Studies on Hysteria*, p. xxix.

20. Breuer, in ibid., pp. 246–47.

21. George Beard, "Neurasthenia, or nervous exhaustion," *Boston Medical and Surgical Journal* 80 (1869): 217–21.

22. Moebius, "Bemerkungen über Neurasthenie, Bibliographie," *Neurologische Beiträge* 2:86–97; Franz Carl Müller, *Handbuch der Neurasthenie* (Leipzig, 1893).

23. Moebius, "Bemerkungen über Neurasthenie," *Neurologische Beiträge* 2:63.

24. Krafft-Ebing, *Nervosität und Neurasthenische Zustände* (Vienna, 1895), p. 34.

25. Charcot, *Leçons du Mardi de la Salpetrière*, 2 vols. (Paris, 1889, 1892).

26. Wilhelm Erb, *Handbuch der Krankheiten des Nervensystems*, 2d ed. (Leipzig, 1878), p. 392.

27. Paul Blocq, "La neurasthénie et les neurasthéniques," *Gazette des Hospitaux*, 1891, pp. 425–34.

28. Krafft-Ebing, *Neurasthenische Zustände*, p. 34.

29. Otto Binswanger, *Die Pathologie und Therapie der Neurasthenie* (Jena, 1896), p. 59.

30. Krafft-Ebing, *Neurasthenische Zustände*, p. 62; *Psychopathia Sexualis*, tr. Charles G. Chaddock, 7th Ger. ed. (Philadelphia and London, 1893), p. 374.

31. Freud, "A Reply to Criticism of My Paper on Anxiety Neurosis" (1895), *Standard Edition* 3:125.

32. Loewenfeld, *Die nervösen Störungen sexuellen Ursprungs* (Wiesbaden, 1891), pp. 61, 75–76.

33. The relevant gynecological literature is reviewed in Alexander Peyer, *Die unvollständige Beischlaf und seine Folgen beim männlichen Geschlechte* (Stuttgart, 1890).

34. Albert Eulenberg, "Über coitus reservatus als Ursache sexualer Neurasthenie bei Männern," *Internationale Centralblatt*, 1892, pp. 3–7.

35. Peyer, *Die unvollständige Beischlaf*, p. 7.

36. Freud, "Review of Averbeck's *Die Akute Neurasthenie*" (1887), *Standard Edition* 1:35; to Martha Bernays, 2 February 1886, *Letters*, p. 213; 10 February 1886, p. 223. Freud to Breuer, 1 September 1886, p. 232; Freud, *Origins*, p. 58.

37. Blocq, "La neurasthénie," p. 434.

38. Freud, "The Neuro-Psychoses of Defence," p. 58.

39. Freud, in Freud and Breuer, *Studies on Hysteria*, p. 257.

40. Ibid.

41. Ewald Hecker, "Ueber larvirte und abortive Angstzustände bei Neurasthenie," *Zentralblatt für Nervenheilkunde* 16 (1893): 565–72; "Zur Behandlung der neurasthenischen Angstzustände," *Berliner klinische Wochenschrift* 29 (1892): 1195–97.

42. Freud, "Draft B," dated 8 February 1893, "Extracts," pp. 179–84.

43. Freud, *Origins*, p. 77.

44. Freud, "On the Grounds for Detaching a Particular Syndrome from Neurasthenia under the Description 'Anxiety Neurosis' " (1895), *Standard Edition* 3:91.

45. Ibid., p. 99.

46. Loewenfeld, "Ueber die Verknupfung neurasthenischer und hysterischer Symptome in Anfallsformen nebst Bemerkungen über die Freud'sche 'Angstneurose'," *Münchener medicinische Wochenschrift* 42 (1895): 282–84.

47. Freud, "A Reply to Criticism," p. 127.

48. Ibid., p. 123.

49. Freud, "Draft C," undated, *Origins*, pp. 73–75.

50. Freud, "On the Grounds for Detaching a Syndrome," pp. 107–08.

51. Ibid., 109.

52. The terms *aktuelle Neurose* and *Aktualneurose* have been translated by most writers, including James Strachey, the editor of the *Standard Edition*, as "actual neuroses." Although it is a mistranslation, this is now established as the conventional rendering.

53. Freud, "Draft H," dated 24 January 1895, "Extracts," p. 207.

54. Freud, "Obsessions and Phobias" (1895), *Standard Edition* 3:80.

55. A synopsis of this unpublished lecture by Freud (delivered before the Verein für Psychiatrie und Neurologie in Vienna, 15 January 1895) appeared in the *Wiener klinische Wochenschrift* 8 (1895): 496.

56. Freud, "On the Grounds for Detaching a Syndrome," p. 97.

57. James Strachey discusses Freud's changing views on phobias in *Standard Edition* 3:83–84.

58. Freud, "Draft G," undated, "Extracts," pp. 200–06.

59. Freud, "On the Grounds for Detaching a Syndrome," p. 99.

60. Freud, "The Etiology of Hysteria" (1896), *Standard Edition* 3:200–01.

61. Freud, in Freud and Breuer, *Studies on Hysteria,* p. 102.

62. Alfred Binet and Charles Féré, *Animal Magnetism* (London, 1887), p. 353.

63. Jules Janet, "Le hystérie et l'hypnotisme."

64. Pierre Janet, *The Mental State of Hystericals,* p. 505.

65. Freud, in Freud and Breuer, *Studies on Hysteria,* p. 104.

66. Ibid., p. 261.

67. Freud, to Fliess, 8 October 1895, *Origins,* p. 126. Freud to Fliess, 15 October 1895, *Origins,* p. 127.

68. Freud, *Origins,* p. 128.

69. Freud, "Heredity and the Etiology of the Neuroses" (1896), *Standard Edition* 3:154–55.

70. Freud, "The Etiology of Hysteria," p. 209.

71. Freud, "Further Remarks on the Neuro-Psychoses of Defence" (1896), *Standard Edition* 3:165.

72. This was one of three lectures on the neuroses given by Freud in October, 1895, before the Wiener medicinisches Doctoren-Collegium but never published. The lectures were reviewed in the *Wiener medizinische Presse,* 1895, p. 1638. The discussion which followed the lectures was reviewed on pp. 1717–18. (Another review of these lectures appeared in the *Wiener klinische Rundschau* [1895], pp. 662–63, 679–80, 696–97; but this review did not mention Freud's reference to infantile sexual traumas.)

73. Freud, "Heredity and the Etiology of the Neuroses," pp. 143–49.

7. Freud's "Project for a Scientific Psychology"

1. Freud, in Freud and Breuer, *Studies on Hysteria,* p. 259.

2. Freud, "Draft K," 1 January 1896, "Extracts," pp. 221–22.

3. Freud to Fliess, 16 August 1895, *Origins,* p. 123.

4. Freud to Fliess, 27 April 1895, 6 August 1895, and 16 August 1895, *Origins,* pp. 118, 122, 123.

5. Jones, *Sigmund Freud,* 1:381.

6. Freud to Fliess, 23 September 1895, *Origins,* pp. 123–24.

7. Freud to Fliess, 1 January 1896, "Extracts," pp. 388–91.

8. Freud, "Project for a Scientific Psychology" (1895), *Standard Edition* 1:295.

9. Freud also uses the designation Q'η. The distinction between Q and Q'η seems to be that the former represents quantities of excitation of the magnitude involved in external sensory stimulation, while Q'η denotes internal, intercellular orders of magnitude. But this difference is not clearly defined and Freud's usage is rather ambiguous. The distinction between Q and Q'η will therefore be ignored in this presentation, and only the term Q will be used.

10. Richet, "Les Reflexes Psychiques," *Revue Philosophique*, 1888, pp. 225–37, 387–422, 500–28.

11. Wilhelm Waldeyer, "Ueber einige neuere Forschungen im Gebiete der Anatomie des Centralnervensystems," *Berliner klinische Wochenschrift*, 1891, p. 691.

12. Freud, "Project," p. 298.

13. Freud used the German word *Besetzung*. The word *cathexis* was coined by Strachey in 1922 as a translation for *Besetzung* and has become a standard psychoanalytic term. (See Strachey's note in *Standard Edition* 3:63n.)

14. Freud, "Project," pp. 298–99.

15. Sigmund Exner, "Zur Kenntniss von der Wechselwirkung der Erregungen in Centralnervensystems," *Archiv für Physiologie* 28 (1882): 487–506.

16. Hippolyte Taine, *Verstand*, tr. L. Siegfried, 2d French ed., (Bonn, 1880), p. 237.

17. Ribot, *Diseases of Memory*, pp. 20–21.

18. Freud, "Project," p. 303.

19. Ibid., p. 312.

20. Griesinger, "Ueber psychische Reflexactionen," *Gesammelte Abhandlungen* (Berlin, 1872) 1: 1–45.

21. Freud, "Project," p. 297.

22. Ibid., pp. 318–19.

23. David Hartley, *Observations on Man* (London, 1791), pp. 37f.

24. Herbert Spencer, *The Principles of Psychology*, 2d ed., 2 vols. (London and Edinburgh, 1870) 1:190.

25. Freud, "Project," p. 323.

26. Ibid., p. 326.

27. Ribot, *Les Maladies de la Volonté*, pp. 13–14.

28. Wernicke, *Der Aphasische Symptomencomplex*, p. 8.

29. Ibid.

30. Ribot, *Les Maladies de la Volonté*, p. 5.

31. Freud, "Project," pp. 328–29.

32. Ibid., p. 332.

33. Ibid., p. 363.

34. Ibid., p. 368.

35. Exner, *Entwurf zu einer physiologischen Erklärung der psychischen Erscheinungen* (Leipzig and Vienna, 1894), pp. 163–71; Henry Maudsley, *The Physiol-*

ogy of Mind (London, 1876) pp. 313ff.; William Carpenter, *Principles of Mental Physiology,* 4th ed. (London, 1877), p. 382.

36. Ribot, *Psychologie des Sentiments,* 3d ed. (Paris, 1899), p. 440.

37. Freud, "Project," p. 320.

38. Ibid., p. 324.

39. Ibid., p. 347.

40. Ibid., pp. 348–49.

41. Ibid., p. 352.

42. Ibid., p. 321.

43. Ibid., p. 354.

44. Freud to Fliess, 20 October 1895, *Origins,* p. 129.

45. Freud to Fliess, 1 January 1896, "Extracts," pp. 388–91.

8. Beyond the Seduction Theory

1. Freud, "Draft K," "Extracts," p. 222.

2. Freud, Review of L. Edinger's "Eine neue Theorie über die Ursachen einiger Nervenkrankheiten, insbesondere der Neuritis und der Tabes," *Wiener klinische Rundschau* 9 (1895): 27–28.

3. Moebius, "Ueber das Wesen der Basedow'schen Krankheit," *Centralblatt für Nervenheilkunde* 10 (1887): 225–29; "Ueber die Basedow'sche Krankheit," *Deutsche Zeitschrift für Nervenheilkunde* 1 (1891): 400–43.

4. Moebius, "Ueber die Basedow'sche Krankheit," p. 439.

5. Freud, "Preface and Footnotes to Charcot," pp. 139–40.

6. Data on the history of endocrinology are from Fritz Lieben, *Geschichte der Physiologischen Chemie* (Hildesheim, 1970), 12, "Die Hormone," pp. 655–711.

7. Freud to Fliess, 2 April 1896, *Origins,* p. 161.

8. Freud to Fliess, 1 March 1896, 30 June 1896, pp. 159, 169.

9. Fliess, *Die Beziehungen zwischen Nase und weiblichen Geschlechtsorganen* (Leipzig and Vienna, 1897).

10. Fliess, "Die nasale Reflexneurose," p. 392.

11. Freud refers to this challenge by Loewenfeld in a letter to Fliess, 1 March 1896, *Origins,* pp. 158–60.

12. Headaches are discussed in several of the letters to Fliess first published in Max Schur, *Freud: Living and Dying* (New York, 1972).

13. Freud, "Draft I," undated, "Extracts," pp. 213–15.

14. Freud to Fliess, 6 December 1896, "Extracts," p. 238.

15. Freud to Fliess, 8 November 1895, 8 December 1895, *Origins,* pp. 133, 137.

16. Freud, "Draft K," "Extracts," p. 222.

17. Freud, "Further Remarks," pp. 169–70.

18. Ibid., pp. 172–73n.

19. Freud to Fliess, 30 May 1896, "Extracts," pp. 229–32; Freud to Fliess, 6 December 1896, ibid., pp. 233–39.

20. Freud, "Draft L," enclosed with letter to Fliess dated 2 May 1897, ibid., pp. 248–50.

21. Freud to Fliess, 28 April 1897, ibid.

22. Freud to Fliess, 2 May 1897, ibid.

23. Freud, "Draft N," enclosed with letter to Fliess dated 21 May 1897, ibid. pp. 254–57.

24. Freud to Fliess, 21 September 1897, ibid., pp. 259–60.

25. Alexander Schusdeck, in an article entitled "Freud's 'Seduction Theory': A Reconstruction" (*Journal of the History of the Behavioral Sciences* 2 [1966]: 159–60), has suggested that the major factor in Freud's rejection of the seduction theory was a recent change in his clinical method. Schusdeck argues that the pressure technique—whereby Freud placed his hand on the patient's forehead and assured him that some forgotten event, crucial to his illness, would be remembered—encouraged the eliciting of seduction stories. Schusdeck maintains that it was the shift to free association as the primary clinical technique that finally allowed Freud to recognize these tales of seduction as fantasies. (Freud's papers and correspondence offer no precise date for the abandonment of the pressure technique; they merely indicate that this occurred some time between 1893 and 1904.) There are a few remarks by Freud which would seem to support Schusdeck's thesis. In particular, Freud states in "An Autobiographical Study" (pp. 33–34) that "under the influence of the technical procedure which I used at that time, the majority of my patients reproduced from their childhood scenes in which they were sexually seduced by some grown-up person." However, it seems likely that the change in technique occurred gradually and was as much a result of modifications in theory as a cause of such modifications. The pressure technique was developed because Freud believed that some traumatic experience must lie at the source of neuroses and that uncovering the pathogenic experience would lead to a cure. This technique was always combined with elements of free association, which were used particularly in attempting to extract memories of childhood events from the dreams, fantasies, and impulses revealed in therapy. With rejection of the seduction theory, the mere revelation of childhood encounters no longer seemed to promise a cure; and it was probably at this point that the special emphasis on eliciting memories gave way to an increased interest in free association per se, with the object of learning more about the nature of neurotic dreams, fantasies, and impulses.

26. Freud to Fliess, 15 October 1897, "Extracts," pp. 263–66.

27. Freud to Fliess, 3-4 January 1899, ibid., p. 276; Freud, "Screen Memories" (1899), *Standard Edition* 3: 303–22; Freud, "My Views on the Part Played by Sexuality in the Etiology of the Neuroses" (1906), *Standard Edition* 7:271–79.

28. Freud, "Fragment of an Analysis of a Case of Hysteria" (1905), *Standard Edition* 7:7–122.

29. Freud, *Three Essays on the Theory of Sexuality* (1905), *Standard Edition* 7:135–243.

30. Freud, "On the History of the Psycho-Analytic Movement" (1914), *Standard Edition* 14:7–66.

31. An example is Binet's explanation of fetishes in *Études de psychologie expérimentale: le fetischisme dans l'amour* (Paris, 1888).

32. Freud, "Draft K," "Extracts," p. 221.

33. Freud to Fliess, 6 December 1896, ibid., p. 238.

34. Freud to Fliess, 14 November 1897, ibid., pp. 268–69.

35. Krafft-Ebing, *Psychopathia Sexualis*, p. 31.

36. Ernst Chambard, "Du somnambulisme en general; nature, analogues, signification, nosologique et etiologique avec sept observations de somnambulisme hysterique" (Thesis, Paris Faculty of Medicine, 1881).

37. Moll, *Die Conträre Sexualempfindung*, 2d ed. (Berlin, 1893); Moll, *Untersuchungen über die libido sexualis* (Berlin, 1897).

38. S. Lindner, "Das Saugen an den Fingern, Lippen, etc., bei den Kindern (Ludeln)," *Jahrbuch für Kinderheilkunde* 14 (1879): 68–91.

39. Krafft-Ebing, *Psychopathia Sexualis*, pp. 37–38.

40. Wilhelm Stekel, "Coitus im Kindersalter," *Wiener medizinische Blätter* 18 (1895): 247–49.

41. Freud, *Three Essays*, p. 203.

42. Ibid., p. 232.

43. Freud, "My Views," p. 277; Freud, *Three Essays*, pp. 237–38.

44. Freud, "Sexuality in the Etiology of the Neuroses" (1898), *Standard Edition* 3:263–85.

45. Freud, "My Views," p. 275.

46. Freud, "Fragment of an Analysis," p. 113.

47. Freud, *Three Essays*, p. 177.

48. Freud, "My Views," p. 278.

49. Krafft-Ebing, "Zur Erklärung der contraren Sexualempfindung," *Jahrbücher für Psychiatrie* 12 (1894): 338–65; 13 (1895): 1–16.

50. Freud, *Three Essays*, p. 143n.

51. Ibid., p. 219.

52. Freud, "Fragment of an Analysis," p. 82n.

53. Freud, *Three Essays*, p. 221.

54. Freud to Fliess, 4 January 1898, *Origins*, p. 242; Freud to Fliess, 7 August 1900, ibid., pp. 333–35.

55. Freud, "Fragment of an Analysis," pp. 40–41, 53, 113.

56. Freud, "My Views," pp. 278–79.

9. The Interpretation of Dreams

1. Meynert, "On the Collaboration of Parts of the Brain." Also, Meynert, "Zum Verstandnis der functionellen Nervenkrankheiten."

2. Freud, *The Interpretation of Dreams* (1899), *Standard Edition* 4 and 5; quoted material from pp. 100–01.

3. See letters to Martha Bernays in *Letters*.

4. The dream of "Irma's Injection" is discussed at length by Freud in *The Interpretation of Dreams*. See especially pp. 106–21; quoted material from pp. 118–19. Max Schur, in *Freud: Living and Dying*, presents excerpts from some previously unpublished letters to Fliess which throw additional light on the dream.

5. Freud to Fliess, 12 June 1900, *Origins*, pp. 321–22.

6. Freud, *The Interpretation of Dreams*, p. 134.

7. Griesinger, *Mental Pathology and Therapeutics*, pp. 108–09.

8. Freud, "Project," p. 336.

9. Freud to Fliess, 30 May 1896, "Extracts," p. 232.

10. Freud to Fliess, 16 May 1897, *Origins*, p. 200.

11. Freud, "The Neuro-Psychoses of Defence."

12. Freud, "Draft N," "Extracts," p. 256.

13. Freud to Fliess, 19 February 1899, "Extracts," p. 278.

14. Freud to Fliess, 7 July 1897, ibid., p. 258; Freud to Fliess, 21 September 1897, *Origins*, pp. 215–18.

15. Freud, *The Interpretation of Dreams*, pp. 605–06.

16. Ibid., p. xxiii.

17. Ibid., p. 592.

18. Ibid., p. 104.

19. Ibid., p. 588.

20. Freud, "Fragment of an Analysis," pp. 10–11.

21. Freud, *The Interpretation of Dreams*, p. 135.

22. Ibid., pp. 152–53.

23. Ibid., p. 160.

24. Ibid., pp. 196–97.

25. Maudsley, *The Physiology of Mind*, p. 291.

26. Freud, *The Interpretation of Dreams*, p. 567.

27. Freud to Fliess, 6 December 1896, "Extracts," pp. 234–35.

28. Ibid., p. 235.

29. Freud, *The Interpretation of Dreams*, p. 579.

30. Ibid., pp. 580–81.

31. Ibid., p. 528.

32. Ibid., p. 588.

33. When the terms which have been translated Preconscious (*Vorbewusst*) and Unconscious (*Unbewusst*) first appeared in Freud's correspondence (in notes written in May, 1897—about six months after the letter to which the topographical model can be traced), they were used in a discussion of symptom formation and designated simply two types of thought processes, rather than processes together with specific contents.

34. Freud, *The Interpretation of Dreams*, p. 597.

35. Ibid., pp. 599–600.

36. Ibid., p. 604.

37. Ibid; p. 606n.

38. Ibid., p. 604.

39. Kris, "The Significance of Freud's Earliest Discoveries." Also, Kris, "New Contributions to the Study of Freud's *The Interpretation of Dreams,* A Critical Essay," *Journal of the American Psychoanalytic Association* 2 (1954): 180–91; and Kris's introduction to *Origins.*

40. Bernfeld, "Freud's Earliest Theories and the School of Helmholtz." Bernfeld wrote this paper before the "Project" was published. But he maintained in the paper that the concepts of mental functioning utilized by Freud in *The Interpretation of Dreams* and later works were drawn largely from the physiology Freud had learned as a medical student. The publication of the "Project," with its physiological formulation of the same concepts, served to reinforce his argument.

41. Amacher, *Freud's Neurological Education,* p. 73.

42. Fancher, "The Neurological Origin of Freud's Dream Theory."

43. Holt, "Freud's Biological Assumptions." Also, Holt's comments in Modell, "The Concept of Psychic Energy."

Bibliography

Primary Sources

Averbeck, H. "Die Akute Neurasthenie." *Deutsche medizinal Zeitung* 7 (1886): 293–96, 301–05, 313–15, 325–28.

Azam, Etienne. "Les Alterations de la personnalité." *Revue Scientifique,* 3d ser.(1883): 610–18.

———. *Amnésie périodique ou dédoublement de la Personnalité.* Bordeaux: Feret, 1877.

———. "Amnésie périodique, ou dédoublement de la vie." *Revue Scientifique,* 2d ser. (1876): 481–89.

———. *Hypnotisme, Double Conscience et Alterations de la Personnalité.* Paris: Librairie J.-B. Baillière et Fils, 1887.

Bain, Alexander. *The Senses and the Intellect.* 3d ed. London: Parker, 1868.

Bastian, Charleton. "On Different Kinds of Aphasia." *British Medical Journal* 2 (1887): pp. 931–36, 985–90.

Beard, George. "Neurasthenia, or Nervous Exhaustion." *Boston Medical and Surgical Journal* 80 (1869): 217–21.

———. *Sexual Neurasthenia.* Edited by A. D. Rockwell. New York: E. B. Treat, 1884.

Benedikt, Moriz. "Aus der Pariser Kongresszeit. Erinnerungen und Beobachtungen." *Internationale klinische Rundschau,* 1889, pp. 1531–33, 1573–76, 1611–14, 1657–59, 1699–1703, 1858–60.

———. *Elektrotherapie.* Vienna: Tendler and Co., 1868.

———. *Hypnotismus und Suggestion.* Leipzig and Vienna: Breitenstein, 1894.

———. "Second Life. Das Seelen-Binnenleben des gesunden und kranken Menschen." *Wiener Klinik,* 1894, pp. 127–38.

———. "Ueber Neuralgien und neuralgische Affektionen und deren Behandlung." *Klinische Zeit- und Streitfragen,* 1892, pp. 67–106.

———. "Ueber Neurasthenie." *Wiener medizinische Blätter* 14 (1891): 33–34.

———. "Zur Therapie der Neurasthenie und die funktionellen Neurosen uberhaupt." *Internationale klinische Rundschau,* 1891, pp. 177–82.

"Berliner medicinische Gesellschaft." *Berliner klinische Wochenschrift,* 1879, p. 125.

Bernard, Claude. *An Introduction to the Study of Experimental Medicine.* 1865. Translated by Henry Copley Green. New York: Dover, 1957.

Bernheim, Hippolyte. *Suggestive Therapeutics,* 1887. Translated by Christian Herter. Westport, Conn.: Associated Booksellers, 1957. (First edition appeared in 1884.)

Binet, Alfred. *Alterations of Personality.* Translated by Helen Green Baldwin. London: Chapman and Hall, 1896.

——. *Études de psychologie expérimentale: le fetischisme dans l'amour.* Paris: Doin, 1888.

——."L'inhibition dans les phénomènes de conscience." *Revue philosophique* 30 (1890): 136–56.

——. *On Double Consciousness.* Chicago: Open Court, 1890.

——. "Recherches sur les alterations de la conscience chez les hystériques." *Revue philosophique* 27 (1889): 135–70.

Binet, Alfred, and Joseph Delboeuf. "Les diverses ecoles hypnotiques." *Revue philosophique* 22 (1886): 532ff.

Binet, Alfred, and Charles Féré, *Animal Magnetism.* London: Kegan, Paul, Trench, 1887.

——. "Expériences sur hypnotisme et les images associées." *Revue philosophique* 21 (1886): 159–63.

——. "L'hypnotisme chez les hystériques." *Revue philosophique* 19 (1885): 1–25.

Binswanger, Otto. *Die Pathologie und Therapie der Neurasthenie.* Jena: Gustav Fischer, 1896.

Block, Iwan. *Beiträge zur Aetiologie der Psychopathia Sexualis.* Dresden: H. R. Dohrn, 1902.

Blocq, Paul. "La neurasthénie et les neurasthéniques." *Gazette des Hopitaux,* 1891, pp. 425–34.

Bouveret, L. *Die Neurasthenie.* Translated from French into German by Otto Dornbluth. Leipzig and Vienna: Franz Deuticke, 1893.

Braid, James. *Neurypnology.* London: John Churchill, 1843.

Breuer, Josef. "Autobiography of Josef Breuer." Edited and translated by C. P. Oberdorf. *International Journal of Psychoanalysis* 34 (1953): 64–67.

Briquet, Paul. *Traité clinique et thérapeutique de l'Hystérie.* Paris: J.-B. Bailliére et Fils, 1859.

Brodie, Benjamin. *The Works of Sir Benjamin Brodie.* Collected and arranged by Charles Hawkins. 3 vols. London: Longman, Green, Longman, Roberts and Green, 1865.

Brown-Sequard, C. E. *Lectures on the Diagnosis and Treatment of Functional Nervous Affections.* Philadelphia: J. B. Lippincott, 1868.

Brücke, Ernst. *Vorlesungen über Physiologie.* Vienna: Wilhelm Braumüller, 1876.

Carpenter, William. *Principles of Mental Physiology.* 4th ed. London: Henry S. King, 1877.

Carter, Robert Brudenell. *On the Pathology and Treatment of Hysteria.* London: John Churchill, 1853.

Chambard, Ernst. "Du somnambulisme en general; nature, analogues, signification, nosologique et etiologique avec sept observations de somnambulisme hysterique" Thesis, Paris Faculty of Medicine, 1881.

Charcot, Jean Martin. *Clinical Lectures on Diseases of the Nervous System.* Translated by Thomas Savill. London: New Sydenham Society, 1889.

——. *Leçons du Mardi de la Salpetriére.* 2 vols. Paris, Progres Medical, 1892, 1889.

——. *Lectures on Localization in Diseases of the Brain.* Translated by E. P. Fowler. New York: William Wood, 1878.

——. *Lectures on the Localization of Cerebral and Spinal Diseases.* Translated by W. B. Hadden. London: New Sydenham Society, 1883.

——. *Lectures on the Pathological Anatomy of the Nervous System.* Translated by Cornelius Comegys. Cincinnati: Peter G. Thomson, 1881.

——.*Poliklinische Vorträge.* Translation by Max Kahane of vol. 2 of *Leçons du Mardi.* Leipzig and Vienna: Franz Deuticke, 1895.

——. *Poliklinische Vorträge: Schuljahr 1887/1888.* Translation by Sigmund Freud of vol. 1 of Charcot's *Leçons du Mardi.* Leipzig and Vienna: Franz Deuticke, 1892.

——. "Sur les divers états nerveux determinés par l'hypnotisation chez les hystériques." *Comptes Rendues des Séances de l'Académie des Sciences* 94 (1882): 403–05.

Charcot, Jean Martin, and Georges Gilles de la Tourette. "Hypnotism in the Hysterical." In *Dictionary of Psychological Medicine,* edited by Hack Tuke, 1:606–10. Philadelphia: P. Blakiston, 1892.

Charcot, Jean Martin, and Pierre Marie. "Hysteria." In *Dictionary of Psychological Medicine,* edited by Hack Tuke, 1:627–41. Philadelphia: P. Blakiston, 1892.

Cullen, William. *First Lines in the Practice of Physic.* 2 vols. Edinburgh: Reid and Scott, 1802.

Danilewsky, B. "Die Hemmungen der Reflex- und Willkürbewegungen, Beiträge zur Lehre vom thierischen Hypnotismus." *Archiv für der gesammte Physiologie* 24 (1881): 489–525.

Darwin, Charles. *The Expression of the Emotions in Man and Animals.* 1872. Reprint. Chicago: University of Chicago Press, 1965.

Delbouef, Joseph. *De l'entendue de l'action curative de l'hypnotisme.* Paris: F. Alcan, 1890.

——.*Le magnétisme animal.* Paris: Anciènne Librairie Germer Baillière, 1889.

——. *De l'origine des effets curatifs de l'hypnotisme.* Paris: F. Alcan, 1887.

Erb, Wilhelm. *Handbuch der Krankheiten des Nervensystems.* Vol. 1, 2d half, 2d ed. Leipzig: F. C. W. Vogel, 1878.

Esquirol, J. E. D., *Mental Maladies: A Treatise on Insanity.* Translated by E. K. Hunt. Facsimile of the English edition of 1845. New York: Hafner, 1965.

Eulenberg, Albert. "Über coitus reservatus als Ursache sexualer Neurasthenie bei Männern." *Internationale Centralblatt,* 1892, pp. 3–7.

288　　Bibliography

Exner, Sigmund. *Entwurf zu einer physiologischen Erklärung der psychischen Erschei-nungen.* Leipzig and Vienna: Franz Deuticke, 1894.

———. "Zur Kenntniss von der Wechselwirkung der Erregungen in Central-nervensystems. *Archiv für Physiologie* 28 (1882): 487–506.

Falret, Jeanne Pièrre. *Des maladies mentales et des asiles d'aliènes.* Paris: J.-B. Baillière, 1864.

Fechner, Gustav. *Einige Ideen zur Schöpfungs- und Entwicklungsgeschichte der Orga-nismus.* Leipzig: Breitkopf und Hartel, 1873.

———. Elements of Psychophysics. Translated by Helmut E. Adler. Vol. 1. New York: Holt, Rinehart and Winston, 1966.

Féré, Charles. "Choc moral chez les enfants." *Bulletin de la Société de Médecine Mentale,* 1894, pp. 333–40.

———. "A Contribution to the Pathology of Dreams and of Hysterical Para-lyses." *Brain* 9 (1887): 488–93.

Flechsig, Paul. *Der körperliche Grundlagen der Geistesstörungen.* Leipzig: von Veit, 1882.

Fliess, Wilhelm. *Die Beziehungen zwischen Nase und weiblichen Geschlechtsorganen.* Leipzig and Vienna: Franz Deuticke, 1897.

———. "Die nasale Reflexneurose." *Verhandlungen des Congresses für innere Medi-cin* 12: 384–94. Weisbaden: J. F. Bergmann, 1893.

———. *Neue Beiträge zur Klinik und Therapie der nasale Reflexneurose.* Leipzig and Vienna: Franz Deuticke, 1893.

Forel, Auguste. *Briefe, Correspondance.* Edited by Hans Walser. Bern and Stutt-gart: Hans Huber, 1968.

———. "Gehirn und Seele." *Zeitschrift für Hypnotismus* 3 (1895) 171ff.

———. *Der Hypnotismus.* Stuttgart: Ferdinand Enke, 1889.

———. *Der Hypnotismus.* 2d ed. Stuttgart: Ferdinand Enke, 1891.

———. *Out of My Life.* Translated by Bernard Miall. New York: W. W. Norton, 1937.

Freud, Sigmund, *The Standard Edition of the Complete Psychological Works of Sig-mund Freud.* Translated and edited by James Strachey, assisted by Alix Strachey and Alan Tyson. 24 vols. London: Hogarth Press, 1953–1966. Hereafter cited as *Standard Edition.*

———. "Abstracts of the Scientific Writings of Dr. Sigmund Freud." 1897. In *Standard Edition* 3:227–56.

———. "Aphasie." In *Handwörterbuch der gesammten Medizin,* edited by A. Villa-ret, 1: 88–90. Stuttgart: Ferdinand Enke, 1888.

———. "An Autobiographical Study." 1925. In *Standard Edition* 20:7–70.

———. "Beyond the Pleasure Principle." 1920. In *Standard Edition* 18:7–64.

———. "Charcot." In *Standard Edition* 3:11–23. (Originally published in *Wiener medizinische Wochenschrift,* 1893, pp. 1513–20.)

———. *The Cocaine Papers.* Vienna: Dunquin, 1963.

———. "The Etiology of Hysteria." In *Standard Edition* 3:191–221. (Originally published as "Zur Ätiologie der Hysterie." *Wiener klinische Rundschau,* 1896, pp. 379–81, 395–97, 413–15, 432–33, 450–52.)

————. "Extracts from the Fliess Correspondence." In *Standard Edition* 1:177–280, 388–91.

————. "Fragment of an Analysis of a Case of Hysteria." In *Standard Edition* 7:7–122. (Originally published as "Bruchstück einer Hysterie-Analyse." *Monatsschrift für Psychiatrie und Neurologie*, 1905, pp. 285–310, 408–67.)

————. "Freud's Psycho-Analytic Procedure." In *Standard Edition* 7:249–54. (Originally published as "Die Freud'sche Psychoanalytische Methode." In *Die psychische Zwangserscheinungen*, edited by Leopold Loewenfeld, pp. 545–51. Wiesbaden: Bergmann, 1904.)

————. "Further Remarks on the Neuro-psychoses of Defence." In *Standard Edition* 3:162–85. (Originally published as "Weitere Bemerkungen über die Abwehr-Neuropsychosen." *Neurologisches Zentralblatt*, 1896, pp. 434–48.)

————. "Gehirn." In *Handwörterbuch der gesammten Medizin*, edited by A. Villaret, 1:68–97. Stuttgart, Ferdinand Enke, 1888.

————. "Heredity and the Etiology of the Neuroses." In *Standard Edition* 3:143–56. (Originally published as "L'hérédité et l'etiologie des nevroses." *Revue neurologique*, 1896, pp. 161–69.)

————. "Hypnosis." In *Standard Edition* 1:105–14. (Originally published as "Hypnose" in *Therapeutisches Lexikon*, edited by Anton Bum, pp. 724–32. Vienna: Urban and Scharzenberg, 1891.)

————. "Hysteria." In *Standard Edition* 1:41–57. (Originally published as "Hysterie" in *Handwörterbuch der gesammten Medizin*, edited by A. Villaret, pp. 886–92. Stuttgart: Ferdinand Enke, 1888.)

————. "Hystero-Epilepsy." In *Standard Edition* 1:58–59. (Originally published as "Hysteroepilepsie," in *Handwörterbuch der gesammten Medizin*, edited by A. Villaret, p. 892. Stuttgart: Ferdinand Enke, 1888.)

————. *The Interpretation of Dreams.* 1899. In *Standard Edition* 4–5.

————. *Jokes and Their Relation to the Unconscious.* 1905. In *Standard Edition* 8.

————. *Letters of Sigmund Freud.* Translated by Tania and James Stern. Edited by Ernst Freud. London: Hogarth Press, 1970.

————. "My Views on the Part Played by Sexuality in the Etiology of the Neuroses." In *Standard Edition* 7:271–79. (Originally published as "Meine Ansichten über die Rolle der Sexualität in der Ätiologie der Neurosen." In *Sexualleben und Nervenleiden*, edited by Leopold Loewenfeld. 4th ed. Wiesbaden: Bergmann, 1906.)

————. "The Neuro-Psychoses of Defence." In *Standard Edition* 3:45–61. (Originally published as "Die Abwehr-Neuropsychosen." *Neurologisches Zentralblatt*, 1894, pp. 362–64, 402–09.)

————. "Observation of a Severe Case of Hemi-Anaesthesia in a Hysterical Male." In *Standard Edition* 1:25–31. (Originally published as "Beobachtungen einer hochgradigen Hemianästhesie bei einem hysterischen Manne." *Wiener medizinische Wochenschrift*, 1886, pp. 1633–38.)

————. "Obsessions and Phobias." In *Standard Edition* 3:74–82. (Originally published as "Obsessions et Phobias." *Revue neurologique*, 1895, pp. 33–38.)

———. *On Aphasia.* 1891. Translated by Erwin Stengel. New York: International Universities Press, 1953.

———. "On Dreams." In *Standard Edition* 5:633–86. (Originally published as "Über den Traum." In *Grenzfragen des Nerven- und Seelenlebens,* edited by L. Loewenfeld and H. Kurella, pp. 307–44. Wiesbaden: Bergmann, 1901.)

———. "On Psychotherapy." In *Standard Edition* 7:257–68. (Originally published as "Über Psychotherapie." *Wiener medizinische Presse,* 1905, pp. 9–16.)

———. "On the Grounds for Detaching a Particular Syndrome from Neurasthenia under the Description 'Anxiety Neurosis'." In *Standard Edition* 3:90–115. (Originally published as "Über die Berechtigung, von der Neurasthenie einen bestimmten Symptomenkomplex als 'Angstneurose' abzutrennen." *Neurologisches Zentralblatt,* 1895, pp. 50–66.)

———. "On the History of the Psycho-Analytic Movement." 1914. In *Standard Edition* 14:7–66.

———. "On the Psychical Mechanism of Hysterical Phenomena." In *Standard Edition* 3:27–39. (Originally published as "Über den psychischen Mechanismus hysterischer Phänomene." *Wiener medizinische Presse, 1893, pp. 121–26, 165–67.)*

———. "On the Psychical Mechanism of Hysterical Phenomena: Preliminary Communication." In *Standard Edition* 2:3–17.(Originally published as "Über den psychischen Mechanismus hysterischer Phänomene [Vorläufige Mitteilung]." *Neurologisches Zentralblatt,* 1893, pp. 4–10, 43–47.)

———. *The Origins of Psycho-Analysis.* Translated by Eric Mosbacher and James Strachey. Edited by Marie Bonaparte, Anna Freud, and Ernst Kris. London: Imago Press, 1954.

———. "Preface and Footnotes to the Translation of Charcot's *Leçons du Mardi de la Salpetrière, 1887–8.*" 1892–1894. In *Standard Edition* 1:133–43.

———. "Preface to the Translation of Bernheim's *De la* Suggestion." 1888. In *Standard Edition* 1:75–85.

———. "Preface to the Translation of Charcot's *Leçons sur les Maladies du Système Nerveux:* Tome Troisième." 1886. In *Standard Edition* 1:21–22.

———. "Project for a Scientific Psychology." 1895. In *Standard Edition* 1:295–387.

———. "The Psychical Mechanism of Forgetfulness." In *Standard Edition* 3:289–97. (Originally published as "Zum psychischen Mechanismus der Vergesslichkeit." *Monatsschrift für Psychiatrie und Neurologie,* 1898, pp. 436–43.)

———. "Psychical (or Mental) Treatment." In *Standard Edition* 7:283–302. (Originally published as "Psychische Behandlung [Seelen-Behandlung]." In *Die Gesundheit,* edited by R. Kossmann and J. Weiss. Stuttgart: Union Deutsche Verlagsgesellschaft, 1890.)

———. *Psychopathology of Everyday Life.* In *Standard Edition* 6. (Originally published as "Zur Psychopathologie des Alltagsleben." *Monatsschrift für Psychiatrie und Neurologie,* 1901, pp.1–32, 95–132.)

———. "A Reply to Criticism of My Paper on Anxiety Neurosis." In *Standard Edition* 3:123–39. (Originally published as "Zur Kritik der 'Angstneurose'." *Wiener klinische Rundschau* 9 (1895): 417–19, 435–37, 451–52.)

———. "Report on My Studies in Paris and Berlin." 1886. In *Standard Edition* 1:5–15.

———. "Review of Auguste Forel's *Hypnotism*." In *Standard Edition* 1:91–102. (Originally published in *Wiener medizinische Wochenschrift*, 1889, pp. 1097–1100, 1892–96.)

———. "Review of Averbeck's *Die Akute Neurasthenie*." In *Standard Edition* 1:35. (Originally published in *Wiener medizinische Wochenschrift*, 1887, p. 138.)

———. Review of L. Edinger's "Eine neue Theorie über die Ursachen einiger Nervenkrankheiten, insbesondere der Neuritis und der Tabes." *Wiener klinische Rundschau* 9 (1895): 27–28.

———. "Review of Weir Mitchell's *Die Behandlung gewisser Formen von Neurasthenie und Hysterie*." In *Standard Edition* 1:36. (Originally published in *Wiener medizinische Wochenschrift*, 1887, p. 138.)

———"Screen Memories." In *Standard Edition* 3:303–22. (Originally published as "Über Deckerinnerungen." *Monatsschrift für Psychiatrie und Neurologie*, 1899, pp. 215–30.)

———. "Sexuality in the Etiology of the Neuroses." In *Standard Edition* 3:263–85. (Originally published as "Die Sexualität in der Ätiologie der Neurosen." *Wiener klinische Rundschau*, 1898, pp. 21–22, 55–57, 70–72, 103–05.)

———. "Sketches for the 'Preliminary Communication.'" 1892. In *Standard Edition* 1:147–54.

———. "Some Points for a Comparative Study of Organic and Hysterical Paralyses." In *Standard Edition* 1:160–72. (Originally published as "Quelques considerations pour une étude comparative des paralysies motrices organiques et hystériques." *Archives de Neurologie*, 1893, pp. 29–43.)

———. "A Successful Case of Treatment by Hypnotism." In *Standard Edition* 1:117–28. (Originally published as "Ein Fall von hypnotischer Heilung." *Zeitschrift für Hypnotismus*, 1892–1893, pp. 102–07, 123–29.)

———. *Three Essays on the Theory of Sexuality*. 1905. In *Standard Edition* 7:135–243.

Freud, Sigmund, and Josef Breuer. *Studies on Hysteria*. 1895. In *Standard Edition* 2.

Gilles de la Tourette, Georges. *Die Hysterie nach den Lehren der Salpetrière*. Translated into German by Karl Grube. Leipzig and Vienna: Franz Deuticke, 1894.

Griesinger, Wilhelm. *An Introductory Lecture Read at the Opening of the Clinique for Nervous and Mental Diseases in the Royal Charite in Berlin*. 1866. Translated by John Sibbald. London: J. E. Adler, 1867.

———. *Mental Pathology and Therapeutics*. Translated from the second German edition by C. Lockhart Robertson and James Rutherford. Facsimile of the English edition of 1867. London: Hafner, 1965.

————. *Die Pathologie und Therapie der psychischen Krankheiten.* 2d ed. Stuttgart: Adolph Krabbe, 1861.

————. "Ueber psychische Reflexactionen." *Gesammelte Abhandlungen* 1:1–45. Berlin: A. Hirschwald, 1872.

Gyurkovechky, Victor. *Pathologie und Therapie der männliche Impotenz.* Vienna and Leipzig: Urban and Schwarzenberg, 1889.

Hartley, David. *Observations on Man.* 1749. Reprint. London: J. Johnson, 1791.

Hecker, Ewald. "Ueber larvirte und abortive Angstzustände bei Neurasthenie." *Centralblatt für Nervenheilkunde* 16 (1893): 565–72.

————. "Zur Behandlung der neurasthenischen Angstzustände." *Berliner klinische Wochenschrift* 29 (1892): 1195–97.

Hegar, Alfred. *Der Zusammenhang der Geschlechtskrankheiten mit nervösen Leiden und die Castration bei Neurosen.* Stuttgart: Ferdinand Enke, 1885.

Heidenhain, Rudolph. *Der sogenannte thierische Magnetismus.* Leipzig: Breitkopf und Hartel, 1880.

Herbart, Johann Friedrich. *A Textbook in Psychology.* Translated by Margaret K. Smith. New York: D. Appleton and Co., 1891.

Jackson, John Hughlings. *Selected Writings of John Hughlings Jackson.* Edited by James Taylor. New York, Basic Books, 1958.

James, Alexander. "The Reflex Inhibitory Centre Theory." *Brain,* 1881, pp. 287–302.

Janet, Jules. "Le hystérie et l'hypnotisme, d'après la théorie de la double personnalité." *Revue scientifique* 41 (1888): 616–23.

Janet, Pierre. "Les acts inconscients et le dédoublement de la personnalité pendant le somnambulisme provoqué." *Revue philosophique* 22 (1886): 577–92.

————. *The Mental State of Hystericals.* Translated by Caroline Rollin Corson. New York and London: G. P. Putnam, 1901.

————. "Quelques définitions récentes de l'hystérie." *Archives de Neurologie,* 1892, pp. 417–38; 1893, pp. 1–29. Reprinted as the final chapter of *Etats mental des hysteriques* (1894).

Jerusalem, Wilhelm. *Die Urteilsfunction.* Vienna: Wilhelm Braumüller, 1895.

Kaan, Hanns. *Der Neurasthenische Angstaffect bei Zwangsvorstellungen von der primordiale Grübelzwang.* Vienna and Leipzig: Franz Deuticke, 1892.

King, A. F. A. 'Hysteria." *American Journal of Obstetrics* 24 (1891): 513–32.

Kraepelin, Emil. *One Hundred Years of Psychiatry.* 1917. Translated by Wade Baskin. London: Peter Owen, 1962.

————. *Psychiatrie.* 3d ed. Leipzig: Ambrose Abel, 1889.

————. *Der Richtungen der Psychiatrischen Forschung.* Leipzig: F. C. W. Vogel, 1887.

Krafft-Ebing, Richard. "Die Entwicklung und Bedeutung der Psychiatrie als klinischer Wissenschaft." *Wiener klinische Wochenschrift,* 1889, 817–20, 843–45.

————. *An Experimental Study in the Domain of Hypnotism.* Translated by Charles G. Chaddock. New York: G. P. Putnam, 1889.

————. *Lehrbuch der Psychiatrie auf klinische Grundlage.* Stuttgart: Ferdinand Enke, 1879.

————. *Nervosität und Neurasthenische Zustände.* Vienna: Alfred Holder, 1895.

————. *Psychopathia Sexualis.* Stuttgart: Ferdinand Enke, 1886.

————. *Psychopathia Sexualis.* Translated by Charles Gilbert Chaddock, from the 7th German edition. Philadelphia and London: F. A. Davis, 1893.

————. "Ueber Nervösen und Psychosen durch sexuelle Abstinenz." *Jahrbücher für Psychiatrie* 8 (1889): 1–6.

————. "Ueber Neurasthenia sexualis beim Männe." *Wiener medizinische Presse,* 1887, pp. 161–65, 201–05.

————. "Zur Erklärung der contraren Sexualempfindung." *Jahrbücher für Psychiatrie* 12 (1894): 338–65; 13 (1895): 1–16.

Laennac, R. T. H., "Anatomie Pathologique." In *Dictionnaire des sciences medicales* 2:46–61. Paris: C. L. F. Panckoucke, 1812.

Laycock, Thomas. *Mind and Brain.* New York: D. Appleton, 1869.

————. "On the Reflex Function of the Brain." *British and Foreign Medical Review* 19 (1845): 298ff.

Leidesdorf, Max. *Lehrbuch der psychischen Krankheiten.* Erlangen: Ferdinand Enke, 1865.

Lewes, George Henry. *The Physical Basis of Mind.* London: Trübner and Co., 1877.

Lindner, Gustav Adolf. *Manual of Empirical Psychology As an Inductive Science.* Translated by Charles DeGarmo. Boston: D. C. Heath and Co., 1889.

Lindner, S. "Das Saugen an den Fingern, Lippen, etc., bei den Kindern (Ludeln)." *Jahrbuch für Kinderheilkunde,* n.s. 14 (1879): 68–91.

Loewenfeld, Leopold. *Die nervösen Störungen sexuellen Ursprungs.* Wiesbaden: J. F. Bergmann, 1891.

————. *Pathologie und Therapie der Neurasthenie und Hysterie.* Wiesbaden: J. F. Bergmann, 1894.

————. "Ueber die Verknupfung neurasthenischer und hysterischer Symptome in Anfallsformen nebst Bemerkungen über die Freud'sche 'Angstneurose'." *Münchener medicinische Wochenschrift* 42 (1895): 282–84.

Magnan, Valentin, and J. M. Charcot. "Inversion du Sens Génital." *Archives de Neurologie,* 1882, pp. 53–60, 296–322.

Mandl, Emil. Review of lecture [May 24, 1893] on article "Some Points for a Comparative Study of Organic and Hysterical Paralyses" by Sigmund Freud. *Internationale klinische Rundschau,* 1893, pp. 868–69.

Maudsley, Henry. *The Physiology of Mind.* London: Macmillan and Co., 1876.

Meynert, Theodor. "Der Bau der Gross-Hirnrinde und seine ortlichen Verschiedenheiten, nebst einem pathologisch-anatomischen Corollarium." Neuwied and Leipzig: J. H. Heuser'schen, 1868.

————. "Beitrag zum Verstandniss der traumatischen Neurose." *Wiener klinische Wochenschrift,* 1889, pp. 475–76, 498–503, 522–24.

————. Manuscripts, previously unpublished, dating from 1868 and 1870 appear in "Psychiatry on a Neuropathological Basis: Th. Meynert's Application for the Extension of His Venia Legendi," by Otto Marx. *Clio Medica* 6 (1971): 139–58.

———. "On the Collaboration of Parts of the Brain." 1890. In *Some Papers on the Cerebral Cortex.* Translated by Gerhard von Bonin. Springfield, Illinois: Charles C. Thomas, 1960.

———. *Sammlung von Populär-Wissenschaftlichen Vorträgen über den Bau und die Leistungen des Gehirns.* Vienna and Leipzig: Wilhelm Braumüller, 1892.

———. *Skizzen über Umfang und wissenschaftliche Anordnung der klinischen Psychiatrie.* Vienna: Wilhelm Braumüller, 1876.

———. *Ueber Fortschritte in Verstandniss der krankhaften psychischen Gehirnzustände.* Vienna: Wilhelm Braumüller, 1878.

———. "Ueber functionelle Nervenkrankheiten." *Anzeiger der K.K. Gesellschaft der Aerzte in Wien,* 1883, pp. 158–61.

———. "Ueber hypnotische Erscheinungen." *Wiener klinische Wochenschrift,* 1888, pp. 451–53, 473–76, 495–98.

———. "Ueber Zwangsvorstellungen." *Wiener klinische Wochenschrift,* 1888, pp. 109–12, 139–41, 170–72.

———. "Zum Verstandnis der functionellen Nervenkrankheiten." *Wiener medizinische Blätter,* 1882, pp. 481–84, 517–18.

Moebius, Paul. *Die Basedow'sche Krankheit.* In *Specielle Pathologie und Therapie,* edited by Hermann Nothnagel, 22. Vienna: Alfred Holder, 1896.

———. *Neurologische Beiträge.* 2 vols. Leipzig: Ambrose Abel, 1894.

———. "Ueber das Wesen der Basedow'schen Krankheit." *Centralblatt für Nervenheilkunde* 10; (1887): 225–29.

———. "Ueber den Begriff der Hysterie." *Centralblatt für Nervenheilkunde* 11 (1888): 66–71. Also published in *Neurologische Beiträge* 1:1–7.

———. "Ueber die Basedow'sche Krankheit." *Deutsche Zeitschrift für Nervenheilkunde* 1 (1891): 400–43.

———. "Ueber die gegenwartige Auffassung der Hysterie." *Monatsschrift für Geburtshilfe und Gynaekologie* 1 (1895): 12–21.

Moll, Albert. *Der Hypnotismus.* Berlin: Fischer's Medicinische Buchhandlung, 1889.

———. *Der Hypnotismus.* 2d. ed. Berlin: Fischer's Medicinische Buchhandlung, 1890.

———. "Der Hypnotismus in der Therapie." *Berliner klinische Wochenschrift,* 1887, pp. 871–73.

———. *Die Conträre Sexualempfindung.* 2d ed. Berlin: Fischer's Medicinische Buchhandlung, 1893. (1st ed., 1891).

———. *Untersuchungen über die libido sexualis.* Berlin: Fischer's Medicinische Buchhandlung, 1897.

Morel, Benedict Augustin. "Des caractéres de l'héréditè dans les maladies nerveuses." *Archives Générales de Médecine* 14 (1859): 257–83.

Müller, Franz Carl. *Handbuch der Neurasthenie.* Leipzig: F. C. W. Vogel, 1893.

Obersteiner, Heinrich. "Experimental Researches in Attention." *Brain*, 1879, pp. 439–51.

———. *Der Hypnotismus.* Vienna: M. Breitenstein, 1887. (Reprinted from *Klinische Zeit- und Streitfragen*, 1: 49–79.)

———. *Die Lehre von Hypnotismus.* Leipzig and Vienna: M. Breitenstein, 1893.

Oppenheim, Hermann. "Thätsachliches und Hypothetisches über das Wesen der Hysterie." *Berliner klinische Wochenschrift*, 1890, pp. 553–56.

———. *Die traumatischen Neurosen.* Berlin: August Hirschwald, 1889.

Page, Herbert W. *Injuries of the Spine and Spinal Cord without Apparent Mechanical Lesion, and Nervous Shock.* London: J. and A. Churchill, 1883.

Peyer, Alexander. *Die nervosen Affectionen des Darmes bei der Neurasthenie des männlichen Geschlechtes.* Vienna: Urban und Schwarzenberg, 1893.

———. *Der unvollständige Beischlaf und seine Folgen beim männlichen Geschlechte.* Stuttgart: Ferdinand Enke, 1890.

Review of three unpublished lectures on the neuroses given by Freud in October, 1895, before the Wiener medicinisches Doctoren-Collegium: *Wiener medizinische Presse*, 1895, pp. 1638–41, 1678–79. Discussion which followed lectures was reviewed on pp. 1717–18. The three lectures were also reviewed in *Wiener klinische Rundschau*, 1895, pp. 662–663, 679–80, 696–97.

Reviews of unpublished lecture "On Male Hysteria" given by Freud in October, 1886, before the Vienna Medical Society: *Allgemeine Wiener medizinische Zeitung* 31 (1886): 506–07; *Anzeiger der K. K. Gesellschaft der Aerzte in Wien* 25 (1886): 149–51; *Münchener medicinische Wochenschrift* 33 (1886): 768; *Wiener medizinische Blätter*, 1886, pp. 1292–93: *Wiener medizinische Presse* 27 (1886): 1407–09; *Wiener medizinische Wochenschrift* 36 (1886): 1445–47.

Review of two unpublished lectures on hypnosis and suggestion, given by Freud in April and May, 1892, before the Wiener medizinischen Klub: *Internationale klinische Rundschau*, 1892, pp. 814–18, 853–56.

Reynolds, Russell. "Remarks on Paralyses and Other Disorders of Motion and Sensation, Dependent on Ideas." *British Medical Journal* 2 (1869): 483–85.

Rheinstadter, August. "Ueber weibliche Nervosität." in *Volkmann's Sammlung klinischer Vorträge, Gynäkologie*, 56: 1493–1510.

Ribot, Theodule. *Diseases of Memory.* London: Kegan, Paul, Trench, 1882.

———. *Les Maladies de la Personnalité.* Paris: Anciènne Librairie Germer Baillière, 1885.

———. *Les Maladies de la Volonté.* Paris: Librairie Germer Baillière, 1883.

———. *Psychologie des Sentiments.* 3d ed. Paris: Librairie Germer Baillière, 1899.

Richet, Charles. "Du Somnambulisme Provoqué." *Journale de l'anatomie et de le physiologie normales et pathologiques* 11 (1875): 348–78.

———. "Les Reflexes Psychiques." *Revue philosophique*, 1888, pp. 225–37, 387–422, 500–28.

Romberg, M. H. *Diseases of the Nervous System.* Translated by Edward Sieveking. London: New Sydenham Society, 1853.

Rosenthal, Moriz. *Klinik der Nervenkrankheiten.* 2d ed. Stuttgart: Ferdinand Enke, 1875.

——. "Untersuchungen und Beobachtungen über Hysterie." *Wiener medizinische Presse,* 1879, pp. 569–72, 604–07, 633–36, 670–72, 737–41, 801–05.

——. "Untersuchungen und Beobachtungen über Hysterie und Transfert." *Archiv für Psychiatrie* 12 (1882): 201–31.

——. "Zur Charakteristik der Hysterie." *Allgemeine Wiener medizinische Zeitung,* 1887, pp. 571–72, 584–85.

von Schrenck-Notzing, A. Freiherrn. *Suggestions-Therapie bei krankhaften Erscheinungen des Geschlechtssinnes.* Stuttgart: Ferdinand Enke, 1892.

Sechenov, Ivan M. *Reflexes of the Brain.* 1873. Translated by S. Belsky. Cambridge, Mass.: M. I. T. Press, 1965.

Spencer, Herbert. *The Principles of Psychology.* 2d ed. 2 vols. London and Edinburgh: Williams and Norgate, 1870.

Stekel, Wilhelm. "Coitus im Kindersalter." *Wiener medizinische Blätter* 18 (1895): 247–49.

Strümpell, Adolph. *Ueber die Entstehung und die Heilung von Krankheiten durch Vorstellungen.* Erlangen: Junge, 1888.

——. "Ueber die traumatischen Neurosen." *Berliner Klinik* 3 (1888): 1–29.

——. "Ueber die traumatischen Neurosen." In *Verhandlungen des Congresses für innere Medicin,* 12:83–98. Wiesbaden: J. F. Bergmann, 1893.

Synopsis of Freud's unpublished lecture "Mechanismus der Zwangsvorstellungen und Phobien" (delivered before the Verein für Psychiatrie und Neurologie in Vienna, January 15, 1895). *Wiener klinische Wochenschrift* 8 (1895): 496.

Taine, Hippolyte. *Verstand.* Translated into German from the second French edition by L. Siegfried. Bonn: Emil Strauss, 1880.

Thomsen, Robert, and Hermann Oppenheim. "Ueber das Vorkommen und die Bedeutung der sensorischen Anästhesie bei Erkrankungen des zentralen Nervensystems." *Archiv für Psychiatrie* 15 (1884): 559–83, 633–80, 656–67.

Tuke, Hack. "Imperative Ideas." *Brain,* 1894, pp. 192–94.

"Ueber die traumatischen Neurosen." In *Verhandlungen des Congresses für innere Medicin,* 12:143–66. Wiesbaden: J. F. Bergmann, 1893.

Valenta, Alois. "Ueber den sogenannten Coitus Reservatus als eine Hauptursache der chronischen Metritus und den weiblichen Nervosität." *Memorabilien: Monatshefte für rationelle praktische Aerzte* 25 (1880): 481–85.

"Verhandlungen ärztlicher Gesellschaften." *Berliner klinische Wochenschrift,* 1884, p. 725.

Virchow, Rudolph. *Cellular Pathology.* Translated by Frank Chance. Philadelphia: J. B. Lippincott, 1863.

Wernicke, Carl. *Der Aphasische Symptomencomplex.* Breslau: Max Cohn und Weigert, 1874.

——. *Lehrbuch der Gehirnkrankheiten für Aerzte und Studirende.* 3 vols. Kassel and Berlin: Theodor Fischer, 1881.

————. "Ueber die traumatischen Neurosen." In *Verhandlungen des Congresses für inner Medicin,* 12:98–143. Wiesbaden: J. F. Bergmann, 1893.

————. *Ueber den wissenschaftlichen Standpunkt in der Psychiatrie.* Cassel: Theodor Fischer, 1880.

Westphal, Carl. *Gesammelte Abhandlungen.* Edited by A. Westphal. Berlin: Hirschwald, 1892.

————. "Nekrolog" for Wilhelm Griesinger. *Archiv für Psychiatrie und Nervenkrankheiten* 1 (1869): 765–66.

Wunderlich, Carl August. *Wien und Paris: Ein Beitrag zur Geschichte und Beurtheilung der gegenwärtigen heilkunde in Deutschland und Frankreich.* Stuttgart: Ebner und Seubert, 1841. (Presently being edited for reprinting by H. M. Koelbing at the Institute for the History of Medicine in Zurich.)

Wundt, Wilhelm. "Hypnotismus und Suggestion." *Philosophische Studien* 8 (1892):1–85.

Critical Bibliography

Ackerknecht, Erwin. "Josef Breuer über seinen Anteil an der Psychoanalysis." *Gesnerus* 14 (1957):169–71.

————. *Medicine at the Paris Hospital: 1794–1848.* Baltimore: Johns Hopkins Press, 1967.

————. *A Short History of Psychiatry.* Translated by Sulammith Wolff. New York: Hafner, 1959.

Alexander, Franz G., and Sheldon T. Selesnick. *The History of Psychiatry.* New York: Harper and Row, 1966.

Amacher, Peter. *Freud's Neurological Education and Its Influence on Psychoanalytic Theory.* Psychological Issues, vol. 4, no. 4. New York: International Universities Press, 1965.

————. "Thomas Laycock, I. M. Sechenov and the Reflex Arc Concept." *Bulletin of the History of Medicine* 38 (1964): 168–83.

Andersson, Ola. *Studies in the Prehistory of Psychoanalysis.* Stockholm: Svenska Bokforlaget, 1962.

Anzieu, Didier. *L'Auto-Analyse.* Paris: Presses Universitaires de France, 1959.

Bernfeld, Siegfried. "Freud's Earliest Theories and the School of Helmholtz." *Psychoanalytic Quarterly* 13 (1944): 341–62.

————. "Freud's Scientific Beginnings." *American Imago* 6 (1949): 163–96.

————. "Sigmund Freud, M.D., 1882–1885." *International Journal of Psychoanalysis* 32 (1951): 204–17.

Bernfeld, Siegfried, and Suzanne Cassirer Bernfeld. "Freud's First Year in Practise, 1886–1887." *Bulletin of the Menninger Clinic* 16 (1952): 37–49.

Binswanger, Ludwig. "Freud und die Verfassung der klinische Psychiatrie." *Schweizerisches Archiv für Neurologie und Psychiatrie* 37 (1936) 177–99.

Bloch, Ernst. "Zur Geschichte der traumatischen Neurose." *Medizinische Klinik* 45 (1906): 1167–68.

298   Bibliography

Brazier, Mary. "The Rise of Neurophysiology in the Nineteenth Century." *Journal of Neurophysiology* 20 (1957): 212–26.

Brett, G. S., *History of Psychology.* Edited and abridged by R. S. Peters. Cambridge, Mass.: M. I. T. Press, 1965.

Brun, R. "Sigmund Freuds Leistungen auf dem Gebiet der organischen Neurologie." *Schweizerisches Archiv für Neurologie und Psychiatrie* 37 (1936): 205ff.

Bry, Ilse, and Alfred H. Rifkin. "Freud and the History of Ideas: Primary Sources, 1886–1910." In *Science and Psychoanalysis,* edited by J. Masserman, 5:6–36. New York: Grune and Stratton, 1962.

Buggle, Franz, and Paul Wirtgen. "Gustav Fechner und die psychoanalytischen Modellvorstellungen S. Freuds." *Archiv für die gesamte Psychologie,* 1969, pp. 148–201.

Bunker, Henry. "From Beard to Freud: A Brief History of the Concept of Neurasthenia." *Medical Review of Reviews* 36 (1930): 108–14.

Buxbaum, Edith. "Freud's Dream Interpretation in the Light of His Letters to Fliess." *Bulletin of the Menninger Clinic* 15 (1951): 197–212.

Chertok, L. "Freud in Paris: A Crucial Stage." *International Journal of Psychoanalysis* 51 (1970): 511–20.

———. "From Liebeault to Freud." *American Journal of Psychotherapy* 22 (1968): 96–101.

Cranefield, Paul F. "Freud and the 'School of Helmholtz'." *Gesnerus* 23 (1966): 35–39.

———. "Josef Breuer." In *The Dictionary of Scientific Biography,* edited by Charles C. Gillispie, 3:445–50. New York: Charles Scribner, 1971.

———. "Josef Breuer's Evaluation of His Contribution to Psychoanalysis." *International Journal of Psychoanalysis* 39 (1958): 319–22.

———. "Some Problems in Writing the History of Psychoanalysis." In *Psychiatry and Its History: Methodological Problems in Research,* edited by George Mora and Jeanne L. Brand, pp. 41–55. Springfield, Ill.: Charles Thomas, 1970.

Crocker, D. "Sigmund Freud: His Medical Education and Development." *Bulletin of the Cleveland Medical Library,* 1956, pp. 35–45.

Decker, Hannah. "The Medical Reception of Psychoanalysis in Germany, 1894–1907: Three Brief Studies," *Bulletin of the History of Medicine* 45 (1971): 461–81.

Delay, Jean. "Le Jacksonisme de Ribot." *Encéphale* 40 (1951): 185–216.

Dorer, Maria. *Historische Grundlagen der Psychoanalyse,* Leipzig: Felix Meiner, 1932.

Eissler, K. R. *Sigmund Freud und die Wiener Universität.* Bern and Stuttgart: Hans Huber, 1966.

Ellenberger, Henri. "Charcot and the Salpetrière School." *American Journal of Psychotherapy,* 1965, pp. 253–67.

———. *The Discovery of the Unconscious.* New York: Basic Books, 1970.

———. "The Evolution of Depth Psychology." In *Historic Derivations of Modern Psychiatry,* ed. Iago Galdston, pp. 159–84. New York: McGraw-Hill, 1967.

———. "Fechner and Freud." *Bulletin of the Menninger Clinic* 20 (1956): 201f.

———. "The Story of 'Anna O.': A Critical Review with New Data." *Journal of the History of the Behavioral Sciences,* 1972, pp. 267–80.

Erikson, Eric. "The Dream Specimen of Psychoanalysis." *Journal of the American Psychoanalytic Association* 2 (1954): 5–56.

Faber, Knud. *Nosography.* New York: Paul B. Hoeber, 1930.

Fancher, Raymond. "The Neurological Origin of Freud's Dream Theory." *Journal of the History of the Behavioral Sciences* 7 (1971): 59–74.

Fearing, Frank. *Reflex Action: A Study in the History of Physiological Psychology.* Cambridge, Mass., and London: M. I. T. Press, 1970. (First published in 1930.)

Fischer-Homberger, Esther. *Ursachen der Traumatischen Neurose von der "Railway-Spine" bis nach dem Ersten Weltkrieg.* Inaugural dissertation, University of Zurich, n.d.

Gedo, John E. "Freud's Self-Analysis and His Scientific Ideas." *American Imago* 25 (1968): 99–118.

Gedo, John E., Melvin Shabshin, Leo Sadow, and Nathan Schlesinger. "*Studies in Hysteria:* A Methodological Evaluation." *Journal of the American Psychoanalytic Association* 12 (1964): 734–51.

Genil-Perrin, Georges. "L'idée de dégénérescence en médecine mentale." Thesis, Paris Faculty of Medicine, 1913.

Gicklhorn, Josef and Renée Gicklhorn. *Sigmund Freuds akademische Laufbahn.* Vienna: Urban und Schwarzenberg, 1960.

Glick, Burton S. "Freud: The Problem of Quality and the 'Secretory Neurone'." *Psychoanalytic Quarterly* 35 (1966): 84–97.

Greenblatt, Samuel H. "The Major Influences on the Early Life and Work of John Hughlings Jackson." *Bulletin of the History of Medicine* 39 (1965): 346–76.

Grinstein, Alexander. *On Sigmund Freud's Dreams.* Detroit: Wayne State University, 1968.

Hahn, G. "Charcot et son influence sur l'opinion publique." *Revue des questions scientifiques.* 2d ser. 6 (1894): 230–61, 353–79.

Haymaker, Webb, and Frances Schiller, eds. *The Founders of Neurology.* Springfield, Ill.: Charles C. Thomas, 1970.

Hillman, R. G. "A Scientific Study of Mystery: The Role of the Medical and Popular Press in the Nancy-Salpetrière Controversy on Hypnotism." *Bulletin of the History of Medicine* 39 (1965): 163–82.

Hoff, H., and F. Seitelberger. "History of the Neurological School of Vienna." *Journal of Nervous and Mental Diseases* 116 (1952): 495–505.

Holt, Robert R. "A Critical Examination of Freud's Concept of Bound and Free Cathexis." *Journal of the American Psychoanalytic Association* 10 (1962): 475–525.

———. "Freud's Biological Assumptions." In *Psychoanalysis and Current Biological Thought,* edited by Norman S. Greenfield and William C. Lewis, pp. 93–121. Madison, Wis.: University of Wisconsin Press, 1965.

Hunter, Richard, and Ida Macalpine. *Three Hundred Years of Psychiatry:* 1535–1860. London: Oxford University Press, 1963.

Jackson, Stanley. "The History of Freud's Concepts of Regression." *Journal of the American Psychoanalytic Association* 17 (1969) 743–84.

———. Review of Amacher's *Freud's Neurological Education and Its Influence on Psychoanalytic Theory. Journal of the History of Medicine* (1966), pp. 202–03.

Jelliffe, S. E. "Sigmund Freud As a Neurologist." *Journal of Nervous and Mental Diseases* 85 (1937): 696–711.

Jones, Ernest. *The Life and Work of Sigmund Freud.* 3 vols. New York: Basic Books, 1953.

Karpinska, Luise von. "Ueber die psychologischen Grundlagen des Freudismus." *International Zeitschrift für ärztliche Psychoanalyse* 2 (1914): 305ff.

Kris, Ernst. "New Contributions to the Study of Freud's *The Interpretation of Dreams:* A Critical Essay." *Journal of the American Psychoanalytic Association* 2 (1954): 180–91.

———. "The Significance of Freud's Earliest Discoveries." *International Journal of Psychoanalysis* 31 (1950); 108–16.

Lesky, Erna. *Die Wiener medizinische Schule.* Cologne: Hermann Bohlaus, 1965.

Lieben, Fritz. *Geschichte der Physiologischen Chemie.* Hildesheim: George Olms, 1970.

Lopez Pinero, Jose Maria, and Jose Maria Morales Meseguer. *Neurosis y Psicoterapia.* Madrid: Espasa-Calpe, 1970.

Marx, Otto. "Aphasia Studies and Language Theory in the Nineteenth Century." *Bulletin of the History of Medicine* 40 (1966) 328–47.

———. "Freud and Aphasia: An Historical Analysis." *American Journal of Psychiatry,* 1967, pp. 214ff.

———. "Nineteenth-Century Medical Psychology: Theoretical Problems in the Work of Griesinger, Meynert and Wernicke." *Isis,* 1970, pp. 355–70.

———. "Psychiatry on a Neuropathological Basis: Th. Meynert's Application for the Extension of His Venia Legendi." *Clio Medica* 6 (1971) 139–58.

Modell, Arnold H. "The Concept of Psychic Energy." *Journal of the American Psychoanalytic Association* 11 (1963): 605ff.

Nemiah, John. "The Development of the Concept of Intrapsychic Conflict in Freud's Writings." *International Journal of Psychoanalysis* 46 (1965): 367–71.

Owen, A. R. G. *Hysteria, Hypnosis, and Healing: The Work of J. M. Charcot.* London: Dennis Dolson, 1971.

Riese, Walther. "Freudian Concepts of Brain Function and Disease." *Journal of Nervous and Mental Diseases* 127 (1958): 287–307.

———. *A History of Neurology.* New York: MD Publications, 1959.

———. "The Pre-Freudian Origins of Psychoanalysis." In *Science and Psychoanalysis,* edited by J. Masserman. New York: Grune and Stratton, 1958.

Riese, Walther, and Ebbel C. Hoff, "A History of the Doctrine of Cerebral Localization." *Journal of the History of Medicine* 5 (1960): 51–71; 6 (1961): 439–70.

Sachs, Heinrich. "Die Entwicklung der Gehirnsphysiologie in neunzehnte Jahrhundert." *Zeitschrift für pädagogische Psychologie* 3 (1901): 255–80.

Sadow, Leo, John Gedo, Julian Miller, George Pollock, Melvin Shabshin, and Nathan Schlesinger. "The Process of Hypothesis Change in Three Early Psychoanalytic Concepts." *Journal of the American Psychoanalytic Association* 16 (1968): 245–73.

Schlesinger, Nathan, John E. Gedo, Julian Miller, George H. Pollock, Melvin Shabshin, and Leo Sadow. "The Scientific Style of Breuer and Freud in the Origins of Psychoanalysis." *Journal of the American Psychoanalytic Association* 15 (1967): 404–22.

Schoenwald, Richard L. "Recent Studies of the Younger Freud." *Bulletin of the History of Medicine* 29 (1955): 261–68.

———. "A Turning Point in Freud's Life: *Zur Auffassung der Aphasien.*" *Osiris* 11 (1954): 119–26.

Schultz, J. H. "Psychoanalyse. Die Breuer-Freudschen Lehren, ihre Entwicklung und Aufnahme." *Zeitschrift für angewandte Psychologie* 2 (1909): 440–97.

Schur, Max. "Some Additional 'Day Residue' of 'The Dream Specimen of Psychoanalysis'." In *Psychoanalysis-A General Psychology: Essays in Honor of Heinz Hartmann,* edited by R. M. Loewenstein, L. M. Newman, M. Schur, and A. J. Solnit, pp. 45–85. New York: International Universities Press, 1966.

———. *Freud: Living and Dying.* New York: International Universities Press, 1972.

Schusdeck, Alexander. "Freud's 'Seduction Theory': A Reconstruction." *Journal of the History of the Behavioral Sciences* 2 (1966): 159–66.

Sigerist, H. "Psychiatry in Europe in the Middle of the Nineteenth Century." In *One Hundred Years of American Psychiatry,* edited by J. K. Hall. New York: Columbia University Press, 1944.

Spehlmann, Rainier. *Sigmund Freuds neurologische Schriften.* Berlin: Springer, 1953.

Stengel, Erwin. "A Re-Evaluation of Freud's Book 'On Aphasia'." *International Journal of Psychoanalysis* 35 (1954): 85–89.

Stewart, Walter A. *Psychoanalysis: The First Ten Years.* New York: Macmillan, 1967.

Sullivan, John. "From Breuer to Freud." *Psychoanalytic Review* 46 (1959): 69–90.

Veith, Ilza. *Hysteria: The History of a Disease.* Chicago and London: University of Chicago Press, 1965.

Vogel, Paul. "Zur Aphasielehre Sigmund Freuds." *Monatsschrift für Psychiatrie und Neurologie* 128 (1954): 256–64.

Waldeyer, Wilhelm. "Ueber einige neuere Forschungen im Gebiete der Anatomie des Centralnervensystems." *Berliner klinische Wochenschrift,* 1891, p. 691.

Whyte, Lancelot Law. *The Unconscious Before Freud.* New York: Basic Books, 1960.

Wyrsch, Jacob. *Zur Geschichte und Deutung der Endogenen Psychosen*. Stuttgart: Georg Thieme, 1956.

Wyss, Dieter. *Depth Psychology*. Translated by Gerald Onn. New York: W. W. Norton, 1966.

Young, Robert M. *Mind, Brain, and Adaptation in the Nineteenth Century*. Oxford: Clarendon Press, 1970.

Zilboorg, Gregory, and G. W. Henry. *A History of Medical Psychology*. New York: Norton, 1941.

Index

Pick's disease, 33

Pinel, Phillipe, 16, 17, 47

Pituitary gland, 188, 190

Pleasure, 272 n.60; and nervous excitation, 164; Freud on, 164–65; and nervous system, 164–65; and unpleasure, 164–65; and infantile sexual trauma, 205; and sexual toxins, 217. *See also* Unpleasure

Preconscious, 252, 282 n.33; and wish-fulfillment, 235–36; and dreams, 236–38, 244; and unconscious, 238; and infantile thoughts, 240, 242–43; and excitation, 240–41; and neuroses, 241; and psychic process, 244; and cathexis, 245; and inhibition 245–46; and unpleasure, 245–46

Premature ejaculation, 130–32. *See also* Sexuality

Presenile dementia, 33

"Project for a Scientific Psychology," 7, 8, 9, 11, 71, 157–59, 171, 177, 184, 191, 192, 193, 236, 237, 239–40, 243, 245, 246–47, 249, 250, 254; and wish-fulfillment, 222–23; and dreams, 224

Psychiatry, 3, 4, 57, 74, 110, 123, 129, 253; anatomically oriented, 5; academic, 5, 47, 255; and neurophysiology, 6, 12; and pathoanatomical approach, 16–19, 19–23, 29, 37, 256, 265 n.60; German, 19–23, 24; Meynert on, 25, 29; Westphal on, 29–30; and hypnosis, 49. *See also* Neuropsychiatry; Pathoanatomical approach

Psychic model; 237, 272 n.60; multiple psychic states, 10, 11, 13; Freud on, 232–46, 247–49; and mental thought, 249–50; and cultural factors, 256

"Psychical (or Mental) Treatment," 65

Psychical primary process, Freud's theory of, 183, 249, 250; and reflex, 168; and infantile behavior, 169, 170–71; and thought, 173; and primary defense, 176; and hysteria, 180; and wish-fulfillment, 222–23; and preconscious, 244; and unconscious, 244; and dreams, 224, 245–46; physiological model of, 246–47; psychological model of, 246–47

Psychical secondary process, Freud's theory of, 168, 183, 249, 250; and maturation, 169–71; and wish-fulfillment, 222–23; and preconscious, 244; and unconscious, 244; physiological model of, 246–47; psychological model of, 246–47

Psychoanalytic theory, 10, 219, 228–29, 231

Psychological model, 9–12, 64–93, 160, 246–55. *See also* Hysteria; Neurophysiology; Neuroses

Psychology, 3, 4, 74, 89, 255. *See also* Psychological model

Psychoneuroses, 185n, 193, 194–95; and somatic sexual excitation, 184–85; and infantile experience, 203; and infantile sexual impulses, 203–04, 205, 212–13, 254; and repression, 211, and heredity 215; and sexual physiology, 219–20; and dreams, 224, 232; Freud on, 228; and sexuality, 246. *See also* Hysteria; Obsessional neuroses; Neuropsychoses

The Psychopathology of Everyday Life, 13, 230

Psychophysiology, 153–54, 156, 157, 158, 159–77. *See also* Neurophysiology; "Project for a Scientific Psychology"

Psychoses, 27, 28, 129, 130, 200; hallucinatory, 103

Psychotherapy, 8, 111, 117, 127, 133, 140, 143, 254

Puberty, 130, 132, 148, 180–83, 185, 193–94, 197–98, 203, 211, 217–18, 227, 247

Pyromidal nuclei, 26

Q. *See* Nervous excitation, quantity of

Railway spine, 40

Reflex motions, 64, 71, 90, 106, 250; and suggestion, 68; and inhibitory control, 69, 72–74, 168–71; and brain, 72; and nervous system, 168–71; physiological model of, 168–71; and thought, 173, 223; and unpleasure, 176, 182; and memory, 223; and psychic excitation, 236

"A Reply to Criticism of My Paper on Anxiety Neurosis," 139–40

"Report on My Studies in Paris and Berlin," 55, 64

Repression (*Verdrangung*), 13, 94, 106, 107, 108, 109, 145; and hysteria, 14, 147, 193–96; and infantile sexuality, 14, 202, 205–07, 212, 217–18, 229; and inhibition, 108, 157, 158–59, 182–83, 246–47; and sexuality, 112, 125–27, 147, 180, 214–15, 225–26, 227–28, 241; and phobias, 143; and catharsis, 148–49; and trauma, 154, 156, 208; psychological model of, 155; and somatic sexual excitation, 155, 156, 159, 182–83; and neurodynamics, 157–58; and defense, 157,